Artificial Intelligence

for CBSE Class X

Reema Thareja
Assistant Professor
Shyama Prasad Mukherji College
University of Delhi

Universities Press

ARTIFICIAL INTELLIGENCE FOR CBSE CLASS X

UNIVERSITIES PRESS (INDIA) PRIVATE LIMITED

Registered office
3-6-747/1/A & 3-6-754/1, Himayatnagar, Hyderabad 500 029, Telangana, India
info@universitiespress.com; www.universitiespress.com

Distributed by
Orient Blackswan Private Limited

Registered office
3-6-752 Himayatnagar, Hyderabad 500 029, Telangana, India

Other offices
Bengaluru, Chennai, Guwahati, Hyderabad, Kolkata,
Mumbai, New Delhi, Noida, Patna, Visakhapatnam

First published 2023

ISBN: 978-81-954009-6-6

501864

Typeset in Adobe Garamond Pro 10.5 by
SRS Publishing Services, Puducherry

Printed in India by
SS Colour Impression Pvt Ltd, Chennai 600 106

Published by
Universities Press (India) Private Limited
3-6-747/1/A & 3-6-754/1, Himayatnagar, Hyderabad 500 029, Telangana, India

I dedicate this book to my family and my uncle Mr B L Thareja,
who is a well-known author himself.

ARTIFICIAL INTELLIGENCE (SUBJECT CODE 417)

CLASS – X (SESSION 2022–2023)

Total Marks: 100 (Theory-50 + Practical-50)

	Units	Max. Marks for Theory and Practical	Refer Chapter No.
PART A	**Employability Skills**		
	Unit 1: Communication Skills-II*		1
	Unit 2: Self-management Skills-II	3	1
	Unit 3: ICT Skills-II	3	2
	Unit 4: Entrepreneurial Skills-II	4	1
	Unit 5: Green Skills-II*		1
	Total	**10**	
PART B	**Subject-specific Skills**		
	Unit 1: Introduction to Artificial Intelligence	10	3
	Unit 2: AI Project Cycle	10	4
	Unit 3: Natural Language Processing	10	13
	Unit 4: Evaluation of Models	10	14
	Total	**40**	
PART C	**Practical Work** • Advanced Python • Data Science • Computer Vision		5–12
	Practical Examination	35	
	Viva Voce		
	Total	**35**	
PART D	Project Work / Field Visit / Practical File / Student Portfolio Viva Voce	15	5
	Total	**15**	
	GRAND TOTAL	**100**	

Note

Units marked with * are to be assessed through Internal Assessment/ Student Activities. They are not to be assessed in Theory Exams.

Contents

Preface

Artificial Intelligence (AI) is a niche technology that has been gaining significant importance over the past three decades. This is because, it provides solutions to a diverse variety of problems using big dataset in every industry. Hence, it is imperative for high-school students to understand AI and have the ability to use AI and big data to solve real-world problems.

Besides understanding the topics discussed in the AI curriculum, it is very important for the student to be aware of the ethics associated with the usage of AI to get maximum benefit. Students should know that they are already using AI in their day-to-day lives – from virtual assistance to the recommendation of videos on YouTube. Learning AI at school has the following benefits:

- It boosts creative thinking in students at an early age.
- It prepares children to lead in the future.
- It provides new strategies to effectively solve real-world problems.
- It improves the qualities of patience and perseverance among students.
- It helps students to learn by reasoning rather than by rote memory.

Hence, this book has been designed to introduce the basic concepts of AI to the student with focus on the subject syllabus prescribed by CBSE for Class X. In addition, the book also covers Python, which is an open-source, excellent, easy, high-level, interpreted, interactive, object-oriented and a reliable language that uses English-like words. It is also a versatile language that supports development of a wide range of applications ranging from simple text processing to WWW browsers to games. Moreover, programmers can embed Python within their C, C++, COM, ActiveX, CORBA, and Java programs to give 'scripting' capabilities for users.

Python has a huge user base that is constantly growing. The strength of Python can be understood from the fact that this programming language is the most preferred language of companies like Nokia, Google, YouTube and even NASA for its easy syntax. The support for multiple programming paradigms, including object-oriented programming, functional Python programming, and parallel programming models makes it an ideal choice for the programmers.

However, no student can learn to program just by reading a book; rather it is a skill that must be developed by practice. So, after learning the rudiments of program-writing, students will find a number of examples and exercises that would help them to learn to design efficient programs. The book presents various programming examples that have already been implemented and tested using Python 3.8.3.

KEY FEATURES

This book is aimed at serving as a textbook for students enrolled in Class X of CBSE. The objective of this book is to introduce the concepts of Communication, Entrepreneurship, Self-management, Sustainable Development, Green Technology, and the basics of Artificial Intelligence before introducing the Python Programming language as a multifaceted tool with diverse functions. Salient features of the book include:

Pictorial Approach: Well-labelled diagrams are provided throughout the text for clear understanding of the concepts.

Easy to understand: The book uses a very simple language to explain the concepts and breaks down technical jargons to simpler terms for the student's benefit.

Practical orientation: The book has numerous solved examples and chapter-end exercises in the form of objective type questions and review questions to help students face their exams with confidence.

Comprehensive Coverage: The book provides comprehensive coverage of all the topics prescribed by CBSE in its Class X syllabus for Artificial Intelligence.

Glossary: A list of key terms included is provided at the end of each chapter to facilitate revision of important topics learned.

Informative Textboxes: Theory discussions are interspersed with ample hints and explanations given in well-placed textboxes for ease of understanding.

AI Lab Sessions and Activities at the end of all chapters to familiarize the student with the various AI-powered applications that are currently in use and to highlight the immense potential of this emerging technology.

Programmer's Zone examples are used in context to help the students understand the technique of programming.

Complementary App: Students can download the free mobile app Jruma from Google Play Store or Apple Store for additional learning resources. The app would help them to recapitulate and test their understanding of the concepts learnt, right from Class I. The app will also be useful for the students to hone their Computer Science (CS) and Logical Reasoning (LR) skills.

ACKNOWLEDGMENTS

The writing of this text book was a mammoth task for which a lot of help was required from many people. Fortunately, I have had the fine support of my family, friends and fellow members of the teaching staff at the Shyama Prasad Mukherji College.

My special thanks would always go to my father Late Sh. Janak Raj Thareja, my mother Smt. Usha Thareja, my brother Pallav and sisters Kimi and Rashi who were a source of abiding inspiration and are a divine blessing for me. I am especially indebted to my son Goransh, who has been very patient and cooperative in letting me realize my dreams. I am obliged to my uncle Mr B L Theraja for his inspiration and guidance in writing this book.

Last but not the least, my acknowledgements will always be incomplete if I do not thank the editorial team at Universities Press (India) Private Limited that gave me this brilliant opportunity to utilize my writing skills.

Reema Thareja
reema_thareja@yahoo.com

About the Author

Reema Thareja is Assistant Professor at Shyama Prasad Mukherji College, University of Delhi. She has over 17 years of experience, teaching computer science for various courses including BA, BSc, MSc, BBA, MBA, BCA and MCA. She has authored several books, including those on Computer Fundamentals, C Programming, OOPS with C++, Data Structures, Data Warehousing and Python Programming, which are well-accepted across the globe. She has also written books on Data Science and Machine Learning in R for the current academic session.

Dr Thareja has published more than 20 research papers in journals of national and international repute. A recipient of 64 Google Scholar Citations, she has launched a Computer Science Learning and Quizzing mobile app, Jruma, for both Android and iOS devices to promote incentive-based learning through quizzing.

A recipient of the Nobel Laureate Maria Goeppert–Mayer Inspiring Woman of the Year 2021 Award in the field of Computer Science by International Multi-disciplinary Research Foundation (IMRF), Dr Thareja was also among "India's Top 50 Women Leaders in the Education Industry" recognized by uLektz Wall of Fame for the year 2020. She has conducted several faculty development programs, student workshops and webinars in India and US, and participated in the International Dialogue on Empowered Future – Women's Role on the eve of International Women's Day 2021.

A member of the Computer Society of India and Editorial Board and Keynote Speaker of the IMRF Conference Board, Dr Thareja is a skilled motivator who helps students utilize their untapped skills and reinvent themselves. She was also conferred with the Knowledge Mobilization Award at the Seventh Annual Research Awards event organized by Shri Param Hans Education and Research Trust and was invited as a speaker at the Global Virtual Summit held recently in New York. She has received multiple awards and recognitions for her contributions in the field of education.

Communication, Self-management, Entrepreneurial and Green Skills

1

Chapter Objectives

This chapter talks about communication, entrepreneurial, self-management and green skills. Important concepts discussed in this context include:

- Characteristics and barriers of effective communication
- Inculcating self-management skills and improving self-confidence
- Entrepreneurial motivation and some interesting business ideas
- Sustainable business development, goals and initiatives

In class 9, we have already studied about vital skills that one must possess to excel as an individual, professional, entrepreneur and a concerned citizen. Moving further on the same discussion, in this chapter, we will learn about:

- Effective communication
- Self-management and self confidence
- Motivation and aim of an entrepreneur
- Sustainable development.

1.1 CHARACTERISTICS OF EFFECTIVE COMMUNICATION

Several researchers have highlighted the relevance of communicating one's feelings effectively. As breathing is important to life, effective communication is crucial for ordered social structure. Hence, it becomes very important to understand the characteristics that are relevant for effective communication. Our messages should be:

Clear: Every communication – oral or written – must be very clear. For this, one must keep in mind the following points:

- Use short and simple sentences
- Use active voice rather than passive voice
- Use bullet points to convey several messages together.

Concise: Today everyone lacks time. The normal attention span is just a few minutes long. Long and lengthy communique is boring and avoided by a majority of the people. So, instead of making a beautiful, but long presentation or speech, focus on presenting summary reports in a clear and lucid way.

Concrete: An idea backed by facts or data is more valued. So, whatever you say or write, defend it by giving references, analysis results or any other information that makes the communication well-footed. Remember that a tangible argument is always easy to understand and difficult to criticize

Coherent: You enjoy a story only if you know it from the first line. What if you join a story-telling session in the middle of the session or what if you know the end of a mystery movie? To get involved in a session, the story should be well-narrated. Similarly, when communicating with others, be coherent. Think ahead and maintain an appropriate flow of information. You must be very clear about what to say, when and where. The key to a coherent communication is being well-planned to present the information in a logical and sequential manner. The main ideas in a communication should be differentiable and they should follow each other in a way that is derivative of some rules.

Courteous: We must be formal in all our business communications. Be honest, respectful, considerate, open and polite when interacting with people. A rude person can never attract a large audience even if he/she is communicating vital and critical information. Never use offensive words. Do not reveal your political affinity. Do not be racist or misogynist or any other personality that creates a bad impression on the audience. Even when cracking a joke, make sure that nobody feels hurt.

Listening and Understanding: Effective communication is not just about presenting or delivering information. It is also about receiving it. Be a good listener. Try to deeply understand the meaning of what is being conveyed. A good listener not only focuses on what a person says but also gives attention to the speaker's non-verbal cues.

A good listener must be practical, emotionally intelligent and mature and a highly focused individual. He/she should be good at analyzing information but should never be carried away with his own personal judgments of either the topic or the presenter. Such a listener queries or responds only after a thorough understanding of the subject being discussed.

Focus and Attention: Today, life has become so fast that we all need to be multi-tasking. No longer do we have to communicate through a single medium. We have to communicate through emails, calls, social media, etc. Any misplaced communication can prove to be disastrous. Also, while receiving information, missing out even a single message may create a mountain of problems.

Emotional Awareness and Control: The most important aspect of effective communication is having full control over our emotions. Whether we are receiving or delivering information, we have to be emotionally stable and exhibit emotional maturity and emotional intelligence.

1.2 BARRIERS TO EFFECTIVE COMMUNICATION

The entire communication process can be affected by multiple barriers. These barriers can disturb and distort a communication by causing misunderstandings and result in a total failure of realizing its goal(s). Some common barriers to effective communication include linguistic, psychological, emotional, physical, and cultural limitations.

Linguistic Barriers: This is the main barrier limiting effective communication. Since language is the most commonly used tool of communication (Fig. 1.1) and every major region has its own language, even a thick dialect may become ineffective if people are unable to understand each other's ideas due to a different language being used.

In a big country like India, dialects of even neighbouring regions change within a few kilometers. Even in the same workplace, employees may have different linguistic skills. People proficient in a particular language may under-estimate the ones who lack language proficiency. This may affect the effectiveness of the communication across the organization.

Verbal Communication is the exchange of words to convey a thought, idea or just express your feeling.

Tips to Build

- Hear what others have to say
- Think before you talk
- Don't fake it
- Speak with confidence
- Control the tone
- Know your listeners
- Use your gestures
- Be humble

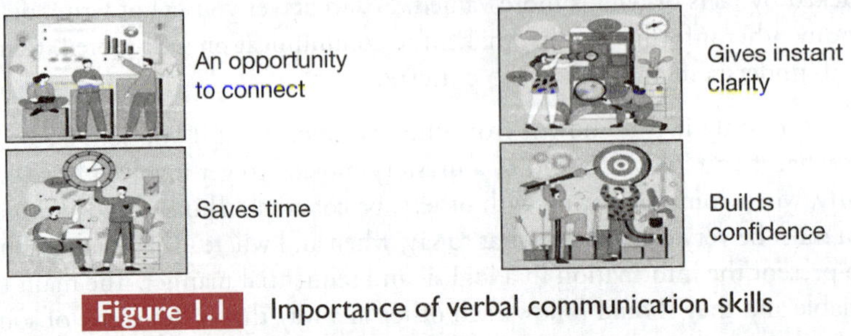

Figure 1.1 Importance of verbal communication skills

Psychological Barriers: Mental and psychological factors like stage fear, speech disorders, phobia, depression, etc. are major barriers to effective communication and are, at times, really difficult to manage.

Emotional Barriers: The emotional IQ of an individual can be related to the ease and comfort with which he/she can communicate. To communicate effectively, one must be emotionally mature. Of course, in addition to emotions, concrete facts must be used in communication.

People who talk immaturely and allow their emotions to take over the communication face lot of difficulties in their personal as well as professional lives. Emotions like anger, frustration and bad humor can adversely affect the decision-making capabilities of a person and impact the effectiveness of his/her communication.

Physical Barriers: These barriers are the most obvious barriers that can be easily removed. Physical barriers include noise, poor network, closed doors, faulty equipment, etc. In a big organization, physical separation between employees combined with the factors discussed above may result in severe barriers to effective communication.

Cultural Barriers: With globalization, all big organizations have their offices in several cities of different countries with employees coming from varied cultures, backgrounds, regions and religions with an absolutely different style of eating, dressing, talking and working. Hence, the organization must be very particular in maintaining harmony amidst cultural diversity. Employees should be taught to be courteous and tolerant to people with a different background. For this, many MNCs make it mandatory for their employees to take up special courses offered at the orientation stages that make them aware about other cultures and teach them how to work as a team despite all variations.

Organizational Structure: Every organization has a rigid organizational structure. There is a path in which information flows. This can however adversely affect communication and result in misinformation or lack of appropriate transparency available to the employees.

Attitude: While some people are introvert, others are extroverts. Some like to live alone while others want to be very social. There are also people who have a lot of ego or are absolutely inconsiderate about others. All these factors cause severe strains in communication. Therefore, companies must run special courses to help employees overcome their problems of shyness, anger, social anxiety, ego, etc. through proper training.

Perception: The ability of people perceiving the same thing differently can be an advantage but, at the same time, it can be a factor hampering effective communication. Knowledge of the perception levels of the audience helps to have an effective communication. In general, every word that you say must be clear enough to be easily understood by everyone.

Physiological: Certain disorders, diseases or limitations also affect communication. For example, shrillness of voice and dyslexia are some common physiological barriers to effective communication. However, these factors can be compensated and removed.

Technological and Socio-religious Barriers: Technology is evolving very fast. Therefore, for many people, it is difficult to keep up with the newest developments in technology and this becomes a barrier to effective communication. Some people cannot afford to invest in the latest technology. Even small organizations may not be able to pay the cost for decent gadgets that assist in communication. Socio-religious barriers are another factor that affects communication. For example, in a patriarchal society, a woman or a transgender may face many difficulties and barriers while expressing themselves.

1.3 IMPORTANCE OF FEEDBACK IN A COMMUNICATION

Feedback facilitates a two-way communication as it conveys information regarding successful delivery of a message. We can understand its importance from the points given below.

- Feedback helps to understand the **attitude** of the receiver and thus forms the basis of problem-solving.
- Feedback follows the principle of **democracy** in which even the receiver participates in the communication process by expressing his/her opinion.

- Feedback supports **effective communication** by ensuring that the message is rightly sent and interpreted.
- Feedback helps the communicator to make necessary **improvements** in his/her communication.
- Feedback creates **better relationship** between sender and receiver of the message. Such a relationship cannot be built in case of a one-way communication.
- Last but not the least, a healthy relationship supports **effective coordination and team work**, which is very necessary for successful completion of any project.

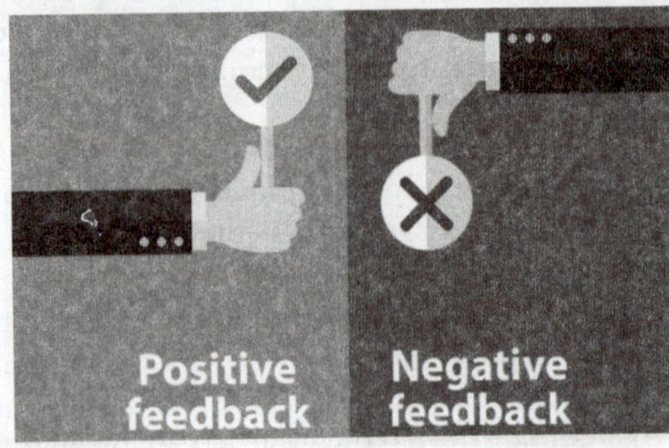

1.4 IMPROVING SELF-MANAGEMENT SKILLS

Anyone can improve their self-management skills in the following ways:

Take Care of Yourself: Be organized. Do not lose temper. Keep your well-being on top priority. For this, eat healthy food, get ample sleep, and exercise regularly. Relax your mind using simple meditation techniques to take care of your mental health.

Practice Being Patient: One can manage himself/herself better if he/she knows how to be patient in the worst of situations. We develop patience only with time through practice. Remember that we, as humans, cannot control everything and everyone. However, it is within our power to be calm and patiently wait for the worst situation to subside.

Focus Your Attention on One Task: No doubt, we need to be multi-tasking but when we have several tasks to complete, we must prioritize them and then complete the top-priority task by focusing our attention and efforts on it. This would avoid unnecessary stress and help us to be calm and more productive.

Reflect on Your Strengths: Take some time off to learn more about yourself – your strengths, your weaknesses, your likes and your dislikes. Work in the areas of your strength. This will help you to have a higher degree of control over your career. For example, if you are good communicator, then you can look for roles that involve more of interacting with people. Embracing strengths help one to feel more confident and at ease.

1.5 USING SELF-MANAGEMENT SKILLS IN THE WORKPLACE

Being conscientious of our actions at work is an important part of self-management. When we act professionally while being considerate, we get more respect. To practice self-control at the workplace, make sure that you always remember to do the following things.

Set Goals: When you set a goal, track and measure your progress, it clearly shows that you have the self-control to manage your time, set your priorities and reach your ambitions. Our goals should be SMART – Specific, Measurable, Achievable, Relevant, and Time-bound.

Plan for Each Workday: Use a calendar to keep you organized. Mark all the tasks that you need to do. Take some time every day to review whether you were able to complete them on time or not. You can even mark the tasks that you need to do in personal life – uniting with friends, going for shopping, etc.

Prepare in Advance for Meetings: A self-organized person prepares well in advance as he/she knows the value of time. During every meeting, take notes; arrive on or even before time. Eat healthy food and sleep on time the day before a crucial meeting.

Think Before You Speak: When discussing ideas or actions, plan and think before you say. Avoid any statement that may hurt others. You may have few critiques around you, but deal with them patiently and professionally to be more productive.

1.6 SELF-CONFIDENCE

Self-confidence is an attitude about our skills and abilities. It allows an individual to accept and trust oneself to exercise some control in our lives. We must be aware about our strengths and weaknesses, set realistic goals, communicate assertively, and handle criticism to develop a positive view of ourselves.

A person with low self-confidence is often passive or submissive and never trusts himself/herself or even others. Such a person feels inferior, unloved and becomes very sensitive to criticism.

We may feel confident in some situations and less confident in others. For example, you may feel very confident when discussing your favorite sport but may feel jittery when academics are discussed. Actually, high or low self-confidence is more about our perceptions (how we think about ourselves) than our actual abilities. We often have low confidence due to,

- some bitter experiences
- growing up in an unsupportive and critical environment
- separation from friends or family
- judging ourself too harshly
- anxiety issues and being afraid of failure.

1.6.1 Increasing Self-confidence

People with low self-confidence often have errors in their thinking. A healthy self-confidence is the key to succeed in both our professional and personal lives (Fig. 1.2). So, it is very important to boost our confidence. This can be done by,

- Identifying our strengths and working on them to make them more prominent.
- Rewarding and praising ourselves for the efforts and progress already made by us.
- Treating ourselves with kindness and compassion when facing difficult situations.
- Telling ourselves that failure is not permanent and trying continuously until we succeed.
- Setting realistic and achievable goals instead of chasing perfection.
- Slowing down when feeling intense emotions.
- Staying calm and thinking logically when faced with challenging situations.
- Not making any assumptions about anything and never judging ourselves, other people and/or situations.
- Expressing our feelings, beliefs and needs directly and respectfully.
- Saying 'NO' to unreasonable requests.
- Not comparing ourselves to others. Understand that everyone has a unique journey and our motive is to be happy and satisfied with whatever we have.
- Never feeling shy or offended to go for individual counseling.
- Being with positive and like-minded people; making friends with those who help us to rise up in life. The types of people we spend time with have a very strong influence on our thoughts and behavior.
- Practicing positive self-talk to foster self-compassion, overcome self-doubt, and take on new challenges. Correspondingly, avoiding negative self-talk that limits our abilities and hampers our confidence. Never saying words, "I can't handle it" or "It is too hard", "I shouldn't even try this.", "This is impossible". Rather, saying to ourselves, "I can do it," "I must try this.", "I can do better next time," "at least I learned something."

Figure 1.2 Self-confidence: the ladder to success

1.6.2 Benefits of Self-confidence

Self-confidence is a big asset as it helps us at home, work, and dealing with our relationships in the following ways.

Better Performance: When we know about strengths, we can invest our time more judiciously to do something we are good at. We will not waste time and energy to handle things that are not in our domain. This improves our performance and further boosts our confidence.

Healthy Relationships: When we feel good, we our happy and satisfied, everyone loves and respects us. This, in turn, gives us strength to positively deal with negative situations/people.

Openness to Try New Things: When we believe in ourselves, we are always keen on trying new things. Being bold helps us to face our fears rather than run away from difficult situations.

Confidence and Behavior

The table given below compares the behavior of a confident person with that of a person having low confidence.

Confident Behavior	Behavior with Low Self-confidence
Stands firm with strong belief in himself/herself even when others are mocking or criticizing them	Carried away easily by others' opinion
Takes risks and goes the extra mile to achieve better things.	Prefers to stay in the comfort zone, fears failure, and avoids risk
Learns from every experience and admits mistakes	Works hard to cover up mistakes so that they are rectified before anyone notices them
Waits for others to congratulate them on their accomplishments	Praises himself/herself
Accepts compliments graciously by saying, "Thanks for appreciating my efforts"	Dismisses compliments by making statements like "It's nothing for me"
Has a sense of inner peace and happiness.	Suffers from issues like anxiety, depression, and other mental health challenges.

1.7 ENTREPRENEURIAL MOTIVATIONS

Motivation drives people to do exceptionally well. Entrepreneurial motivations are required to motivate an individual to start a business. Researchers have listed the following factors that trigger an individual to initiate and run a startup.

While external factors like the economy, the availability of business capital, competitors and government regulations do play a major role in entrepreneurship, there are also a few non-motivational factors that have a strong influence. Some of them are:

a. Unsatisfactory work environment
b. Unwanted and unexpected change in career
c. Urge to do something different or of your own
d. Drive to work independently or to have financial independence
e. A desire to achieve personal goals or a vision to achieve something big
f. To be your own boss, manage your own time and earn more money.

1.7.1 Aims and Objectives of Entrepreneurship

Every entrepreneur must set a goal to help him/her remain focused on the aims and objectives of business growth. This enhances the chances of success.

Setting goals for a business is not really easy. The entrepreneur must have a clear vision of the business. He/she must know why the business exists (to deliver excellent customer service, offer access 24/7, increase brand awareness, increase the business size, sell sustainable locally sourced products) to develop a long-term strategy. While the business goals must be achievable in 3–5 years, business objectives state actions that needs to be performed for achieving business goals. They are the targets and success measures of the business.

1.7.2 Entrepreneurial Development Programme

An entrepreneurial development program is an organized and systematic process of enhancing motivation, knowledge and skills of those who wish to become entrepreneurs. The program is designed to groom individuals to broaden their outlook and emphasizes on operational rather than academic training. It is considered as a tool to grow industrialization and fix the problem of unemployment. The program goes beyond the scope of simple training sessions and includes personal counseling and support (Fig. 1.3).

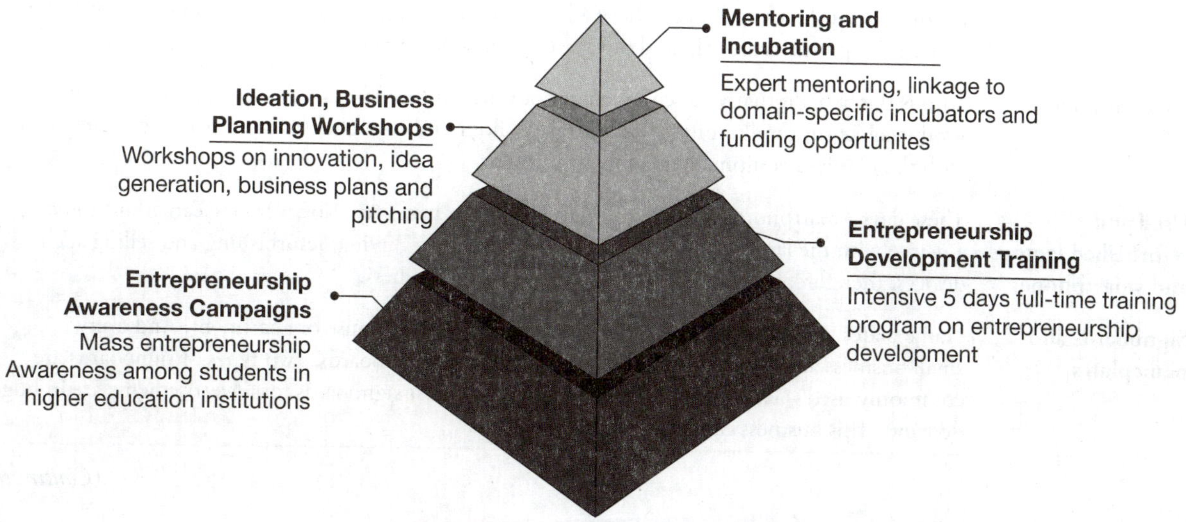

Figure 1.3 Steps for a successful EDP

The main objectives of entrepreneurial development programs include:

Promotion of cottage and small-scale industries The EDP focuses in the rural areas by running special programs to stimulate new ventures and/or expand the reach of existing activities of small- and medium-scale industries.

Generation of employment opportunities EDP encourages self-employment among individuals in the processing of indigenous raw materials for local consumption and for exports. In this way, EDP promotes innovations and harnesses the vast untapped human skills to channelize them into accelerating industrialization. When surplus young energies are directed towards self-employment careers, it also helps the country to grow financially and defuse social tension and unrest among youth.

To create awareness about availability of resources This provides a healthy base for sound economic growth and rapid industrialization. Proper training is given to minimize excessive scraps, defective output and wastage in the production process.

To impart training in managerial understanding and skills It provides post-training assistance and monitoring facilities. The training sessions also remove doubts in the minds of individuals and give them solutions for their problem(s). It helps the entrepreneurs to set or reset the business objectives. The main aim of EDP is to provide a constructive direction to those who wish to have a different career path.

Thus, an EDP creates a **conducive and healthy environment** for the growth of entrepreneurs by providing them the required training, education and reorientation. Government-initiated programs such as NREP (National Rural Employment Program and IRDP (Integrated Rural Development Program etc.), aimed to eliminate/minimize the problems of poverty and unemployment, are examples of EDP.

EDP also **promotes Balanced Regional Development** by supporting small-scale and micro enterprises which require less investment in funds. This not only increases new investment and bring innovations but also stimulates economic growth.

1.7.3 Business Ideas

Religious items	Pictures of deities, incense sticks, cotton wicks for lamps, candles, prayer beads, etc. can be made at home or at a small premise with low investment.
Imported products	Travelers returning to India from a foreign trip can buy products abroad (like fragrances, cosmetics, cigarettes, liquor, chocolates, food items, dresses, etc.) that they can sell locally to make for the cost of their trip. Indians have a big craze for foreign goods. So, you can open a website where such products are sold and purchased at affordable rates.
Soya products	Soya is the best alternative to complement our protein needs in a pure-vegetarian diet. Soya products like soya milk, tofu (soya curd), soya flour and soya chunks can be easily manufactured with the required equipment at a low investment.
Used and refurbished laptops and smartphones	These days, smartphones and laptops have become a necessity. Not everyone can afford to have a device with the latest features and high configuration. Buying, refurbishing and selling such devices, therefore, is a low-investment, high-returns business.
Signboards and nameplates	Name plates are installed outside the door of almost every house or apartment. And every small business and commercial establishment requires signboards. Two types of signboards are commonly used – Painted and Neon. Creative, low-cost signboards for advertisements are in huge demand. This business can be started at low cost.

(Continued)

Manpower supply	Every business and household requires manpower. The attrition rate of unskilled workforce (like waiters, maids, cooks) is very high. You can start a business solving manpower problems in a better way. Senior people in hospitals and homes require caregivers as their children are either busy at work or settled at a far-off place. You can start a business to supply people for such tasks.
Stationery supply	Every business, school and college requires stationery (like files, folders, customized letterheads, business cards, envelopes, invoice books, receipt books) in bulk. With a small investment, you can enter into this evergreen business. You can even start selling stationery products online to retail customers (like students).
Corporate gifts	Every business requires gift items including pens, wallets, mugs and other types of decorative items that could be given to their staff and business associates at different occasions. Usually, these items are printed with the company's name and logo. This is an ever-green business, especially in a country like ours.
Packing services	Small and middle-sized businesses (SMBs) do not have a separate department for packing their products. They usually prefer to outsource this work to small businesses who can pack their stuff with care while adhering to deadlines. To enter this business, you will need packing material (like tapes, cartons), strapping machines, cutters and manpower.
Homemade chocolates	You can start this business with a very low investment and then collaborate with pastry shops and gift stores. Chocolates are always in high demand for corporate gifting and during festive and wedding seasons.
Trending dresses	You can become a part of the fashion designing industry by replicating the dresses worn by Bollywood celebrities. This business can be started at a low investment and it can yield high returns. You can even give these dresses on rent.
Chips and wafers	Chips and wafers are consumed almost everywhere (cinema halls, schools, home, bars, in buses, trains). Manufacturing this food item with potato, raw banana, jackfruit, tapioca and other starchy roots is fairly easy and calls for less investment. Tying up with shops and bars can make this business profitable.
Idli and dosa batter	Idli and dosa are very popular across India. Not everyone can prepare the batter required for making these dishes as it requires a proper blend of rice and cereals and then the batter has to be fermented to the right degree to get a good taste. Packaged Idli and Dosa batter, therefore, can be supplied to home customers and small restaurants.
Electrical devices maintenance	You can sign contracts with business and households to offer maintenance (repair/service) of these electrical appliances.
Employee background checks	Due to high migration of labor, companies and households now prefer to hire employee background checks to verify information (address, work experience, educational qualifications, references, reviews) provided by a jobseeker through an external agency.
Handicrafts	You can create a website to buy and sell handicrafts made in rural areas. Glitzy showrooms charge a lot, so these products can be sold through a mobile app/ website at cheaper rates. Businesses and households extensively use these items for gifting and decoration purposes.
Skin and beauty treatment	With people becoming beauty conscious, you can open a small business providing skin and beauty treatment including therapies for glowing skin, anti-aging and facelifts. Herbal and natural therapies, when provided at low cost, can keep you ahead of competition.

(*Continued*)

Mushroom harvesting	Mushrooms are very nutritious as well as expensive. Therefore, the Indian government is giving a lot of subsidies and facilities to people who can harvest mushrooms. This is a low-investment business idea. You just need to set up a green-house with controlled temperature for getting the right crop. Mushroom spores are readily available from state-run cooperatives and agricultural shops.
Handling broken glass	There is a huge market for broken glass as millions of glass bottles that cannot be recycled, are discarded daily in India. Shards of broken glass are used in building compound walls to keep away robbers and to discourage them from scaling the compound wall. Glass shards also prevent reptiles from slithering over the compound wall.
Apiary and honey	If you have a garden or an open plot of land, then you can set up an apiary to breed honeybees. Homemade honey can be sold at a high price.
Tomato sauce making business	There is a huge demand of tomato sauce, especially in households, canteens, restaurants, fast-food joints, etc. You can start making sauces (like sweet-and-spicy tomato sauce, tomato ketchup, no-garlic–no-onion tomato sauce, organic tomato ketchup and chilli-tomato ketchup) with very low investment
Ginger–garlic paste making business	Knowing the facts that ginger–garlic paste is used in all kinds of dishes and both these crops are produced in almost all the states of India, any entrepreneur can start making ginger–garlic paste on a small scale with a small capital investment. It is an agriculture-related activity, so you can easily get help from government. Apart from domestic cooking, you can collaborate with food chains, restaurants, hotels, fast-food chains, cafes, canteens and street-food stalls for selling your product.
Online marketing	You can advertise or promote products and services of others on social media. Blogging, reviewing and acquiring customers are all a part of online marketing business.
Goat-farming business	This is a very profitable business that employs a large number of unemployed people in rural area. Goat-farming is gaining popularity in India and this is established as a business by livestock management department as goats contribute a lot to the rural economy by providing meat, fibre, milk, skin and high-quality manure.
Toilet-cleaner making business	You can manufacture and then sell products like toilet- and bathroom-cleaner at a very low cost.
T-shirt printing business	Most youngsters like to wear clothes with new designs and colorful printed customized T-shirts are viable attractions for this segment. You can start a small T-shirt printing business with low investment.
School-uniforms business	You can start a business of making school uniforms from home with very low investment and still earn good profits.
Naphthalene balls manufacturing	We all keep naphthalene balls in clothes and bathrooms and toilets to keep our homes/clothes safe from bacteria and to remove bad odor. Manufacture of naphthalene balls, also known as phenyl pills, can earn you good profits.
Flower business	You can sell a variety of flowers, bouquets and can take orders for flower decorations on weddings and special occasions to start a low-investment business yielding a high profit.
Trading of pure cotton clothes	In summer, the weather is very hot and we all prefer to wear pure cotton clothes. You can start a business by contacting the manufacturer of cotton clothes to get clothes at wholesale rate and cheap prices and then selling them to other shops by keeping a profit margin.

(*Continued*)

Detergent powder making business	You can start business with low investment and earn money from home by making detergent powder. This product is always in demand and can be easily sold to consumers.
Tiffin service business	Nobody can eat or even afford to eat outside food daily. So you can start a business to supply home-made food. You can even tie up with Swiggy to deliver the food from your location to the customer's location.
Real estate business	You can start a real estate business dealing with the management, purchase, operation and selling of land, offices, resorts, warehouse, villas and buildings. It also provides a good investment opportunity.
Food parlor	You can start a food parlor to sell snacks, desserts and shakes.
Lawn-care service or landscape design	Lawn-care and landscaping are small-scale profitable businesses that need less equipment and thus less investment. Most bungalows and farm housees prefer to use landscape design for beautification.
Game parlor	Game parlor is very popular among kids and youngsters. Since parents usually do not allow children to download every other game, they can go to a game parlor with friends and enjoy gaming as an activity. Though this business requires high initial investment, it helps you generate good revenue later.
Advertising agency	If you are good at using designer software, able to do digital marketing and have advertising skills, then the best business for you could probably be to open an advertising agency. You can create small ads to capture the customer's attention.
Physical fitness	You can open a gym or work as a yoga instructor or as a trainer for mental and physical relaxation. Such businesses can be started at a low cost but they have a high footfall.

1.8 SUSTAINABLE DEVELOPMENT

Initially, the environment was considered as a separate entity, having no connection with human emotion or action and the term development was used in the context of achieving political goals and economic progress. Ignoring environment in all key policies for growth resulted in environmental degradation.

But now, the government and people have realized the importance of sustainable development. They now understand that the environment in which we live and development done to improve our lives cannot be separate entities. Therefore, Environmental Protection Agencies were added to the existing government structures to address environment issues and rectify the policies that adversely affect our environment.

1.8.1 Sustainability and Sustainable Development

Sustainability is defined as an art of living where protecting our environment is more important than massive developments. It aims to use the available resources only to the extent where they can be replenished and made available for use by the future generation. Sustainability focuses on how human beings can live in peace and harmony with nature without creating ecological disturbance.

> According to United Nations, the objective of sustainable development is society, economy and environment.

Correspondingly, sustainable development meets the needs of the present without compromising on the ability of future generations to use natural resources to meet their demands. All of us need to contribute towards sustainable development by judiciously using resources and by following 4*R*'s and 1*U* of Sustainability. These can be given as,

REFUSE, say 'NO' to use products that may harm the environment.

REDUCE the use of the products that may cause harm to the environment.

REUSE the products as much as possible to reduce the waste generation.

RECYCLE after reusing the product.

UPCYCLE, give a new look to the old product to make it attractive for use. Even an unusable product can be upcycled with creativity and innovation.

1.8.2 Principles of Sustainability

The three main principles of sustainability are:

- Reduce the use of non-renewable resources so their depletion rates do not exceed the development rate of renewable alternatives
- Limit the use of renewable resources so that they are not exploited at a rate higher than their regeneration levels.
- Do not exceed the absorption and regeneration capacity of the natural environment.

1.8.3 Importance of Sustainable Development

Sustainable development focuses on people's welfare along with the maintenance of the environment (Fig. 1.4). Today, adopting sustainable techniques for sustainable development is the only alternative that we have, for otherwise, our future generation will pay the cost of our greed. We can understand its importance as given below.

Judicious Use of Resources: Sustainable development trains people to make optimized use of means and resources for maximum benefit without wastage. This would in turn help us to conserve and promote the environment. For example, the use of mineral oil, drinking water, insecticide, chemical fertilizer and forest products should be minimized.

Balanced Economic Growth: Uneven distribution of available resources across different economic zones creates social imbalance and results in serious crime. To ensure balanced economic growth of all, sustainability is important.

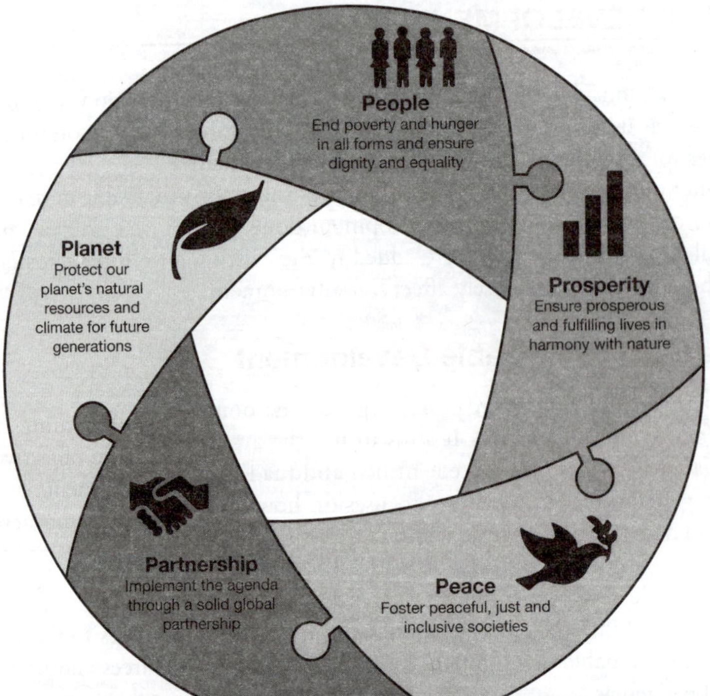

Figure 1.4 The five *P*'s of sustainable development

Source: https://sdg.gdrc.org

Combating Environmental Issues: Environmental problems like climate change and emission of greenhouse gases are alarming. To combat these issues, Sustainable Development is the only viable option.

Develop Positive Attitude: Sustainable development has a positive impact on peoples' behavior, knowledge, attitude and skill. A responsible person who wisely uses and preserves natural resources thinking that they are the common property of all, will create a society in which everybody coordinates and cooperates to conserve natural and social environment.

Overall Development: Sustainable development takes utmost care for overall development of human beings by focusing on the progress of health, education, agriculture, tourism and social reform. This would, in turn, result in economic growth.

Development Based on People's Participation: Sustainable development is possible only with the support of the public and their involvement at all levels of environment protection and promotion. People's participation creates an interest among the local people to work with a feeling of ownership towards development and conservation of the environment.

Limited Development: Limited but optimized use of resources can very well satisfy the basic needs of people. But due to the greed of becoming more powerful and successful, more development works are carried out than required. As a result, non-renewable resources that are already very scarce are depleting at a very fast rate. With sustainable development, policies are made considering the welfare of the people as well as the environment.

Long-lasting Development: Sustainable development provides economic and social development without destroying the earth's resources. It fosters current work while conserving natural resources for the future generation.

1.9 SUSTAINABLE DEVELOPMENT GOALS

To achieve sustainability, the United Nations adopted 17 Sustainable Development Goals (SDGs) in 2015 as a universal call to action to end poverty, protect the planet and ensure that all people enjoy peace and prosperity by 2030. In line with these SDGs, countries are now making policies and regulations to promote sustainable systems needed in all economic sectors to provide a secure, affordable and sustainable economy.

These SDGs proposed by the Open Working Group of the United Nations include,

- **Eradicating poverty** in all its forms everywhere by 2030. When a person has less than $1.25 a day, he is said to be living in poverty
- Putting an **end to hunger** by achieving food security, improved nutrition, and promoting sustainable agriculture by 2030
- Providing **quality education** and promoting life-long learning opportunities for all by 2030
- Ensuring availability and **sustainable management** of water and sanitation for all by 2030
- Accessibility to affordable, reliable, sustainable, and modern energy for all by 2030
- Promoting **sustained economic growth** by providing productive employment and decent work for all
- Sustaining **per capita economic growth** by providing at least 7 percent per annum GDP growth in the least-developed countries
- Encouraging **innovation** by developing quality, reliable, sustainable and resilient infrastructure that supports sustainable industrialization
- Reducing **inequality** within and among countries by 2030
- Making cities and human settlements inclusive, safe, resilient and sustainable by 2030
- Ensuring sustainable consumption and production patterns
- Mitigating and eliminating problems created due to climate change in all countries
- Conserving the oceans, seas and marine resources for sustainable development by 2025
- Justice for all and promoting accountability at all levels.

1.9.1 Society, Sustainability and the Environment

Over the years, our environment has been facing major challenges due to rapid economic development (Fig. 1.5).

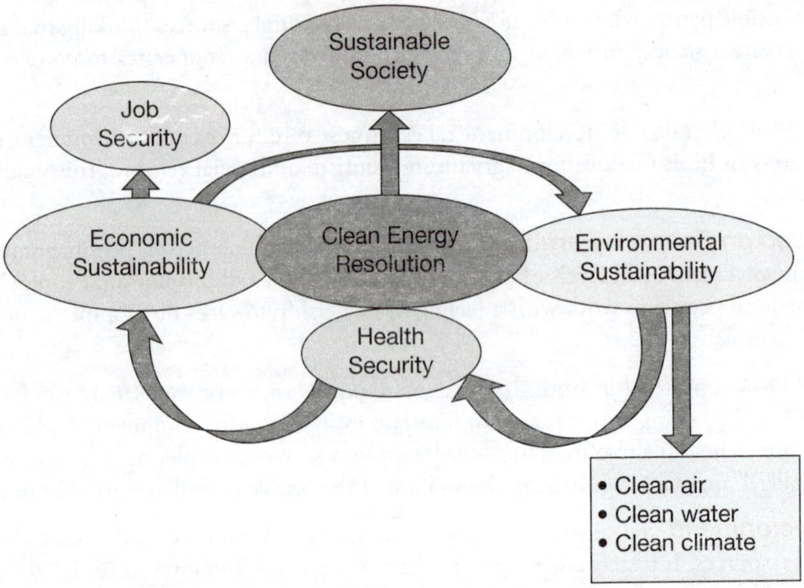

Figure 1.5 Three major problems that elucidate one common goal

For example, to feed an increasing population, high use of fertilizers, insecticides, pesticides and hybrid crops resulted in soil and environmental degradation. In this context, sustainable agriculture consists of environment-friendly techniques of farming that allow the production of agricultural crops or livestock without causing any harm to human beings or the environment. It prohibits the excessive use of chemicals to avoid adverse effects to soil, water and biodiversity.

Just consider the situation when excessive chemicals are disposed in rivers, lakes and ponds from industries. Even the water (containing soil polluted with chemicals) from farm lands flows into the nearby water, polluting the fresh water that is used for drinking. Further, humans are extensively cutting down trees for fuel, paper, rubber, construction of homes and furniture. All this has resulted in extreme weather conditions, such as floods, droughts, and excessive cold or heat.

However, things are more easily said than done. Sustainable development therefore focuses on,

- reducing excessive use of resources
- enhancing resource conservation
- recycling and reusing waste materials
- scientific management of renewable resources, especially bio-resources
- planting more trees
- using environment-friendly material or biodegradable material and
- using environment-friendly technology based on efficient use of resources.

1.10 SMALL SUSTAINABLE DEVELOPMENT INITIATIVES

After plastics were banned by the municipal corporation of Mangalore, an innovator and entrepreneur Mr Avasth Hedge found an eco-friendly, **100% bio-degradable bag** which can dissolve in hot water and decompose in natural environment. Now, this bag is in high demand in many countries.

Narayana Peesapaty, another innovator, wanted to stop the use of plastic spoons, forks, etc. So, he made **edible cutlery** made out of grain. Users can even eat these spoons. The best part of this cutlery is that it can easily decompose in the soil, enriching it.

Shagun Singh started Geeli Mitti to teach the world to build earthquake-proof, environment-friendly, cool and **durable homes with mud and bamboo.**

Prerna Prasad, CEO of Ecoplore, started a green business which urges people to explore nature in an eco-friendly manner and promote healthy living. The venture **promotes hotels** that are at least 30% green inside their boundary and made of non-concrete material.

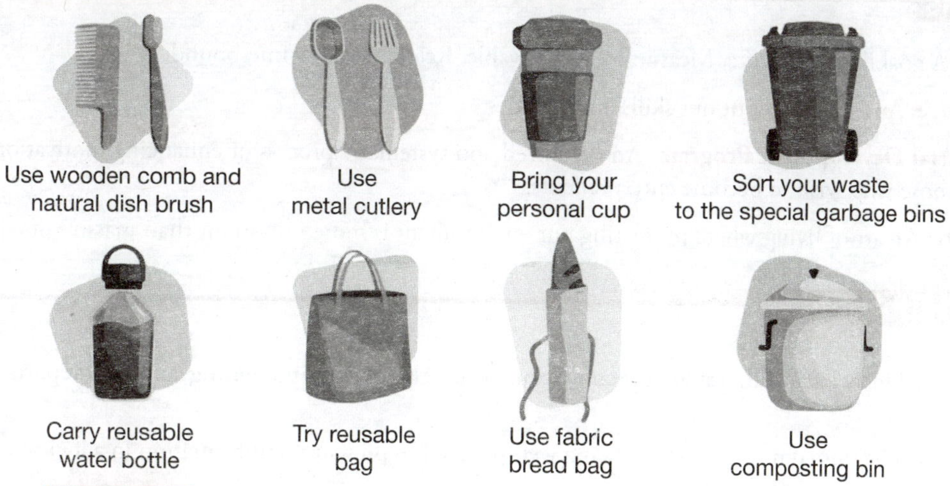

Figure 1.6 Infrastructure should be created taking sustainability into account

Sahar Mansoor is the founder of Bare Necessities which is a zero-waste company that aims to provide a **zero-waste environment**. The company aims to promote products which are powered by natural, bare Indian ingredients, having no harmful impacts on health or the environment. These products are handcrafted by women in Karnataka.

These initiatives by Indian innovators are a few examples of groundwork being done in the right direction to conserve Nature (Fig. 1.6).

1.11 SUSTAINABILITY STEPS TO BE TAKEN BY US

Each one of us can contribute to sustainable development by becoming responsible environment citizens in the following ways:

- Limit the use of facilities and resources.
- Use car-pooling to go to school with friends and not alone.
- Help each other in studies, especially those who wish to drop out of school.
- To overcome inequality issues, be friendly with everyone and play with everyone without thinking about the category to which the other student belongs.
- Build toilets and create awareness towards sanitation.
- Save energy by switching off lights and fans when not in use.
- Use natural light as much as possible.
- Use energy-efficient lights (LED bulbs) and appliances or solar energy as much as possible.
- Reuse paper, glass, plastic, water, etc.
- Do not use plastic.
- Take cloth bags to market.
- Donate things like clothes, books, furniture, food, etc. that you no longer want.
- Buy goods from local manufacturers/producers/sellers.
- Repair leaking taps and pipes to avoid wasting water.

- Sort and treat garbage before disposing.
- Do not throw plastic items into the sea and other water bodies, to protect marine life.
- Plant more and more trees.

Key Terms

Smart Goal: A goal that is Specific, Measurable, Achievable, Relevant, and Time-bound.

Self-confidence: An attitude about our skills and abilities.

Entrepreneurial Development Program: An organized and systematic process of enhancing motivation, knowledge and skills of those who wish to become entrepreneurs.

Sustainability: An art of living where protecting our environment is more important than massive developments.

Chapter Highlights

- Instead of making a beautiful, but long presentation or speech, focus on presenting summary reports in a clear and lucid way.
- The key to a coherent communication is being well-planned to present the information in a logical and sequential manner.
- We must be formal in all our business communications. Be honest, respectful, considerate, open and polite when interacting with people.
- A good listener must be practical, emotionally intelligent, mature and highly focused individual.
- Feedback facilitates a two-way communication as it conveys information regarding successful delivery of a message.
- Being conscientious of our actions at work is an important part of self-management. When we act professionally while being considerate, we get more respect.
- We must set SMART goals – Specific, Measurable, Achievable, Relevant, and Time-bound.
- A person with low self-confidence is often passive or submissive and never trusts himself/herself or even others. Such a person feels inferior, unloved and becomes very sensitive to criticism.
- To achieve sustainability, the United Nations adopted 17 Sustainable Development Goals (SDGs) in 2015 as a universal call to action to end poverty, protect the planet and ensure that all people enjoy peace and prosperity by 2030.

Review Questions

1. Explain the basic characteristics of an effective communication.
2. List any three barriers to an effective communication.
3. What is the role of feedback in an effective communication?
4. Imagine that your friend is very upset because of some family-related reason. What will you suggestions will you give to help her manage herself well and come out of the problems as a stronger person?
5. Assume that you are a project manager in a renowned IT company. Some freshers have joined your project. Tell them how they should be organized in the office.
6. Rishabh's classmate thinks very low of himself. He is too shy to talk to others and always thinks that he will be a failure in whatever he would do. What problem do you think he is suffering from and how can he get rid of it?
7. Write any two sentences that differentiate between positive and negative self-talk.
8. What do you know about EDP?

9. Explain the 4*R*'s and 1*U* of Sustainability.
10. Write any 5 points on which SDGs emphasize.
11. Differentiate between confident behavior and less confident behavior.

Fill in the Blanks

1. A _______ idea that is always backed by facts or data is more valued.
2. Stage fear, speech disorders, phobia and depression are ________ barriers to an effective communication.
3. _______ facilitates a two-way communication as it conveys information regarding successful delivery of a message.
4. _________ helps to understand the attitude of the receiver.
5. Being ________ of our actions at work is an important part of self-management.
6. A self-managed person always sets ________ goals.
7. In a smart goal, SMART means _______, ______, ______, _______ and ______.
8. ________ before you speak.
9. We must stay ____ and think ______.
10. _________ promotes innovations and harnesses the vast untapped human skills, to channelize them into accelerating industrialization.
11. _________ is the art of living where protecting our environment is more important than massive developments.

State True or False

1. We must use bullet points to convey several messages together.
2. A good listener must be practical, emotionally intelligent, mature and a highly focused individual.
3. We should analyze the situation but never make judgments about any person.
4. Anger, frustration and bad humor are psychological barriers to an effective communication.
5. You can control everything and everyone around you.
6. When we act professionally while being considerate, we get more money but not respect.
7. A person with low self-confidence feels inferior and unloved and becomes very sensitive to criticism.
8. When feeling intense emotions, we must not slow down.
9. A person with high level of self-confidence has healthy relationships.
10. EDP supports small-scale and micro enterprises which require less investment in funds.

Multiple Choice Questions

1. Use short and simple sentences to make the communication _______.
   a. clear
   b. courteous
   c. relevant
   d. correct
2. Identify the incorrect option.
   a. We must use active voice rather than passive voice.
   b. Bullet points should be used to convey several messages together.
   c. Presentations should be long and attractive.
   d. Summary reports should be created.

3. A ________ communication is well-planned to have a logical and sequential presentation of the information.
   a. clear
   b. courteous
   c. coherent
   d. correct

4. ________ means we should be honest, respectful, considerate, open and polite when interacting with people.
   a. Clear
   b. Courteous
   c. Coherent
   d. Correct

5. A good speaker should ________.
   a. use offensive words
   b. reveal his/her political affinity
   c. crack jokes to make some people laugh even if a few get hurt
   d. talk precisely

6. Which of the following is not a cultural barrier to effective communication?
   a. Different regions
   b. Different religions
   c. Different lifestyles
   d. Faulty equipment

7. Shrillness of voice and dyslexia, are some common ________ barriers to effective communication.
   a. physiological
   b. psychological
   c. physical
   d. perception

8. Identify the incorrect statement about feedback.
   a. The receiver participates in the communication.
   b. It ensures that the message is rightly sent and interpreted.
   c. It supports effective coordination and team work.
   d. None of these.

9. What should be the priority of your life?
   a. Family
   b. Studies
   c. Health
   d. Wealth

10. To manage ourselves, we must not be ________.
    a. organized
    b. calm
    c. focused on one thing at a time
    d. multi-tasking always

11. Your daily time-table must not include ________.
    a. time for study
    b. time for play
    c. time for chatting with friends
    d. None of these.

12. Suppose you have an important business meeting at the office. What should you not do?
    a. Eat heavy and fried food on the night before the meeting so that you don't feel hungry
    b. Prepare well in advance
    c. Arrive on or even before time
    d. Sleep on time the day before.

13. ________ is an attitude about our skills and abilities.
    a. Self-management
    b. Self-confidence
    c. Self-motivation
    d. Self-learning

14. We develop low self-confidence due to ________.
    a. growing up in an unsupportive and critical environment
    b. separation from friends or family.
    c. anxiety issues and being afraid of failure.
    d. All of these.

15. Our goals should not be ________.
    a. perfect
    b. realistic
    c. unachievable
    d. practical

16. To boost self-confidence, we should
    a. not make any assumptions.
    b. never judge ourselves.
    c. not compare ourselves to others.
    d. All of these.

17. Which of the following is not an entrepreneurial motivation factor?
    a. Unsatisfactory work environment
    b. Unwanted and unexpected change in career
    c. Urge to do something different or of your own
    d. To work under someone.

18. Which of the following is not correct about EDP?
    a. It enhances motivation.
    b. It narrows the outlook of individuals.
    c. It fixes the problem of unemployment.
    d. It provides personal counseling and support.

19. Identify the incorrect point about sustainable development.
    a. It meets the needs of the present generation.
    b. It saves resources for future generations to use them to meet their demands.
    c. Resources are used only to the extent where they can be replenished.
    d. It focuses on the use-and-throw concept.

20. We must ________ to use products that may harm the environment.
    a. refuse
    b. recycle
    c. reduce
    d. reuse

21. ___________ gives a new look to the old product to make it attractive for use.
    a. Recycle
    b. Upcycle
    c. Reuse
    d. All of these.

22. Sustainability does not promote ______.
    a. balanced economic growth
    b. safety of environment
    c. welfare of humans
    d. unlimited development

Group Discussion

1. Discuss how we can support sustainable development in our daily lives.
2. Business ideas – do we have to innovate something?
3. If given support, what business would you like to start and why?

Class Activity

Design a poster inviting students from classes VI–VIII in your school to participate in an IT Quiz. Email this poster to class monitors of all the sections.

Project Work

1. Draw posters to promote the concept of 4*R*'s and 1*U* of sustainability.
2. Make a PowerPoint presentation on SDG of the United Nations.

Answers

Fill in the Blanks

1. concrete
2. psychological
3. Feedback
4. Feedback
5. conscientious
6. SMART
7. Specific, Measurable, Achievable, Relevant, and Time-bound
8. Think
9. calm, logically
10. Entrepreneurial Development Programme
11. Sustainability

State True or False

1. True
2. True
3. True
4. False
5. False
6. False
7. True
8. False
9. True
10. True

Multiple Choice Questions

1. a
2. c
3. c
4. b
5. d
6. d
7. a
8. d
9. c
10. d
11. d
12. a
13. b
14. d
15. c
16. d
17. d
18. b
19. d
20. a
21. d
22. d

ICT Skills

2

Chapter Objectives

The chapter recapitulates some important ICT skills that students have already learnt in their junior classes. Topics covered in this chapter include:

- Different types of operating system like batch processing, multi-programming, time sharing, multi-user, multi-processing, distributed, real-time, mobile and embedded operating system
- User interface – CUI and GUI
- Understanding file management concepts and managing files on computer
- Permanently deleting data and restoring deleted files
- Commandments of computer care
- Computer hardware and software maintenance

2.1 TYPES OF OPERATING SYSTEM

ICT stands for Information Communication Technology. In this chapter, we will read about different types of operating systems that were available in the market. This will help you to realize that this technology has come a long way to make our work simpler and faster.

2.1.1 Batch Processing Systems

In this type of operating system, there is no direct interaction between user and the computer. It was used decades ago. The user submits his work (better known as job) written on cards or tape to a computer operator (Fig. 2.1).

The computer operator collects several jobs and makes batches of similar jobs (jobs written in the same language and having similar requirements). The batches are then submitted to the computer for execution (as shown in Fig. 2.2). No doubt, the performance of such systems is very slow as a lot of time is wasted to create batches.

Figure 2.1

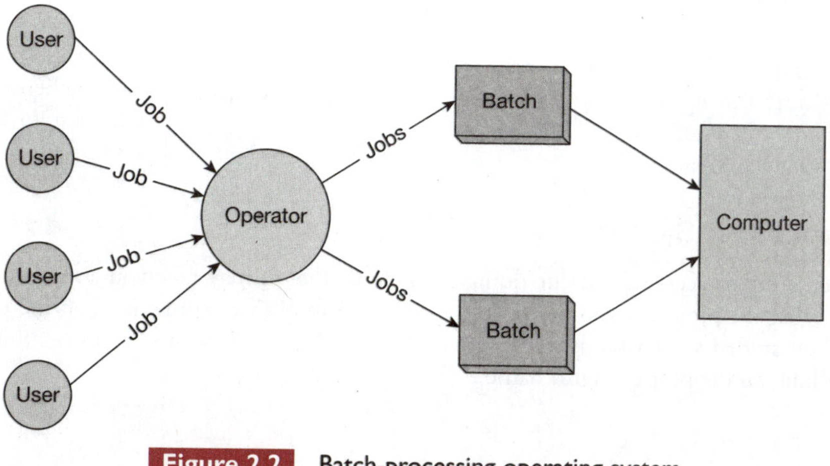

Figure 2.2 Batch-processing operating system

2.1.2 Single-user, Single-task Operating System

As the name implies, these operating systems work on a single task at a time and only a single user can use it at a time. MS-DOS, Palm OS used on handheld computers and mobile OS are examples of single-user, single-task operating system.

Example: MS-DOS.

2.1.3 Multi-programming Systems

What happens when you have a mock test in class? The teacher asks the student a question. If he/she is not able to answer, she immediately asks it to another student. This saves the teacher's time. Had the teacher been asking questions to every student individually, then one student will go to her, the teacher will ask questions, then the student will go back and send the other student. This will waste a lot of time as the teacher will be idle and waiting for the next student to arrive.

Same is the case in a single processing system in which only one program resides in the main memory. However, in a multi-programming operating system as shown in Fig. 2.3, two or more programs can reside in the main memory at the same time. ***The moment one program is executed, the CPU immediately takes the next program for execution. So, the main focus in a multi-programming system is to maximize the CPU usage.*** For this, the operating system decides which process will get memory when and how much.

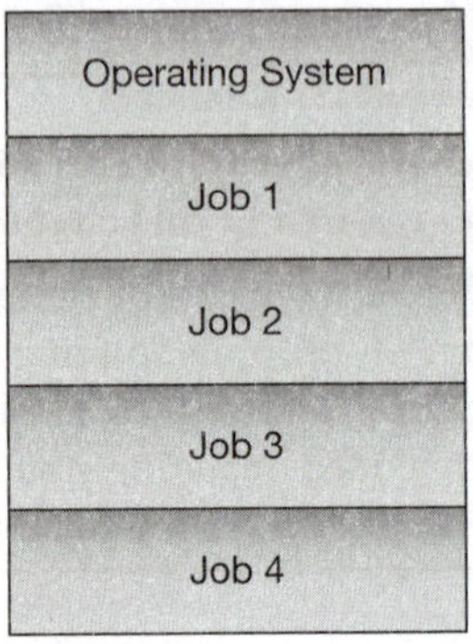

Figure 2.3 Multi-programming operating system

2.1.4 Time-sharing Systems or Multi-tasking Operating Systems

Time-sharing system goes one step ahead of multi-programming systems. In time sharing-systems, the main aim is to minimize the response time. And for this, multiple processes are executed at the same time by switching between them. However, switches occur at a very fast pace so that users get an immediate response from the computer. For example, if there are 5 processes to be executed, the CPU will run each of them for less than one second. That is, it will place them in a queue. The first process is executed for say 0.001 seconds, then the second for 0.001 seconds, and so on. After the fifth process, it will return to the first process to execute it for another 0.001 seconds. This will be repeated until all the processes are completely executed.

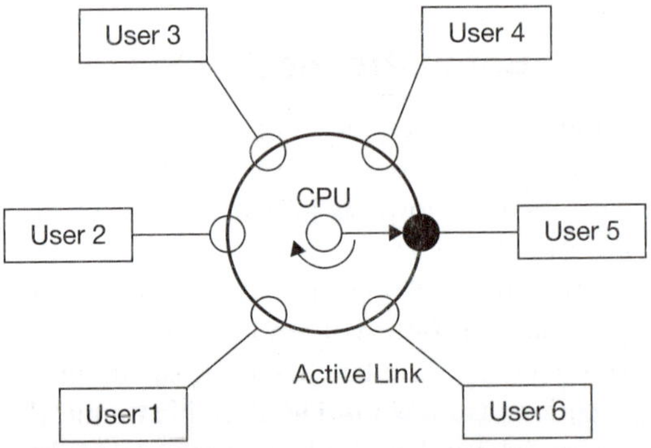

Figure 2.4 Time-sharing operating system

Time-sharing operating systems are also known as single-user, multi-tasking operating system as only one user can use the computer but he can run a number of applications at the same time. All modern-day computers support time-sharing system. For example, we can listen to music while typing a document in Word.

Example: Mac OS, MS Windows.

> Response time is the time elaspsed between submission of a request to the time the first response is produced.

2.1.5 Multi-processor Systems

When you are given a big project and you are doing it all alone, then it may take you a month to complete it. But if your teacher says that the project has to be completed by a group of three students, then the project work will be divided amongst three students. So, what is the advantage here? The project is complete in less time as you have more than one brain working on the project, right? Same is the case with computer systems.

In a multi-processor system (Fig. 2.5), several processors or CPUs are used. They all share a common memory. A multi-processor system provides higher computing power and speed. This is because multiple processors work together under a single operating system.

Therefore, we can say that with multi-processor system, we get better performance by speeding up execution.

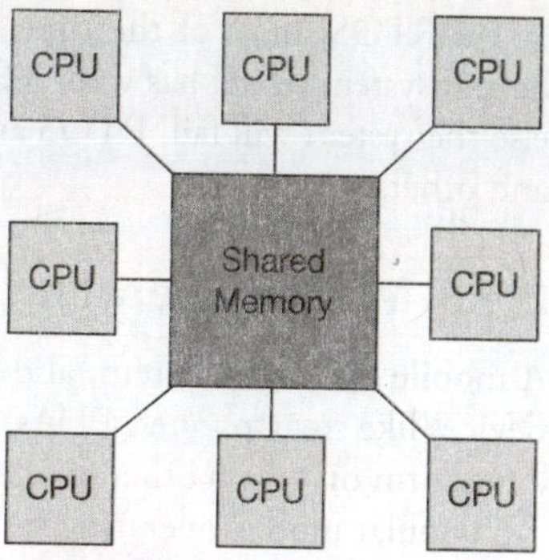

Figure 2.5 Multi-processor operating system

2.1.6 Distributed Operating Systems

The advancement in technology and decline in cost of computer systems have made it possible to design and develop distributed systems. A distributed system (Fig. 2.6) comprises of many computers that are connected by a network. In this type of operating system, a user working on one computer can utilize the resources (including data or devices) of another computer on the same network. The main advantage of distributed system is that it enables fast processing and does not put the entire load of work on one machine.

> The main difference between distributed system and multi-processor system is that in multiprocessor system there are multiple processors which share a common memory. But in a distributed system, there are multiple computer systems. No memory is shared.

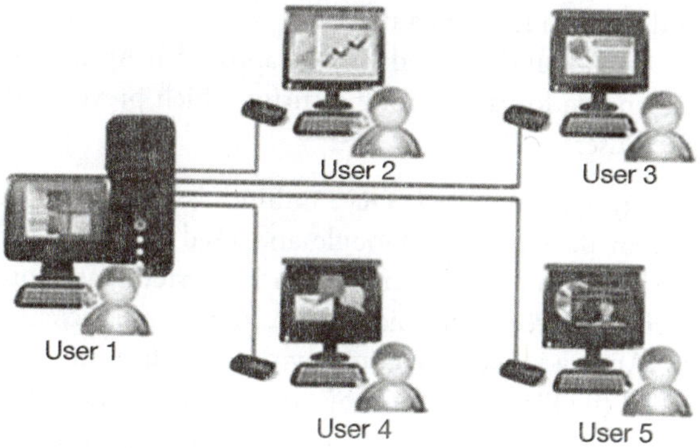

Figure 2.6 Distributed operating system

The most common example of a distributed system is the client–server system (as shown in Fig. 2.7) in which clients send requests to perform an action, and the server performs the action and returns the result to the client.

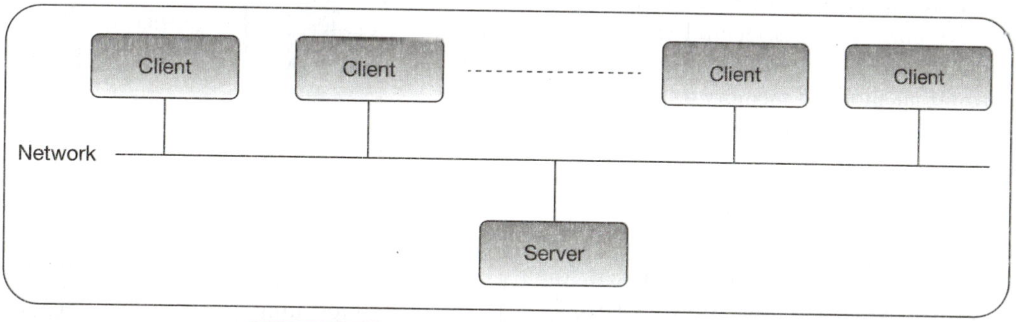

Figure 2.7 Distributed client–server system

In a distributed operating system, all the computers work in co-operation with each other. Such an operating system manages all the computers and makes them appear to be a single computer system.

Example: Unix, Linux.

2.1.7 Real-time Operating System

Real-time Operating Systems (RTOS) are systems which demand very fast and quick response. For example, RTOS is used in a petroleum refinery to measure temperature and send warnings if the temperature gets too high and demand immediate attention to avoid an explosion.

In RTOS, most of the time, processes remain in primary memory to provide immediate response. It is a time-bound system which has well-defined time constraints. Processing must be complete within the defined constraints or else the system will fail. RTOS are widely used in embedded systems, industrial robots, scientific research equipment and others.

2.1.8 Mobile Operating Sytem

A mobile operating system, also known as mobile OS, is an operating system that is specifically designed for mobile devices like smartphones, PDAs, tablet computers and other handheld devices. The mobile operating system provides a platform on which other applications (known as apps) can run.

Popular mobile operating systems are Android, Symbian, iOS, BlackBerry OS and Windows Mobile.

A mobile OS is similar to a computer operating system (like Windows, Linux, and Mac) but it is relatively simple and light. Two popular mobile operating system are:

Apple iOS Apple's iOS is the second most popular smartphone operating systems. It runs on Apple devices only like iPhones, iPad tablets and iPod Touch media players.

Users can download various apps from Apple App Store. iOS apps are known for their strong security, which prevents access by unauthorized users.

> Chromium is an operating system by Google, which is used with chromebooks.
>
> 
>
> Google chromebooks

Google's Android OS Android is the most popular operating system developed by Google and used in smart phones and tablets. Android is an open-source operating system based on Linux. The user interface of Android is very simple and efficient.

Android, like iOS, comes with an application and media store called the Play Store built by Google. Some phone manufacturers and other organizations also offer their own stores to install software and media.

Handheld operating systems (shown in Fig. 2.8) are used in handheld devices like PDAs, tablets, smartphones. These systems have a comparatively small amount of memory, include slow processors, and have small display screens. Therefore, the operating system must manage memory and other resources efficiently. This includes returning all allocated memory to the memory manager, once the memory is no longer being used.

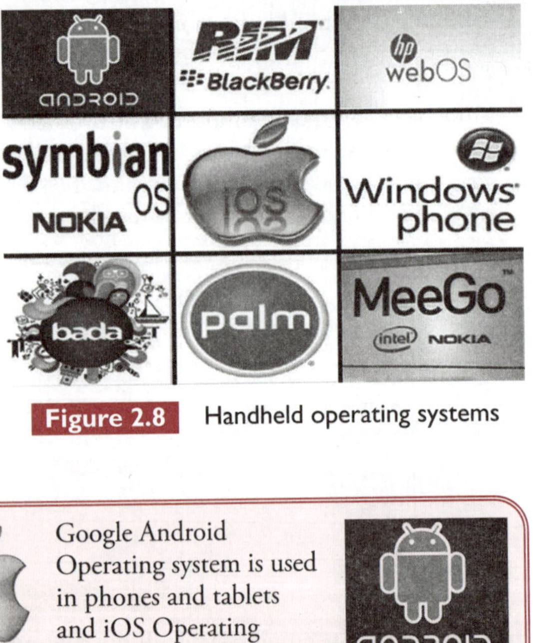

Figure 2.8 Handheld operating systems

2.1.9 Embedded Operating System

Embedded operating system, as the name suggests, is embedded in a device. In an embedded system, the operating system is located in the ROM. Generally, embedded systems do not have many resources. They are widely used in appliances like microwaves, washing machines, traffic control systems, cars, ATMs, airplane controls, point-of-sale (POS) terminals, digital cameras, GPS navigation systems, elevators, etc.

> Google Android Operating system is used in phones and tablets and iOS Operating system used with the Apple iPhone and iPads.

2.2 TYPES OF OPERATING SYSTEM BASED ON USER INTERFACE

We now know that the operating system acts as an interface or intermediary between the user and the computer hardware. This means that the operating system provides an interface through which users can give commands to the computer. Thus, based on the type of interface, operating systems can be classified into two groups.

2.2.1 Command Line Interface (CLI) or Character User Interface (CUI)

In this type of operating system, the users type commands to give instructions to the computer.

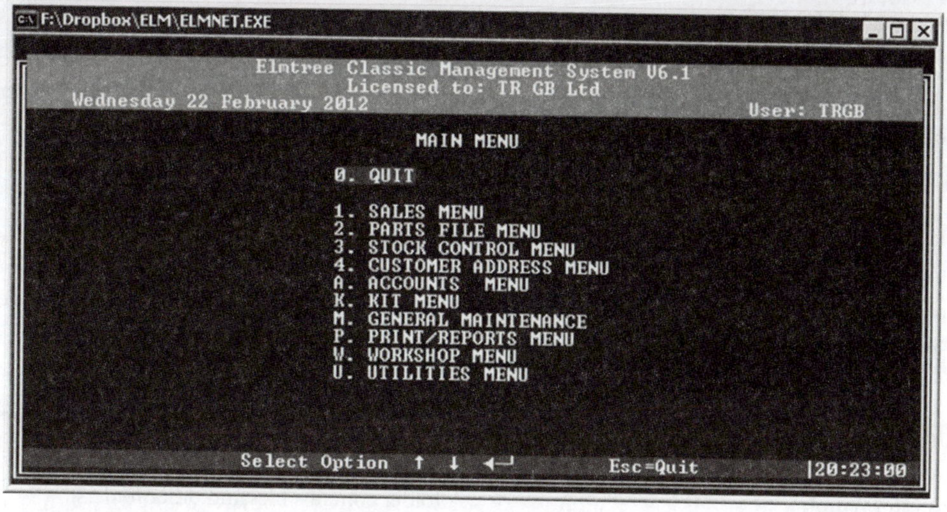

2.2.2 Graphical User Interface (GUI)

Modern operating systems are all based on GUI. In this type of operating system, users interact with the operating system by giving commands using the mouse. That is, to give commands or instructions to the computer, users move the mouse to click **icons, buttons,** and **menus,** or other such tabs that are displayed on the screen. For example, to open the MS Paint program you just double-click on its icon. To save a file, you just click on the File Menu and then click on the Save option.

Table 2.1 shows the difference between command liner interface (CLI) and graphical user interface (GUI).

Table 2.1 Comparison of CLI and GUI

Command Line Interface (CLI)	Graphical User Interface (GUI)
The user must learn all the commands to use the computer.	The user does not need to learn any commands.
The users must type full commands.	Users can even use shortcuts; for example, to save a file, he/she can either click on menus or press Ctrl + S keys.
Since the user has to learn lot of commands; it is difficult to work with.	Since users have to just click and not learn, it is very easy to work with.
Only people having good knowledge of computer can work with CLI.	Even children and those who don't know much about computers can work with GUI.
Only keyboard is used as the input device.	Mouse and other pointing devices are also used as input devices.
Consumes less memory as there are no pictures, menus or icons.	Consumes more memory as there are lot of colors, pictures, menus and other items.
Example, MS DOS	Example, MS Windows, Linux, Ubuntu

2.3 FILE MANAGEMENT

We have been reading about the terms files, folders, etc., in our previous classes. Let us quickly recapitulate the basic terminology that we had been using.

Drive: A drive is a computer storage device that can store our files, folders and programs. The top-level Drive (also known as the Root Directory) is usually designated with a letter such as C:\ in Windows. The C drive refers to the hard drive of the computer.

Folder: A folder is a storage location within a drive. It can have other files or folders inside it.

Sub-folders: A folder inside another folder is called a sub-folder.

File: A file is used to store related information. This information can be text, picture, audio, video, or just any other thing. Files are typically associated with a program or software application that is needed in order to open them. The difference between a file and folder is given in Table 2.2

Table 2.2 Difference between file and folder

File	Folder
A file contains information.	A folder contains files and other folders.
A file name has an extension.	A folder name does not have any extension.
The icon of files varies depending on the program in which it is created.	The icon of all the folders is same.

File Name: A computer identifies every file by its name. This name is known as the file name. Files in the same folder must have unique names. This means that we cannot have two files with name File.docx in our folder.

File Extension: The file extension comprises of those characters that appear after the dot in the file name. File extension indicates the program in which the file is created. For example, the file extension ".docx" indicates that the file is a Microsoft Word document. Some commonly used file extensions are shown in Table 2.3

Table 2.3 Common file extensions

Extension	Type of File
.txt	Text file created in WordPad
.docx	Text File. Can contain pictures. Created in MS Word
.pptx	Presentation File created in MS PowerPoint
.jpg, .bmp, .gif	Picture File created in MS Paint
.wav,..mp3, .aiff, .wma	Sound or audio file
.avi, .mp4, .wmv, .mov, .flv	Video file
.rar, .tar	Compressed files
.xlsx, .odx	Spreadsheet file
.bak, .cur, .ico, .tmp, .sys	Operating system file
.pdf	Portable Document Format

Path: Every file or folder in the computer has a unique path which helps us to easily locate it in the computer. We can specify the path in two ways – using the absolute path or relative path.

The ***absolute path*** contains the full path to the file. The location starts from a particular drive and ends at the name of the file.

The ***relative path***, on the other hand, specifies the path of the file with respect to the current working directory. It does not give the complete path.

Table 2.4 compares the two forms of path specification.

Table 2.4 Absolute path and relative path

Absolute Path	Relative Path
It specifies the complete path of the file in the computer.	It specifies a partial path of the file in the computer.
It is not specified with respect to the current working directory.	It is specified with respect to the current working directory.
The path starts from the name of the drive (or the root directory) and ends at the name of the file.	The path may begin from any directory (or folder) and end at the name of the file.
Example, D:\Teachers\File 2.pptx	Example, File2.pptx If the user is currently working in Teachers folder, then it means the file D:\Teachers\File 2.pptx

2.3.1 File Management Utility

A *File Management Utility* is a computer program provided by the operating system. For example, Windows 10 has the File Explorer utility. File Explorer provides users a graphical interface using which they can organize their files and folders on the computer's storage device.

Zipping or Compressing Folders Zipping or compressing a folder means packaging a folder that contains multiple files into a single file. This file is called compressed folder or zipped folder. A zipped folder not only combines multiple files into one but also takes less space as compared to the space taken by individual files.

A zipped folder is especially useful when we have to email multiple files to someone. It has a ".zip" or ".rar" file extension. The receiver has to first unzip the folder to view the files. To compress a folder, follow the steps given below:

Step 1: Open File Explorer.

Step 2: Locate the folder to be compressed.

Step 3: Right-click on the folder and click on Add to FolderName.rar option from the pop-up menu (Fig. 2.9).

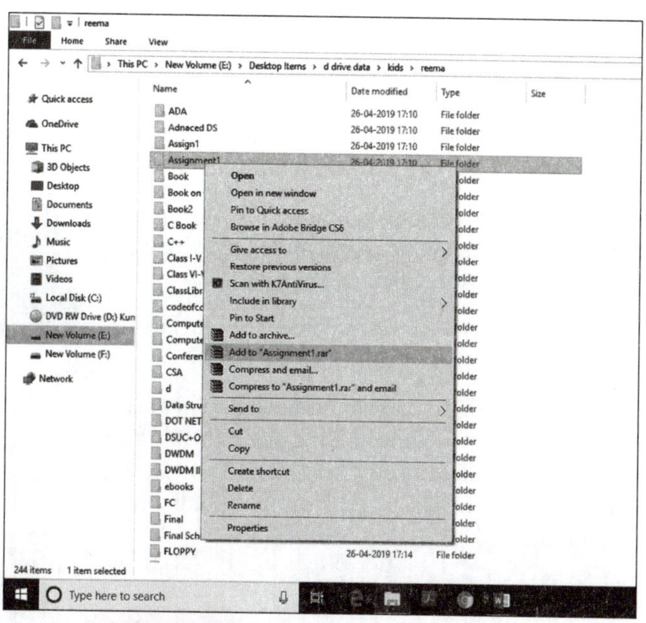

Figure 2.9 Steps to compress a folder

The folder will be zipped.

To unzip or uncompress the folder, right-click on the compressed folder and click on Extract to FolderName\ option form the pop-up menu (Fig. 2.10).

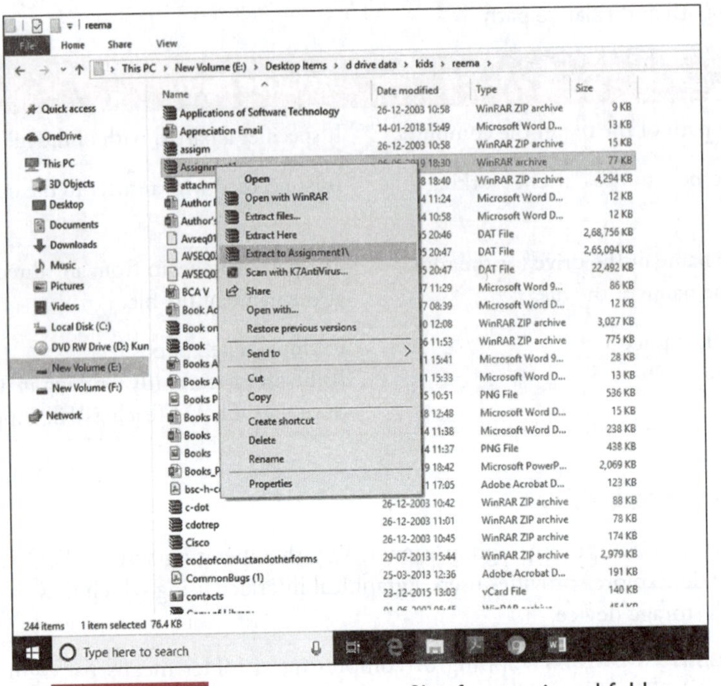

Figure 2.10 Steps to extract files from a zipped folder

File Management File management includes methods for creating, naming, storing, sorting, arranging, accessing, moving, editing and organizing files to store information for easy retrieval. A file management system like that of File Explorer allows users to browse through folders and access the different files stored in them.

2.4 TRANSFERRING FILE(S) FROM PEN DRIVE TO YOUR COMPUTER

In the previous classes, we have studied that to **copy or move files** we just have to right-click on the file(s) in the File Explorer and select Copy (to copy) or Cut (to move) the files. Then we have to locate the destination folder, right-click on it and select Paste option from the pop-up menu.

Similarly, to **delete, rename or compress** files or folders, we have to right-click on that file or folder and select the desired option. Now to copy files(s) from a pen drive to your computer, follow the steps given below:

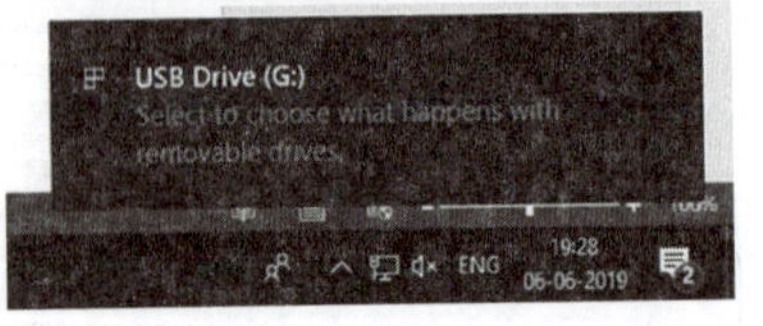

Step 1: Plug the flash drive into USB port of your computer. You will get a message at the bottom right corner of the screen notifying that the USB drive has been connected as G:\ drive (or any other drive). Click on the message.

Step 2: A menu will appear on the screen. Click on open Folder to view Files to open the File Explorer.

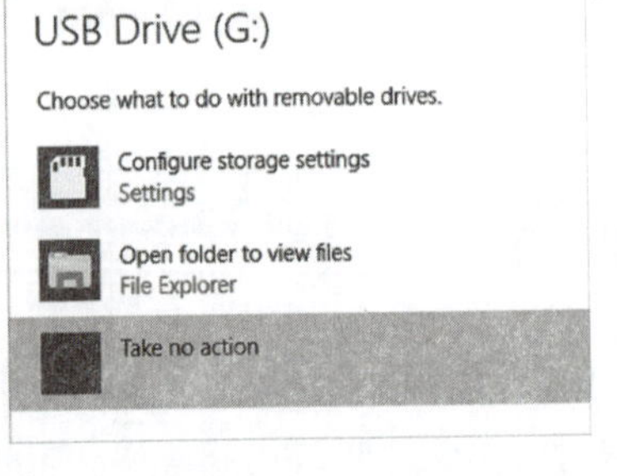

Step 3: Select file(s) or folder(s) to be copied. To select multiple adjacent (placed next to each other) files or folders, click on them while holding down the Shift key on the keyboard. To select all the files or folders, press Ctrl + A keys on the key-board. To select multiple non-adjacent files or folders, click on them individually while holding down the Ctrl key on the keyboard.

Step 4: Right-click and select Copy from the pop-up menu.

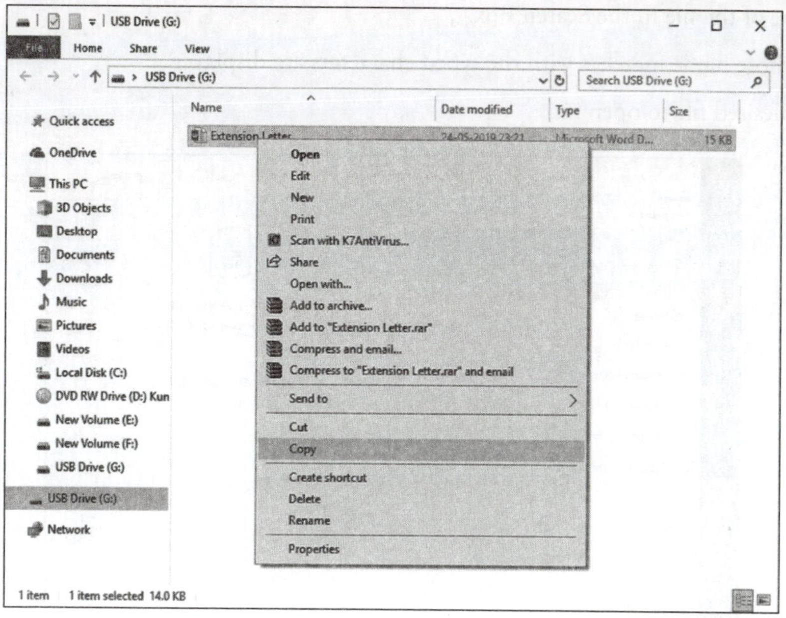

Step 5: Select the folder into which you want to copy the selected files or folders from the pen drive.

Step 6: Right-click on the folder and select Paste from the pop-up menu.

Once you are done with transferring files from your pen drive, you must eject it properly. Eject means removing it from the computer. If you don't eject properly then it may corrupt (spoil or affect) the data stored in it.

To eject the pen drive, follow the steps given below.

Step 1: Click on the Show Hidden Icons in the right corner of the Task Bar.

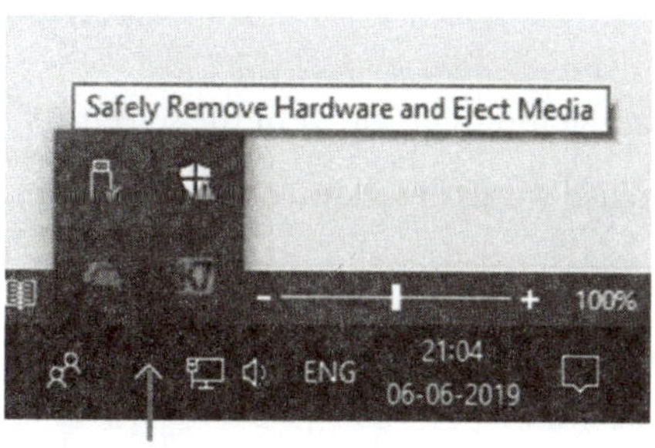

Show Hidden Icon

Step 2: Click on Safely Remove Hardware and Eject Media.

Step 3: Click on Eject Mass Storage Device.

Step 4: Wait for a moment. You will get a notification that the flash drive is safe to remove. Now you can remove the pen drive from your computer by gently pulling on it.

To copy files or folders from the computer in to pen drive, first select the files and folders from your computer. Then, right on G:\ and select Paste from the pop-up menu.

2.5 SEARCHING FILE(S) OR FOLDER(S) IN WINDOWS 10

We all have countless files and folders in our computer. To search for a particular file or folder may take a very long time and it may be just impossible, at times. To make our search easy, Windows 10 allows users to use the Search box (Fig. 2.11). Follow the steps given below to search for a particular file on your computer:

In Windows 11, Microsoft has done away with putting the Search box in the taskbar by default. To get the Search box on the taskbar, follow the steps given below:

Step 1: Press and hold (or right-click) the taskbar and select Taskbar settings.

Step 2: Select Taskbar items to expand the section, then toggle the Search switch to On.

Step 1: Type the name of the file in the Search Box.

Step 2: All the files whose name matches with the typed characters are displayed.

Step 3: Click on the desired file to open it.

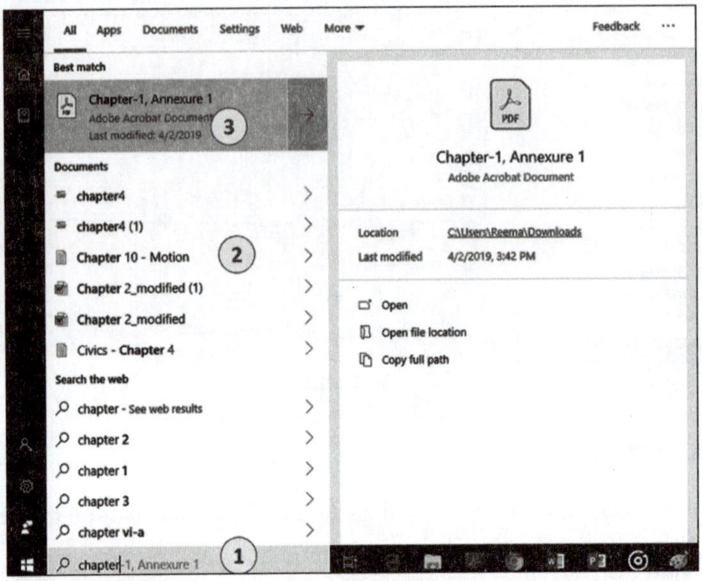

Figure 2.11 Search for a file or folder in the Search Box

Another Way of Searching Files or Folders

An alternative way to search for files/folders on the computer is to use the File Explorer. Follow the steps given below to search using File Explorer:

Step 1: Open the File Explorer by clicking on its icon in the taskbar.

Step 2: Type the file name or part of the file name in the Search Box present at the top right corner of the screen.

Windows 10 will find the files matching the typed query and highlight the matched words in yellow colour (Fig. 2.12).

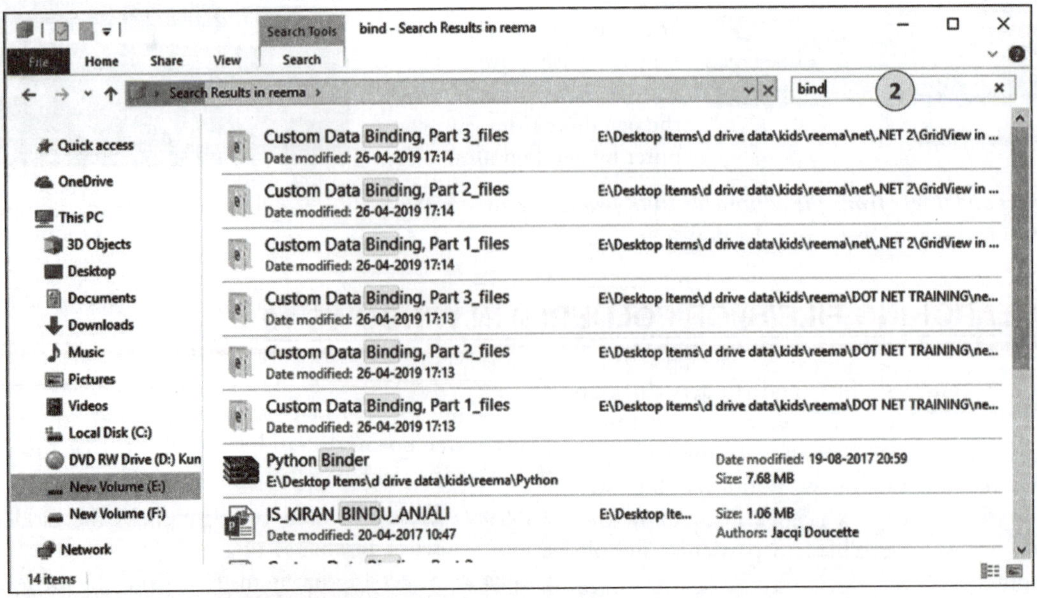

Figure 2.12 Search for a file or folder in the Search Box

2.5.1 Efficient Serarching of Files Using Wildcard Characters

We can use the following wildcard characters to search for our files and folders accurately and efficiently. If we don't use wildcards then Windows will, by default, use all possible combinations. This will not only take more time to find our files but also give us a huge list of files from which we will have to find the desired file. So using wildcard characters, narrows down (or reduces) the list of files or folders returned by the Windows Search program. Table 2.5 shows the common wildcard characters used in Windows.

Table 2.5 Common wildcard characters

Wildcard Character	Purpose	Example
*	Matches any string of characters (including the empty string) of any length.	C*t will match cat, cabt or any number of characters between c and t.
?	Matches for any single character or symbol.	C?t will match cat, c1t, c_t or any filename with a single character between c and t.
!	Excludes the given file name pattern	!*.docx will search for any file except MS Word files.

2.5.2 More Examples of Wildcard Characters

T????.pptx will search all PowerPoint presentations with a five-character filename starting with *T*.

.xls? will locate all files with a four-character file extension, where the first three characters have to be xls. Therefore, *Budget 2020.xlsx* will match but *Target.xls* will not match.

> A ? also matches a space. Therefore b???ba?? Will match bat ball.

r??????.* will find all files with a seven-character filename that starts with *r*.

chap* will return any files or folders whose name starts with *chap*.

ter will return any files or folders whose name ends with *ter*.

p* will return all files or folders that have a *p* anywhere in the name.

> The question mark substitutes for one letter or symbol but the asterisk is used to substitute for many letters and symbols.

cha*.*s returns any file or folder whose name starts with *cha* and has a file extension that ends with *s*.

ch*er will return all files or folders whose name starts with *ch* and ends with *er*.

c?????r will return any file or folder whose name has c?????r anywhere in the name. For example, this will match *chapter1 Edited.docx* as well as *New_chapter1.docx.*

pter will find any file or folder that has *pter* anywhere in the file or folder name.

r.txt will find all files whose name ends with *r* and have an extension *.txt.*

r*.txt will find all files whose name starts with *r* and have an extension *.txt.*

.pptx will find all files with extension *.pptx*.

Chapter.* will find all files with name *Chapter* and any extension.

. will find all files irrespective of their name and extension.

2.6 COPYING AND MOVING FILES

Copy a file means to create a duplicate copy of the file. Copy operation preserves or retains the original copy of the file. Follow the steps given below to copy a file from one folder to another:

Step 1: Click on File Explorer icon on the Task Bar to open it.

Step 2: Open the folder from which you want to copy the file(s).

Step 3: Click on the file that you want to copy. To select multiple files hold the Ctrl key on the keyboard pressed while clicking on the files.

Step 4: Right-click and select Copy from the menu (Fig. 2.13).

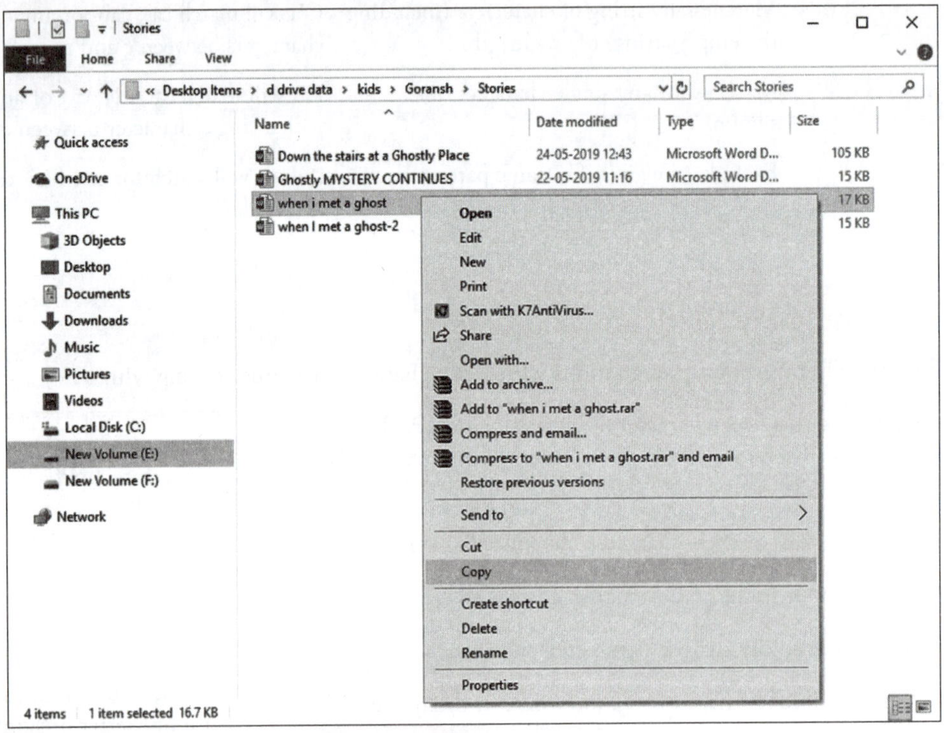

Figure 2.13 Copying a file

Step 5: Open the folder in which you want to copy the file(s).

Step 6: Right-click on an empty space and click on Paste option from the menu.

Moving a file means performing cut-paste operations. That is, deleting a file from the original location and moving it to another location.

Step 1: Click on File Explorer icon on the Task Bar to open it.

Step 2: Open the folder from which you want to move file(s).

Step 3: Click on the file that you want to move. To select multiple files hold the Ctrl key on the keyboard pressed while clicking on the files.

Step 4: Right-click and select Cut from the menu.

Step 5: Open the folder in which you want to move the file(s).

Step 6: Right-click on an empty space and click on Paste option from the menu.

2.6.1 Permanently Deleting Files

Formatting a hard drive and wiping it clean are two different things. Since deleted files can still be retrieved from a formatted hard drive, you must take an extra step to overwrite the data with special software.

But in case of wipe cleaning the hard drive, always back up any file(s) that you think you may need in future. This is important because once the drive is wipe cleaned, it will be impossible or very expensive to retrieve any lost data later. Wipe cleaning the hard drive must be done to protect personal information before selling/recycling, giving, donating a computer or cleaning out unnecessary files.

2.7 RECOVERY OF DELETED DATA

Data once deleted can be easily recovered and restored from the Recycle Bin or data backup storage. In fact, there are file recovery software that can recover even those files that have been permanently removed without any backup.

To recover a file deleted in Windows, follow the steps given below:

Step 1: Right-click on the Recycle Bin icon on the desktop.

Step 2: Select the file(s) to restore.

Step 3: Right-click on the selected files.

Step 4: Click the Restore option from the pop-up menu (as shown in Fig. 2.14).

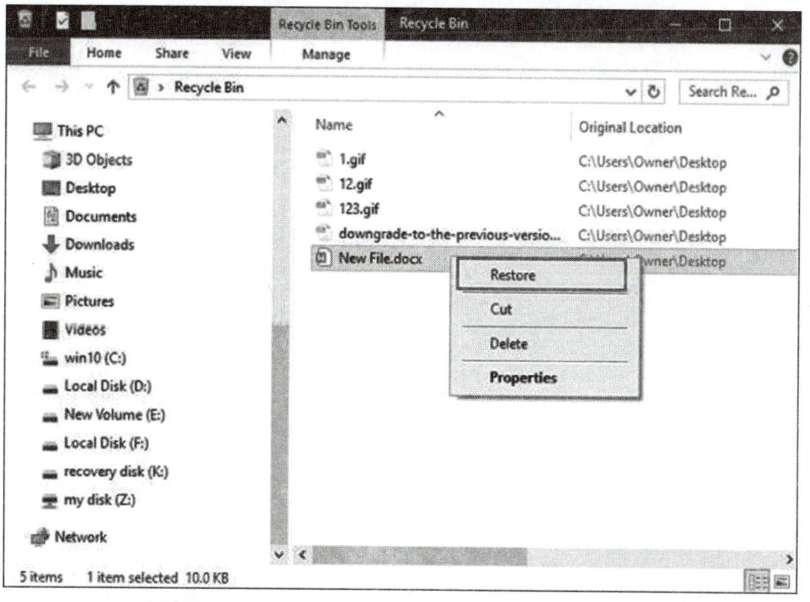

Figure 2.14 Restoring files/folders from recycle bin

This will retrieve deleted files and restore them to their original location. However, after restoration, you can move the files to any other drive or folder as you like.

2.8 CREATING A FOLDER IN C:

Follow the steps given below to create a folder in C:.

Step 1: Open the File Explorer. The simplest way to do is just click on the File Explorer icon on the Task Bar.

Step 2: Click on C: in the left pane of the File Explorer window.

Step 3: Right-click on any blank area in the right pane of the File Explorer window and then click on New from the pop-up menu.

Step 4: Click on Folder.

Step 5: Type a relevant name for your folder and press the Enter Key on the keyboard.
In the same way, you can make a folder in any drive or on the Desktop. Figure 2.15 shows the screenshots for creating a new folder.

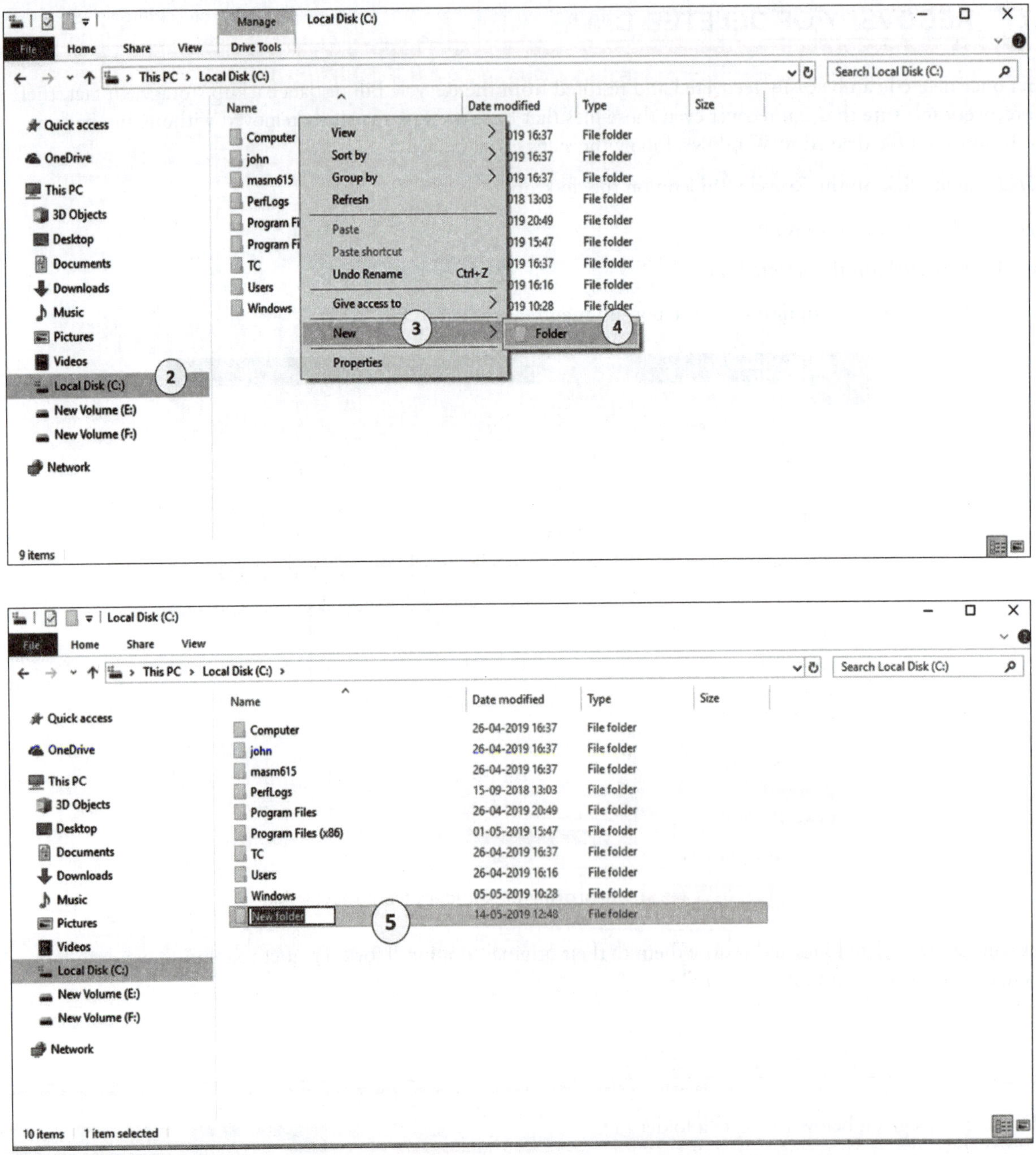

Figure 2.15 Creating a new file in C

2.9 DELETE A FOLDER OR SUB-FOLDER

Follow the steps given below to delete a folder:

Step 1: Open the File Explorer.

Step 2: In the left pane, click on the Drive.

Step 3: Navigate to the folder or the sub-folder to be deleted and select it in the right pane.

Step 4: Right-click on the folder or sub-folder to be deleted and click on Delete from the pop-up menu.

> If you simply delete a file, folder or a sub-folder, it will go in the Recycle Bin. But it you want it to be completed deleted from your computer and you don't want it to go even in the Recycle Bin, then left-click on the file or the folder and press the Shift Key and Delete key together on the keyboard.

Step 5: Windows will ask you whether you are sure that you want to delete or not. This is because if you delete a folder, all files and other sub-folders in that folder will also be deleted. Click on YES if you want to delete and NO otherwise.

The folder or the sub-folder will deleted along with its entire contents.

Figure 2.16 shows the screenshot for deleting a file

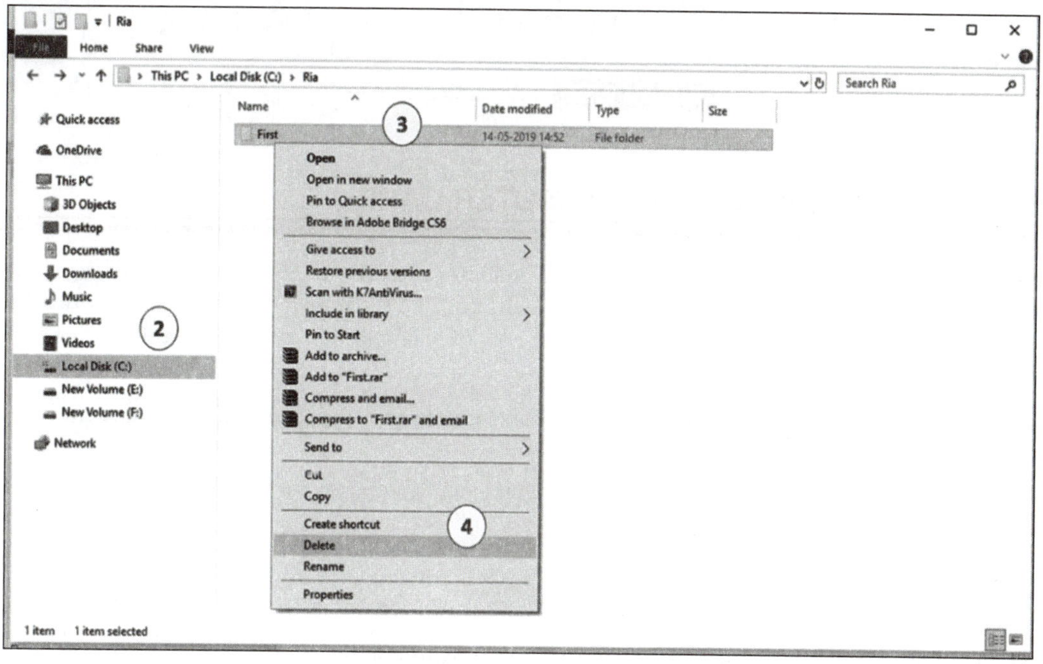

Figure 2.16 Deleting a file

2.10 RENAME A FOLDER OR SUB-FOLDER

Follow the steps given below to delete a folder:

Step 1: Open the File Explorer.

Step 2: In the left pane, click on the Drive.

Step 3: Navigate to the folder or the sub-folder to be renamed and select it (by left-clicking on it) in the right pane.

Step 4: Right-click on the folder or sub-folder to be reamed and click on Rename from the pop-up menu as shown in Fig. 2.17.

Step 5: Type a name for the folder or the sub-folder and press the Enter key on the keyboard.

The desired folder will be renamed.

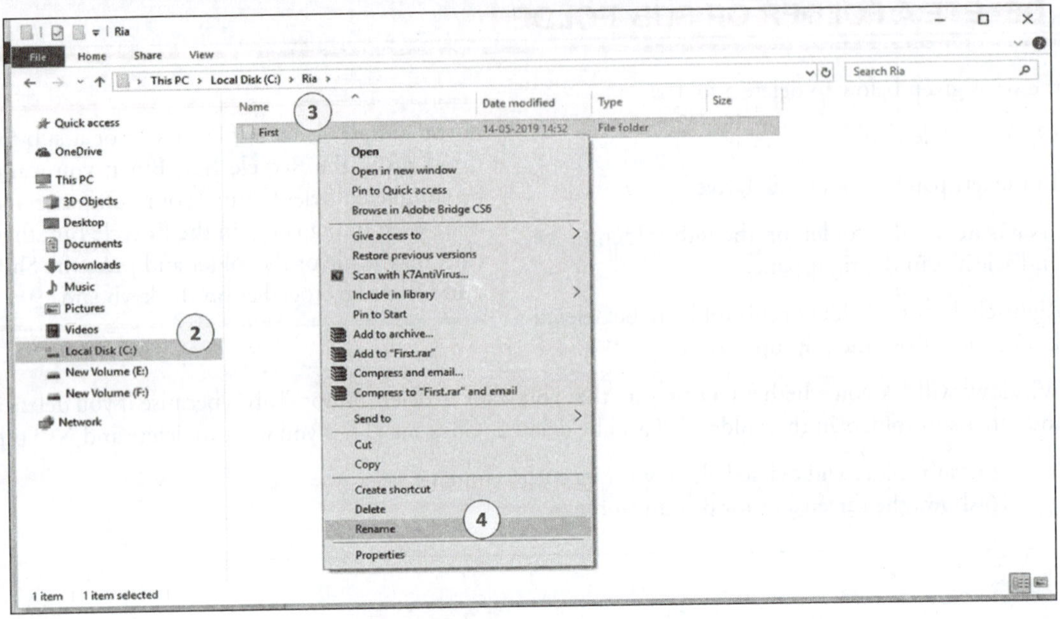

Figure 2.17 Renaming a folder

2.11 THE COMMANDMENTS OF COMPUTER CARE

Computers, like any other electronic device, need regular maintenance. As we go for annual medical check-up program, the computer also needs scheduled maintenance of hardware and software for an extended lifespan. This is often referred to as preventative maintenance. Before discussing how to maintain our computer, let us first understand why we should do it.

Address Issues before they become problems. Minor issues can easily aggravate into problems and they can adversely impact the performance of your computer.

Prevent Security Threats to keep your computer as well as yourself safe.

Improve Speed and Overall Performance of the computer. Designing a hardware maintenance calendar can actually extend the life of your computer system. So, to properly tune your hardware, you need to do the following things:

Install Antivirus Software. It is required to detect malware in your computer. An antivirus software will not allow any malware content to attack your computer. In case the computer is already infected with a malware, then the anti-virus software will remove the malware and protect the computer from its ill-effects. You may have to purchase a good anti-virus software, but that is worth it.

Perform Regular Software Updates. This helps in smooth running of the machine. Updates generally contain fixes for bugs and glitches as well as better security features.

Run Computer Maintenance. Regularly defragment the hard disk of your computer, clean the registry and do a full-system scan.

Backup Files. Regularly backup all your data on an external hard drive so that if something happens to your computer, at least the important files are safe.

Activate Screen Saver to protect your display monitor. Screen saver recycles the color and eliminates the outline burned image in the monitor.

Use a Surge Protector to protect your system from electric spikes and ensure a steady flow of electricity to your computer. This will protect your computer from damage or data loss due to fluctuations in voltage supply.

Use Uninterruptable Power Supplies (UPS) to your computer system and data when there is a power cut. With a UPS, you get ample time to save your files and properly turn off your computer during power loss.

> While cleaning your computer, make sure that you do not knock out any cords or damage internal components.

Avoid Extreme Temperatures The best room temperature for a computer is 68 to 71 degrees Fahrenheit. Make sure that you do not leave your laptop in a hot car or a cold, damp basement for instance.

Carry Laptops in Cases Preferably, these cases should be padded to protect computers from scratches and dents, and exposure to dust and debris inside the fans, vents, etc.

2.12 COMPUTER HARDWARE MAINTENANCE

We know that all the physical components of a computer (like keyboard, hard drives, internal CD or DVD drive, fans, etc.) constitute its hardware. We need to perform preventative maintenance programs for the visible as well as not-so-visible components of the computer at the system level and the physical level.

2.12.1 Physical Level Maintenance

This is where you clean the physical components of the computer. Clean the keyboard to ensure that you remove the dust sitting between the keys. It is important to remove and clean the fans that help maintain CPU temperature. Also, wipe off the monitor and blow out the dust sitting inside the CPU.

Make sure you complete this entire cleaning process carefully. Using any type of liquid or solvent can cause damage to the physical parts. Instead, it is important to use a soft cloth and the right type of solvent. During the maintenance process, do not expose the physical components to extreme temperature changes.

Keep your keyboard crumb-free. Do not eat or drink while working on the computer. It is very common to see food particles getting into keyboard or water or any liquid getting spilled on the keyboard.

Do not expose the computer to hazardous or toxic fumes since it can cause both internal and external damage to the system.

Clean the screen. Do it gently using a soft cloth or wipes specifically made for electronics.

Remove dust from vents and fans If you don't do it, then your computer may run very slow.

Figure 2.18 Avoid getting any liquid spilled on the keyboard

Clean the outer surface with the use of moderate soap and water. But make sure that the liquid does not penetrate to the internal parts. Avoid using harmful chemicals like alcohol (unless it has been instructed in the manual).

Gently swipe brush in between the keys to clean the keyboard. You must open the CPU once in a while to clear up the dust. This can be done using a vacuum. Do not touch the computer screen while cleaning it. Gently wipe it with a soft cloth. Try to avoid using any cleaning solution.

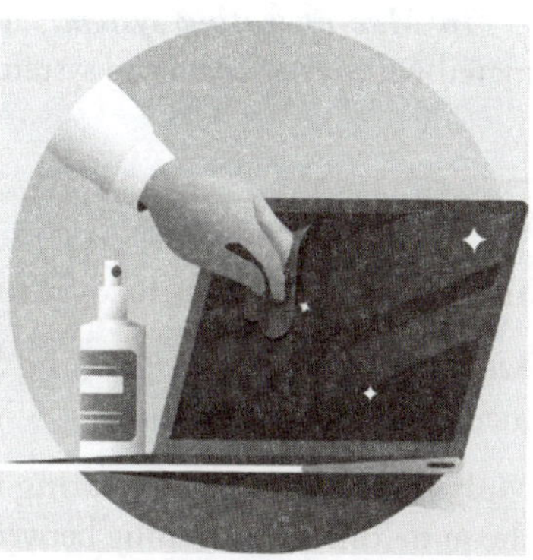

Cover your computer when not in use to protect it from dust. Too much dust can result in overheating of the parts. It is always recommended to use computer in an air-conditioned room or to place a fan in front of it to prevent overheating.

Do not hold or touch your computer, specifically the keyboard, with wet hands.

Make sure that the cord is free from breakage.

2.12.2 System Level Maintenance

System-level maintenance ensures that the operating system is optimized and the latest versions of hardware drivers and operating system are installed. Delete all the programs in your computer that you do not use. By freeing the disk space used by those programs, you can install other useful programs.

Update the anti-virus and anti-malware software as an outdated one can pose a substantial threat to the operating system.

Don't Shutdown Your Computer Too Often Although it is a good habit to shut down your computer to give a chance for the internal components to cool down, shutting down too frequently is also not good.

When shutting down the computer, do it from the start menu rather than doing a forced shut down by pressing the power button. Forced shut down should be done only when the system is unresponsive and can't be shutdown normally.

Do not Charge Your Laptops All the Time Ideally, you must charge to 80%, then let it drain to 40%. This will be helpful to promote the laptop's batter life by four times.

Constant heat also puts undue stress on the batteries. So, you must use computers, especially laptops, in a cool place or can remove the battery charger once it reaches maximum power.

2.13 COMPUTER SOFTWARE MAINTENANCE

If you have installed *Windows operating system*, then update it every week. Windows Updates contain patches, security fixes, and software/driver updates that are required to run your system smoothly. Many modern computer systems automatically update Windows. Also make sure that all other vital software installed in your computer (like anti-virus, database, etc.) are also up-to-date. But it never hurts to check that the installation completed correctly.

2.13.1 Disk Cleanup and Disk Defragmenter

These two tasks must also be done regularly. While disk cleanup deletes all unwanted files from the disk that are consuming lot of space (including files in Recycle Bin contents, temporary internet files, and memory dump files), Disk Defragmenter, on the other hand, recognizes files on the hard disk to consolidate them to run them more efficiently (Fig. 2.19).

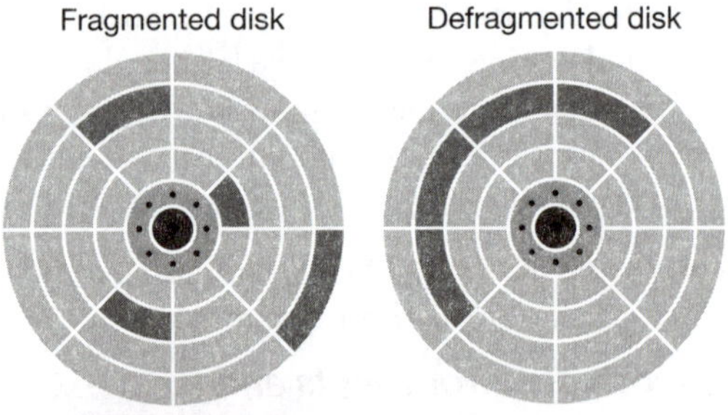

Figure 2.19 Disk defragmentation

Files on the disk get fragmented when we save, change, or delete files. Fragmentation slows down the computer as it has to look in different places to open a single file. Therefore, it is always recommended to schedule Disk Cleanup and Defragmenter.

Newer versions of Windows automatically notify users when the level of fragmentation is above 10%.

In Mac operating system, the maintenance process is automated within the operating system. It facilitates users to update the software and uninstall unnecessary apps.

Key Terms

Single-tasking Operating System: Operating System in which only one program resides in the main memory.

Multi-programming Operating System: Operating System in which two or more programs can reside in the main memory at the same time.

Multi-Processing/Time-sharing Operating System: Operating System in which multiple processes are executed at the same time by switching between them.

Response time: Time elapsed between the submission of a request and the first response produced.

Multi-processor Operating System: The Operating System in which several processors or CPUs are used.

Mobile Operating System: The Operating System specifically designed for mobile devices like smartphones, PDAs, tablet computers and other handheld devices.

Operating System: An interface or intermediary between the user and the computer hardware.

Drive: A drive is a computer storage device that can store our files, folders and programs.

Folder: A folder is a storage location within a drive.

Sub-folders: A folder inside another folder is called a sub-folder.

File: A file is used to store related information. This information can be text, picture, audio, video, or just any other thing.

Path: Every file or folder in the computer has a unique path which helps us to easily locate it in the computer.

Chapter Highlights

- A distributed system comprises of many computers that are connected by a network. A user working on one computer can utilize the resources of another computer on the same network.
- Real-time Operating Systems (RTOS) are systems which demand very fast and quick response.
- In Character User Interface (CUI) operating system, users type commands to give instructions to the computer.
- In Graphical User Interface (GUI), users interact with the operating system by giving commands using the mouse.
- Zipping or compressing a folder means packaging a folder that contains multiple files into a single file.
- While disk cleanup deletes all unwanted files from the disk that consume a lot of space (including files in Recycle Bin contents, temporary internet files, and memory dump files), Disk Defragmenter, on the other hand, recognizes files on the hard disk to consolidate them to run them more efficiently.
- File management includes methods for creating, naming, storing, sorting, arranging, accessing, moving, editing and organizing files to store information for easy retrieval.
- Formatting a hard drive and wiping it clean are two different things.

Review Questions

1. How does batch operating system work?
2. A multi-processor system provides higher computing power and speed. Justify this statement.
3. Give two areas where RTOS is used.
4. With the help of relevant examples, explain the utility of wildcard characters.
5. Why is preventive maintenance important in computer systems?
6. Give three ways by which you can properly tune your hardware.
7. Why should we cover the computer system?
8. Why must you use the computer in an air-conditioned room?
9. Differentiate between:
   a. Single-tasking and Multi-tasking Operating System
   b. Single-user and Distributed Operating System
   c. CUI and GUI
   d. Folder and Sub-folder
   e. File and Folder
   f. Absolute and Relative Path

Fill in the Blanks

1. In ________ operating system, there is no direct interaction between the user and the computer.
2. The main aim of multi-programming system is to maximize the _____ usage.
3. In a multi-processing operating system, a ________ of processes is maintained.
4. A distributed system comprises of many computers that are connected by a _______.
5. ______ uses fixed time constraints.
6. The operating system acts as an interface or intermediary between the _______ and the _______.
7. In ________ User Interface operating system, users type commands to give instructions to the computer.
8. The top-level drive of the computer is also known as the _____ Directory.
9. The _______ path contains the full path to the file.
10. __________ a folder means packaging a folder that contains multiple files into a single file.
11. ________ characters to search our files and folders accurately and efficiently.
12. _____ will find all files whose name ends with t and has an extension txt.
13. ______ will find all files created in MS Excel.
14. _________ software protects computer from malware attack.
15. With a ______, you get ample time to save your files and properly turn off your computer during power loss.

State True or False

1. MS-DOS and Palm OS are examples of mobile operating system.
2. Response time is the time elapsed between submission of a request and the final response.
3. All modern-day computers support time-sharing system.
4. Multi-processing operating system gives better performance than multi-processor system.
5. In a distributed system, a user working on one computer is confined to using the resources of only that computer.
6. In an embedded system, the operating system is located in RAM.
7. Modern operating systems are all based on CUI.
8. The C drive refers to the pen drive in the computer.
9. We can have multiple folders within a folder.
10. Files in the same folder must have unique name.
11. Relative path gives the complete path.
12. Zipped folder takes less space as compared to space taken by individual files.
13. Formatting a hard drive and wiping it clean are two different things.
14. We cannot restore files in the Recycle Bin.
15. Disk cleanup recognize files on hard disk to consolidate them to run them more efficiently.

Give an Example of Each

1. Single-user Operating System ___________
2. Multi-user Operating System ___________
3. Single-tasking Operating System _________
4. Multi-tasking Operating System ____________
5. Multi-programming Operating System _________
6. Distributed Operating System ___________
7. Mobile Operating System ____________
8. Open-source operating system based on Linux _______
9. CUI Operating System ____________
10. GUI Operating System ____________

Multiple Choice Questions

1. In which operating system, the main aim is to minimize the response time?
   a. Single-user b. Single-tasking
   c. Multi-programming d. Time-sharing
2. Time-sharing operating systems are also known as ___________ Operating System.
   a. Single-user b. Multi-tasking
   c. Both of these. d. None of these.
3. In _________ Operating System, several processors or CPUs are used.
   a. Multi-processor b. Multi-processing
   c. Multi-programing d. Multi-tasking
4. Several computers share memory in a _______ Operating System.
   a. Distributed b. Multi-processor
   c. Multi-processing d. All of these.
5. Embedded systems, industrial robots and scientific research equipment use _____ Operating System.
   a. RTOS b. Distributed
   c. Single-tasking d. Multi-tasking
6. _________ Operating Systems have a comparatively small amount of memory, include slow processor, and have a small display screen.
   a. RTOS b. Mobile
   c. Single-user d. Distributed
7. Microwaves, washing machines, traffic control systems, cars, ATMs, digital cameras, elevators use _______ Operating System.
   a. RTOS b. Mobile
   c. Single-user d. Embedded
8. ______ input device is used to give commands in a CUI Operating System.
   a. Keyboard b. Mouse
   c. Joystick d. Touch-screen
9. A zipped folder has ______ extension.
   a. .zip b. .rar
   c. Both of these. d. None of these.

10. File management does not include ______.
    a. creating b. storing
    c. sorting d. None of these.

11. Which wildcard character is a match for any single character or symbol?
    a. * b. ?
    c. ^ d. !

12. Identify the incorrect statement.
    a. We should wipe the computer screen with a cotton cloth.
    b. We should not touch the keyboard with wet hands.
    c. We must swipe a brush in between the keys to clean the keyboard.
    d. We can eat but cannot take coffee near a computer.

13. Identify the incorrect statement about system-level maintenance.
    a. We must keep the operating system updated.
    b. We must update anti-virus software regularly.
    c. Our laptops must be 100% charged always.
    d. Forced shutdown may adversely affect our computer.

14. ________ deletes all unwanted files from the disk that consume a lot of space.
    a. Operating System b. Disk Defragmenter
    c. Utility Programs d. Disk Cleanup

Fill the Table

S.No.	Extension	Type of File
1.	.txt	
2.	.docx	
3.	.pptx	
4.	.jpg, .bmp, .gif	
5.	.wav,..mp3, .aiff, .wma	
6.	.avi, .mp4, .wmv, .mov, .flv	
7.	.rar, .tar	
8.	.xlsx, .odx	
9.	.bak, .cur, .ico, .tmp, .sys	
10.	.pdf	

Class Activity

1. Create a folder containing files of different types such as sound, text, presentation, spreadsheet and video.
2. Note down the extension of each file.
3. Write their absolute and relative paths.
4. Zip the folder and email it to your friend.
5. Copy a file from another folder to your folder.

6. Rename the file (copied from another folder).
7. Delete the file that was renamed.
8. Restore this file.
9. Transfer at least three files to a pen drive.

Answers

Fill in the Blanks

1. batch
2. CPU
3. queue
4. network
5. RTOS
6. user, computer hardware
7. Character
8. Root
9. absolute
10. Zipping or compressing
11. Wildcard
12. *t.txt
13. *.xlsx
14. Antivirus
15. UPS

State True or False

1. False
2. False
3. True
4. False
5. False
6. False
7. False
8. False
9. True
10. True
11. False
12. True
13. True
14. False
15. False

Give an Example of Each

1. MS DOS
2. Linux
3. MD DOS
4. Windows
5. Windows
6. Unix
7. Android
8. Ubuntu
9. MS DOS
10. Windows

Multiple Choice Questions

1. d
2. c
3. a
4. b
5. a
6. b
7. d
8. a
9. c
10. d
11. b
12. d
13. c
14. d

Fill the Table

1. Text file created in WordPad
2. Text File. Can contain pictures. Created in MS Word
3. Presentation File created in MS PowerPoint
4. Picture File created in MS Paint
5. Sound or audio file
6. Video file
7. Compressed files
8. Spreadsheet file
9. Operating system file
10. Portable Document Format

Introduction to Artificial Intelligence 3

Chapter Objectives

The chapter introduces Artificial Intelligence and its underlying technologies including,

- Neural networks
- Machine learning – supervised, unsupervised learning
- Reinforcement learning
- Deep learning
- Natural language processing
- Computer vision
- Weak and strong AI
- Reactive machines, theory of mind, limited memory and self-awareness
- Applications of AI in different areas

3.1 WHAT IS ARTIFICIAL INTELLIGENCE?

From a layman's view, Artificial Intelligence (AI) simply means the intelligence demonstrated by machines that help them to mimic the actions of humans. AI simulates natural intelligence in machines that are programmed to learn from experiences, adjust to new inputs and perform human-like tasks.

From a researcher's view, AI is a set of algorithms that generates results without having to be explicitly instructed to do so, thereby making machines capable of thinking and acting rationally and humanely.

> Most AI examples, from chess-playing computers to self-driving cars, heavily depend on deep learning and natural language processing techniques.

AI applications perform specialized tasks by processing large amounts of data and recognizing patterns in it. Besides learning from experience, AI applications can recognize objects, understand and respond to language and make decisions to solve real-world problems. AI performs tasks that normally require human intelligence. The main focus of this technology is to build machines and algorithms, which are capable of performing computational tasks that would otherwise require human-like brain functions.

> **NITI Aayog: National Strategy for Artificial Intelligence has defined AI as follows:**
> AI refers to the ability of machines to perform cognitive tasks like thinking, perceiving, learning, problem-solving and decision-making. Initially conceived as a technology that could mimic human intelligence, AI has evolved in ways that far exceed its original conception. With incredible advances made in data collection, processing and computation power, intelligent systems can now be deployed to take over a variety of tasks, enable connectivity and enhance productivity.

3.2 HOW ARTIFICIAL INTELLIGENCE (AI) WORKS

Building an AI system is a process of reverse-engineering human traits and capabilities in a machine. AI is a broad field of study that includes many theories, methods and technologies. To understand how Artificial Intelligence actually works, we must look into its various sub-domains. All these domains have one thing in common. They all process large amounts of data with fast and intelligent algorithms to allow the software to learn automatically from patterns or features in the data. We shall now take a closer look at these sub-domains.

3.2.1 Neural Networks

Neural Networks work in the same way as human neural (brain) cells. A series of nodes capture the relationship between various underlying variables and processes the data. Every node (or neuron) processes information by responding to external inputs and relaying information between each unit. The entire process of learning requires multiple passes at the data to derive meaning from undefined data (refer Fig. 3.1).

Note that even the most basic neural network consists of the following layers:

1. An ***input layer***, which is the layer from where data enters the network.
2. At least one ***hidden layer***, where machine learning algorithms process the inputs. Weights, biases and thresholds are applied to the received inputs and the results of processing are passed to the output layer.
3. An ***output layer***, where the final result is displayed.

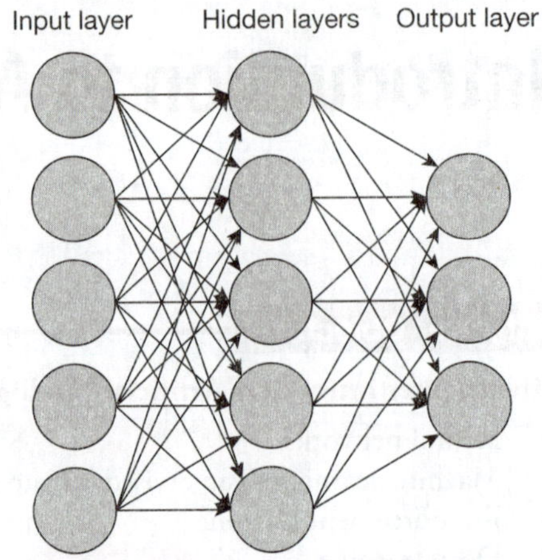

Figure 3.1 Basic neural network

Artificial Intelligence is broadly classified as shown in Fig. 3.2.

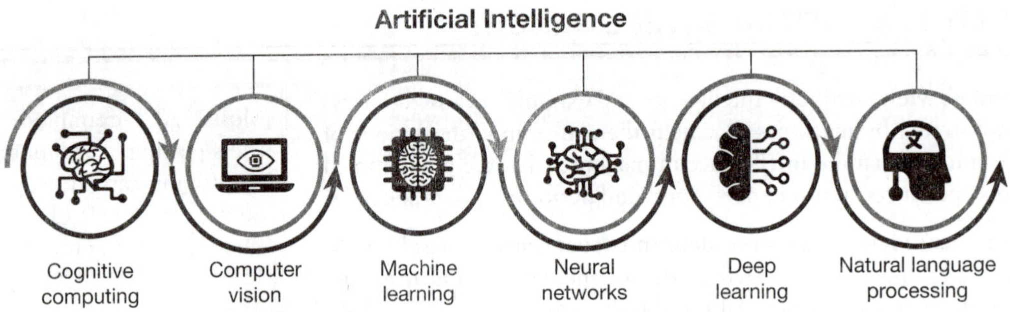

Figure 3.2 Classification of artificial intelligence

3.2.2 Machine Learning

Machine Learning (ML) is a branch of computer science that analyzes data and identifies patterns to teach a machine to make inferences and decisions without any human intervention. It is an approach or subset of Artificial Intelligence that is based on the idea that machines can be given access to data along with the ability to learn from it (Fig. 3.3). ML algorithms learn from experiences rather than instructions. They automatically learn and improve by reviewing their output. For this, humans do not have to write instructions to produce the desired output. They learn by analyzing the given data sets and comparing them with the final output. In case of any error, the learning process is repeated until the accuracy of the outputs improve. This automation not only saves human time and effort but also helps to make better decisions. Machine learning algorithms can be categorized as follows:

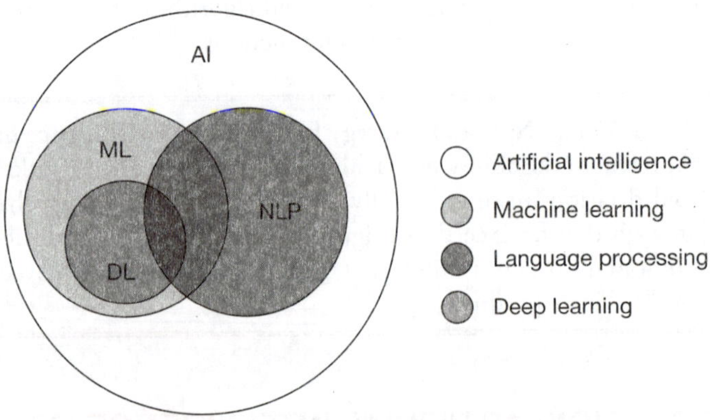

Figure 3.3 Sub-domains of artificial intelligence

Unsupervised Learning Supervised machine-learning algorithms, as the name indicates, has a supervisor as teacher. These algorithms apply learning from past data (or experiences) to new data using labelled examples.

> Supervised learning should be used when output of data in the training set is known.

These algorithms start with analyzing a known training dataset, to produce an inferred function that can be used to predict future data values. The learning algorithm then compares the predicted output with actual output to find errors and modify the model accordingly.

For example, if you have a basket filled with different variety of fruits, then the first step is to train the machine to identify a fruit. Now, our machine can easily identify, say, an apple and a banana.

Unsupervised Learning Unsupervised learning trains the machine to use information that is neither classified nor labeled. In this case, the machine learning algorithm works on the given information without any guidance. The unsorted information is grouped based on similarities, patterns and differences without any prior training of data. For example, if we give an image of mango and an orange, then initially the machine has no idea about how a mango looks and how the orange looks (Fig. 3.4).

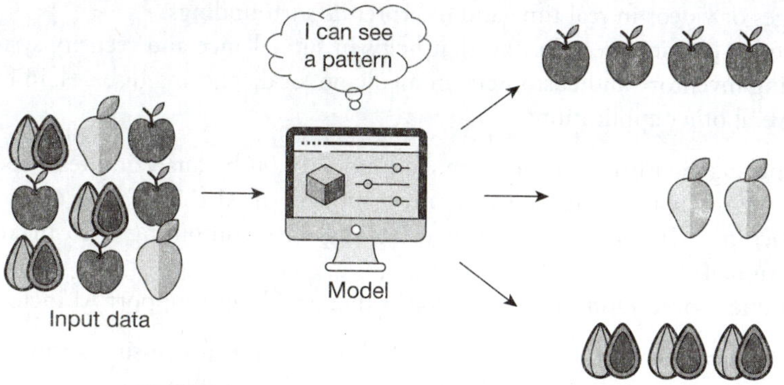

> Semi-supervised machine learning algorithms fall somewhere between supervised and unsupervised algorithms since they use both labeled and unlabeled data for training. These algorithms improve accuracy.

Figure 3.4 Unsupervised machine learning

Unsupervised machine learning algorithm learns through observation and finds structures in the data. That is, the model automatically finds patterns and relationships in the dataset by creating clusters in it. For example, if given a dataset of pictures of both mangoes and oranges, the algorithm can make two clusters – one containing only pictures of oranges and the other of mangoes. What unsupervised machine learning cannot do is to specify labels to the clusters. That is, it can only segregate the pictures but cannot tell that this is a real-world orange or that is a mango.

Deep Learning Deep Learning (DL) is a ML technique that teaches a machine to process inputs through layers to more accurately classify, infer and predict the outcome. DL creates huge neural networks with several layers of processing units to take full advantage of advances in computing power and improved training techniques. This helps the algorithm to learn complex patterns in large amounts of data. Some applications of DL include image and speech recognition.

Deep learning models are based on *deep neural networks,* that is, neural networks with multiple hidden layers (Fig. 3.5). In such a network, each hidden layer further processes the temporary outputs received from the previous layer. This movement of computations through the hidden layers to the output layer is known as ***forward propagation***.

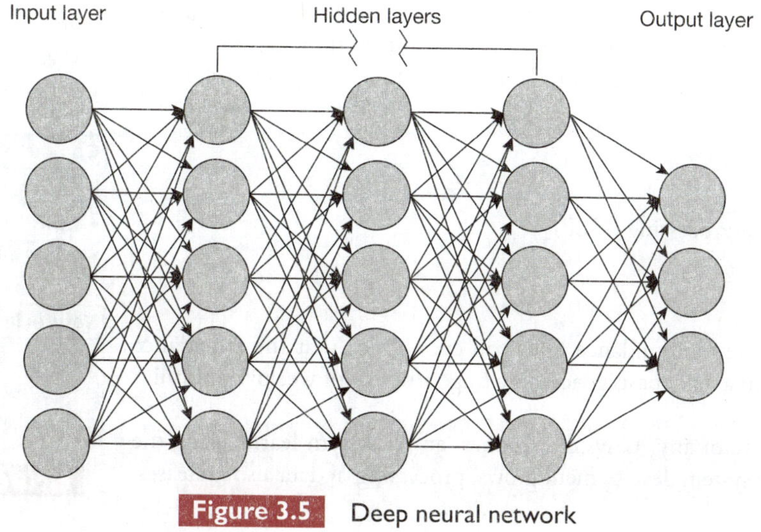

Figure 3.5 Deep neural network

Once the final result is produced by the output layer, its accuracy is calculated. In case of unsatisfactory results, errors are identified, weights assigned to each node are updated, and pushed back to the previous layers to refine or train the model. This process of moving backward to update weights of all nodes is known as ***backward propagation***.

Deep learning models can work with labeled as well as unlabeled data. This means that deep learning supports both supervised and unsupervised learning.

Natural Language Processing NLP is a science in which a machine is made to read, understand, interpret and respond to a human language. This is specifically done to make the machine capable of communicating with a human.

Computer Vision Computer vision is a branch of AI that tries to understand an image by breaking it down into several parts and then studying each part of the image. This helps the machine to classify and learn from a set of images so that it can make better decisions based on previous observations. For example, when a machine can process, analyze and understand images, it can capture images or videos in real time and interpret its surroundings.

Computer vision techniques are used today for facial recognition that helps in surveillance and security systems, autonomous vehicles, retail stores for tracking inventory and customers, in medicine for diagnosing diseases, in financial institutions to prevent fraud, and in several other applications.

Cognitive Computing Cognitive computing algorithms try to mimic a human brain by analyzing text, speech, images or objects in the same way to give the desired output. It is basically a subfield of AI that is used to provide a natural, human-like interaction with machines. The ultimate goal of using cognitive computing is to make the machine speak coherently in response to a human.

Apart from the above-mentioned techniques, some additional technologies that enable and support AI include:

Graphical processing units that provide heavy computing power required for iterative processing and training neural networks.

Internet of Things to generate massive amounts of data from connected devices. Usually, this data remains unanalyzed. Automating models with AI helps to analyze this data and extract useful information from it. **Advanced algorithms** can be used to analyze data faster at multiple levels to identify and predict rare events, understand complex systems and optimize unique scenarios.

Application Programming Interfaces (or APIs), which are portable packages of code, are used to add AI functionality to existing software. For example, image recognition capabilities can be added to home security systems along with Q&A capabilities to describe data, create captions and headlines to identify interesting patterns and insights in data.

3.3 AI DOMAINS FOR HUMAN–MACHINE INTERACTIONS

Humans interact with computers while working on them to perform a specific task or operation. In human–machine interactions, hardware and software both play a vital role in communication. The interface of such an interaction should be very user-friendly. In AI, human–machine interactions are done using the following domains (Fig. 3.6):

1. Data
2. Computer Vision (CV)
3. Natural Language Processing (NLP)

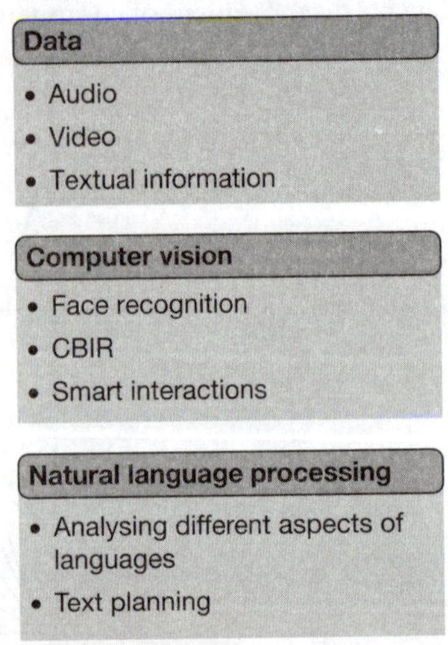

Figure 3.6 AI domains

3.3.1 Data

Today, data is everywhere in abundance. Did you ever notice that the attendance taken by your teacher on a daily basis generates a huge amount of weekly/ monthly/ yearly data?

Data is the backbone of any AI system. In fact, an AI system learns using the underlying data. As the system development grows, processing of data also increases.

This data can be in any form – text, audio, video, images or big data for predictions, insights, forecasts, decision making, etc. For example, a computer program can be written to play the game **Rock–Paper–Scissor** with the user.

3.3.2 Computer Vision (CV)

Computer vision is a field of science that helps computers gain a high level of understanding from digital images or videos. It is done by acquiring images, processing them, analyzing them and finally understanding the information they are conveying.

Once the images are understood, computer vision is then used in the following areas.

Facial recognition Facial recognition systems recognize faces in images and videos. Applications like Google Photos, Snapchat, Facebook, Instagram, etc. use facial recognition system to identify people (Fig. 3.7).

Almost every smart phone these days use facial-recognition algorithms to unlock phones. Facebook uses facial recognition to identify users in the posted pictures. In China, this technology is integrated with **payment technology** to allow users do cashless payment.

Some government agencies in different countries are also using facial technology for **surveillance**. Though use of this has raised concerns among rights and privacy advocates, facial recognition techniques and applications are on a constant rise.

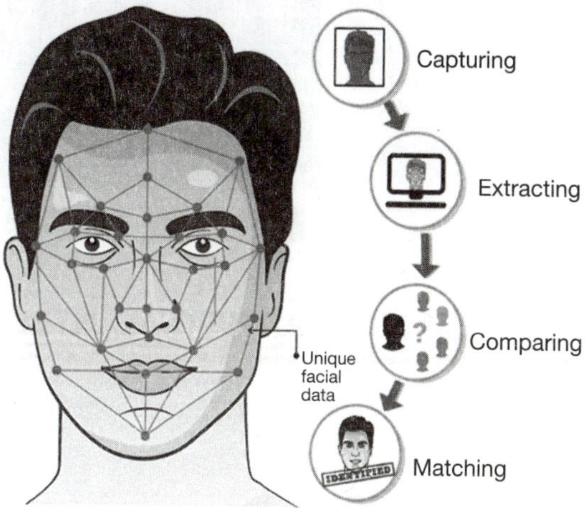

Figure 3.7 Facial recognition

Content-based Image Retrieval systems Content-based image retrieval (CBIR) systems identify images by using image properties like composition, color, texture etc. Search engines like Google and Bing, and software analyzing CT scans and MRIs in hospitals, etc. use CBIR systems.

Computer Vision is extensively used in smart interactions to give input to computers. This is especially helpful in **gaming software** and in systems designed for differently abled individuals.

Software used in **home security systems**, office security systems, drone-based surveillance systems, etc., also use computer vision techniques.

Computer vision is the heart of **augmented reality apps** that detect physical objects in real-time to place virtual objects within the physical environment. For example, when you use apps like Snapchat, you can place your image on any background, you can put any hair-style, facial features (eyes, lips, ears, etc), accessories (earings, hairbands, lipstick, etc) and a lot more.

Many agricultural organizations use computer vision techniques to **monitor the harvest** and solve common agricultural problems including weed emergence or nutrient deficiency (Fig. 3.8). Images collected from satellites, drones, or planes are processed by computer vision algorithms to **detect potential problems** in the early phase, thereby avoiding unnecessary loss at a later stage.

Figure 3.8 Use of computer vision in agriculture

Self-driving cars (like Tesla) use computer vision to learn from their surroundings. Every smart vehicle has cameras to capture videos from different angles. These videos act as an input to the computer vision software that processes them to detect objects like road marking, pedestrians or other cars, traffic lights, etc.

Websites like Facebook perform **content moderation** using computer vision techniques. Billions of posts by users every day are reviewed and any images/videos that contain violence, extremism, or pornography are immediately removed.

Ninety percent of medical data is present in the form of images. So, most of the diseases can be easily diagnosed by processing images available in the form of **X-rays, MRI, mammography**, etc. For example, computer vision algorithms can detect diabetic retinopathy (Fig. 3.9), which is the most prevalent cause of blindness. Going further, these algorithms can also process pictures of the back of the eye and rate their severity (in case a disease is detected). Computer vision algorithms can even detect cancer with much higher precision than human doctors.

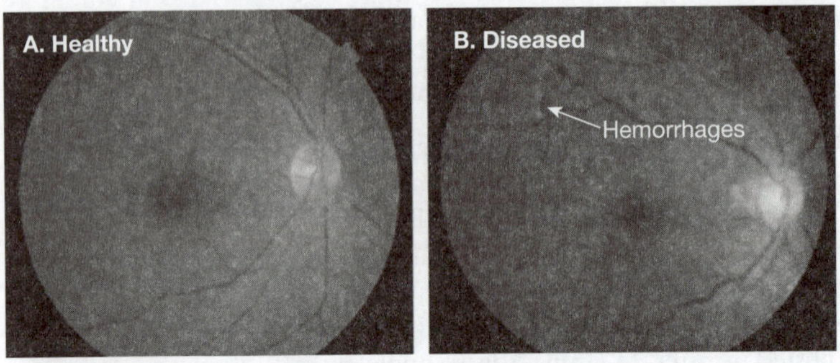

Figure 3.9 Use of computer vision software in medical imaging

3.4 TYPES OF ARTIFICIAL INTELLIGENCE

We can categorize artificial intelligence applications into two broad categories based on capabilities and functionality of AI as shown in Fig. 3.10.

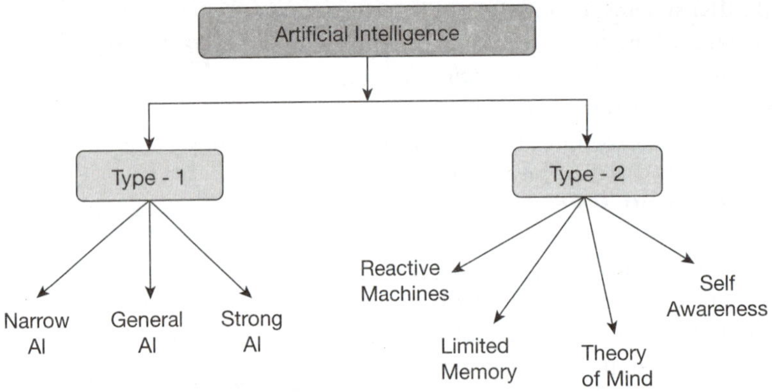

Figure 3.10 Types of AI

3.4.1 AI Type-1: Based on Capabilities

Based on capabilities, AI applications can be classified as Weak AI (or Narrow AI), General AI and Strong AI (or Super AI).

Narrow AI Narrow AI is the most commonly used type of AI these days. Narrow or Weak AI, performs a dedicated task with intelligence. But it cannot perform any other task as it is specifically trained for a specific task only.

Narrow AI does not mimic or replicate human intelligence. It just simulates human behavior based on a narrow range of parameters and contexts. Narrow AI is close to human functioning but in very specific contexts, and many times, it can even surpass them. However, narrow AI works well only in very controlled environments with a limited set of parameters.

Examples of Weak AI include,

- Virtual assistants like Siri by Apple, Alexa by Amazon, Cortana by Microsoft that use narrow AI as they work with a limited pre-defined range of functions.
- IBM's Watson supercomputer, which is an expert system that combines machine learning and natural language processing techniques.

- AI systems used in medicine to diagnose cancer and other diseases with greater accuracy by using cognition and reasoning techniques.
- Chatbots that use NLP to interpret human language and interact with humans.
- Other examples, are playing chess, purchasing suggestions on e-commerce site, self-driving cars, speech recognition, and image/facial recognition. Moreover, manufacturing robots, drones, email spam filters, social media monitoring tools, and marketing content recommendations based on watch/listen/purchase behavior also make use of narrow AI to perform their specified task.

General AI General AI performs any intellectual task with efficiency like a human. General AI takes smart decisions without human intervention. As of now, there is no system that falls under this category as there is no machine that can perform any task as perfect as a human. But researchers worldwide are actively working to develop machines with General AI.

A General AI system has a human-level of cognitive function across a wide variety of domains such as language processing, image processing, computational functioning and reasoning and so on (Fig. 3.11).

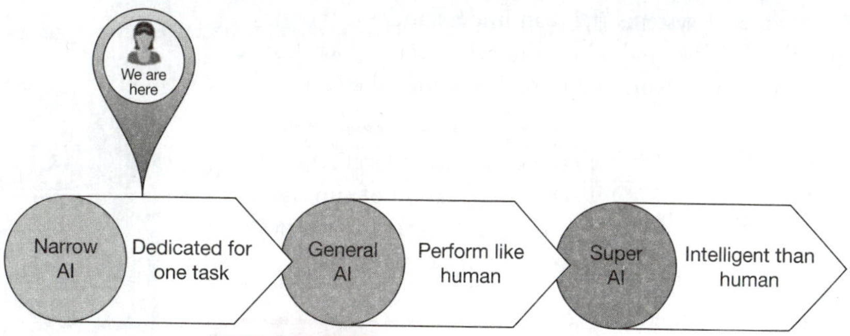

Figure 3.11 Future evolution of AI

Super AI Super AI or Strong AI is a level of intelligence of systems at which machines could surpass human intelligence. The main aim here is to make machines use their cognitive properties to perform any task better than humans.

Super AI systems have the ability to think, reason, solve the puzzle, make judgments, plan, learn, and communicate on its own. However, like General AI, even Super AI is a hypothetical concept of Artificial Intelligence and develop ment of such systems is still a big challenge.

Table 3.1 summarizes the difference between Weak AI and Strong AI.

Table 3.1 Comparison of weak and strong AI

Weak AI	Strong AI
It supports a narrow range of applications with a limited scope.	It supports a wider range of application with a wide scope.
This application is good at specific tasks.	This application has an incredible human-level intelligence.
It uses supervised and unsupervised learning to process data.	It uses clustering and association techniques to process data.
Example: Siri, Alexa.	Example: Advanced Robotics

3.4.2 Artificial Intelligence Type-2: Based on Functionality

Based on functionality, AI can be classified as reactive machines, limited theory, theory of mind and self-awareness.

Reactive Machines They are the most basic types of Artificial Intelligence machines. As the name indicates, such systems focus on current scenarios and react to them in the best possible way. They do not store past experiences for future actions. Examples of such AI systems are: IBM's Deep Blue system and Google's AlphaGo.

IBM's Deep Blue (Fig. 3.12) defeated chess grandmaster Garry Kasparov. It is a reactive machine that sees the chess-board pieces and reacts to them. It has no way to refer to any of its prior experiences so that it can improve its performance. It just identifies the pieces on a chessboard and tries to predict its opponent's as well as its own next moves.

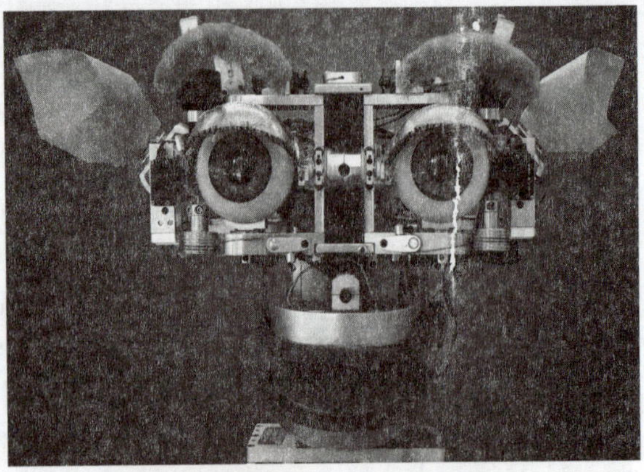

Figure 3.12 IBM's Deep Blue

Limited Memory As evident from the name, such AI systems do have a memory, though limited in size, to store past experiences or some data for a short period of time. Self-driving cars are one of the best examples of such AI systems. These cars store recent speed of nearby cars, the distance of other cars, speed limit, and other vital information that is necessary to navigate the road.

Theory of Mind These are AI systems that can understand human emotions, people, beliefs, and also interact socially like humans. Though researchers are aggressively working on such systems, they are still not developed yet.

One real-world example of the theory-of-mind AI is Kismet, which is a robot head made in the late 90s by a Massachusetts Institute of Technology (MIT) researcher. The robot mimics human emotions and recognizes them. However, it can still not follow gazes or convey attention to humans.

Another robot, Sophia (Fig. 3.13), applies the theory-of-mind AI. Cameras are fitted inside Sophia's eyes. Pictures taken by the camera when processed with AI algorithms, allow her to see, sustain eye contact, recognize individuals, and follow faces.

> Theory-of-mind level AI is not about replication or simulation; it is about training machines to truly understand humans.

> Strong AI uses a theory-of-mind AI framework to ensure that robots possess the capability to discern needs, emotions, beliefs and thought processes of other intelligent entities.

Figure 3.13 Sophia applies the theory of mind AI

Self-awareness As of today, self-awareness AI systems is a hypothetical concept. But such systems are said to be the future of AI systems. These machines will be super intelligent, having their own consciousness, sentiments, and self-awareness. Such machines are expected to be much smarter than the human mind.

3.5 APPLICATIONS OF ARTIFICIAL INTELLIGENCE

Artificial Intelligence is widely being used by companies to improve their process efficiencies, automate resource-heavy tasks, and to make business predictions by analyzing data. Today, data is all around us. Especially with the Internet of Things (IoT) and sensors collecting every bit of data and possessing the ability to harness that data, artificial intelligence (AI) can be extensively used to learn interesting patterns in the data and automate tasks for a variety of business benefits. Some of them are discussed below.

3.5.1 Automating Repetitive Tasks

AI automates repetitive learning and discovery through data. But AI is different from hardware-driven, robotic automation. While a robot automates manual tasks, AI can be used to perform frequent, high-volume, computerized tasks reliably without fatigue. In such a system, human intervention is still required to set up the system.

3.5.2 Adding Intelligence

AI can be used to add intelligence to existing products. AI is not usually sold as an individual application; rather, it is used within existing products to improve their capabilities. For example, Siri was added as a feature to a new generation of Apple products. Automation, bots and smart machines can be used at home and in the workplace for anything ranging from security intelligence to investment analysis.

Example: Consider an AI-based application that predicts a student's marks in the final exams based on certain facts. Such a system can help the student to know how much more hard work needs to be put in to get the expected results (Fig. 3.14).

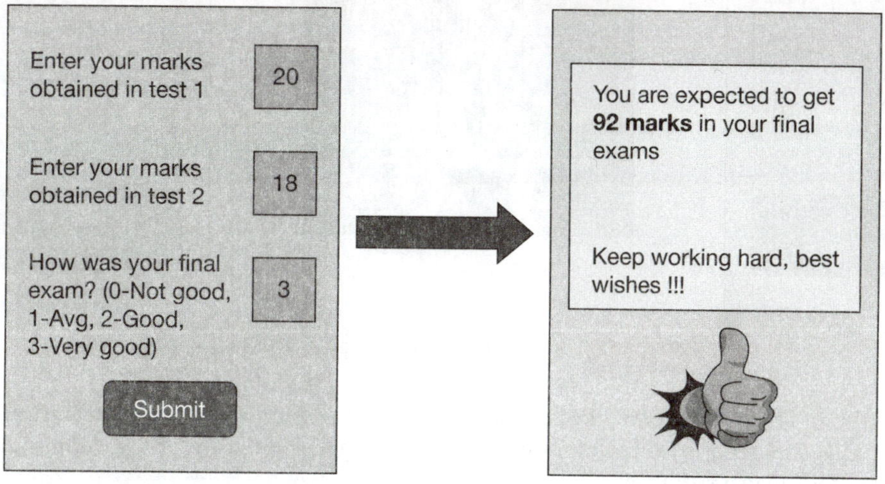

Figure 3.14 A simple AI system that asks the student to enter the marks obtained in two class tests to predict the marks that can be obtained in the final exam

Fraud Detection AI analyzes tons of data using neural networks and deep neural networks with multiple hidden layers to detect fraud and other unwanted activity. The more data you feed to an AI system, the more accurate they become (Fig. 3.15).

Figure 3.15 Fraud detection using AI

AI systems do all their work with incredible accuracy using deep neural networks. For example, your interactions with Alexa, Google Search and Google Photos are all based on deep learning. In the medical field, deep learning, image classification and object recognition, which are all a part of AI techniques, are used to find cancer on MRIs, with the same accuracy as highly trained radiologists.

AI gets the most out of data. When we use self-learning techniques, the data itself becomes intellectual property. Huge volumes of data are rigorously analyzed to extract otherwise hidden, useful information and create a competitive advantage. In any industry, a company having best data wins despite tough competition.

Healthcare In the healthcare industry, AI systems are used to analyze the patient's information efficiently. They are also used in,

Telemedicine In non-emergency situations, patients can use AI systems to analyze their symptoms and assess if there is a need for medical attention (Fig. 3.16). This not only helps the patient but also reduces the pressure on medical professionals since only critical cases will be forwarded to them.

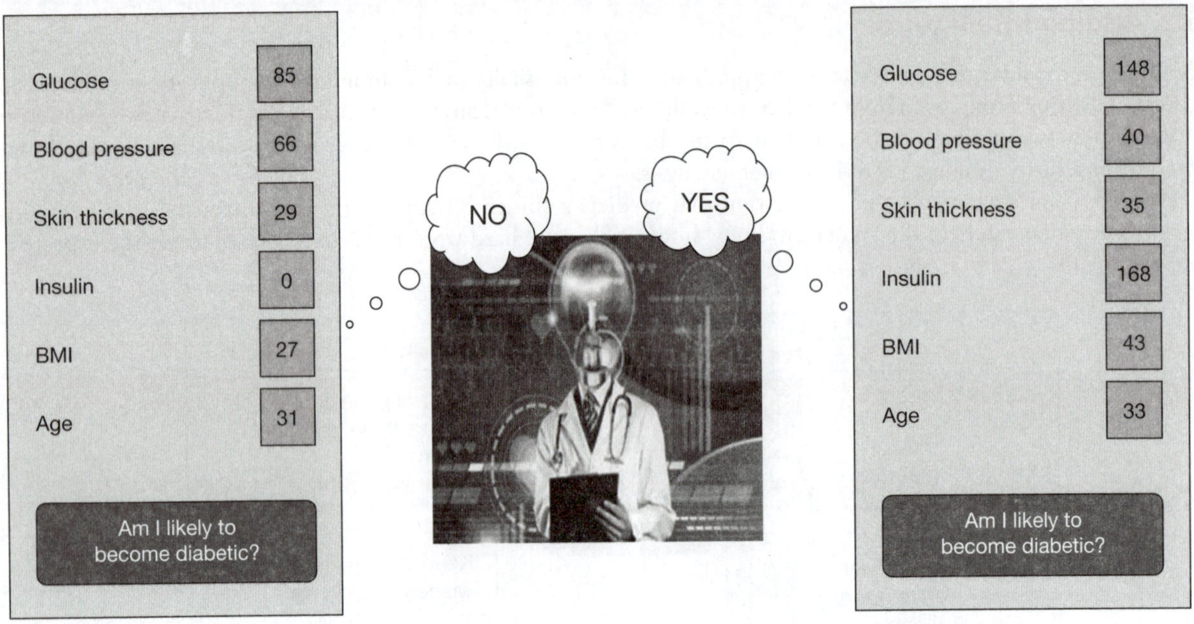

Figure 3.16 Example for application of telemedicine

Assisted Diagnosis: Using techniques like computer vision and neural networks, AI systems can easily interpret information from MRI scan reports to check for tumors and other malignant growths, with almost the same accuracy but at a much faster pace than a radiologist.

Robot-assisted surgery: Robots, when used for doing surgeries, can perform their task very precisely with negligible margin of error, round-the-clock, without getting tired. Robotic surgeries not only reduce the time to conduct a surgery but also reduce the amount of time spent by patients to recover after a surgery.

Wearable Health Monitoring Gadgets. A person's state of health is an ongoing process, and it needs to be continuously monitored. For this, wearable devices that are continuously collecting and analyzing this data are available in the market. They can predict health fluctuations even before the patient is aware about some serious illness within his/her body and can even save lives in critical cases.

E-commerce: In e-commerce, AI techniques are extensively used for recommending products/services. Even social networking sites use it to recommend friends or useful connections to a user. Companies are also using AI to predict demand for different products at different times of the year so that companies can efficiently manage their stocks to meet the demand. They also use AI to create targeted recruitment ads and predict an applicant's suitability to the company. AI-powered employment services help job seekers to explore the opportunities available in various avenues (Fig. 3.17).

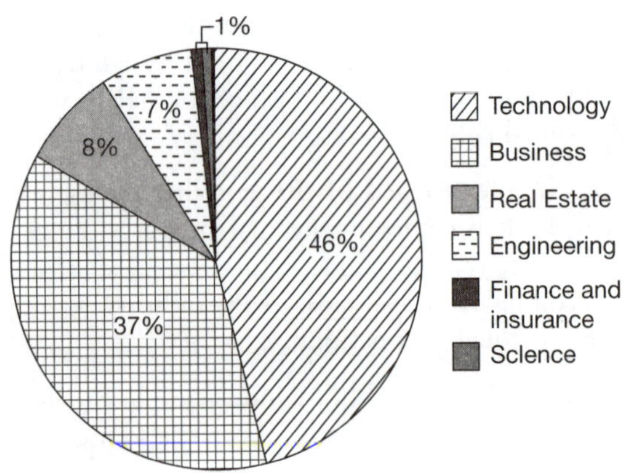

Figure 3.17 Industries referencing AI in job postings

Chatbots On e-commerce or most other websites, these days there are assisted programs designed to serve customers at odd-hours and during peak hours thereby reducing the workload of limited human resources.

Filtering Spam and Fake Reviews: Websites like Amazon get a very high number of reviews and some of them may be fake and thus need to be filtered. At times, it is impossible for humans to do this job. But using NLP, AI systems can scan these reviews to identify suspicious activities and filter them out to provide a better buyer experience.

Today's virus and spam detection software also use deep neural networks to detect new types of virus and spam with great speed and higher accuracy.

Speech recognition: Also known as speech-to-text (STT), this AI technology recognizes spoken words and converts them to digitized text. Such a software is used in computer dictation apps, TV voice remotes, voice-enabled text messaging, GPS, and voice-driven phone-answering menus.

Automated stock trading: AI is used to optimize stock portfolios. An AI system can make thousands or even millions of trades per day without human intervention.

Ride-share services: Uber, Lyft, and other ride-share services use AI techniques to help passengers collaborate with drivers to minimize wait times and even eliminate the need for surge pricing during peak hours.

Autopilot technology: Autopilot technology using AI is being used in flying commercial and military aircraft. Autopilot aircrafts use sensors, GPS technology, image recognition techniques, collision avoidance technology, robotics, and natural language processing to guide an aircraft safely through the skies.

Advanced navigation systems not only save time but also adapt to the changing conditions in the ocean, which might be dangerous for cargo ships.

Automated Transportation In automated transportation, many options are available to the users. For example, AI can be used to drive the car alone in the absence of a driver. **Tesla's AutoPilot** and **Nissan's ProPilot,** both provide the steering, acceleration and braking systems. However, in case of failure, the driver needs to take control. So, in this case, the driver needs to be alert and keep an eye on the road.

Audi's A8L can take up full driving responsibility in slow-moving traffic.

Fully self-driven cars can drive independently without any driver. Google's Waymo project is one such car, which is already operating in the US.

Autonomous transportation requiring absolutely no human interaction will be a reality soon. **Robotic taxi** is one such project.

Optimizing search The success of any e-commerce website depends on what users are looking for and what they are able to find. AI techniques can optimize search results to reduce the gap between the demand and supply of results.

Human Resource Management: AI is used to analyze employee data to place the right talent in the right team, assign projects based on their competencies, collect feedback about the workplace, and even try to predict if any employee is thinking of quitting the company.

Using NLP, an AI system can easily scan thousands of CVs in just few seconds to shortlist really good candidates. This can be done without any human errors or biases, thereby shortening the length of hiring cycles.

Robotics: AI has helped man to innovate and improve the design and capabilities of robots. Robots in AI have found applications across verticals and industries in the manufacturing and packaging industries. For example, robots are now used for the following jobs:

- In **assembly related jobs**, AI, along with computer vision techniques, is used to make the robots learn which path is best for a certain process while it is performing its operation.
- **Robots** providing Customer Service use NLP to interact with customers, just like a human.
- AI-enabled robots are used in the packaging industry to enable quicker, cheaper, and more accurate packaging. Movements of robot to do a particular task can be optimized to achieve best performance.

> Speedfactory is an entirely robot-enabled manufacturing plant. It aims to reduce errors in manufacturing and shipping time. Companies like Faulhaber Micromo, USA, have even started working on robots that could diffuse bombs.

Bitmojis and Criminal Identification: A bitmoji is a personalized cartoon avatar that is created to look just like the user. The bitmoji app translates an image to a cartoon that has similar properties to the image (Fig. 3.18). When working with this app, you can either choose to use your or any other person's face photo to translate it into an emoji or can choose only the eyes, nose, lips, etc.

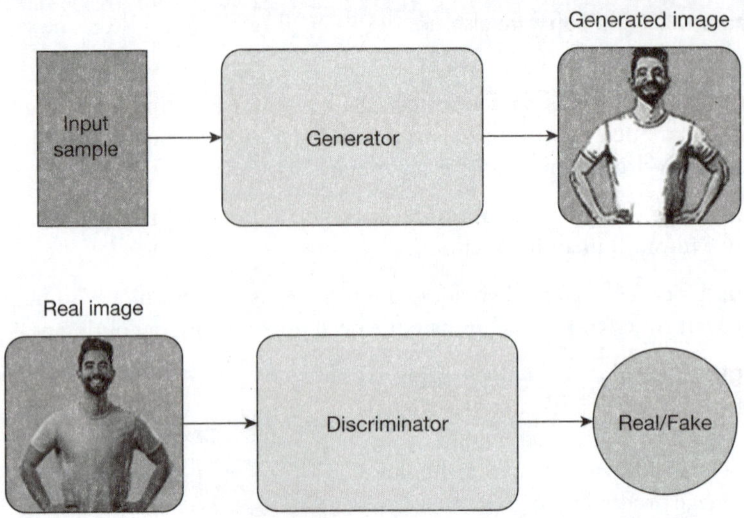

Figure 3.18 Use of bitmoji

This technique can also be used prove useful in criminal identification. The eyewitnesses or policemen can create an avatar of the criminal. This is far simpler and more accurate than creating regular sketches. Moreover, with this technique any cartoon avatar, can be translated into a photo again, which looks closely like the face.

Battlefield Surveillance: AI can be used to get updated information about hostile zones for a military response, especially when getting such updates are difficult owing to high danger. For example, AI-operated drones are already used to provide instant alerts when they notice an anomaly or even conduct pre-emptive strikes.

Movie Industry: Science fiction movies use Artificial intelligence to a great extent (Fig. 3.19). The first movie portraying AI as a movie character was a German movie Metropolis released in 1927. Since then, AI characters like HAL:9000 from 2001: A Space Odyssey (1968), the Skynet from the Terminator series or Ultron from Avengers: Age of Ultron (2015) have been raising concerns of people regarding this technology.

Figure 3.19 Science fiction movie with robots

However, some AI characters loved by people for their mannerisms, helpful nature, good deeds and pleasing personalities include R2-D2 and C-3PO from the Star Wars series and WALL-E from the movie WALL-E (2008).

Ghost in a Shell, an animated movie released in 1995 having fictional characters, changed how people viewed AI and their possible synergy with humans. Similarly, I, Robot released in 2005, showed billions of AI-operated robots acting as personal and public servants. Though these robots were built on the 'three principles of AI' to prevent them from harming humans, the outcome was not what was perceived.

Education: These days, students can be educated by AI teacher robots. Such a technology has proved very beneficial for visually challenged students who can learn using voice assistants.

AI techniques can be used to monitor a student's performance at regular intervals and also recommend content based on the past experience.

Disaster Management: The havoc created by disasters can be minimized by using AI to get constant alarm alerts right from the time when even a minute potential risk is detected.

The importance of AI can be understood from the fact that President Putin of Russia said that, "The fronttunner in the field of artifical intelligence would be likely to become the leader of the world".

Besides this,

- Robots are used to perform **custom tasks**, based on a specific application like small-scale agriculture.
- Smart computer systems can easily **detect forgery** as compared to humans.
- Researchers from Stanford could use AI to **predict voting behavior** in elections by analyzing images from Google Street View.
- Facebook knows when you are dating someone even before even you write something about it on the platform. Facebook also automatically suggests users to tag their friends, based on their facial features in their images. Similarly, Amazon's **predictive shipping** technique that uses AI allows it to send you a package before you know you want it.
- Google uses AI to **translate text** from one language to another. Moreover, Google's **predictive search algorithm** keeps track of data entered by a user in the past to predict what the user would type next in the search bar. Similarly, Netflix uses past data to recommend what movie a user might want to see next. This knowledge helps the website to hook the user onto the platform to increase watch time.
- Even **plagiarism checkers and tools** use AI to identify text that is taken from other websites, books or any other sources.
- Scientists are working on robots that can provide **medical care to senior citizens**.

3.6 ADVANTAGES AND DISADVANTAGES OF ARTIFICIAL INTELLIGENCE

We have seen that AI has made our life better by making recommendations, mapping directions and preventing fraud, but there are always two sides to a coin, and that holds true even with AI. Let us look into some advantages as well as disadvantages of this technology.

Advantages of AI	Disadvantages of AI
• Reduction in human error • Available 24×7 • Helps in tirelessly performing repetitive work • Faster and accurate decisions • Improved security • Efficient communication, also provides digital assistance • AI robots reduce human risks by performing all risky tasks. For example, robots are used in places like coal mines, exploring the deepest parts of the ocean, sewage treatment, and nuclear power plants to avoid any disaster involving precious human life	• AI systems are expensive as compared to their traditional counterpart. • Less talent available in this area. • Can lead to disaster, if misused. • AI systems do not make decisions based on emotions, compassion, and empathy.

3.7 ETHICS IN AI

The current world is quickly getting transformed by artificial intelligence and those who use this technology are living a richer and easy-going life. But this is possible only when we talk about ethical AI, not just AI.

The term 'Ethical AI' is composed of two words, Ethical and AI. We are now already familiar with the term AI. 'Ethical' means one that is according to ethics. And ethics relates to moral principles that govern the behavior and actions of a group or individual. So, ethical AI is the theory behind developing computer systems that can perform tasks that require human intelligence. It focusses on how right, how fair and how just is the AI's output, outcome and impact.

Example: We know that AI can produce biased results if it is trained with biased data or if it does not do anything to avoid bias. So, any AI system that works on biased data is actually not ethical (or unethical). For example, Microsoft released a chatbot called Tay on Twitter in 2016, to learn by engaging people in dialogue through tweets or direct messages. However, trolls made Tay learn all negative words that spread hatred for women, a particular race and all sorts of biased data within hours. Tay was also taught to give repulsive and toxic responses. This aroused anger of Twitter users and finally Microsoft had to silence Tay forever in even less than 24 hours.

An ethical AI system designed to solve a particular problem, uses unbiased data and is trained in using the right learning model for the problem. It is monitored to evaluate if the results produced by it are right and fair.

3.7.1 Why Is Ethical AI Important?

Since AI is used in areas like medicine, law enforcement, recruiting, data privacy, military defense and self-driving vehicles, it is mandatory that the AI system must produce accurate, transparent and understandable results that are in synchronization with the ethical standards and norms of our society. To understand the need of ethical AI systems, we must first understand that a biased or incorrect output from AI system, if used by law enforcement, job recruitment, defense work or self-driving vehicles can result in eroding people's privacy (by misusing data in unintended ways). It may be impossible for people to understand the decisions taken based on faulty AI inputs to accept liability for damages when harm is caused.

Apart from being unbiased and accurate, the credibility of AI systems also depends how we choose to develop and use it. We can just hope that AI will be used for purposes that benefit mankind. But there is nothing that can stop a person from creating systems that can be disastrous for humanity.

Nonetheless, efforts are being made by numerous agencies, committees, coalitions, and expert groups to ensure that we are on the right track to make AI systems do more to heal than harm. For example, the IEEE Global Initiative on Ethics of Autonomous and Intelligent Systems that put out *Ethically Aligned Design*, a publication from 2016, outlines the guiding standards for developing and administering ethical AI solutions. Therefore, ethical AI aims to *ensure that AI is doing good for the planet.*

Going further on this, the European Commission High-level Expert Group on AI identified seven guiding principles for creating Trustworthy AI. These guidelines are:

- AI systems should support human autonomy and decision-making.
- AI systems should be technically robust and safe to use. It must have a fallback plan that can be used when something goes wrong.
- AI systems should ensure data privacy by protecting users' data, and providing adequate mechanisms to maintain the quality and integrity of the data.
- AI systems should not work on biased data. The system should be clear, explicable and transparent about its underlying data and the models.
- AI systems should be trained with diverse, non-discriminatory and fair data and models to avoid unfair bias.
- AI systems should be designed to benefit everyone, now and in future. They must focus on societal and environmental wellbeing to be sustainable and environmentally friendly.
- An AI system should have the accountability to ensure accurate, unbiased outcomes, with utmost responsibility.

Key Terms

Artificial Intelligence (AI): Intelligence demonstrated by machines that help them to mimic the actions of humans.

Input layer: Layer from where data enters the network.

Hidden layer: *Layer in which* machine learning algorithms process the inputs. Weights, biases and thresholds are applied to the received inputs and the results of processing are passed to the output layer.

Output layer: Layer that gives the final result to be displayed.

Machine learning: A branch of computer science that analyzes data and identifies patterns to teach a machine to make inferences and decisions without any human intervention.

Deep learning: ML technique that teaches a machine to process inputs through layers to more accurately classify, infer and predict the outcome.

Backward propagation: In case of unsatisfactory results, errors are identified, weights assigned to each node are updated, and pushed back to the previous layers to refine or train the model. This process of moving backward to update weights of all nodes is known as *backward propagation.*

Natural language processing*:* Science which makes a machine capable to read, understand, interpret and respond to a human language.

Computer vision*:* A branch of AI that tries to understand an image by breaking it down into several parts and then studying each part of the image.

Bitmoji: A personalized cartoon avatar that is created to look just like the user.

Ethics: Moral principles that govern the behavior and actions of a group or individual.

Ethical AI: Study that focusses on how right, how fair and how just is the AI's output, outcome and impact.

Chapter Highlights

- Supervised machine learning algorithms apply learning from past data (or experiences) to new data using labeled examples.
- ML algorithm then compares the predicted output with actual output to find errors and modifies the model accordingly.
- Unsupervised learning trains the machine to use information that is neither classified nor labeled.
- Narrow or Weak AI, performs a dedicated task with intelligence.
- General AI performs any intellectual task with efficiency like a human. General AI takes smart decisions without human intervention.
- Super AI or Strong AI is a level of intelligence of systems at which machines could surpass human intelligence.
- Reactive machines focus on current scenarios and react to them in the best possible way. They do not store past experiences for future actions.
- Theory-of-Mind AI systems can understand human emotions, people, beliefs, and interact socially like humans.

Review Questions

1. Define Artificial Intelligence.
2. How do neural networks learn?
3. Explain the different types of AI systems.
4. Write any three applications of AI.
5. Highlight how AI can be used in the healthcare industry.
6. How can our military forces use AI to protect our country from intruders and terrorists?
7. What do you understand by the term 'Ethical AI'?
8. Write short notes on:

   a. NLP b. Computer Vision

9. Differentiate between the following:
   a. Supervised and Unsupervised Learning
   b. Forward and Backward Propagation
   c. Weak AI and Strong AI

Fill in the Blanks

1. In a neural network, processing is done in ________.
2. Neural Networks learn from the ________ produced by the machine.
3. ________ learning trains the machine using information that is neither classified nor labeled.
4. Huge and complex neural networks are better known as ________.
5. ____________ is a science which makes a machine capable to read, understand, interpret and respond to a human language.
6. __________ processing units provide heavy computing power required for iterative processing and training neural networks.
7. __________ generate massive amounts of data from connected devices.
8. _______ apps detect physical objects in real-time to place virtual objects within the physical environment.
9. ________ focus on current scenarios and react on them in the best possible way without storing past experiences for future actions.
10. _________ machines will be super-intelligent, having their own consciousness, sentiments, and self-awareness.
11. Social networking sites use AI techniques to ________ friends to a user.
12. A _______ is a personalized cartoon avatar that is created to look just like the user.
13. ________ AI focusses on how right, how fair and how just is the AI's output, outcome and impact.
14. ________ will surpass human intelligence.

State True or False

1. ML algorithms learn from experiences rather than instructions.
2. Supervised machine-learning algorithms apply learning from past data (or experiences) to new data using unlabeled examples.
3. Deep learning algorithms can work with textual data only.
4. Deep learning models can work with labeled as well as unlabeled data.
5. Self-driving cars make extensive use of NLP.
6. Narrow AI does not mimic or replicate human intelligence.
7. General AI system exists only theoretically.
8. Advanced robotics uses general AI.
9. Limited memory AI systems can understand human emotions, people, beliefs, and interact socially like humans.
10. Plagiarism checkers use AI to identify text that is taken from other websites, books or any other sources.
11. Ethical AI system works on biased data.
12. We can use AI to identify fake news.
13. Machine Learning and NLP are sub-domains of Artificial Intelligence.
14. You must acquire advanced skills to create AI applications.

15. Open-ended AI systems do not exist so far.
16. AI is a sub-field of robotics.
17. We can expect a large number of IoT devices to be used worldwide due to increased use of 3G Internet.
18. It is easy to analyze unstructured data than analyzing structured data.
19. AI-powered surveillance systems use facial recognition techniques.
20. Smart cities use Strong AI applications.
21. Smart buildings do not require maintenance.
22. We can use AI to identify fake news.

Multiple Choice Questions

1. ML algorithms learn from experiences rather than instructions Data is processed in ________ layer of the neural network.
   a. input b. output c. hidden d. Any of these.
2. ML algorithm compares the ________ output with ________ output to find errors and modify the model accordingly.
   a. predicted, actual b. predicted, predicted
   c. actual, actual d. actual, predicted
3. Movement of computations through the hidden layers to the output layer is known as ________ propagation.
   a. backward b. forward c. bi-directional d. linear
4. To update weights of nodes, ________ propagation is performed.
   a. backward b. forward c. bi-directional d. linear
5. ________ is a branch of AI that tries to understand an image by breaking it down into several parts and then studying each part of the image.
   a. Neural Network b. Decision Tree c. NLP d. Computer Vision
6. ________ AI performs a dedicated task with intelligence.
   a. Narrow b. Strong c. General d. Super
7. Virtual assistants like Siri by Apple, Alexa by Amazon, Cortana by Microsoft are examples of ________ AI.
   a. Narrow b. Strong c. General d. Super
8. Virus detection software uses ________ to detect new types of virus.
   a. Deep Neural Networks b. Decision Tree
   c. NLP d. Computer Vision
9. Self-driving car Vaymo is being produced by ________.
   a. Microsoft b. Google c. Amazon d. Tesla
10. AI system must produce ________ results.
    a. accurate and ethical b. transparent c. understandable d. All of these.
11. Amazon Alexa uses ________ technique to perform its task.
    a. Image Recognition b. Speech Recognition
    c. Neural Networks d. Robotics
12. Which of the following is not a sub-domain of AI?
    a. Machine Learning b. Deep Learning
    c. Neural Networks d. Python Programming
13. ________ mimics the operation of the human brain.
    a. Intelligent Network b. Decision Support System
    c. Neural Network d. NLP

AI Domain Identification

Identify the domain of AI used in the following applications:

Number plate detection ____________________

Email spam filter ____________________

Google translator ____________________

Google photos ____________________

Emoji scavenger hunt ____________________

Group Discussion

1. Drones have been used to attack airbases in Jammu. What should we do in this context?
2. If your parents allow you to buy a robot, for what purpose will you buy it?
3. Almost all virtual assistants have a female voice. Isn't this an AI bias?

Project Work

Ask the students to collect information about how robots are used to perform tasks that can endanger human lives.

Brainstorm Activity

1. The government has decided to use drones to monitor all activities taking place during rallies, processions and protests. Discuss the ethical issues involved. Is it justified to keep a check on citizens' behavior?
2. Every human has got nine types of intelligence as shown in the figure given below. Compare it with that of computers. What do you think, how many types of intelligence does the computer exhibit?

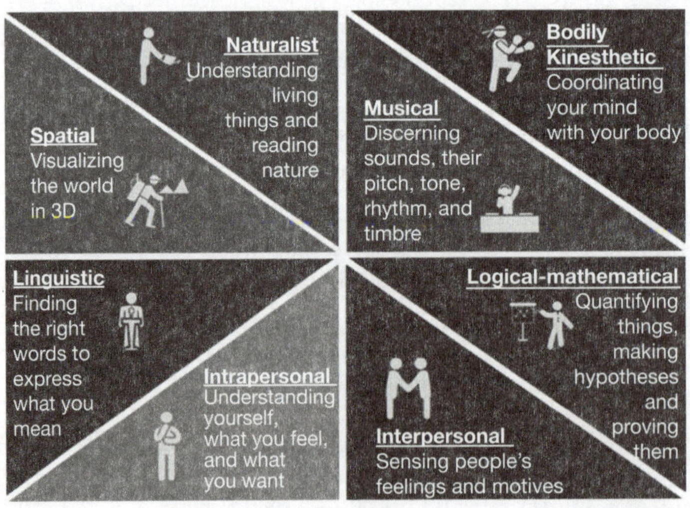

Case Study Discussion

Neyon is a Class V student. His brain is developing and he has immense intelligence and creativity. Till class 4, his imagination knew no bounds. In class V, his parents started using a virtual assistant at home. Neyon also wanted to portray himself as a tech-savvy person. He started asking the assistant to answer his questions. Soon, Neyon became habituated to getting his homework answers provided by the virtual assistant and he used to quickly write them in the notebook. A good intelligent boy turns into a smart cheater.

How can we control the misuse of AI by students?

AI Lab Session – NSynth Sound Maker

The AI-powered application helps users to create unusual new sounds using machine learning techniques. The application trained a neural network on over 300,000 instrument sounds. NSynth combines sounds, like a bass and flute, into a new, hybrid bass-flute sound. Visit the link

https://experiments.withgoogle.com/sound-maker to explore work with NSynth.

Test Your IQ

1. A girl shot her husband in a hotel and later that night, they had a candle-lit dinner together. How is this possible?
2. The robbers, while robbing a bank, left a clue by writing numbers 10, 03, 08, 11 on the calendar. There are the five suspects – John, Oman, Karan, Charanpreet, Arnav. Can you guess the robber?
3. Mr. Bajaj was murdered on a Sunday morning. The police came and enquired about who was doing what, at the time of the murder. The reply was as follows: the wife was in bed, the butler was polishing the silverware, the gardener was trimming trees, the maid was taking mails, and the cook was preparing breakfast. Whom do you suspect?
4. On Thursday afternoon, a woman was found dead in her house. The police found two packages, unopened letters, Monday's newspaper, junk mail, and a flyer for a plumbing service. Whom do you suspect and why?
5. A serial killer kidnaps people and asks them to take one of the two identical pills that he offers. The killer says that one of the two pills is poisonous. When the victim takes any one pill, the killer takes the other one. The victims always die after swallowing the tablet with water but the killer is always safe. How is this possible?
6. Poor people have it. Rich people need it. If you eat it you die. What is it?
7. It is yours but others use it more than you. What is it?
8. It sits in a corner and travels around the world. What is it?
9. A participant in a race quickly passes the person in the second place. At what position is that participant coming?
10. Saina is standing behind Goransh. And Goransh is standing behind Saina. How is this possible?

11. Manav has to cross a river and take with him a wolf, a deer and some grass. He has a boat, in which only he can sit and either the wolf, deer or the grass. He cannot leave wolf and deer on the same shore as the wolf will eat the deer. If the deer and grass are alone on the shore, then deer will eat the grass. How can Manav bring the three across the river safely?

12. A thief is taken before the king to be punished. The king says, "Say a statement. If it is true, you will be killed by lions. If it is false, you will be killed by a herd of wild buffaloes. If it is neither true nor false, you will be set free." What statement should the thief give to be free?

Answers

Fill in the Blanks

1. nodes
2. output
3. Unsupervised
4. deep neural networks
5. Natural Language Processing
6. Graphical
7. Internet of Things
8. Augmented Reality (AR)
9. Reactive machines
10. Self-awareness
11. recommend
12. bitmoji
13. Ethical
14. Strong AI

State True or False

1. True
2. False
3. False
4. True
5. False
6. True
7. True
8. False
9. False
10. True
11. False
12. True
13. True
14. True
15. True
16. False
17. False
18. False
19. True
20. False
21. False
22. True

Multiple Choice Questions

1. c
2. a
3. b
4. c
5. d
6. a
7. a
8. a
9. b
10. d
11. b
12. d
13. c

Test Your IQ

1. She shot with the camera
2. Oman – 10 for 'O', 03 for 'M', and so forth.
3. The maid, as no mails come on a Sunday
4. Newspaperman as he knows that the newspaper will no be longer required after Monday.
5. The poison is in the water.
6. Nothing
7. Your name
8. Stamp
9. Second place
10. They are standing back-to-back.
11. First, Manav will takes the deer across. He returns alone and then takes the wolf across, but returns with the deer. Then he takes the grass across, leaves it with the wolf and returns alone to get the deer.
12. "I will be killed by a herd of buffaloes."

AI Project Cycle

4

Chapter Objectives

The chapter brings forward the challenges in collecting Big Data and creating Machine Learning Models for AI projects. It gives a detailed explanation on the AI Project Cycle, before presenting a detailed coverage on Supervised, Unsupervised, Semi-Supervised and Reinforcement Learning to enable the student choose the appropriate algorithm for the AI project at hand. The chapter also discusses the stages of an AI Project. These stages include:

- Problem scoping
- Data acquisition
- Feature analysis to create a system map
- Data exploration
- Data modelling using rule-based, learning-based and decision-tree approaches
- Evaluation and deployment

4.1 WHAT IS BIG DATA?

Data is everywhere. Our phones, credit/debit cards, software applications, vehicles, records, websites, and digital media store, transmit and process massive amounts of data to generate incredibly valuable information. This data, also known as Big Data, therefore refers to huge amounts of complex data that may be structured or unstructured. This data is rapidly and continuously generated from a wide variety of sources.

Analytical systems capable of handling complex data for analysis integrate Big Data into existing processes to provide insights into data that can help to make vital business decisions. Big Data is used in nearly every industry to identify patterns, trends, understand customer behavior, make complex decisions to grow business, enhance research, make predictions and target key audiences for advertising.

> One gigabyte is equivalent to a seven-minute video in HD and One zettabyte is equal to 250 billion DVDs.

For example, companies can collect and analyze customer reviews and shopping behavior for recommending other products/brands and enhance sales. Remember the 3*V*'s of Big Data, namely.

- **Volume** means enormous amounts of data being stored. While the size of traditional data is measured in units like megabytes, gigabytes and terabytes, Big Data's size varies from petabytes to zettabytes.
- **Velocity** refers to the speed at which large amounts of data is processed and analyzed. Organizations must harness data and derive useful information from it in real time to reap its true benefits. While some data can be collected and then processed at a later point of time, others may require immediate action for the best outcome. For example, data collected from sensors fitted in health devices can collect and process health data to provide physicians with potentially life-saving information.
- **Variety** indicates different sources and forms from which data is collected. This data can be numbers, text, video, images, audio and text.

The 3*V*'s of Big Data can be visualized as shown in Fig. 4.1. These days, data is continuously generated whenever we use an app, search Google or open GPS to track our location in real time. This data needs to be managed, stored, visualized and analyzed.

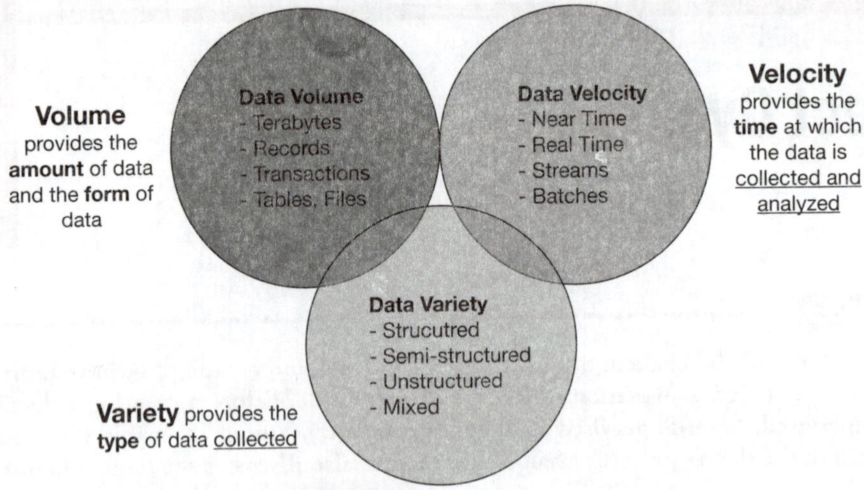

Figure 4.1 3V's of Big Data

4.1.1 How Big Data Works

> 10^{21} bytes equal to 1 zettabyte or one billion terabytes forms a zettabyte.

Big Data provide users an opportunity to extract important pieces to discover new opportunities and business models. To work with Big Data, we need to perform three key actions:

- **Integrate:** Big Data is a collection of data from different varieties of sources and applications.
- **Manage:** Big Data requires huge storage. These days, data is usually stored on the cloud.
- **Analyze:** Data is visualized and explored in detail using machine learning models and artificial **intelligence.** Results of data analysis are then put into action.

4.1.2 Challenges of Big Data

> Statistics shows that 500+ terabytes of new data is added to the databases of social media site Facebook every day in the form of photo and video uploads, message exchanges, comments, etc.

We have seen that enormous amount of data is being generated every second from business transactions, sales figures, customer logs, and stakeholders. Though this huge data is the fuel that drives companies, there are certain challenges that need to be tackled wisely.

Many companies get stuck at the initial stage of their Big Data projects. This is because they are neither aware of the challenges of Big Data nor equipped to tackle those challenges. Let us take a closer look at these challenges and the ways to overcome them.

Lack of Proper Understanding of Big Data Companies often are not able to fully utilize Big Data technologies as the employees themselves do not understand what data is, its storage, processing, importance, and sources. For example, if employees are not aware about the importance of data storage, then they may not know the techniques to properly store and retrieve data efficiently.

Solution Big Data workshops, seminars and training programs must be arranged for all the employees who are involved in Big Data projects.

Data Growth Issues Data grows exponentially with time and becomes so huge that it becomes difficult to handle.

Solution Employees must be trained to compress data for reducing the number of bits in the data, thus reducing its overall size, and removing redundant or unwanted data from a data set. Moreover, with data tiering, companies can store data in different storage tiers to ensure that the data is residing in the most appropriate storage space. For example, depending on the data size and importance, data tiers can be public cloud, private cloud, and flash storage.

Lack of Data Professionals There is a scarcity of talent in the new technologies. Skilled data professionals including data scientists, data analysts and data engineers having sufficient experience in working with the techniques are difficult to find.

Solution Companies are investing more money in the recruitment and regular training of skilled professionals. They are also using AI tools that can be run by professionals who are not an expert in this area.

Securing Data Companies get so engrossed in collecting, transforming, visualizing, analyzing and interpreting data that maintaining security of this data is a real big challenge. Unprotected data acts as breeding grounds for malicious hackers. According to a study, companies can lose up to $3.7 million for a stolen record.

Solution Companies are recruiting more cybersecurity professionals to protect their data. They are also using techniques like data encryption, access control, end-to-end security, real-time security monitoring and Big Data security tools (like IBM Guardian) to maintain security of data.

Integrating Data from a Variety of Sources Data in an organization comes from a variety of sources. Combining all this data is a challenging task.

Solution Companies are solving their data integration problems by deploying appropriate tools for data integration like Talend Data Integration, Centerprise Data Integrator, ArcESB, IBM InfoSphere, Xplenty, Informatica PowerCenter, CloverDX, Microsoft SQL, QlikView and Oracle Data Service Integrator.

> A single jet engine can generate 10+ terabytes of data in 30 minutes of flight time. With many thousand flights per day, generation of data reaches up to many Petabytes.

Poor Quality Data Analyzing wrong, incorrect, incomplete data is more harmful than not performing any data analytics. In the absence of good-quality input, the output will be unreliable. The main reason for having inaccurate data is manual errors made during data entry. Another reason for presence of incorrect data is updating data in one system but not using the updated data when working on another system, which may have the previous version of the data. This makes the final output outdated and inconsistent.

Solution: Companies are using centralized data storage to eliminate using inconsistent data. There is only one copy of data in such systems. So, whenever a piece of information is updated, the change(s) will be reflected everywhere at all times. Moreover, data is now input automatically with mandatory or drop-down fields, leaving little room for human error.

4.2 NEED FOR ARTIFICIAL INTELLIGENCE

We all know that human beings are the most intelligent species on this planet. Humans can think, evaluate and solve complex problems. Therefore, humans now want to impart this intelligence to machines so that even they can think, analyze and act to deduce solutions to otherwise complex problems.

To this end, AI and machine learning aim at making the machines take decisions based on data, with efficiency and scale particularly to automate the data-driven decision-making process. Some factors that escalate the growth and application of machine learning techniques are discussed below:

1. Lack of availability of human expertise or in situations where it is not safe or practically feasible for humans to work. For example, navigation in unknown territories or spatial planets.
2. Dynamic scenarios where conditions keep changing fast and humans are quite slow to respond. Apart from other reasons, it may also be due to limited network connectivity or inadequate availability of infrastructure in the organization.
3. Difficulty faced by humans to provide 100% accurate results, especially for computational tasks. For example, in applications like handwriting recognition, voice recognition, face recognition, and so on.

4.3 MACHINE LEARNING MODEL

We can better understand the role of machine learning techniques through a very simple definition given by professor Mitchell –

"A computer program is said to learn from experience E with respect to some class of tasks T and performance measure P, if its performance at tasks in T, as measured by P, improves with experience E." Based on this definition, the Machine Learning Model can be given as shown in Fig. 4.2. Here,

- **Task(T),** is the real-world problem to be solved. For example, predicting the sales of a product, classifying an email as spam or not a spam, etc. Technically, examples of ML-based tasks are Classification, Regression, Clustering, Recognition, etc.
- **Experience** (E) is the knowledge gained from data provided to the algorithm or model. Once data is provided, the model runs iteratively to learn some inherent patterns. Therefore, like humans, machines now learn from experience by analyzing situations, relationships etc. Supervised, unsupervised and reinforcement learning are some ways to learn or gain experience. Experience acquired through ML model or algorithm is used to solve task T.
- **Performance** (P) is a measure that indicates how well a particular ML algorithm has performed the given task T using experience E. Performance is analyzed based on well-defined metrics including accuracy, F1, confusion matrix, precision, recall, sensitivity etc.

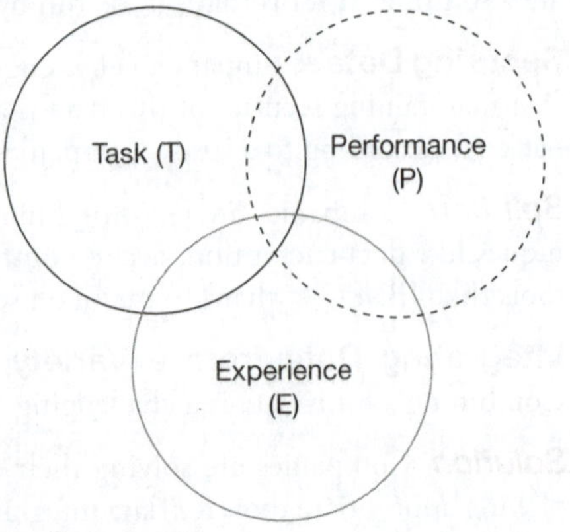

Figure 4.2 Machine learning model

4.3.1 Challenges in Machines Learning

All is not good with respect to machine learning. There are multiple issues with respect to cybersecurity. Apart from this, there are several other significant factors:

- Availability of good-quality data for application of ML algorithms.
- Time-consuming and exhaustive set of tasks involved in data acquisition, feature extraction and retrieval.
- Lack of expertise, as machine learning is still in its infancy stage.
- No clear objective for formulating business problems to make them amenable for applying ML techniques.
- Issue of over-fitting and under-fitting the model.
- Too many features or variables or columns in the data set pose a big challenge.

4.3.2 Applications of Machines Learning

As stated before, Machine Learning is a nascent technology. We are constantly discovering new areas where it could be applied to solve real-world problems. These days, ML is extensively being used for:

- Emotion analysis
- Sentiment analysis
- Error detection and prevention
- Weather forecasting and prediction
- Stock market analysis and forecasting
- Speech synthesis
- Speech recognition
- Customer segmentation
- Object recognition
- Fraud detection and prevention
- Recommendation of products to customer in online shopping
- Identifying profitable opportunities or dangerous risks
- Forming a recommendation engine to personalize online ad delivery in almost real time
- Spam filtering
- Detection of network security threat.

In addition, ML is being used by social media networks, HR systems, automotive industries, and in the field of medicine.

- Facebook's News Feed feature uses machine learning to personalize each member's feed. If a user frequently tags or writes on the wall of a particular friend, the News Feed changes its behavior to display more content from that friend.
- Human resource (HR) systems use machine learning algorithms to identify the characteristics of effective employees and use this knowledge to select the best suitable candidate from the set of all the applicants for a particular vacant post.

- Self-driving cars use deep learning neural networks to identify objects and determine optimal actions for safely steering a vehicle down the road.
- Tumor detection, drug discovery, and DNA sequencing
- To diagnose diseases (like diabetes, cancer) based on the symptoms of patients
- To predict the price and load of electricity that will be consumed in an area
- Voice recognition system
- To identify frequently selling products or products that sell well together so that lucrative discounts can be given to boost their sales.

4.4 TYPES OF MACHINE LEARNING ALGORITHMS

Machine learning algorithms can be categorized as supervised or unsupervised.

4.4.1 Supervised Learning

Supervised machine learning algorithms, as the name indicates, has a supervisor as teacher. These algorithms apply learning from past data (or experiences) to new data using labelled examples.

Technically, supervised learning algorithms learn an association between input data and output. For example, if we have input variable(s) X and output variable Y, then the mapping function from input to output can be given as, $Y = f(X)$. This mapping function can be used to predict the output value for any new input after learning from the existing data.

For example, if you have a basket filled with different varieties of fruits, then the first step is to train the machine to identify the fruit. Now, our machine can easily identify an apple and a banana. Supervised learning algorithms can be further classified into two categories:

> Supervised learning should be used when output of data in the training set is known.

Classification Algorithm A classification algorithm classifies data into a particular group. Classification techniques predict discrete categories. The output will be based on what the model has learnt in the training phase.

For example, a fruit as either an apple or a banana. In real-world applications, classification can be used in medical imaging, speech recognition, hand-writing recognition, credit scoring, predicting if an incoming email is authentic or spam, or whether a tumor is cancerous or benign.

Classification algorithms are best used if data can be tagged, categorized, or separated into specific groups or classes.

Regression A regression algorithm predicts a real value. The output value is based on what the model has learnt in its training phase. In contrast to classification algorithms, regression predicts continuous values. For example, the cost of a product, the value of a stock, changes in temperature or fluctuations in power demand.

> In supervised learning, clear instructions are given specifying what needs to be learnt and how it needs to be learnt.

Thus, in supervised machine learning algorithm, data input and the desired output, along with a feedback about the accuracy of predictions during algorithm training, are provided. Data scientists can select variables or features that can be used by the model to analyze data and make predictions. For example, supervised learning can be used by a company to identify customers who are likely to churn. It can also be used by insurance companies to predict the likelihood of occurrence of a mishap and determine the Total Insurance Value.

4.4.2 Unsupervised Learning

Unsupervised learning trains the machine using information that is neither classified nor labelled. In this case, the machine learning algorithm works on that information without any guidance. The unsorted information is grouped based on similarities, patterns and differences without any prior training of data. For example, if we give an image of mango and an orange, then initially the machine has no idea about how a mango looks and how the orange looks.

Unsupervised machine learning algorithm learns through observation and finding structures in the data. That is, the model automatically finds patterns and relationships in the dataset by creating clusters in it. For example, if given a dataset of pictures of both mangoes and oranges, the algorithm can make two clusters – one containing only pictures of oranges and the other of mangoes (Fig. 4.3). What an unsupervised machine learning cannot do is specifying labels to the clusters. That is, it can only segregate the pictures but cannot tell that this is a real-world orange or that is a mango.

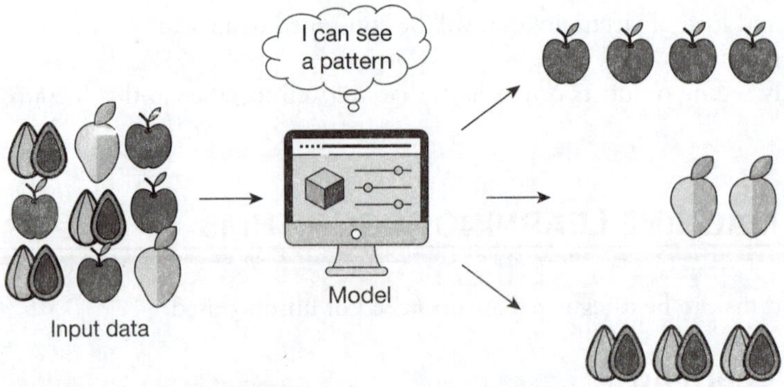

Figure 4.3 Unsupervised learning

Unsupervised learning can be categorized into two sets of algorithms:

Clustering In clustering, the aim is to discover inherent groupings in the data or discover hidden patterns. It is one of the most useful unsupervised machine learning technique as it finds similarity as well as relationship in the underlying data. For example, a company may like to group its customers by their purchasing behavior, a cell phone company can use clustering to optimally decide on the locations where they can build cell phone towers (these clusters can depict the number of people relying on their towers). Other applications include gene sequence analysis, market research, and object recognition.

Association Analysis: In association mining (or analysis), the aim is to discover rules that describe large portions of data. For example, a company can use association analysis to conclude that a customer who buys X also buys product Y.

Dimensionality Reduction: It is used to reduce the number of feature variables for the data set. It is done by selecting a set of principal or representative features. Dimensionality reduction is a very important technique, especially when the data set has a large number (millions).

Outlier Detection or Anomaly Detection: This technique is used to find out the occurrences of rare events or observations that generally do not occur. Application of learnt knowledge in anomaly detection techniques helps to differentiate between anomalous and normal data points. Generally, clustering (more specifically, k-nearest neighbor or KNN) is used to detect anomalies based in data.

Thus, unsupervised machine learning algorithms (also called neural networks) are used when the information used to train is neither classified nor labelled. These algorithms use an iterative approach called deep learning to review data and arrive at conclusions. Unsupervised learning algorithms are used for more complex tasks than supervised learning systems. For example, these algorithms are used in image recognition, speech-to-text and natural language processing applications, and to predict the probability of presence of a particular disease. A retailer can use unsupervised learning technique to find out products that are frequently bought by customers or tend to be bought more frequently.

Figure 4.4 shows a pictorial representation of the key difference between supervised and unsupervised learning.

Figure 4.4 Supervised and unsupervised learning

4.4.3 Semi-supervised Learning

Semi-supervised machine learning algorithms fall somewhere between supervised and unsupervised algorithms since they use both labelled and unlabelled data for training. These algorithms improve accuracy.

Semi-supervised learning algorithms use a small amount of pre-labelled data and a large number of unlabelled data for training. Semi-supervised learning techniques can be applied using any of the two approaches given below.

First, we can build the supervised model based on a small amount of labelled data followed by building an unsupervised model by applying the same to large amounts of unlabelled data. The experience gained by generating more labelled data is used to train the model. This process is repeated multiple times.

In the second approach, we can use unsupervised methods to cluster similar data samples, annotate these groups and then use this information to train the model.

Application of the discussed techniques can be summarized in the flowchart shown in Fig. 4.5.

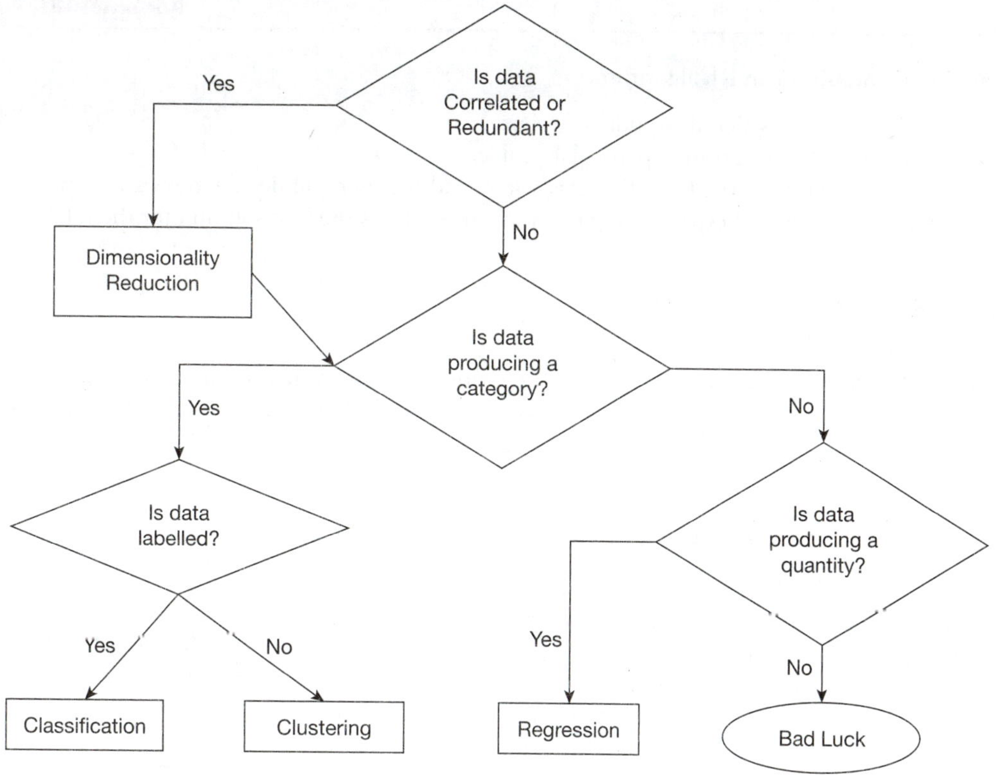

Figure 4.5 Classification of data using machine learning approach

4.4.4 Reinforcement Learning (RL)

These techniques are different from the previously discussed techniques and are rarely used. In a reinforcement learning algorithm, an agent is trained over a period of time so that it can interact with a specific environment.

Reinforcement learning is a type of dynamic programming that trains algorithms using a system of reward and punishment. The agent receives rewards for performing correctly and penalties for performing incorrectly. In this way, the agent learns without any human intervention to maximize its reward and minimize its penalty.

Since RL requires a lot of data, it is mostly used in areas where simulated data is readily available like gameplay and robotics. In these areas, RL is used to find the best possible behavior or path that can be taken in a particular situation.

Reinforcement learning is different from supervised learning. In supervised learning, the training data has labels, so the model is trained with the correct answer but in case of RL, the reinforcement agent decides on what to do to perform the given task. In the absence of a training dataset, it is bound to learn from its own experience.

Example 4.1

In the game shown in Fig. 4.6, there is an agent (robot) and a reward (diamond), with many hurdles (fire) in between. The robot has to learn by trying all the possible paths and then choose the path that gives it the reward with the least hurdles. Each right step earns a reward and every wrong step will subtract the reward of the robot. The total reward is calculated when it reaches the final reward, that is, the diamond.

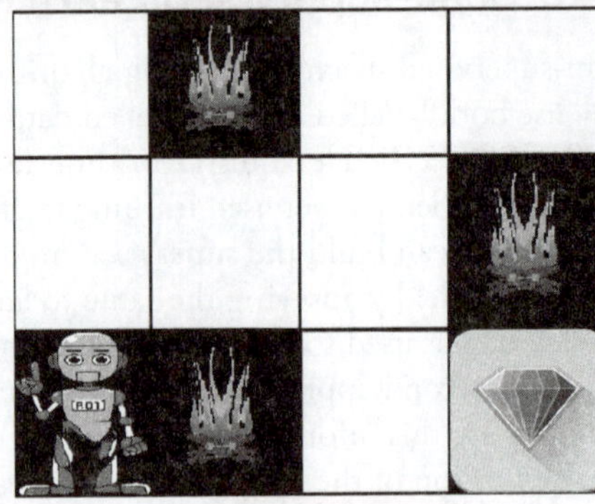

Figure 4.6

To summarize technically, in an RL algorithm,

- Input is an initial state from which the model will start.
- Output is a list of possible outputs for a particular problem.
- Training is based on the input. The model returns a state and the user will decide to reward or punish the model based on its output. The model keeps learning this way until it finds the best solution (or the solution with maximum reward).

Types of Reinforcement

There are two types of reinforcement:

Positive Reinforcement has a positive effect on behavior. It occurs when a particular behavior increases the strength and the frequency of the behavior. Such reinforcement maximizes performance and sustains changes for a long period of time.

Negative Reinforcement is defined as strengthening of a behavior by stopping or avoiding a negative condition.

Applications of Reinforcement Learning RL is used in large environments when a model of the environment is known, but an analytic solution is not available.

- RL can be used in robotics for industrial automation.
- It is used to make machines learn.
- RL is used in data processing applications.
- RL can be used to create training systems that provide custom instruction and materials according to the requirement of students.
- RL is used for creating game playing software (playing chess).
- RL is used in a self-driving car where the car (agent) interacts with its environment, receives a reward depending on how it performs, such as driving to the destination safely. Similarly, the agent receives a penalty for performing incorrectly, such as going off the road or hitting a hurdle.

> An RL agent perceives and interprets its environment, takes actions and learns through trial and error.

4.5 THE AI PROJET CYCLE

- Start with Problem **Scoping**. Set the goal for the AI project by stating the problem.
- **Acquire** or collect data. Data is the fuel that drives any project. This data helps in understanding the features that are related to the problem scoping. Data must be collected from reliable and authentic sources only.
- Create **graphs** for visualizing and easily interpreting large amount of data.
- Develop one or more machine learning **models** to achieve the goal.
- **Test** the models and identify the most efficient one.
- Develop **algorithm** for the most efficient model selected.

Let us discuss all of these points in detail.

4.6 PROBLEM SOLVING IN AI

Any AI project cycle can be divided into various stages including,

1. Problem Scoping
2. Data Acquisition
3. Data Modelling
4. Evaluation and Development

In this section, we will discuss all of these stages in detail.

4.6.1 Problem Scoping

The first stage of AI project cycle is Problem Scoping in which problems are identified. Once the problem is identified, designing, developing and finally testing is performed.

This stage forms the backbone of the entire AI project as incorrect problem scoping will result in failure of the project.

The 4Ws of Problem Scoping For identifying problems accurately, we must focus on 4Ws. These Ws are very helpful in problem scoping. They are:

- **Who?** It helps us to identify who is facing the problem and who are the stakeholders of the problem.
- **What?** Refers to what the problem is and how you noticed it.
- **Where?** Specifies the context/situation/location of the problem.
- **Why?** Helps to know why a solution is required and how the stakeholders will benefit from the solution.

The Problem Statement Template The outcome of problem scoping stage is the problem statement template that contains a summary of the 4Ws. This template is a very useful document as it acts as a guideline for the current as well as all future projects experiencing similar problems.

Activity – Brainstorm Around the Theme and Set a Goal for the AI Project

Given below is a list of themes, select any one for problem scoping.

Select the Theme

The first question then to be answered is,

Why you have selected the theme?

For example, if your theme is

- **Environment**, then enumerate problems such as polluted air, water, and land, etc.
- **Agriculture**, then problems could be excess use of pesticides to increase the production, knowing the appropriate time for sowing and harvesting
- **Traffic**, then think about traffic issues and ways to reduce accidents or any other related problem.

You can take any theme and jot down issues that exist in the context of that theme. The next step is to place the problems into a problem statement template.

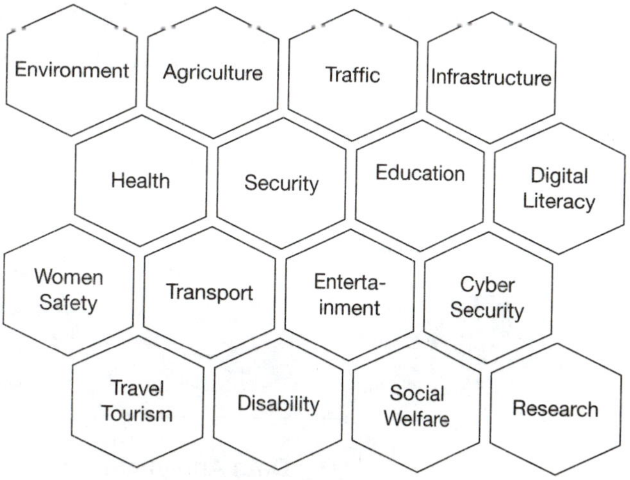

Set up the goal

Once the problem statement is created, set goals that will be fulfilled by the AI project.

For example, if the selected theme is Agriculture, then possible goals can be to identify,

- ***Goal 1:*** Ideal time for seeding
- ***Goal 2:*** Ideal time for harvesting
- ***Goal 3:*** Ideal amount of fertilizer required for the selected crop

Note that the list of goals can be even more. However, before finalizing the goals, let us note two important points.

Do not set the goals with too much enthusiasm as in that case we may set goals that are difficult to achieve and require a lot of time and other resources. This may de-focus the development team (responsible for designing AI-based solution), thereby resulting in delayed projects with a higher budget.

Do not be too skeptical and set goals that are too small to achieve the desired outcome. In such a case, even AI-based solution will be unable to make any effective impact. All the efforts and resources invested in developing a solution would become irrelevant.

To avoid such problems, we must have an expert team that can analyze the problem well, consider the existing measures, talk to customer representatives to gather more information and then finally set a goal that addresses all ethical concerns as well.

Identify the 4Ws Your final problem statement will look like the following table:

Who	**Stakeholders** Farmers, Fertilizer Producers, Laborers, Tractor Companies, Consumer
What	**The problem, Issue, Need** Identify the ideal time for seeding or crop harvesting
When	**Context/Situation** Determine when the crop is mature enough to be harvested.
Why	**Benefits** Farmers will be able to grow and harvest the crop at the most appropriate time and supply it to the consumers on time

4.6.2 Data Acquisition

The term data acquisition consists of two words – data and acquisition, where,

Data refers to the raw facts and figures collected for reference or analysis.

Acquisition means acquiring data for the project from relevant sources. For example, if our theme is Travel Tourism, then we need to collect data from websites, users' reviews, magazines, news reports, survey, cameras, smart devices, sensors, observations, etc., as shown in Fig. 4.7.

(Annexure to this chapter lists some sources of data sets from where crucial data can be freely downloaded for analysis.)

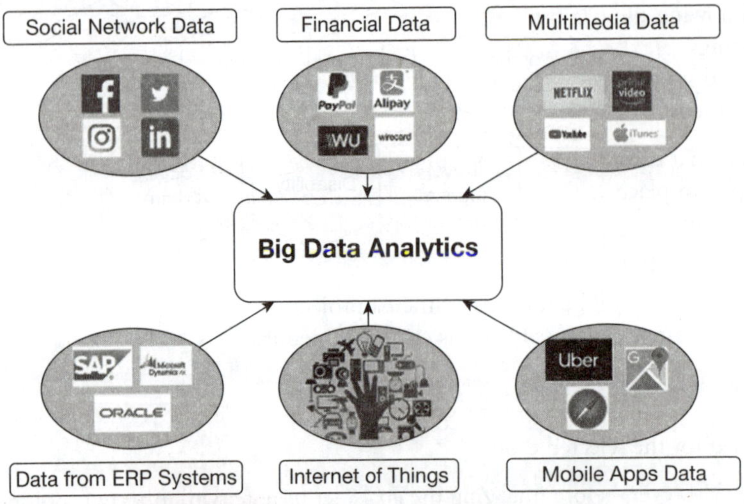

Figure 4.7 Input sources for data analysis

> Extracting anyone's personal data without taking his/her permission is an offence. One of the most reliable and authentic sources of information are the open-sourced websites hosted by the government (like *data.gov.in, india.gov.in*). Data analysts can freely download data from such websites and use it wisely for the benefit of society at large.

4.6.3 Classification of Data

Data can be broadly classified into three broad categories – Basic, Structured and Other (Fig. 4.8). In this section, we will look into all of them in detail.

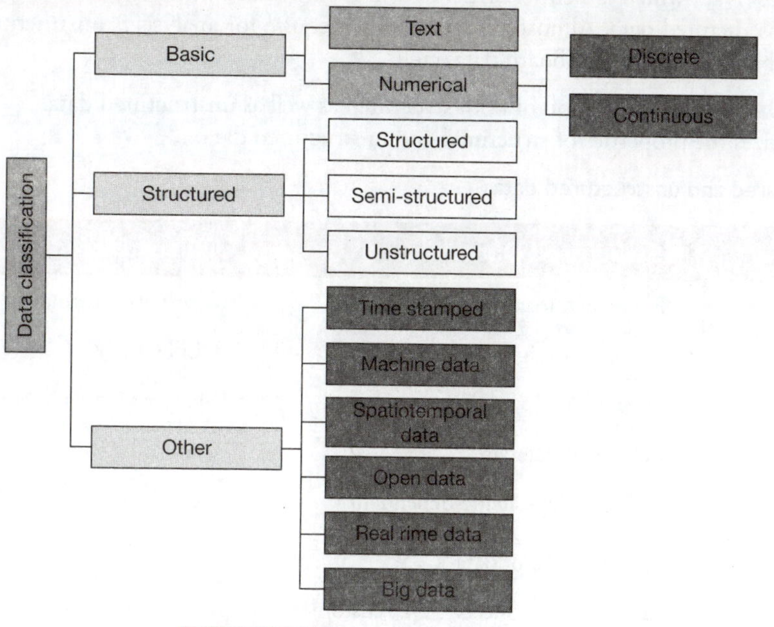

Figure 4.8 Classification of data

Basic Data Basic data can be classified as:

Numeric Data that is mainly used in computations and can be either discrete or continuous.

Discrete data contains integral numeric data that does not have any decimal or fractional value. For example, number of students in a class is 50. In the inter-school quiz competition, 200 students have registered.

Continuous Data that is uncountable represents data in this category. For example, the average weight of class IX boys is 48.5 kgs.

Textual Data is a collection of words that may consist of alphabets, digits and/or special characters. For example, we use textual data to represent names, addresses, subjects, etc.

Structural Classification Data required to train the ML model must follow a specific set of constraints or rules or unique pattern to form the underlying structure of the data. Based on this structure of data, it can be classified into three categories as given below (Fig. 4.9).

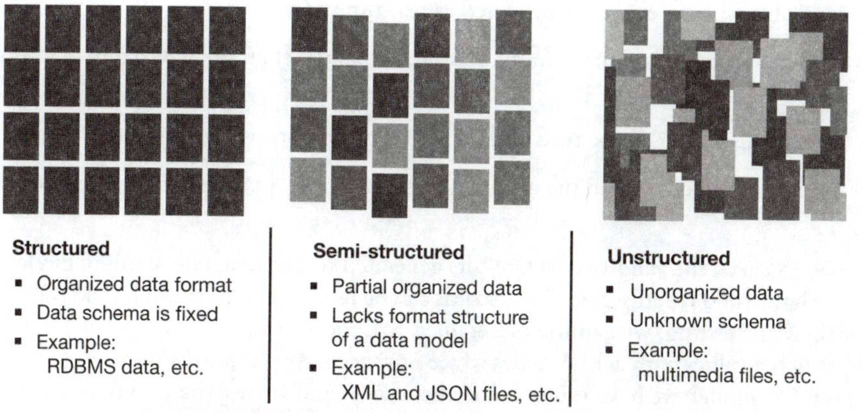

Figure 4.9 Structural classification of data

Structured Data: Structured data has a specific pattern or set of rules. It stores data or values in specific forms like in a tabular format. For example, a list of students, a report card, the cricket scoreboard, the school time-table, an exam datasheet etc.

Unstructured Data: Data which is neither structured in a particular format nor following a specific set of rules can be recorded as unstructured data. Almost all data that we require for analysis is unstructured and is available as YouTube videos, Facebook pictures, Dashboard data, etc.

Semi-structured Data: It is a collection of both structured as well as unstructured data.

Table 4.1 summarizes the properties of structured and unstructured data.

Table 4.1 Structured and unstructured data

Properties	Structured Data	Unstructured Data
Characteristics	Predefined format	Raw/native format
Ease of Searching	Easy and straight-forward	Difficult
Data Types	Defined data types	Many varied data types
Storage	Relational databases	Cannot be stored in relational databases
Flexibility	Not flexible; scheme-dependent	Flexible; not scheme-dependent
Availability	Approx. 20% of data	Approx. 80% of data
Examples	Excel, Google Sheets, SQL, customer data, phone records, transaction history	Text data, social media comments, phone calls transcriptions, various logs files, Images, audio, video

Other Classification Data can be further classified as,

Time-stamped data It follows a specific time-order to define the sequence of events. For example, a student's performance reported every 3 months.

Machine data is obtained as a result or output generated from a specific ML program. Machine data may also be obtained from users' search records, comments, likes and data shared by them, and log records consisting of their interaction with the system.

Spatiotemporal data, as the name suggests, contains information related to geographical location and time. For example, data collected through GPS systems is spatiotemporal data.

Open data is the one that is freely available for anybody to use. For example, various statistics posted by government for analysis by anyone.

Real-time data, available with an event is considered as real-time data.

Big Data means huge amounts of data that cannot be stored by any system or analyzed by traditional data management software.

Data Features Data features refer to the type of data for a specific purpose.

Training data is the data collected to train the machine learning model. In other words, this data makes the machine learn.

Testing data is used to check the validity of the results generated by the machine learning model.

For example, if we have 1000 records then, 700 records can be used to train the model and 300 records can be used for testing the model. While testing, we can use our trained ML model to predict values of a particular variable and then compare the predicted values with actual values to see how accurate the results were.

When creating the ML model, we have values for all the records and we use them to train and test the model. This helps us to use the ML model to predict values for a new record. For example, we can use this model to predict the performance of a new student or the results of the next final exam when the marks in the final exam is not yet known (Table 4.2)

Table 4.2 Training and testing data for Ml model

Marks in Test 1	Marks in Test 2	Unstructured Data	Marks in Final Exams
			Use 70 % values to train ML model to predict final marks
			Use 30 % values to test ML model by comparing predicted with actual values for final marks

Example 4.2

For an Artificially Intelligent system to predict the salary of any employee, we need to input his or her previous salaries in the Machine Learning model. This data would then be used to train the machine. Once the model is ready, it will predict the employee's next salary efficiently. The previous salary data here is known as **Training Data** while the next salary prediction data set is known as the **Testing Data.**

For higher accuracy, the training data must be relevant and authentic; otherwise, the machine will predict wrong values due to incorrect input (training) data.

Data Feature Variable in Machine Learning Now, the important question that arises here is what exactly is a data feature (also known as a data variable or a data attribute). Technically, a feature is a measurable property of the object that is being analyzed. In datasets, features appear as columns.

Roll_no.	Name	Class	Marks	Gender	Grade	Fee_paid

In the above table, we are storing data about students. Each column represents a data feature. So here, the features are: Roll_no., Name, Marks, Gender, Grade and Fee_paid.

Why Feature Variables Are Important Features are the basic building blocks of datasets. The quality of features in a dataset affects the results obtained by applying machine learning algorithms on that dataset. Different business problems may require different features to be analyzed. A good understanding of the business goals and data sets help analysts to select only optimal number of features that are specifically required for the task at hand. Therefore, **feature selection and feature engineering** are performed to contain all essential features that might be required for a specific business problem, leading to the best possible model outcomes and the most beneficial insights. For example, in the above data set, if our goal is to predict marks in the next test, then feature FEE_PAID is irrelevant and must be discarded for analysis.

Creating a System Map Once relevant features are identified, the next step is to create a system map. A system map is used to find the relationships that exist between different elements of the problem. This information about relationship between various features helps the system developer to strategize the solution for achieving the goal of the project.

The developer can visualize complex issues with multiple factors that affect each other. In a system, every element is interconnected and this interconnection is represented using arrows and a specific chain of cause and effect is depicted through a loop. A system may have several chains of causes and effects.

Consider the system map of a water cycle given in Fig. 4.10. In the figure, some arrows are longer than others. This is because that the transition takes a longer time to happen. Technically, this is known as time delay. To change the outcome of a system, we have two options. First, change the elements in a system. Second, change the relationships between the elements. No doubt, changing relationship between the elements in a system is more effective than changing the elements.

The '+' and '–' signs indicates the nature of the relationship between the elements. '+' between two variables means that when the value of one feature increases, the value of the other feature also increases and vice-versa. Correspondingly, a '–' sign means that if the value of one feature increases, the value of the other decreases.

Example 4.3 **Look at the system map of a typical water cycle diagram and write any three inferences that you can deduce from it.**

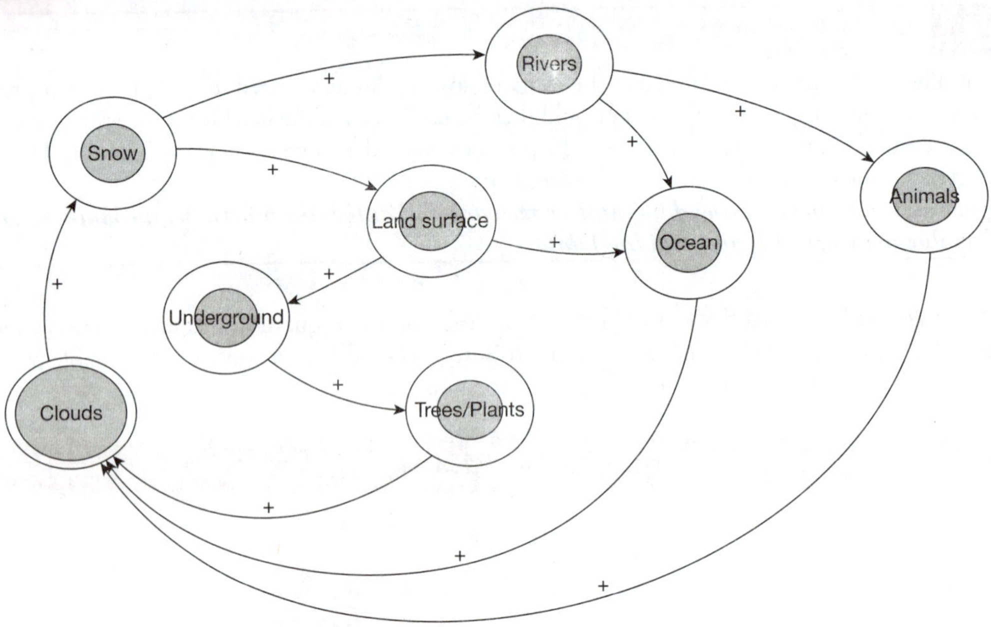

Figure 4.10 System map of a water cycle

Inference 1: More water in rivers means more water in oceans.
Inference 2: More trees/plants contribute to a greater number of clouds.
Inference 3: Trees/plants cause the formation of clouds more rapidly than animals.

Example 4.4 **Create a system map for a simple problem of predicting the grade obtained by a student.**

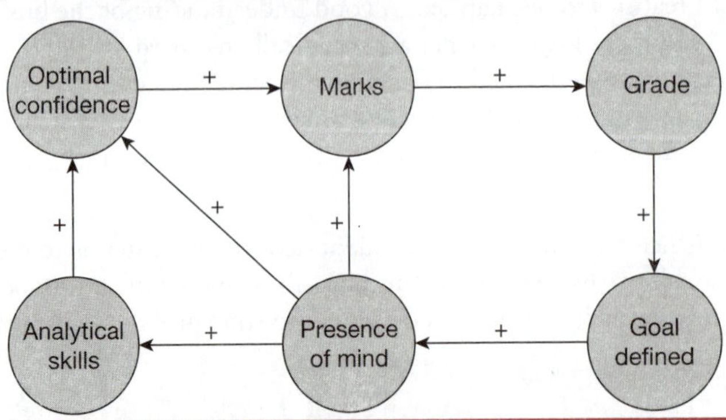

4.7 DATA EXPLORATION

Data exploration refers to the tools and techniques used to easily visualize data that is otherwise difficult to interpret. Acquired data is usually too complex to understand and analyze. Hence, visualization of such data helps users to identify patterns that can be used to predict outcomes. The following are the advantages of data visualization:

- It helps us to get a better understanding and gain insights into the trends followed by data.
- It facilitates user interaction.
- It allows real-time analysis.
- It assists in making business decisions.
- It lowers data complexity.
- It reveals underlying relationships, patterns and trends within data.
- It defines a strategy for your data model.
- It provides an effective way of communication among users.

Select a proper graph for data visualization

There are different types of graphs that can be used to visualize data. However, we need to choose the most appropriate chart for analyzing data in the current context. For example, users can plot following graphs for the given purpose:

1. **Bar graph** for comparing values
2. **Line chart** for comparing trends and visualizing changes over a period of time
3. **Histogram** to visualize distribution of data into different categories
4. **Pie chart** clearly reveals contribution of one particular value in the whole.

Remember that we can create multiple charts also to understand the relationship between data.

4.7.1 Data Modelling

Graphical representation of data not only makes it easy for us to understand it but also assists us in decision making. However, when data has to be accessed and analyzed by machines, machine learning models are used to represent data. The process of creating a model is known as modelling, data modelling or AI modelling.

Three main approaches used for AI modelling are:

1. Rule-based Approach
2. Learning-based Approach
3. Decision tree

Rule-based Approach This approach is based on data and rules fed to the machine. The machine processes data based on the specified rules to produce the desired output. Therefore, rule-based learning model helps machines to learn the relationship or patterns in data according to the rules laid by the developer. Consider the set of rules specified to compute a category of students.

```
IF MARKS < 50, "FAIL"
IF MARKS >= 50 AND MARKS < 60, "AVERAGE"
IF MARKS >= 60 AND MARKS < 70, "GOOD"
IF MARKS >= 70 AND MARKS < 80, "VERY GOOD"
IF MARKS >= 80 AND MARKS < 90, "EXCELLENT"
IF MARKS >= 90 AND MARKS <= 100, "OUTSTANDING"
```

Consider another example. You have a dataset containing 100 images of apples, 100 images of pear and 100 images of bananas. We make a machine learning model to feed this data into the machine so that the machine can accurately label each image as either apple, pear or banana.

Once the model is created, we can test the model by giving it an image of apple. The trained model will compare the image with the trained data and identify the test image as an apple. This is known as rule-based approach. In this approach, rules given to the machine specify the labels for each image in the training dataset (Fig. 4.11).

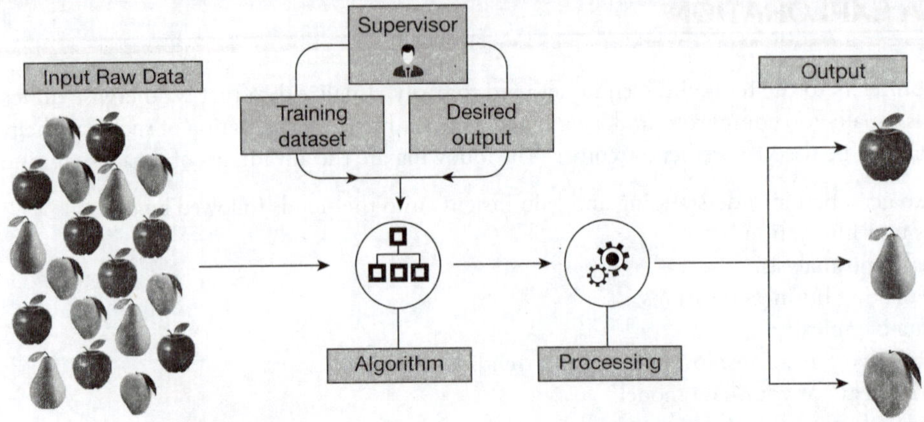

Figure 4.11 Rule-based approach for training dataset

Learning-based Approach In the learning-based approach, the machine is fed with data and the desired output. The machine then automatically designs its own algorithm (or set of rules) to match the input to the desired output.

Therefore, in the learning-based approach, the relationship or patterns in the data is not defined by the developer. Rather, it is left to the machine to identify patterns or required trends.

Generally, this approach is used when the data has no existing labels. In this scenario, the machine looks into the data, extracts similar features out of it and forms clusters of similar datasets. Finally, the machine reveals trends existing in the input (training) data. Therefore, this approach is used to train the data which is either unpredictable or about which the users have no idea.

For example, in a dataset of 1000 images of random stray dogs, you may not have any idea about their breed, color or any other feature. We can feed this into a learning-approach based AI machine that will extract patterns and form clusters of data on the basis of color, size, fur style, etc. Figure 4.12 shows that input data containing a mix of certain shapes, when fixed to ML model, will produce clusters of similar shapes.

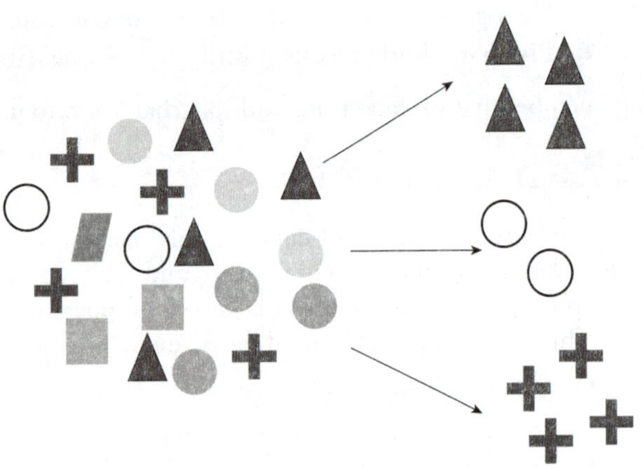

Figure 4.12 Learning-based approach

Decision Trees Do you remember the 'Guess What' game that we used to play in our childhood? One of us will think of something, and the others had to guess what it is. Players can ask close-ended questions, answers of which will be either "Yes" or "No". Based on these clues, the answer is given. For example, consider the tree given in Fig. 4.13. (Note, it is just a sample tree, not a general tree). According to the rules specified, if you are thinking of an animal that is a herbivore and does not live in a forest, then it is a rabbit. The same concept is used to create a **Decision Tree**.

Therefore, a decision tree algorithm forms a tree-like structure to represent decisions. It is similar to a rule-based approach. A decision tree consists of various nodes and follows a top-to-bottom approach. The top-most node of the

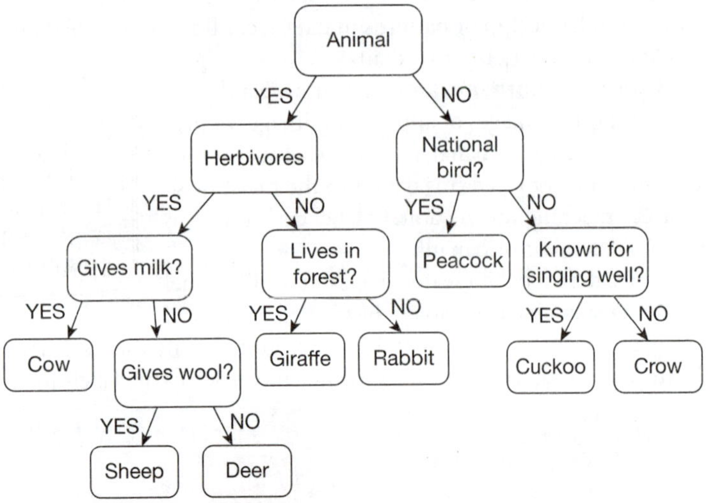

Figure 4.13 A sample decision tree

decision tree is known as **root.** The formation of the tree continues at all levels below the root node by breaking a node to two or more nodes. Nodes in the last level of the decision tree are known as the terminal nodes or leaf nodes. All these nodes are connected with each other by arrow lines.

In a decision tree, nodes represent an event or choice and the edges of the graph represent the decision rules or conditions.

4.7.2 Evaluation and Deployment

Every AI system must be evaluated. In the evaluation phase, the system is tested to make sure that it processes the data accurately without any error(s). The system is verified as well as validated to check that the system meets the stated goals. Any deviation(s) from accuracy or goals may result in modification(s) in the system.

Once the system is thoroughly tested to meet its design goal with efficiency and accuracy, it is deployed (or installed) to allow users reap its benefits. An undeployed system is hardly of any use.

However, the AI project cycle does not end with deployment. Maintenance or System Tuning is a never-ending task that is done at regular intervals for improving the system's effectiveness.

Key Terminology Some important terms that are frequently used in decision trees include:

Root Node: This is the node that performs the first split.

Terminal Nodes/Leaves: These nodes predict the outcome.

Branches: They are depicted by arrows that connect nodes and show the flow from question to answer. Technically, a branch is a sub-section of the entire tree

Splitting: The process of dividing a node into two or more sub-nodes (Fig. 4.14). In a decision tree, splitting done until a user-defined stopping criteria is reached. For example, the programmer may specify that the algorithm should stop once the number of items per node becomes less than 30.

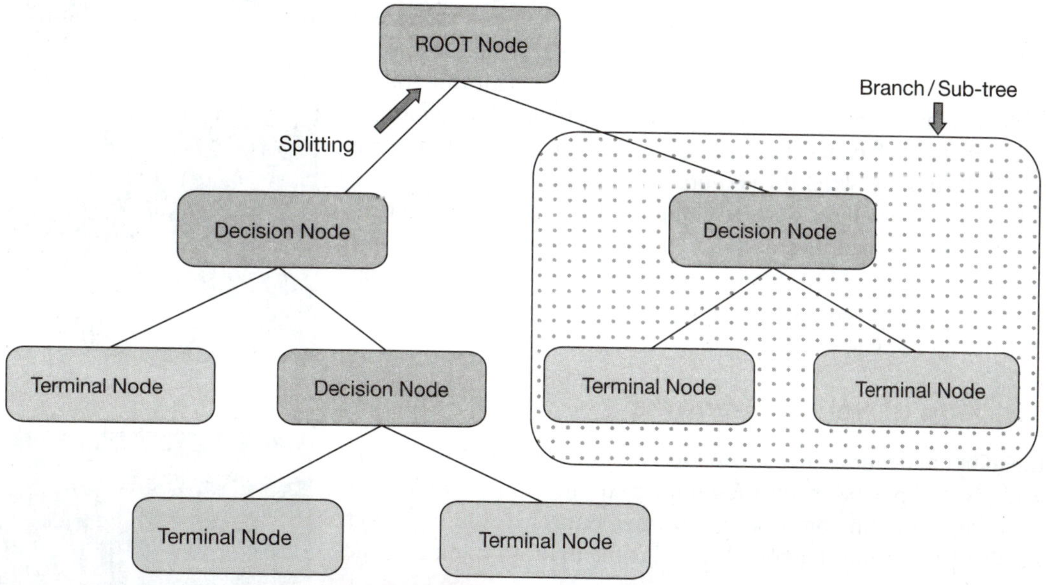

Figure 4.14 Splitting of a node

Decision node: A sub-node that splits into further sub-nodes.

Terminal or leaf node: A sub-node that does not split further.

Parent node: A node which splits into sub-nodes is called a parent node of the sub-nodes (or child of the parent node).

Building a Decision Tree To create a decision tree, remember to follow the points given below.

1. Observe the data carefully.
2. Decide what (data) will be the root node.
3. Decide what (data) will be part of the leaf nodes.
4. Analyze the data and identify unnecessary data (if any).

Example 4.5 **Let us create a simple decision tree which demonstrates your decision whether you should eat Maggi or not (Fig. 4.15).**

In the above decision tree, the first decision that has to be taken is where you are hungry or not. In case the decision is YES, another decision is made whether Maggi is available at home or not. If it is available, the final decision is to cook it and eat.

However, if you are not hungry then you can go and sleep. But if Maggi is not available at home and you are hungry, then immediately take some fruits that are available at home.

Therefore, looking at the above decision tree, we see that there are 3 leaf nodes, thus three decisions – Go to sleep, Cook and eat or Eat some fruits and every decision node has two branches – YES or NO.

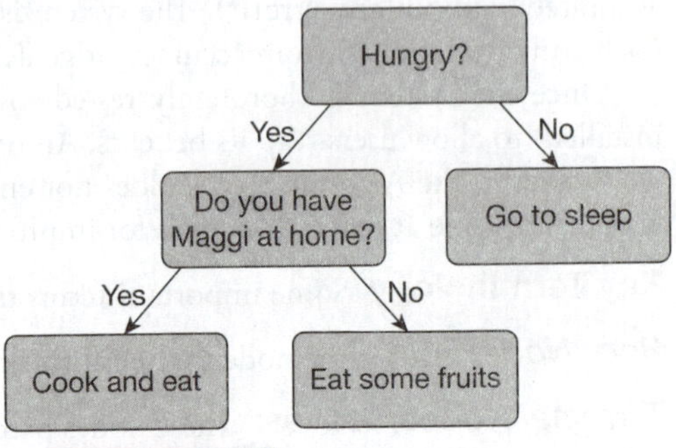

Figure 4.15 A simple decision tree

4.8 NEURAL NETWORKS

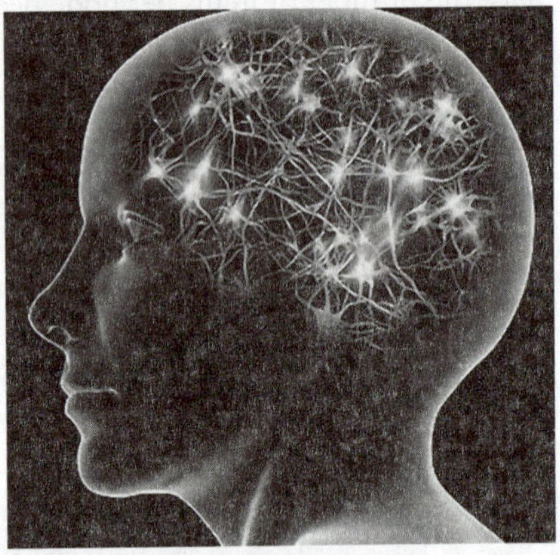

Neural Network (NN) or Artificial Neural Network (ANN) is a machine learning algorithm that is inspired by the biological neuron system and learns by examples. It consists of a large number of highly interconnected processing elements called neurons to solve problems. The algorithm follows a non-linear path and information is processed in parallel throughout the nodes. The best part of neural network is that it can change its internal structure by adjusting the weights of inputs.

Neural network algorithms were developed to solve problems which are easy for humans but difficult for machines. These problems include pattern recognition in which we need to identify similar pictures or patterns. Because of its ability to recognize patterns, neural networks are used for applications that range from optical character recognition to object detection.

4.8.1 Working of Neural Networks

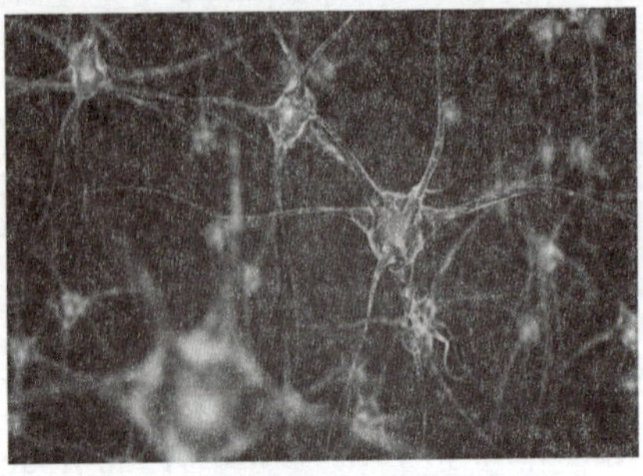

In the human brain, dendrites of a neuron receive input signals from another neuron and give output based on these inputs, to an axon of some other neuron. The human brain comprises of an interconnected web of billions of neurons that process information. This helps the brain to think and take decisions.

Similarly, the neural network algorithm works using a set of connected input/output units. In this structure (Fig. 4.16), each connection has a weight associated with it. In the learning phase, the network learns by adjusting the weights to predict the correct class label of the given inputs.

The learning phase is used along with back propagation error method. Therefore, when error is calculated at the output unit, it is back propagated to all the units because errors at each unit contribute to total error at the output unit. The errors at each unit are then used to optimize the weight at each connection.

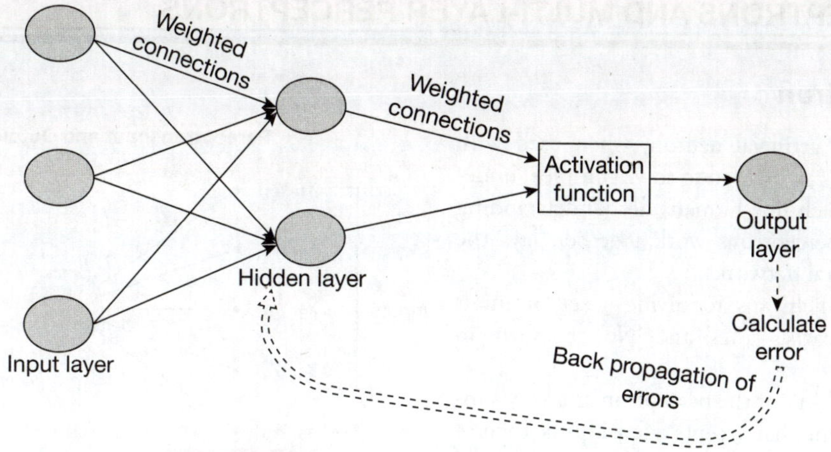

Figure 4.16 A simple neural network model

Forward and Background Propagation We have seen that neural networks take several inputs, process them through multiple neurons from multiple hidden layers, and return the final result using an output layer. This process is known as **Forward Propagation**.

To make a perfect model, we need to minimize the value or weight of neurons that are contributing more to the error. For this, we need to travel back to the neurons of the neural network and find where the error lies. This process is known as **Backward Propagation**. We can reduce the number of iterations to minimize the error by using the 'Gradient Descent' algorithm.

> The output of a neuron is in the range –inf to +inf. So, we need a mapping function, also known as the activation function, that maps inputs to the outputs.

Neural Network with Multiple Hidden Layers In Fig. 4.16, we can see that it is a feedback neural network in which information is passed in both directions (forward as well as backward). The structure of the neural network can change over time based on the inputs. Though the figure shows that there is one input layer, one hidden layer and one output layer, we can have multiple layers of hidden layers as shown in Fig. 4.17.

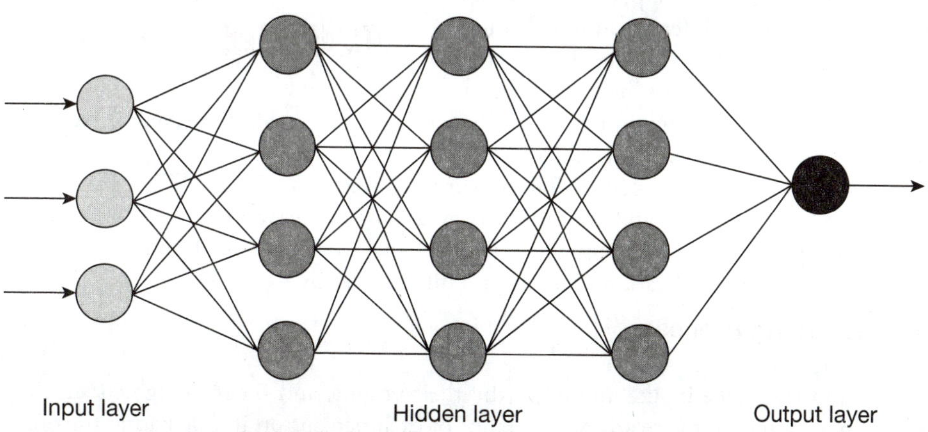

Figure 4.17 Hidden layers of neural network

Here, the input layer is the first layer of the neural network and receives the raw input. It processes the input and passes the processed information to the hidden layers. The hidden layer passes the information to the last layer, which gives the final output.

The output of a neuron can range from –inf to +inf. The neuron does not know the boundary. So, we need a mapping mechanism between the input and output values of the neuron. This mechanism of mapping inputs to output is known as Activation Function. Activation functions decide whether a neuron should be activated or not by calculating the weighted sum and adding bias to it.

4.9 PERCEPTRONS AND MULTI-LAYER PERCEPTRONS

4.9.1 Perceptron

Perceptron or the artificial neuron, when used with other perceptrons, can be used to solve complex, undefined problems much like humans do. Understanding how multi-layer perceptrons work together, lays the foundation of neural networks.

A perceptron helps us to divide a set of input signals into two parts – 'Yes' and 'No' as shown in Fig. 4.18.

Here, we can think of the perceptron as a very simple learning machine that accepts a few inputs, each of which has a weight to signify how important it is, and generates an output decision of '0' or '1'.

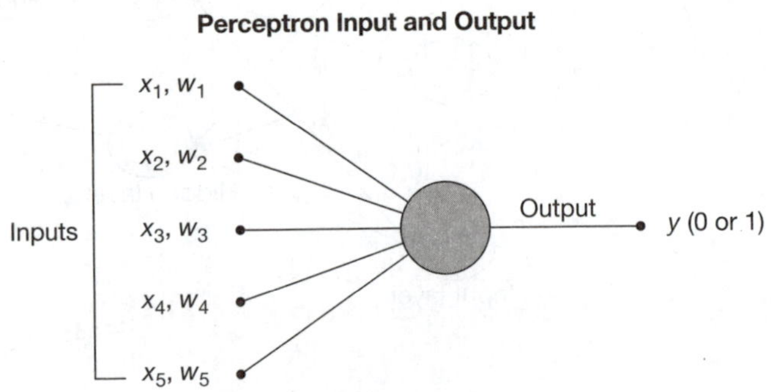

Figure 4.18 Perceptron

4.9.2 Multi-layer Perceptron

A multi-layer perceptron (MLP) or neural network is a perceptron that combines with other perceptrons stacked in several layers, to solve complex problems. For example, Fig. 4.19 given below shows an MLP with three layers. Each perceptron in the first layer on the left (the input layer), sends outputs to all the perceptron in the second layer (the hidden layer), and all perceptrons in the second layer send outputs to the final layer on the right (the output layer). This means that each perceptron sends multiple signals – one signal to each perceptron in the next layer. For each signal, the perceptron uses different weights.

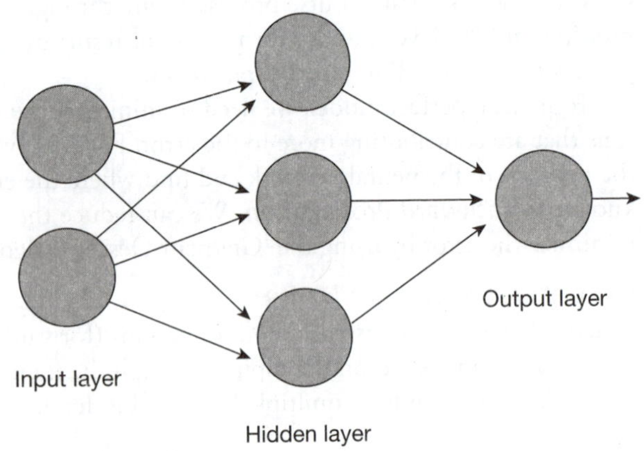

Figure 4.19 Perceptron input and output

In Fig. 4.19, every line going from a perceptron in one layer to the next layer represents a different output. Though this is a very simple figure, a complex one may have a large number of perceptrons in each layer and there can be multiple layers. A three-layer MLP (as shown in figure) is called a **Non-deep** or **Shallow Neural Network**. But, an MLP with four or more layers is called a **Deep Neural Network**.

An interesting point to note here is that neural networks evolved from MLPs. While in the classic perceptron, the decision function is a step function and the output is binary, neural networks, on the other hand, use activation functions to generate outputs of real values, usually between 0 and 1 or between –1 and 1. This helps users to make probability-based predictions or classification of items into different labels.

The Perceptron Learning Process

A perceptron follows these steps:

Step 1: Perceptrons in a layer take input, multiply it by their weight, and then a weighted sum is computed. The weights are assigned depending on the relative importance of each perceptron in calculating the output of that layer. Neural network algorithms learn by finding out better values for these weights to enhance accuracy in the predicted output. Several algorithms including back propagation are used to fine tune the weights.

Step 2: A bias factor is added to fine-tune the numeric output of the perceptron.

Step 3: The sum is fed through the activation function to map the input values to the required output values. For example, input values in the range 1 to 100 may generate outputs as 0 or 1. In a multi-layer perceptron, the activation function also helps the perceptron to learn.

Step 4: The perceptron output, which is usually a classification decision, is produced. Output of the perceptrons, in the 'output layer', is the final prediction of the perceptron learning model.

Pros and Cons

Pros

- Neural networks are flexible algorithms that can be used to solve both regression and classification problems.
- Neural networks perform well on nonlinear dataset with a large number of inputs such as images.
- Neural networks can work with any number of inputs and layers.
- Neural networks work very fast as compared to other classification algorithms since they perform calculations in parallel.

Cons

Algorithms like Decision Tree and Regression that are simple, fast, easy to train, and provide better performance are seen as a preferred choice for classification and regression problems because

- Neural networks require more time for development and needs more computation power.
- Neural networks need more data than any other Machine Learning algorithm.
- Neural networks can be performed only on numerical inputs and non-missing value datasets.

Applications of Neural Networks Neural network algorithms are extensively used in the following fields:

Pattern Recognition applications like facial recognition, object detection, fingerprint recognition, etc. uses neural network algorithms.

Anomaly Detection applications that are specifically designed to detect unusual patterns that don't fit in the general patterns use neural networks because of their ability to perform well in pattern recognition tasks.

Time Series Prediction applications like predicting stock prices and forecasting weather prefer to use neural networks.

Natural Language Processing applications including text classification, Named Entity Recognition (NER), part-of-speech tagging, speech recognition, and spell checking. These are used in a wide range of applications and make use of neural networks algorithms.

Key Terms

Outlier detection or Anomaly detection: Technique used to find out the occurrences of rare events or observations that generally do not occur.

Data acquisition: Acquiring or collecting data for the project from relevant sources.

Structured data: Data that has a specific pattern or set of rules.

Unstructured data: Data which is neither structured in a particular format nor follows a specific set of rules.

Training data: Data collected to train the machine learning model. In other words, this data makes the machine learn.

Testing data: Data used to check the validity of the results generated by machine learning model.

Data exploration: Tools and techniques used to easily visualize data that is otherwise difficult to interpret.

Data modelling: The process of creating a machine learning model is known as modelling, data modelling or AI modelling.

Root node: This is the node that performs the first split.

Terminal nodes/Leaves: These nodes predict the outcome.

Branches: They are depicted by arrows that connect nodes and show the flow from question to answer. Technically, a branch is a sub-section of the entire tree.

Splitting: The process of dividing a node into two or more sub-nodes.

Decision node: A sub-node that splits into further sub-nodes.

Terminal or Leaf node: A sub-node that does not split further.

Parent node: A node which splits into sub-nodes is called a parent node of the sub-nodes.

Multi-layer perceptron (MLP) or neural network: A machine learning algorithm in which a perceptron combines with other perceptrons stacked in several layers, to solve complex problems.

Chapter Highlights

- Data volume means enormous amounts of data being stored. Velocity refers to the speed at which large amounts of data is processed and analyzed. Variety indicates the different sources and forms from which data is collected.
- Supervised machine learning algorithms apply learning from past data (or experiences) to new data using labelled examples. Unsupervised learning trains the machine using information that is neither classified nor labelled.
- In a reinforcement learning algorithm, an agent is trained over a period of time so that it can interact with a specific environment.
- The first stage of AI project cycle is Problem Scoping in which problems are identified. Once the problem is identified, designing, developing and finally, testing is performed.
- The outcome of problem scoping stage is the problem statement template that contains a summary of the 4Ws.
- Once the problem statement is created, the set goals will be fulfilled by the AI project.
- Spatiotemporal data contains information related to geographical location and time. For example, data collected through GPS systems is spatiotemporal data. Open data is the one that is freely available for anybody to use. Big Data means huge amounts of data that cannot be stored by any system or analyzed by traditional data management software.
- Rule-based learning model helps machines to learn the relationship or patterns in data according to the rules laid by the developer.
- In the learning-based approach, the machine is fed with data and the desired output. The machine then automatically designs its own algorithm to match the input to the desired output.

Review Questions

1. What is Big Data? Explain any two challenges faced when working with it.
2. Explain the techniques through which an ML model gains experience.
3. Discuss any five applications of machine learning systems.
4. What is reinforcement learning? Give any three uses of this learning technique.
5. Explain the AI Project Cycle.
6. Give any three reasons highlighting the importance of data visualization.
7. Discuss the different approaches of data modelling.
8. How does the perceptron learn in a neural network?
9. Differentiate between the following:
   a. Supervised and Unsupervised Learning
   b. Positive and Negative Reinforcement
   c. Structured and Unstructured Data
   d. Training and Testing Data.

Fill in the Blanks

1. ________ data is used to identify patterns, trends, gain insights into customers, and make complex decisions to grow business.

2. Three Vs of Big Data are ________, ________ and ________.
3. The size of Big Data varies from ________ to ________.
4. Big Data is stored on ________.
5. ________ algorithms predict continuous values.
6. ________ learning trains the machine using information that is neither classified nor labelled.
7. In reinforcement learning, an agent receives ________ for performing correctly and ______ for performing incorrectly.
8. The outcome of problem scoping stage is ________.
9. ______ Chart clearly reveals the contribution of one particular value in the whole.
10. In a neural network, each node has a ________ associated with it.
11. In neural networks, the output layer receives input from the ________ layer.
12. Artificial neuron is known as ________.
13. Nodes of a neural network layer are arranged in ________.
14. ________ map is used to find the relationship that exists between the different elements of a problem.

State True or False

1. Unsupervised machine learning algorithms apply learning from past data to new data using unlabelled examples.
2. Unsupervised learning algorithms are used for solving tasks that are more complex than those handled by supervised learning systems.
3. The first stage of AI project cycle is Data Exploration.
4. A school timetable is an example of unstructured data.
5. In a decision tree, the root node predicts the outcome.
6. In backward propagation, we minimize the value or weight of neurons that are contributing more to the error.
7. An MLP with more than three layers is called a Non-deep or Shallow Neural Network.
8. Neural networks can solve classification problems only.
9. Goal setting involves identification of reasons for problems.
10. Modelling is the last stage of AI project cycle.
11. AI applications work well with large amounts of data.
12. Machine data is generated by AI systems.
13. Problem Scoping is an important phase in any AI project.
14. All cells in the human brain are connected to each other.
15. Neural networks are the only way of data modelling for AI projects.
16. Edges in the human brain as well as in a neural network can carry data only in one direction.
17. A neural network must have at least three layers.
18. A node in the neural network can accept input from only one node in the previous layer.
19. To check the accuracy of prediction, actual output is compared with predicted output.
20. More the volume of training data, higher is the accuracy of the prediction.

Multiple Choice Questions

1. ________ data can be analyzed by AI application.
   a. Textual b. Visual c. Audio d. All of these.
2. ________ algorithm categorizes data into discrete groups.
   a. Classification b. Regression
   c. Association Analysis d. Outlier Analysis
3. 'A customer who buys X also buys product Y'; such rules are discovered using ________.
   a. Classification b. Regression
   c. Association Analysis d. Outlier Analysis
4. When the data set has a very large set of columns, ________ technique should be used to reduce the number of features.
   a. Classification b. Dimensionality Reduction
   c. Association Analysis d. Outlier Analysis
5. ________ Technique is used to find the occurrences of rare events or observations that generally do not occur.
   a. Classification b. Dimensionality Reduction
   c. Association Analysis d. Outlier Analysis
6. In ________ Learning, an agent is trained over a period of time so that it can interact with a specific environment.
   a. Supervised b. Unsupervised c. Reinforcement d. Machine
7. ________ data follows a specific time-order to define the sequence of events.
   a. Time-stamped b. Spatiotemporal c. Real-time d. Open
8. Which chart will you use for comparing trends and visualizing changes over a period of time?
   a. Bar b. Pie c. Line d. Histogram
9. In ________ Approach, the machine is fed with data and the desired output. The machine then automatically designs its own algorithm (or set of rules) to match the input to the desired output.
   a. Rule-based b. Learning-based c. Decision Tree d. Neural Network
10. In a neural network, ________ are assigned depending on the relative importance of each perceptron.
    a. Bias b. Input c. Output d. Weights
11. Identify the incorrect statement about neural networks:
    a. They require more time for development.
    b. They need more computation power.
    c. They need more data than any other Machine Learning algorithm.
    d. They can perform on numerical as well as textual inputs.
12. Data ________ is an ongoing phase in the development of an AI system.
    a. Collection b. Modelling c. Evaluation d. Maintenance
13. Every AI system must be ________ to ensure that the system meet its goal, that too accurately.
    a. Validated b. Verified c. Both of these. d. None of these
14. Which of the following is not included in one of the Vs of Big Data?
    a. Volume b. Validity c. Variety d. Velocity
15. Which of the following activities are not done as a part of AI system deployment?
    a. Review b. Maintenance c. Testing d. Modelling
16. Errors in the results are identified and the AI system is rectified in the ________ phase.
    a. Data Visualization b. Modelling
    c. Evaluation and Deployment d. Problem Scoping
17. A flight's arrival and departure schedule is an example of ________ data.
    a. Structured b. Unstructured c. Semi-structured d. All of these.

18. Which of the following data is available as the event takes place?
    a. Big Data
    b Real-time data
    c. Spatiotemporal data
    d. Time-stamped data
19. Which of the following is not a stage in the AI Project Cycle?
    a. Problem Scoping
    b. Data Acquisition
    c. Data Exploration
    d. Prototyping
20. ________ enables computers to identify and process images like humans do.
    a. Face Recognition
    b. Model-view-controller
    c. Computer Vision
    d. Eye-in-hand System
21. Data is collected from ________.
    a. Social Media
    b. Smartphone
    c. IoT Devices
    d. All of these.
22. Which sign between two variables means that when value of one feature increases, the value of other also increases?
    a. +
    b. –
    c. ×
    d. /

Group Discussion

Discuss any two features you like the most in a smart TV, smart refrigerator, smart boards, smart security system, smart result evaluation and analysis system.

Project Work

1. Ask students to make a project report on any topic of their interest. Identify the 4 Ws and the goals of the project. Highlight sources from where data will be collected. Which modelling technique would be used to explore the data and why?
2. Ask students to make a Google form and collect data from at least 20 students about any topic of their interest. Analyze this data using charts.

Data Analysis Activity

1. Identify features of the given Employee Data Set. Which features will be used to predict his salary?

Emp No.	Name	Deptt	Desig	Sal	Exp	Loc	Qual

2. Consider the decision trees given below and write down what information you are able to infer from them.

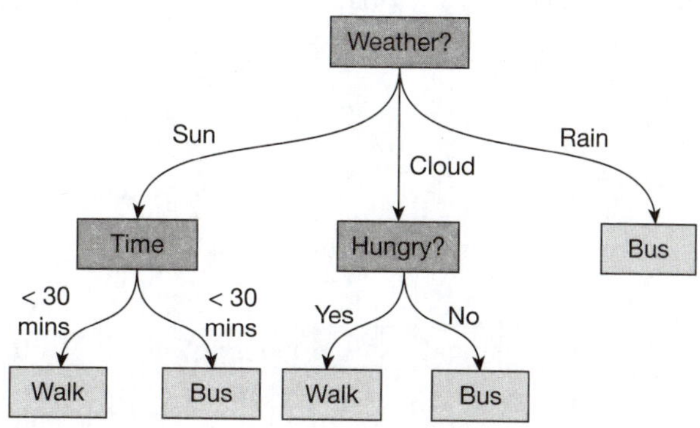

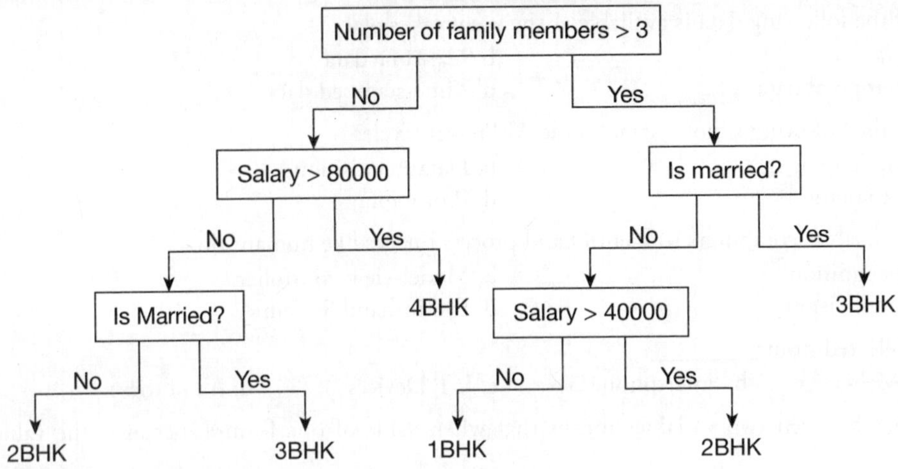

3. Draw a decision tree that represents following rules.
   a. ***Rule 1:*** If it is sunny and humid, then do not go out.
      Rule 2: If it is sunny but not humid, then go out.
      Rule 3: If it is overcast, then go out.
      Rule 4: If it is rainy but not windy, then go out.
      Rule 5: If it is rainy and windy, then do not go out.
   b. ***Rule 1:*** If Reference Rating and Experience < 60% then Not Qualified
      Rule 2: If Reference Rating, Job Experience > 60%, Interview Rating > 40% and Interpersonal Skills > 20% then Eligible
      Rule 3: If Reference Rating, Job Experience > 60%, Interview Rating < 40%, then Not Qualified
   c. ***Rule 4:*** If Reference Rating, Job Experience > 60%, Interview Rating > 40% and Interpersonal Skills < 20% then Not Qualified
4. What information does the following graph give?

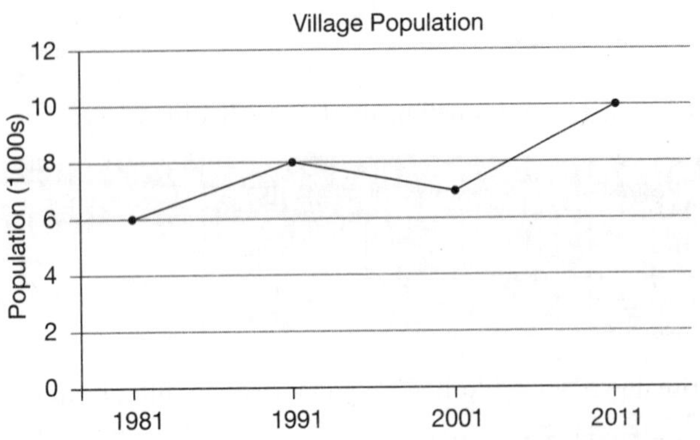

a.

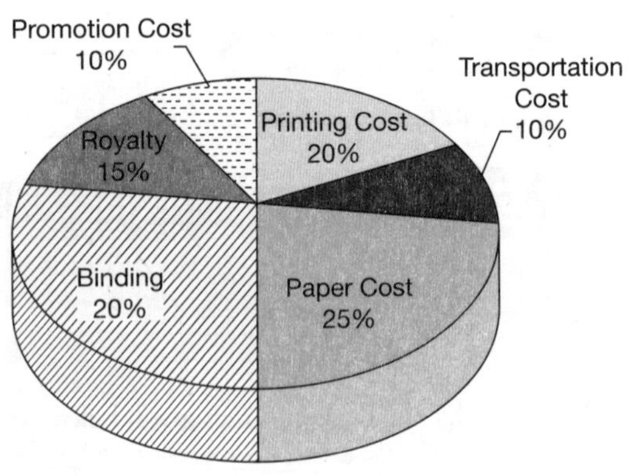

b.

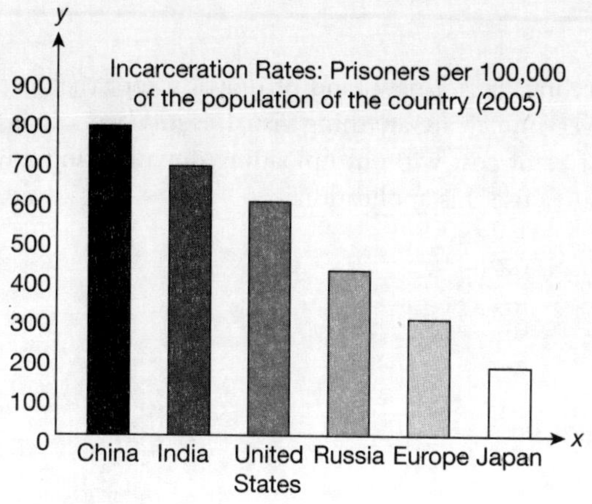

c.

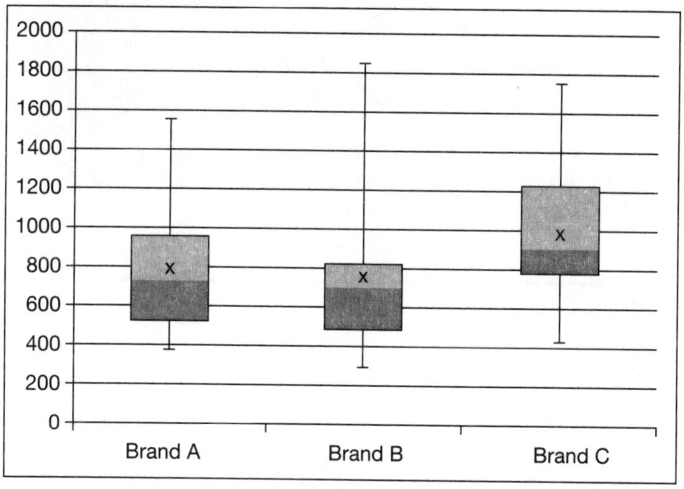

d.

5. Plot graphs for the following data sets.

a. Line graph

X	7	12	28	3	41
Y	14	7	6	19	3

b. Histogram

1.45	2.20	0.75	1.23	1.25
1.25	3.09	1.99	2.00	0.78
1.32	2.25	3.15	3.85	0.52
0.99	1.38	1.75	1.22	1.75

c. Pie chart

1. Dogs (1110 people),
2. Cats (987 people),
3. Rodents (312 people),
4. Reptiles (97 people),
5. Fish (398 people).

d. Box plot

Source data		
2013	**2014**	**2015**
133	195	132
117	199	100
189	177	170
152	194	125
157	123	120
119	120	121
118	135	148
100	194	162
136	120	136
112	135	113
149	185	121
110	183	107
172	156	176

AI Lab Session – AutoDraw

AutoDraw is an AI-powered, fast-drawing application for everyone. It is a new kind of drawing tool that uses ML techniques along with drawings from talented artists to help everyone create anything visual, fast. Users can use this application on their smartphone, tablet, laptop, desktop, etc., free of cost without uploading/downloading any data from the Internet. Just visit the link https://www.autodraw.com/ to use this application.

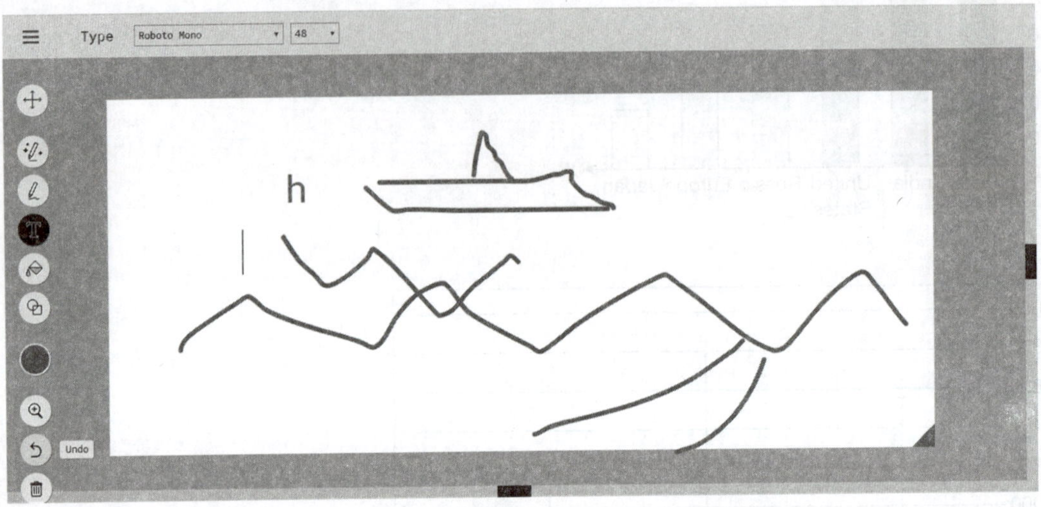

Answers

Fill in the Blanks

1. Big
2. Volume, Velocity, Variety
3. petabytes, zettabytes
4. cloud
5. Regression
6. Unsupervised
7. rewards, penalties
8. problem statement template
9. Pie
10. weight
11. hidden
12. perceptron
13. layers
14. System

State True or False

1. False
2. True
3. False
4. False
5. False
6. True
7. False
8. False
9. True
10. False
11. True
12. False
13. True
14. True
15. False
16. False
17. True
18. False
19. True
20. True

Multiple Choice Questions

1. d
2. a
3. c
4. b
5. d
6. c
7. a
8. c
9. b
10. d
11. d
12. d
13. c
14. b
15. d
16. c
17. a
18. b
19. d
20. c
21. d
22. a

Introduction to Programming Language Python

5

Chapter Objectives

The chapter introduces problem-solving using Python programming language. Topics covered in this chapter include:

- Features and applications of python
- Writing and executing programs
- Tokens in python
- Working with numbers and strings
- Type conversion

Python is a powerful programming language with the right combination of performance and features that makes programming fun and easy. It is a high-level, interpreted, interactive, object-oriented and a reliable language that uses English-like words. It has a vast library of modules to support integration of complex solutions from pre-built components. In this chapter, we will start with a basic introduction of Python.

5.1 FEATURES OF PYTHON

Python is an open-source project, supported by many individuals. It can be used on any operating system. Some of the features which make Python a complete programming language are given below.

Simple: Python is a simple and a small language. Reading a program written in Python feels almost like reading English.

Easy to Learn: A Python program is easy to read and understand. It uses only a few keywords and a clearly defined syntax. This makes it easy for just anyone to pick up the language quickly.

Versatile: Python supports development of a wide range of applications ranging from simple text processing to games.

Free and Open Source: Python is an example of an open-source software. Therefore, anyone can freely distribute it, read the source code, edit it and even use the code to write new (free) programs.

High-level Language: When writing programs in Python, the programmers don't have to worry about the hardware-related details. They just need to concentrate on writing solutions for the current problem at hand.

Interactive: Programs in Python work in interactive mode. Users can give input and get the results accordingly. In this way, users feel as if they are directly communicating with the program.

> Python is being constantly improved upon by a community of users who have always strived hard to take it to the next level.

Portable: Python is a portable language. Hence, the programs behave the same on a wide variety of hardware platforms. The programs work on any of the operating system without requiring any change.

Object Oriented: Python supports object-oriented as well as procedure-oriented style of programming. While object-oriented technique uses classes and objects to bind data and functions that can manipulate that data, *procedure-oriented* technique, on the other hand, builds program by making extensive use of functions (functions are reusable parts of a program).

Interpreted: Python program is processed at runtime (while it is being executed) by the interpreter. The interpreter checks each statement to ensure that there are no syntactical errors. If a statement has one or more errors, then it is reported to the user. After the error is removed or if there is no error in a particular line, the interpreter converts that statement into machine language (comprising of only 0's and 1's) and then processes the next line.

Dynamic: Python program executes dynamically. They can be copied and used for flexible development of applications.

Extensible: Since Python is an open-source software, anyone can add modules to the Python interpreter. These modules enable programmers to add to or customize their tools to work more efficiently.

Embeddable: Programmers can embed Python programs within their C, C++, COM, ActiveX, CORBA, and Java programs for added functionality.

Extensive libraries: Python has a huge library that allows programmers to perform a wide range of applications varying from text processing, maintaining databases to GUI programming.

Besides the above-stated features, Python has a big list of good features, such as

Easy maintenance: Codes written in Python are easy to maintain.

Secure: The Python language environment is secure from tampering.

Robust: Python programmers cannot manipulate memory directly. Moreover, errors can be easily handled through exception handling procedures. For every syntactical mistake, a simple and easy-to-interpret message is displayed. All these things make the language robust.

Multi-threaded: Python supports multi-threading, that is, executing more than one process of a program simultaneously.

Garbage collection: Python performs garbage collection of all objects that are no longer used.

5.2 APPLICATIONS OF PYTHON

Since its origin in 1989, Python has grown to become part of a plethora of web-based, desktop-based, graphic design, scientific, and computational applications. Some of the key applications of Python include:

- Python is used to develop a wide range of applications including *image processing, text processing, web*, and enterprise level using scientific, numeric and data from network.
- 3D software like Maya includes Python which can be used for *automating* small user tasks.
- Python is a popular language for *web development*. For example, websites like Quora, Odoo and Google App engine have their codes written in Python. For web development, Python has frameworks such as Django, Pyramid, Flask and Bottle.
- *GUI-based Desktop Applications* can be easily developed in Python.
- Python is used to make *2D imaging software* such as Inkscape, GIMP, Paint Shop Pro and Scribus. It is also used to make *3D animation* packages, like Blender, 3ds Max, Cinema 4D, Houdini, Lightwave and Maya.
- Features like high speed, productivity and availability of tools (like Scientific Python and Numeric Python) have made Python a preferred language to perform *computation and processing of scientific data*.
- Python has various modules, libraries and platforms that support development of *games*. Games like Civilization-IV, Disney's Toontown Online, Vega Strike, etc. are coded using Python.
- Python is a suitable coding language for *customizing business applications*. For example, Reddit, which was originally written in Common Lips, was rewritten in Python in 2005. A large part of YouTube code is also written in Python.

- Python is also used for *writing codes for operating system.* For example, Ubuntu's Ubiquity Installer, and Fedora's and Red Hat Enterprise Linux's Anaconda Installer are written in Python. Gentoo Linux uses Python for Portage – its package management system.
- Python is used to develop other *languages.* For example, Boo, Apple's Swift, CoffeeScript, Cobra, and OCaml, all have syntax similar to Python.
- Since Python is very easy to learn and an open-source language, it is widely used for *prototype development (that means, for developing user interfaces or screens).*
- Python is used for *network programming* to help users write functions for email processing and support for FTP, IMAP and other Internet protocols.
- Python is a perfect language for teaching programming skills at the introductory as well as advanced level.

5.3 WRITING AND EXECUTING THE FIRST PYTHON PROGRAM

Here onwards, we will be using Python, via the Python console. For that you need to first download Python from www.Python.org. The codes in this book have been developed on Python 3.8.3.

5.3.1 Writing the First Program

To get the interactive interpreter, follow the steps given below.

Step 1: Click on Start button.
Step 2: Type Idle.
Step 3: Click on IDLE (Python GUI).

The IDLE starts. You get a prompt of three right arrows. Type in your instructions at the prompt and press the enter key. **Let us print Hello World!!!** on the screen. For this, simply type the following line on the IDLE.

Example: To print a message on the screen

```
>>> print("Hello World!!!")
Hello World!!!
```

The >>> symbol denotes the Python prompt.

5.4 MORE ABOUT THE `print()` FUNCTION

The `print()` function prints one or more literals (or values) followed by a new line. If you don't want to print on a new line then write end = ' ' after a comma, as shown below.

```
# printing strings
print("Python")
print("Programming")
OUTPUT
Python
Programming
```

```
#printing strings on the same line
print("Python", end= ' ')
print("Programming")
OUTPUT
Python Programming
```

Points to Remember

- To print more than one value, you can use comma or the + sign to separate those values.

```
print("HELLO","GOOD MORNING")
print("PYTHON" + " PROGRAMMING")
OUTPUT
HELLO GOOD MORNING
PYTHON PROGRAMMING
```

- By default, space is inserted between two or more values that are to be printed. Therefore, in the above code, a space is automatically inserted between HELLO and GOOD MORINING in the output.

- The default separator between values, which is the space, can be changed to any other character using the `sep` argument in the `print()` function as shown below. We shall discuss about arguments in a later chapter.

```
print("HELLO","GOOD MORNING","INDIA", sep = '#')
OUTPUT
HELLO#GOOD MORNING#INDIA
```

- The `print()` function prints a string (i.e., a group of characters). If any non-string value is specified in the `print()` function, it automatically converts it to a string before printing.

```
print("Neha's Total Marks = ",98)
OUTPUT
Neha's Total Marks =  98
```

- The `print()` function automatically inserts a new line. So, in case we have multiple `print()` functions in the same program, then output of each `print()` function will be displayed on the next line or the new line.

```
print("HELLO")
print("GOOD MORNING")
OUTPUT
HELLO
GOOD MORNING
```

5.5 WRITING PYTHON PROGRAMS USING THE IDLE EDITOR

In general, the standard way to save and run a Python program is as follows:

Step 1: Open an editor.
Step 2: Write the instructions
Step 3: Save it as a file with the filename having the extension .py.
Step 4: Run the interpreter with the command python program_name.py or use IDLE to run the programs.

> To exit from the IDLE, click on File → Exit, or, press Ctrl + Q keys or type `quit()` at the command prompt.

To execute the program in Python shell, press **F5** key (Fig. 5.1) or click on Run Menu and then select **Run Module**.

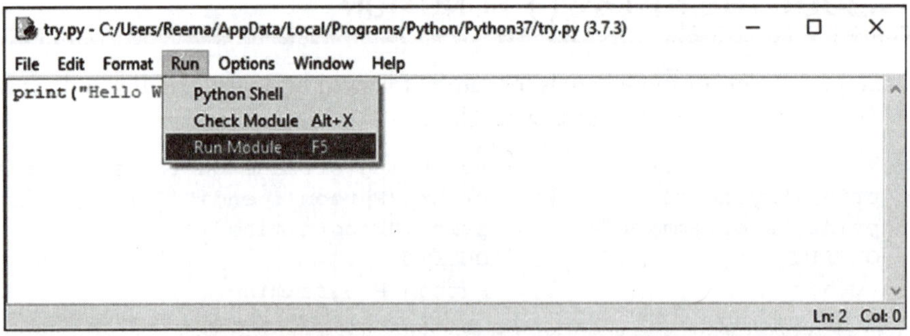

Figure 5.1 Executing Python code in IDLE

5.6 PYTHON TOKENS

Tokens are small units of the programming language (Fig. 5.2). Python supports the following types of tokens. In this chapter, we will read about literals in detail.

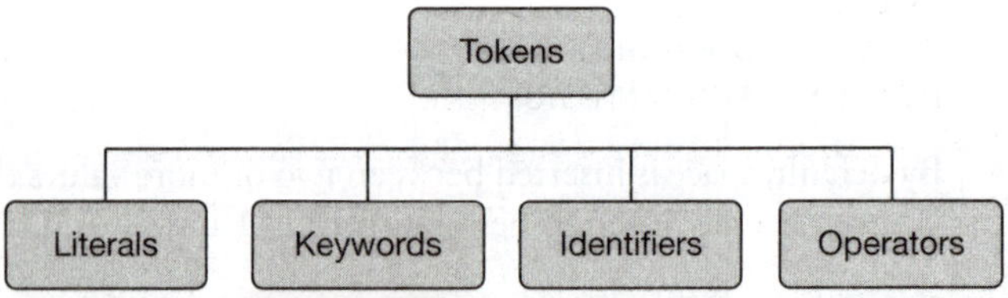

Figure 5.2 Tokens in Python

5.6.1 Literal Constants

The word 'literal' has been derived from 'literally'. The value of a literal constant can be used directly in programs. For example, 7, 3.9, 'A', and "Hello" are examples of literal constants. The number 7 always represents itself and nothing else. Moreover, it is a constant because its value cannot be changed. Hence, it is known as *literal constant*. In this section, we will read about number and string constants in Python.

> You can specify integers in octal as well as hexadecimal number system.

5.6.2 Numbers

Number, as the name suggests, refers to a numeric value. You can use four types of numbers in Python programs. These include integers, long integers, floating-point and complex numbers.

- Numbers like 5 or other whole numbers are referred to as *integers*. Integers can be positive or negative or even equal to zero. They do not have any decimal point.
  Bigger whole numbers are called *long integers*. For example, 535633629843L is a long integer. Note that a long integer must have 'l' or 'L' as the suffix.
- Numbers like are 3.23 and 91.5E–2 are termed as *floating-point numbers*. They are real numbers with a decimal point dividing the integer and fractional parts. The real part of the number can be either negative or positive or even equal to zero.
- Numbers of the form $a + bi$ form (like –3 + 7i) are *complex numbers*, where a is the real part and b is the imaginary part of the number. Both a and b are floating-point numbers and i represents the square root of –1.

> The 'E' notation indicates powers of 10. In this case, 91.5E-2 means $91.5 * 10^{-2}$.

Remember that commas are never used in numeric literals or numeric values. Therefore, numbers like 3,567 1,23.89 –8,904 are not allowed in Python.

Built-in `format()` Function Any floating-point value may contain an arbitrary number of decimal places, so it is always recommended to use the built-in `format()` function to produce a string version of a number with specific number of decimal places. Observe the difference between the following outputs.

# Without using format()	# Using format()
>>> float(16/(float(3))) 5.333333333333333	>>> format(float(16/(float(3))), '.2f') '5.33'

Here, .2f in the `format()` function rounds the result to two decimal places of accuracy in the string produced. For very large (or very small) values, 'e' can be used as a *format specifier*. The `format()` function can also be used to format floating-point numbers in scientific notation. Look at the result of the expression given below.

```
>>> format(3**50,'.5e')
'7.17898e+23'
```

The result is formatted in scientific notation with five decimal places of precision. This feature is especially useful when displaying results in which only a certain number of decimal places is needed. Finally, the `format()` function can also be used to insert a comma in the number as shown below.

```
>>> format(123456.8901,',.2f')
'123,456.89'
```

Simple Operations on Numbers Python can carry out simple operations on numbers. To perform a calculation, simply enter numbers and the type of operations that need to be performed on them directly into the Python console, and it will print the answer, as shown below.

> The spaces around the plus and minus signs here are optional. They are just added to make the statement more readable. The code will execute even if you remove the spaces.

>>> 17 + 56 73	>>> 90 + 50 - 40 100	>>> 35 * 15 525	>>> 108 / 12 9.0	>>> -10 * 14 -140

Dividing a number by zero in Python generates an error, and no output is produced, as shown below.

```
>>> 117 / 0
Traceback (most recent call last):
  File "<pyshell#7>", line 1, in <module>
    117 / 0
ZeroDivisionError: division by zero
```

When a number is divided by another, always a floating-point number is produced.

>>> 15 / 5 3.0	>>> 75 / 15.0 5.0	>>> 39.0 / 3 13.0	>>> 24.0 / 2.0 12.0

You can easily work with a floating-point number and an integer because Python automatically converts the integer to a float. This is known as ***implicit conversion or type conversion****. An implicit conversion is performed by the compiler without the programmer's intervention.*

Quotient and Remainder When a number is divided by another, if you want to know the quotient and remainder, use the floor division (//) and modulo operator (%), respectively. These operators can be used with both floats and integers. Observe the following statements and their output. When we divide 78 by 5 we get a quotient of 15 and a remainder of 3.

>>> 18 // 4 4	>>> 18 % 4 2	>>> 324.0 // 6.0 54.0	>>> 234.567 % 6.5 0.5670000000000073

Exponentiation Besides +, - , *, / Python also supports ** operator. The ** operator is used for exponentiation, i.e., raising of one number to the power of another. Consider the statements given below and observe the output.

>>> 11 ** 3 1331	>>> 5.25 ** 4 759.69140625

5.6.3 Strings

A *string* is a group of characters. We have already printed a string in our first program in which we had printed "HELLO WORLD !!!". In Python, there are three ways in which a string can be used.

- **Using Single Quotes ('):** For example, a string can be written as 'HELLO'.
- **Using Double Quotes ("):** Strings in double quotes are exactly same as those in single quotes. Therefore, 'HELLO' is same as "HELLO".
- **Using Triple Quotes (''' '''):** A multi-line string is specified using triple quotes. We can use as many single quotes and double quotes as required in a string within triple quotes. An example of a multi-line string can be given as,

```
>>> ''' HELLO WORLD !!!
'GOOD MORNING'
"WELCOME TO THE WORLD OF 'PYTHON PROGRAMMING' "
HAPPY LEARNING....'''
' HELLO WORLD !!!\n\'GOOD MORNING\'\n"WELCOME
TO THE WORLD OF \'PYTHON PROGRAMMING\'
"\nHAPPY LEARNING....'
```

Note that all the characters, spaces, tabs, new lines, and quotes (single as well as double) are preserved within triple quotes.

> All spaces and tabs within a string are preserved in quotes (single quote as well as double quote.).

> When two very large floating-point numbers are multiplied, it may result in an *arithmetic overflow*. Arithmetic overflow is a condition that occurs when a calculated result is too large.
>
> Arithmetic underflow occurs when a floating-point number is divided by another. It is a condition that occurs when a calculated result is too small in magnitude to be represented.

>>> 'Hello' 'Hello'	>>> "HELLO" 'HELLO'	>>> '''HELLO''' 'HELLO'

Irrespective of the way in which a string is specified, all strings are ***immutable****. This means that once you have created a string, you cannot change it.*

String literal concatenation Python concatenates two string literals that are placed side by side. Consider the code below wherein Python has automatically concatenated two string literals.

```
>>> 'HELLO' 'WORLD'
'HELLOWORLD'
```

Escape Sequences: Some characters (like , ", \) cannot be directly included in a string. Such characters must be escaped by placing a backslash before them as given below.

```
>>> print('How's life?')
     SyntaxError: invalid syntax
>>> print('How\'s life?')
How's life?
```

The reason for the error was that Python got confused as to where the string starts and ends. So, we need to clearly specify that this single quote does not indicate the end of the string. This indication can be given with the help of an ***escape sequence*** as specified in the second string – *a single quote preceded by a backslash.*

Similarly, to print double quotes in a string enclosed within double quotes, we must precede the double quotes with a backslash as given below.

> When a string is printed, the quotes around it are not displayed.

```
>>> print("Sheena asked,"Will you come with me?"")
SyntaxError: invalid syntax
>>> print("Sheena asked,\"Will you come with me?\"")
Sheena asked,"Will you come with me?"
```

> An escape sequence is treated as a single character.

Other useful escape sequences are given in Table 5.1:

Table 5.1 Some of the escape sequences used in Python

Escape Sequence	Purpose	Example	Output
`\\`	Prints Backslash	`print("\\")`	`\`
`\'`	Prints single-quote	`print("\'")`	`'`
`\"`	Prints double-quote	`print("\"")`	`"`
`\a`	Rings bell	`print("\a")`	Bell rings
`\f`	Prints form feed character	`print("Hello\fWorld")`	Hello World
`\n`	Prints newline character	`print("Hello\nWorld")`	Hello World
`\t`	Prints a tab	`print( "Hello\tWorld")`	Hello World
`\o`	Prints octal value	`print("\o56")`	.
`\x`	Prints hex value	`print("\x65")`	e

Multi-line strings When specifying a string, if a single backslash (\) is added at the end of the line then it indicates that the string is continued in the next line, but no new line is added otherwise. For example,

```
>>> print("Hello World,\
Good Morning !!!")
Hello World,Good Morning !!!
```

Raw Strings If you want to specify that a string should not handle any escape sequences and want it to be displayed exactly as specified then you need to specify that string as a ***raw string***. A raw string is specified by prefixing r or R to the string.

> Raw strings are not processed in any special way, not even escape sequences.

```
>>> R"How\'s life at your end?"
"How\\'s life at your end?"
```

String Concatenation Like numbers, we can also add two strings in Python. The process of combining two strings is called ***concatenation***. Two strings, whether created using single or double quotes, are concatenated in the same way.

`>>>'HI... and ....'+'BYE'`
`HI... and .... BYE`
	`>>>'''PYTHON'''+'''`
	`PROGRAMMING''')`
	`'PYTHONPROGRAMMING'`
		`>>>'''PYTHON'''+'''`
		`PROGRAMMING''')`
		`'PYTHONPROGRAMMING'`

Slice a String A substring of a string is called a **slice**. You can extract subsets of strings by using the slice operator ([ ] and [:]). You need to specify index or the range of index of characters to be extracted. The index of the first character is 0 and the index of the last character is $n - 1$, where n is the number of characters in the string.

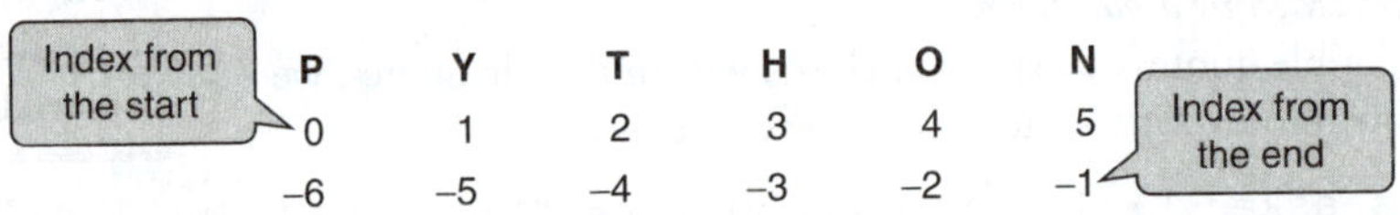

The syntax of slice operation is s[start:end:stride], where start specifies the beginning index of the substring and end is the index of the last character of the string s. *Omitting either start or end index by default takes start or end of the string. Omitting both means omitting the entire string.*

If you want *to extract characters starting from the end of the string, then you must specify the index as a negative number.* For example, the index of the last character is –1.

Specifying Stride while Slicing Strings: In the slice operation, you can specify a third argument as the ***stride.*** The stride specifies the number of characters to move forward after the first character is retrieved from the string. By default, the value of stride is 1, which means that every character between two index numbers is retrieved. If stride is 2, then every second character is accessed; if stride is 3 then every third character is accessed, and so on.

```
#Slice operation on string
>>> str = "Python Programming is Fun"
>>> str[0]                      #prints the first character
P
>>> str[4:10]                   #prints characters from 4 to 9
on Pro
>>> str[5:]                     #prints all characters staring from fifth character
n Programming is Fun
>>> str[-1]                     #prints the last character
n
>>> str[:-1]                    #prints all except the last character
Python Programming is Fu
>>> str[-7:]                    #prints last seven characters
is Fun
>>> str[3:15:2]                 #prints every 2nd character from 3rd - 15th character
'hnPorm'
```

Did you notice that when we use the slice operator, elements are accessed from left towards right? For any index n (positive or negative), $s[:n] + s[n:] = s$. This means that the slice operation always partitions the string into two parts in such a way that all characters are conserved.

Even the whitespace characters are skipped as they are also a part of the string. ***If you omit the first two arguments and only specify the third one, then the entire string is used in steps.*** We can even have a negative value in the stride. For example, if the value of stride is –1 then the string is printed in reverse order.

#print every third character	#print string in reverse	#print every third character in the #reversed string
`str="Python programming is fun"` `print(str[::3])` **OUTPUT** Ph oai n	`str="Python programming is fun"` `print(str[::-1])` **OUTPUT** nuf si gnimmargorp nohtyP	`str="Python programming is fun"` `print(str[::-2])` **OUTPUT** nfs nmagr otP

5.7 TYPE CONVERSION

In Python, it is just not possible to complete certain operations that involve different types of data. For example, it is not possible to perform "4" + 7 since one operand is an integer and the other is of string type.

Another situation in which type conversion is a must is when you want to accept a non-string value (integer or float) as an input. The `input()` function which accepts input(s) from the user takes it as a string. In case the user has to enter a numeric value then the string value must be explicitly typecasted to numbers (integers or floats), so that calculations can be performed on them. In such situations, you must perform conversions between data types.

```
>>>"7"+"4"      >>>int("7")+int("3")
'74'            10
```

```
x = input("Enter the first number : ")
y = input("Enter the second number : ")
print(x + y)
OUTPUT
Enter the first number : 7
Enter the second number : 4
74
```

```
x = int(input("Enter the first number : "))
y = int(input("Enterthe second number : "))
print(x + y)
OUTPUT
Enter the first number : 7
Enter the second number : 4
11
```

Python provides several built-in functions to convert a value from one data type to another. These functions return a new object representing the converted value. Some of them are given in Table 5.2.

Table 5.2 Some commonly used built-in functions in Python

Function	Description	Example
`int(x)`	Converts x to an integer	int(3.5) gives 3
`float(x)`	Converts x to a floating-point number	float('123') gives 123.0
`str(x)`	Converts x to a string	str(123.45) gives '123.45'
`tuple(x)`	Converts list x to a tuple	tuple([1,2,3]) gives (1, 2, 3)
`list(x)`	Converts tuple x to a list	list((1,2,3)) gives [1, 2, 3]
`set (x)`	Converts x to a set	set([1,2,3]) gives {1, 2, 3}
`ord(x)`	Converts a single character to its integer value	ord('D') gives 68
`oct(x)`	Converts an integer to an octal string	oct(9) gives '0oll'
`hex(x)`	Converts an integer to a hexadecimal string	hex(1234) gives '0x4d2'
`chr(x)`	Converts an integer to a character	chr(70) gives 'F'
`complex(x)`	Converts to a complex number	complex(3,-8) gives (3-8j)

However, before using type conversions to convert a floating-point number into an integer number, remember that `int()` converts a float to an `int` by truncation (discarding the fractional part) and not by rounding to the nearest whole number. The `round()` works more appropriately by rounding a floating-point number to the nearest integer as shown below. The `round()` can even take a second, optional argument, which is usually a number that indicates the number of places of precision to which the first argument should be rounded.

```
>>> int(3.7)            >>> round(3.7)          >>> round(1234.56789012,2)
3                       4                       1234.57
```

Note that each argument passed to a function has a specific data type. If you pass an argument of the wrong data type to a function, it will generate an error. For example, you cannot find the square root of a string. If you don't know what type of arguments a function accepts, you should use the `help()` before using the function.

Key Terms

Statement: A statement in Python is an instruction given to the computer to perform any kind of action.

String: A string is a group of characters.

String concatenation: The process of combining two strings.

Slice: A substring of a string is called a slice.

Chapter Highlights

- GIGO means Garbage-in–garbage-out. It means that if we give incorrect data or instructions, then it will give wrong results.
- Python is a high-level, interpreted, interactive, object-oriented and a reliable language.
- Once installed, the Python console can be accessed in several ways. We have discussed two of them in this chapter. First, using the command line and running the Python interpreter directly. Second, using a GUI software that comes installed with Python, called IDLE.
- If you want to execute the program in Python shell, then press **F5** key or click on Run Menu and then select **Run Module**.
- The character set of a language is a set of valid characters that the language can recognize. Such characters may be digits, alphabets, or any other symbol.
- Tokens are the small units of the programming language. Python supports literals, keywords, identifiers and operators as tokens.
- Number, as the name suggests, refers to a numeric value. You can use four types of numbers in Python programs. These include integers, long integers, floating-point numbers and complex numbers.
- Any floating-point value may contain an arbitrary number of decimal places, so it is always recommended to use the built-in `format()` function to produce a string version of a number with specific number of decimal places. It can also be used to control the display of strings.
- A raw string does not handle any escape sequence. It is specified by prefixing r or R to the string.

Review Questions

1. Explain the features of Python.
2. Give some applications of Python.
3. What do you understand by the term 'Python character set'?
4. Write a short note on literals in Python.
5. What problems can pop up while dealing with floating-point numbers?
6. With the help of an example, explain the use of `format()` function.

7. What is a string in Python? Explain the different ways in which you can define a string.
8. Differentiate between implicit conversion and explicit type conversion.
9. What is an escape sequence? Give examples. Why are they called so?
10. Write the commands to display the text 'I love programming' in a width of 50 characters when the text is left-justified, right-justified and centre-aligned.
11. Write a command to print a string in reverse.
12. Justify the statement: 'Python is a free and open-source programming language'.
13. Which of the following expressions would result in overflow or underflow error? Justify your answer.
    a. `1.23e+150*4.56e+100`   b. `6.78e-100/4.67e+200`
14. Identify the expressions which will involve coercion and the ones which will involve explicit type conversion
    a. `5.0+2`   b. `6.5*3.0`   c. `7.0+float(8)`   d. `6.2*5.0`   e. `5.7+int(9.0)`
15. Find and correct the error (if any).
    a. `>>> print('It is Teacher's Daty today ')`
    b. `>>> print("Rohan knows "Hindi","English","Punjabi"")`

Fill in the Blanks

1. A ________ in Python is an instruction given to the computer to perform any kind of action.
2. ________ means that if we give incorrect data or instructions, then it will give wrong results.
3. ________ means looking for patterns in the puzzles and categorizing them.
4. Python files are stored with a ______ extension.
5. The ______ function prints one or more literals (or values) followed by a newline.
6. To execute Python script file, ______ key is pressed.
7. ______ are the small units of the programming language.
8. Large floating-point numbers are efficiently represented in ________ notation.
9. ______ denotes that an arithmetic overflow has occurred.
10. ________ function is used to produce a string version of a number with specific number of decimal places.
11. The ____ prefix specifies that the file contains text written in language other than English.
12. A ________ is specified by prefixing r or R to the string.
13. The process of combining two strings is called __________.
14. The ______ specifies the number of characters to move forward after the first character is retrieved from the string.

State True or False

1. Python is an interpreted programming language.
2. Python is an open-source programming language.
3. Programmers can embed Python programs within their C, C++ codes.
4. Parallel processing can be done in Python.
5. Integers can be specified as octal and hexadecimal numbers also.
6. Arithmetic underflow is a condition that occurs when a calculated result is too large.

7. Strings are mutable in Python.
8. When specifying a string, if a single backslash (\) at the end of the line is added then it indicates that the string is continued in the next line, but no new line is added otherwise.
9. A Unicode string does not handle any escape sequence. It is specified by prefixing r or R to the string.
10. `format()` function can be used to control the display of strings.
11. The default value of stride is 0.
12. Whitespace characters are also counted as a character in the string.
13. Computational thinking means thinking like a computer or to give instructions to a computer.
14. Coding is not a part of computational thinking.
15. Computational thinking involves considering different options carefully before deciding upon the best one.
16. \r represents a newline.
17. An escape sequence is treated as a single character.
18. In Python, the `print()` function is used to accept data from users.

Multiple Choice Questions

1. Python is a __________ language.
   a. high-level b. interpreted
   c. object-oriented d. All of these.
2. Python programs work on any of the operating system without requiring any change. This means that Python is _________.
   a. interactive b. simple
   c. portable d. dynamic
3. Which of the following is not a valid token in Python?
   a. Character set b. Literals
   c. Identifiers d. Keywords
4. Which of the following is not a valid literal constant in Python?
   a. 1.2 b. 5
   c. H5 d. "H5"
5. Which of the following is not a valid number in Python?
   a. 50000000000L b. 5E10
   c. 5000000000.123455D d. 3 – 8i
6. The value ______ indicates that an arithmetic underflow has occurred.
   a. -inf b. inf
   c. 0.0 d. All of these.
7. Which of the following is known as the exponentiation operator?
   a. % b. //
   c. ** d. ^
8. By default, the `format()` function uses _____ character to fill the specified width.
   a. blank spaces b. >
   c. < d. ^
9. A string can be sliced using which of the following operators?
   a. [] b. [:]
   c. Both a and b. c. None of these.

10. The index of the first character is ____ and the index of the last character is ____, where *n* is the number of characters in the string.
    a. 0, *n*
    b. 0, *n* – 1
    c. 1, *n*
    d. 1, *n* – 1

11. The index of the last character is ______.
    a. –1
    b. 0
    c. *n* – 1
    d. *n*

12. Which of the following statements is syntactically not correct?
    a. a = input ( )
    b. a = input (“enter a number”)
    c. a = input (enter a number)
    d. a = INPUT (“enter a number”)

13. Which of the following statement is correct?
    a. a = 10 * 5
    b. 50 = 10 * 5
    c. 15 + 60 = y
    d. print 3 * 4

14. Identify the invalid string literal.
    a. 'PYTHON'
    b. "PYTHON"
    c. '''PYTHON'''
    d. ""PYTHON""

15. Identify the valid floating-point value.
    a. 9
    b. 23/4
    c. 123,456.67
    d. 1.2

16. Which of the following is a valid long floating-point value?
    a. 1.2e
    b. 1.2e2.3
    c. 1.2e01
    d. 1,234e9

17. Which of the following is not a valid integer literal in Python?
    a. 0o123
    b. 0x123
    c. 0X123
    d. 0123

18. Which of the following statements is incorrect about Python?
    a. Python is available free of cost.
    b. Python is a machine level language.
    c. We can create games using Python
    d. Python programs can be executed on any operating system.

19. In Python, all keywords are written in __________ case.
    a. upper
    b. lower
    c. sentence
    d. toggle

Give the Output

1.
```
print("Hello")
print("My Dear Students", end = ' ')
print("Let us learn Python")
print("Programming")
```

2. `>>> format(10**25,'.2e')`

3. `>>> format(987654321.315978,',.3f')`

4. `>>> 'PYTHON'`

5. `>>> "PROGRAMMING IN PYTHON"`

6.
```
>>> ''' I ENJOY PROGRAMMING
IN
PYTHON'''
```
7.
```
>>> 'PYTHON' "PROGRAMMING"
```
8.
```
>>> print("Python Programming \
is FUN !!!!")
```
9.
```
>>> print(R'It is Teacher's Day today ')
```
10.
```
>>> "I" + 'LOVE' + '''PROGRAMMING'''
```
11.
```
str = "I Love Programming in Python"
print(str[0])
print(str[7])
print(str[-5])
print(str[7:10])
print(str[::2])
print(str[3:11:3])
print(str[:-7])
print(str[-6:])
```
12.
```
>>> print(type(int('10')))
```
13.
```
>>> str(print())+"abc"
```
14.
```
>>> print(print("abc"))
```
15.
```
>>> str(print("abc"))+"xyz"
```
16.
```
>>> print(print("abc",end=" "))
```
17.
```
(10<20) and (20 < 10) or (5 < 30) and not (15 < 40)
```

AI Lab Session – Scroobly

Scroobly is a Google experiment that is used to create fun animations in real-time with your camera. The application uses machine learning (ML) models to map the user's live motion to the screen doodle. This means that the ML system updates the animation seen on screen according to the user's movement. Using Scroobly, users extensively use artificial intelligence as a creative tool to become a digital animator. All this can be easily done without any prior knowledge of computer coding. Visit the link https://www.scroobly.com/ to experiment with Scroobly.

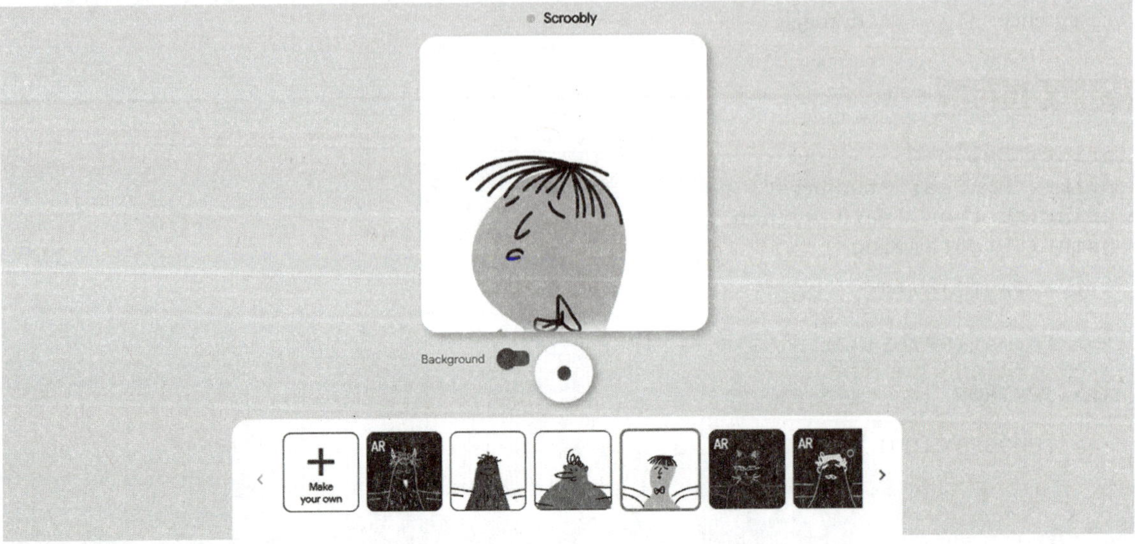

Answers

Fill in the Blanks

1. Statement
2. GIGO
3. Pattern recognition
4. .py
5. `print()`
6. F5
7. Tokens
8. scientific
9. Infinity (inf)
10. `format()`
11. 'U'
12. raw string
13. string concatenation
14. stride

State True or False

1. False
2. True
3. True
4. True
5. True
6. False
7. True
8. True
9. False
10. True
11. False
12. True
13. False
14. True
15. True
16. False
17. True
18. False

Multiple Choice Questions

1. d
2. c
3. a
4. c
5. c
6. c
7. c
8. a
9. c
10. b
11. a
12. c
13. a
14. d
15. d
16. c
17. d
18. b
19. b

Give the Output

1. **OUTPUT**
```
Hello
My Dear Students Let us learn Python
Programming
```
2. `'1.00e+25'`
3. `'987,654,321.316'`
4. `'PYTHON'`
5. `'PROGRAMMING IN PYTHON'`
6. `'I ENJOY PROGRAMMING\nIN\nPYTHON'`
7. `'PYTHONPROGRAMMING'`
8. `Python Programming is FUN !!!!`
9. `It is Teacher's Day today`
10. `'ILOVEPROGRAMMING'`
11. **OUTPUT**
```
I
P
y
Pro
ILv rgamn nPto
o o
I Love Programming in
Python
```
12. `<class 'int'>`
13. `'Noneabc'`
14.
```
abc
None
```
15.
```
abc
'Nonexyz'
```
16. `abc None`
17. `False`

Python – Building Blocks

6

Chapter Objectives

In this chapter, we discuss topics that sit at the core of Python language. We will read about:

- Variables and identifiers
- Data types of the identifiers
- Assigning and initializing variables
- Multiple assignment
- Input function
- Comments
- Reserved words
- Indentation
- Operators and expressions

We have already seen that a statement in Python is an instruction that performs an action. A statement may or may not display a value. For example, the statement, sum = 2 + 3, adds two values but does not display any value. But the statement, `print(sum)` displays the value that we obtain after adding 2 and 3.

In Python, no symbol is used to terminate a statement. Users just have to press the Enter key after typing the statement. Although we can type multiple statements in a single line using semi-colon (;) between the two statements, it is always better to type one statement in a single line for more clarity. So, avoid writing the two statements as,

> A line in Python can contain maximum 79 characters.

```
>>> sum = 2 + 3; print(sum)
5
```

In the last chapter, we had started learning about tokens in Python. We have already covered literals. In this section, we will read about other tokens like keywords, identifiers and operators.

6.1 VARIABLES AND INDENTIFIERS

Using just literal constants, nothing much can be done in programs. For developing complex programs, we must store information to manipulate it as and when required. This is where *variables* can help.

Variable, in simple terms, means something that may change. We can store any piece of information in a variable and this information may change. For example, a variable `today_temp` may have value = `30` today but tomorrow it may be `29` or `31`.

Thus, we see that in Python, variable represents a named location that has a value which can be processed as and when required (as for calculating values).

To be identified easily, each variable is given an appropriate name. Variable names are examples of **identifiers**. *Identifiers*, as the name suggests, are names given to identify something. This something can be a variable, function, class, module or other objects. For naming any identifier, there are some basic rules that you must follow. These rules are:

> Python is a case-sensitive language.

- The first character of an identifier must be an underscore ('_') or a letter (upper or lowercase).
- The rest of the identifier name can be underscores ('_'), letters (upper or lowercase), or digits (0-9).
- Identifier names are case-sensitive. For example, myvar and myVar are **not** the same.
- Punctuation characters such as @, $, and % are not allowed within identifiers.

Examples of valid identifier names are sum, __my_var, num1, r, var_20, First, etc.

Examples of invalid identifier names are 1num (starting with a digit), my-var (punctuation and special characters not allowed), %check (first character should be an alphabet or an underscore) , Basic Sal (space not allowed), H#R&A (special characters not allowed), etc.

6.1.1 Creating Variables

To create a variable in Python, just assign a value to the identifier using the equal to sign (also known as the assignment operator). For example, the following statements create variables with different values in Python.

```
num = 7
float_num = 12.34
ch = 'A'
str = "ABC"
print(num)
print(float_num)
print(ch)
print(str)
```

OUTPUT

```
7
12.34
A
ABC
```

When we create a variable, Python creates labels referring to those values as shown in Fig. 6.1.

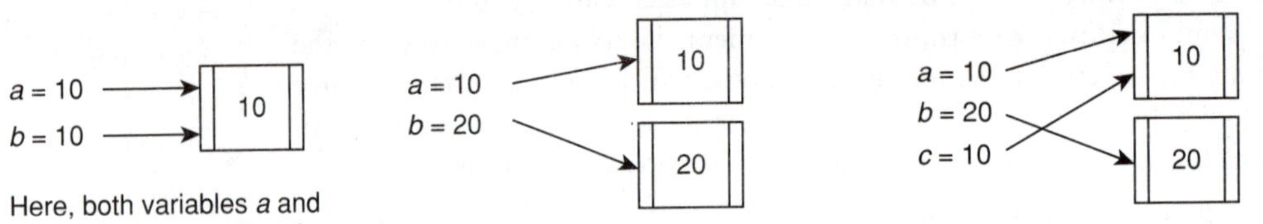

Here, both variables *a* and *b* have the same value. A label with value 10 is created and both variables point to the same label.

Here, the value of the variables are changed. Both variables *a* and *b* have different values. A label with value 20 is created and both variables point to their respective labels.

Here, both variables *a* and *b* have different values. A label with value 10 and another with value 20 are created and both variables point to their respective labels. When the variable *c* is created with same value as that of *a*, it points to the label to which *a* is pointing.

Figure 6.1 Creating labels

Do you know that Python IDLE remembers variables and their values? Just type the following lines in the command console of IDLE and observe the output.

```
>>> x = 10
>>> y = 20
>>> str1 = "HELLO"
>>> print(str1)
HELLO
>>> print(x * y)
200
```

6.2 DATA TYPES OF IDENTIFIERS

In any programming language, data type is a classification that specifies which type of value a variable has. It also specifies the type of mathematical, relational or logical operations that can be applied to it without causing an error. For example, a string data type is used to hold textual data. An integer is a data type that can store whole numbers.

Python has various standard data types that are used to define the operations possible on them and the storage method for each of them. Based on the data type of a variable, the interpreter reserves memory for it and also determines the type of data that can be stored in the reserved memory.

The five standard data types supported by Python include numbers, string, list, tuple, and dictionary. We can even create our own data types in Python (like classes). In this chapter, we will learn about numbers and strings. Other data types will be explored in subsequent chapters.

> Python is a purely object-oriented language. It refers to everything as an object including numbers and strings.

6.2.1 Assigning or Initializing Values to Variables

In Python, programmers need not explicitly declare variables to reserve memory space. The declaration is done automatically when a value is assigned to the variable using the equal sign (=). The operand on the left side of equal sign is the name of the variable and the operand on its right side is the value to be stored in that variable.

Program to display data of different types using variables and literal constants

```
age = 27
salary = 1234567
gender = 'M'
name = "Siva"

print("NAME : " + name)
print("AGE : " + str(age))          # To convert integer to a string
print("SALARY : " + str(salary))
print("GENDER : " + gender)         # To concatenate or to join two strings
```

OUTPUT

```
NAME : Siva
AGE : 27
SALARY : 1234567
GENDER : M
```

To run this program, type the code in IDLE. Save it with a suitable name with an extension .py. Press F5 or click on *Run* and then on *Run Module.*

In the code, the program assigns literal constant 27 to the variable age using the assignment operator (=). Similarly, we have assigned literal constants to other variables and then printed their values.

In Python, you can reassign variables as many times as you want to change the value stored in them. You may even store value of one data type in a statement and then a value of another data in a subsequent statement. This is possible because Python variables do not have specific types, so you can assign an integer to a variable, and later assign a string to the same variable.

Program to Reassign Values to a Variable

```
age = 27              # age is an integer
print("AGE : ", age)

age = 'TWELVE'        # age is a string
print("AGE : ", age)

age = 15.6            # age is a floating-point number
print("AGE : ", age)
```

OUTPUT

```
AGE : 27
AGE : TWELVE
AGE : 15.26
```

While re-assigning values to variables, be cautious for ensuring that the right type of value is used in operations. This is very much evident from the code given below.

```
a = 10
a = a*10
print (a)
a = "PYTHON"
a = a/10
print(a)
```

OUTPUT

```
100
Traceback (most recent call last) :
  File "C : \Python37\try .py" , line 5, in <module>
    a = a/10
TypeError: unsupported operand type(s) for /:
' str ' and ' int'
```

6.2.2 Multiple Assignment

Python allows programmers to assign a single value to more than one variable simultaneously. For example,

```
sum = flag = a = b =0
```

In the above statement, all four integer variables are assigned a value 0. You can also assign different values to multiple variables simultaneously as shown below.

```
sum, a, b, mesg = 0, 3, 5, "RESULT"
```

Here, variable sum, *a*, and *b* are integers (numbers) and `mesg` is a string. `sum` is assigned a value 0, *a* is assigned 3, *b* is assigned 5 and `mesg` is assigned "RESULT".

Remember that *trying to reference a variable that has not been assigned any value causes an error.* This may happen if you have mistakenly used a variable without assigning it a value prior to its use or have deliberately deleted or removed a variable using the `del` statement and then tried to use it later in your code. The examples given below illustrate this concept.

Also remember that, right-hand side expression is evaluated before assignment is done and if there are multiple expressions in a statement separated by commas then expressions on the RHS are evaluated from *left to right* and assigned in the same order.

```
x,y = 10,20
y,y = y+5, y-20      # last value of y persists
print("x = ",x, " y = ",y)
OUTPUT
x =  10  y =  0
```

Programs to assign and access variables

```
>>> name = "Kartik"
>>> age = 15
>>> print(name)
Kartik
>>> print(grade)
Traceback (most recent call last):
   File "<pyshell#8>",line 1, in <module>
      print(grade)
NameError: name 'grade' is not defined
```

Variable not declared prior to use

```
>>> name = "Kartik"
>>> age = 15
>>> grade = 'O'
>>> print(name)
Kartik
>>> del age
>>> print(age)
Traceback (most recent call last):
   File "<pyshell#14>",line 1, in <module>
     print(age)
NameError: name 'age' is not defined
```

Variable being used after it is deleted

6.3 DATA TYPE BOOLEAN

Boolean is another data type in Python. A variable of Boolean type can have one of the two values – *True* or *False*. Similar to other variables, the Boolean variables are also created while we assign a value to them or when we use a relational operator on them.

Remember that Boolean variables are also created by comparing values using the == operator.

>>>Boolean_var = True >>>Boolean_var True	>>> 30 == 50 False	>>>"HELLO" == 'HELLO' True
>>> 10 != 10 False	>>"Python3.7" != "Python3.4" True	>>>50>80 False
>>> 20 <= 20 True	>>> 13 == 13.0 False	>>>13 >= 13.0 True

6.4 INPUT OPERATION

Real-world programs need to be interactive. By interactive, we mean that you need to take some sort of input or information from the user and work on that input to give the desired result.

To take input from the users, Python makes use of the `input()` *function.* The `input()` function prompts the user to provide some information on which the program can work and give the result. However, we must always remember that the *input function takes the user's input as a string.* So, whether you input a number or a string, it is treated as a string only.

Program to read variables from the user

```
name = input("What's your name?")
age = input("Enter your age:")
print(name+ ",you are" +age+ " years old")
```

OUTPUT

```
What's your name? Goransh
Enter your age : 13
Goransh, you are 13 years old
```

To read integers or floating-point numbers using the `input()` function, you must use the `int()` and the `float()` function respectively. The `int()` function is used to convert a non-integer value to an integer. Similarly, the `float()` function is used to convert a non-floating-point value into a floating-point value. Hence, the output of the `input()` function which returns a string value can be passed to the `int()` or `float()` function to get a numeric value.

```
a = int (input ("Enter a number : "))
a = a + 10
print(a)
```

OUTPUT

```
Enter a number : 10
20
```

```
marks = float(input("Enter your total marks : "))
avg = marks/5.0
print (avg)
```

OUTPUT

```
Enter your total marks : 495
99.0
```

6.5 COMMENTS

Comments are added in a program to describe the statements in the program code. They make the program easily readable and understandable by the programmer as well as other users who are seeing the code. In Python, a hash sign (#) that is not inside a string literal begins a comment. *All characters following the # and up to the end of the line are part of the comment.*

Program to use comments

```
#Program to find the cost of a dozen pens
price_1 = int(input("Enter the price of 1 pen : "))
price_12 = price_1 * 12 # dozen means 12
print("Price of a dozen pens = ", price_12)
```

OUTPUT

```
Enter the price of 1 pen : 10
Price of a dozen pens = 120
```

Some important points to remember about comments are:

- Comments are the non-executable statements in a program.
- The interpreter simply ignores the comments.
- When the program is run, comments are not displayed.
- Comments can be either typed in a new line or on the same line after a statement or expression.
- A program can have any number of comments.

6.5.1 Multi-line Comments

In Python, multi-line comments are also known as docstring. They can be specified in two ways. First, by using three single quotes (or apostrophe) and second, by using three double quotes. They are used when explanation of the statements cannot be sufficiently given in one line. The code given below demonstrates the use of multi-line comments.

```
''' adding two
numbers'''
sum = 2 + 3
print(sum)
```

```
""" calculating average
of the two numbers
"""
avg = sum/2.0
print(avg)
```

OUTPUT

```
5
2.5
```

Did you notice that comments are not printed?

6.6 RESERVED WORDS

In every programming language, there are certain words which have a pre-defined meaning. These words, also known as reserved words or keywords, cannot be used for naming identifiers. Table 6.1 shows a list of Python keywords.

All the Python keywords contain lowercase letters only.

Table 6.1 Reserved Words

and	assert	break	class	continue	def	del	elif	else	except
exec	finally	for	from	global	if	import	in	is	lambda
not	or	pass	print	raise	return	try	while	with	yield

6.7 INDENTATION

Whitespace at the beginning of the line is called ***indentation***. These whitespaces or indentation are very important in Python. In a Python program, the leading whitespace including spaces and tabs at the beginning of the logical line determines the indentation level of that logical line.

The level of indentation groups statements to form a block of statements. This means that statements in a block must have the same indentation level. Python very strictly checks the indentation level and gives an error if indentation is not correct.

In the code below, there is a tab at the beginning of the second line. The error indicated by Python tells us that there is an indentation error. Python does not allow you to arbitrarily start new blocks of statements.

```
a = 10
  a = a+1        #Indentation Error
print(a)
```

```
a = 10
a = a + 1
print(a)
```

OUTPUT

```
11
```

Use a single tab for each indentation level.

Like other programming languages, Python does not use curly braces ({...}). Therefore, to indicate blocks of code for class and function definitions or for flow control (discussed later in the book), it uses only indentation to form a block. *All statements inside a block should be at the same indentation level.*

6.8 OPERATORS

Operators are the constructs that are used to manipulate the value of operands. Some basic operators include +, -, * and /. An expression in a programming language is any valid combination of tokens that represents a value. There are two types of expressions,

Simple expressions in which there are only values. For example, 29.

Complex expressions in which one or more operators are used on operand(s) to generate a value. For example, in the expression sum = 2 + 4. Here, 2 and 3 are operands and + is the operator. 10 * 8 / 2 is another example of a complex expression.

Operands are values on which operators are applied to generate a value.

Different operators supported by Python include:

a. Arithmetic operators
b. Comparison (Relational) operators
c. Assignment operators
d. Logical operators
e. Comparison operators
f. Membership operators

6.8.1 Arithmetic Operators

Some basic arithmetic operators are +, –, *, /, %, ** and //. You can apply these operators on numbers as well as on numeric variables to perform the corresponding operations. For example, if $a = 10$ and $b = 20$, then the result of operations can be given as shown in Table 6.2.

Table 6.2 Arithmetic operators

Operator	Description	Example	Output
+	Addition – Adds the operands	`>>> print(a + b)`	30
–	Subtraction – Subtracts operand on the right from the operand on the left of the operator	`>>> print(a - b)`	-10
*	Multiplication – Multiplies the operands	`>>> print(a * b)`	200
/	Division – Divides operand on the left side of the operator with the operand on its right. The division operator returns the quotient.	`>>> print(b / a)`	2.0
%	Modulus – Divides operand on the left side of the operator with the operand on its right. The modulus operator returns the remainder.	`>>> print(b % a)`	0

//	Floor Division – Divides the operands and returns the quotient. It also removes the digits after the decimal point. If one of the operands is negative, the result is floored (rounded away from zero towards negative infinity).	`>>> print(24//5)`
		`>>> print( 24.0//5.0)`
		`>>> print(-37//4)`
		`>>> print(-17.0//3)`
			4
			4.0
			-10
			-5.0

**	Exponent – Performs exponential calculation. That is, it raises the operand on the right side to the operand on the left of the operator.	`>>> print(a**b)`	1020

6.8.2 Comparison Operators

A comparison operator, also known as *relational* operator, is used to compare the values on its either side and determine the relation between the compared values. For example, assuming $a = 10$ and $b = 20$, we can use the comparison operators on them as specified in Table 6.3.

Table 6.3 Comparison operator

Operator	Description	Example	Output
==	Returns true if the two values are exactly equal.	>>> print(a == b)	False
!=	Returns true if the two values are not equal.	>>> print(a != b)	True
>	Returns true if the value of the operand on the left side of the operator is greater than the value on its right side	>>> print(a > b)	False
<	Returns true if the value of the operand on the right side of the operator is greater than the value on its left side.	>>> print(a < b)	True
>=	Returns true if the value of the operand on the left side of the operator is either greater than or equal to the value on its right side.	>>> print (a >= b)	False
<=	Returns true if the value of the operand on the right side of the operator is either greater than or equal to the value on its left side.	>>> print (a <= b)	True

6.8.3 Assignment and In-place or Shortcut Operators

Assignment operator, as the name suggests, assigns value to the operand. In-place operators, also known as *shortcut* operators that include +=, -=, *=, /=, %=, //= and **=, allow you to write a code like num = num + 10 more concisely, as num += 3. The different types of assignment and in-place operators are given in Table 6.4.

> Remember that <, > operators can also be used to compare strings lexicographically.

Example 6.1 **Application of the += operator on strings**

```
>>> str1 = "PYTHON"
>>> str2 = "PROGRAMMING"
>>> str1 += str2
>>> print(str1)
PYTHONPROGRAMMING
```

Table 6.4 Assignment and In-place operator

Operator	Example
=	c = a, assigns value of a to c
+=	a += b is same as a = a + b
-=	a -= b is same as a = a - b
*=	a *= b is same as a = a * b
/=	a /= b is same as a = a / b
%=	a %= b is same as a = a % b
//=	a //= b is same as a = a // b
**=	a**= b is same as a = a** b

6.8.4 Logical Operators

Python supports three logical operators—logical `and`, logical `or`, and logical `not`. As in case of arithmetic expressions, the logical expressions are evaluated from left to right.

Logical and: Logical and operator is used to simultaneously evaluate two conditions or expressions with relational operators. If expressions on both the sides (left and right side) of the logical operator are true, then the whole expression is true; else it is false. For example, (a > b) and (a > c), will return TRUE only if the value of a is greater than the values of b and c.

The and *operator tests the second operand only if the first operand is true.*

Logical or: Logical `or` operator is used to simultaneously evaluate two conditions or expressions with relational operators. If one or both the expressions of the logical operator is/are true, then the whole expression is true. This means that the expression is false only if both the expressions are false. For example, (a > b) or (a != b) will return TRUE if a is either greater than b or less than b. It will return FALSE if a is equal to b.

> Remember that the truth table of Logical `and`, `or` and `not` is exactly same as that of Bitwise `AND`, `OR` and `NOT` operators.

Logical not: The logical `not` operator takes a single expression and negates the value of the expression. Logical `not` produces a zero if the expression evaluates to a non-zero value and produces a 1 if the expression produces a zero. In other words, it just reverses the value of the expression. For example,

```
>>> a = 10
>>> b = not a
>>> print(b)
False
```

a is non-zero (or TRUE) so b is FALSE

```
>>> a = 0
>>> b = not a
>>> print(b)
True
```

a is zero (or FALSE) so b is TRUE

It can be noted that the *logical expressions operate in a shortcut (or lazy) fashion and stop the evaluation when it knows the final outcome for sure.* For example, in a logical expression involving logical and, if the first operand is false, then the second operand is not evaluated as it is certain that the result will be false. Similarly, for a *logical expression involving logical* `or`, *if the first operand is true, then the second operand is not evaluated as it is certain that the result will be true.* The truth table for logical operators is given in Table 6.5.

Table 6.5 Truth table for logical operators

A	B	A and B	A	B	A or B	A	B	A xor B	A	!A
0	0	0	0	0	0	0	0	0	0	1
0	1	0	0	1	1	0	1	1	1	0
1	0	0	1	0	1	1	0	1		
1	1	1	1	1	1	1	1	0		

6.8.5 Membership Operators

Python supports two types of membership operators – **in** and **not in**. These operators, as the name suggests, test for membership in a sequence such as strings, lists, or tuples that will be discussed in later chapters and are listed below.

```
>>> str1="HELLO"
>>> 'L' in str1
True
>>> 'T' in str1
False
```

```
>>> str1="HELLO"
>>> 'e' not in str1
True
>>> 'E' not in str1
False
```

in operator: The operator returns True if a variable is found in the specified sequence and False otherwise.

not in operator: The operator returns True if a variable is not found in the specified sequence and False otherwise.

```
>>> a = "r"
>>> str = "Good Morning"
>>> a in str
True
>>> 'R' in str
False
```

6.8.6 Operator Precedence and Associativity

When an expression has more than one operator, then it is the relative priorities of the operators with respect to each other that determine the order in which the expression will be evaluated.

Remember that,
Operators are associated from left to right. This means that operators with same precedence are evaluated in a left-to-right manner.

Parentheses can change the order in which an operator is applied. The operator in parenthesis is applied first even if there is a higher priority operator in the expression.

Priority of operators can be given as,

```
>>>5*6+3
33
>>>5+6*3
23
```

> * has higher precedence than +. Hence, first the operands will be multiplied and then addition will be performed.

Table 6.6 Operator precedence chart

Operators	
*, /, %, //	HIGHEST PRIORITY
+,-	
<=, <, >, >=	
!=, , ==, <>	
=, %=, /=, //=, -=, +=,*=, **=	
in, not in	
not, or, an	LOWEST PRIORITY

Let us try some more codes to see how operator precedence works in our expressions.

`>>> (5o + 40) * 10 / 20` `45.0`	`>>> ((50+ 40) * 20) / 10` `180.0`	`>>> (50+ 40) * (20 / 1o)` `180.0`
`>>> 50+ (40 * 10) / 20` `70.0`	`>>> 50*100/5//4` `250.0`	`>>> (((50*100)/15)//4)` `250.0`
`>>> 50*(100/(5//14))` `5000.0`		

6.9 EXPRESSIONS IN PYTHON

In any programming language, an expression is any legal combination of symbols (like variables, constants and operators) that represents a value. Every language has its own set of rules that define whether an expression is valid or invalid in that language. *In Python, an expression must have at least one operand (variable or constant) and can have one or more operators. On evaluating an expression, we get a value.*

Operand is the value on which operator is applied. These operators use constants and variables to form an expression. A * B + C – 5 is an example of an expression, where, +, *, – are operators; A, B and C are variables and 5 is a constant. Some valid expressions in Python are: x = a / b, y = a * b, z = a ** b, x = a > b, etc. When an expression has more than one operator, then the expression is evaluated using the operator precedence chart.

An example of an illegal expression can be a+ – b or < y + +. When a program is compiled, the validity of all expressions is checked. If an illegal expression is encountered, an error message is displayed.

In Python, we can categorize expressions based on the data type of the result obtained on evaluating an expression. These types of expressions include,

- *Constant Expressions* that involve only constants. Example: 8 + 9 – 2
- *Integral Expressions* that produce an integer result. Example:
  a = 10, b = 5
  c = a * b
- *Floating-point Expressions* produce floating-point results. Example: a * b / 2
- *Relational Expressions* return either True or False value. Example: c = a > b
- *Logical Expressions* combine two or more relational expressions and return a value as True or False. Example: a > b and y! = 0.
- *Assignment Expressions* assign a value to a variable. Example: c = 10.
- Lvalues are expressions that come on the left side of the assignment operator.
- Rvalues are expressions that come on the right side of the assignment operator.

> Remember that deleted variables can be used again in the code if and only if you reassign them some value.

PROGRAMMER'S ZONE

1. **Write a program to enter a number and display its hex and octal equivalent and its square root.**

```
num = int(input("Enter a number : "))
print("Hexadecimal of " + str(num) + "  : " + str(hex(num)))
print("Octal of " + str(num) + "  : " + str(oct(num)))
print("Square root of " + str(num) + " : " + str(num**0.5))
```

OUTPUT

```
Enter a number : 17
Hexadecimal of 17  :  0x11
Octal of 17  : 0o21
Square root of 17 : 4.123105625617661
```

2. **Write a program to read and print values of variables of different data types.**

```
num = int(input("Enter Roll Number : "))
fees = float(input("Enter Fees : "))
grade = input("Enter the grade : ")
name = input("Enter the name : ")
#Print the values of variables
print(ROLL NUMBER = ,num)
print(NAME = ,name)
print(FEES = ,fees)
print(GRADE = ,grade)
```

OUTPUT

```
Enter Roll Number : 1
Enter Fees : 99999
Enter the grade : A
Enter the name : Priya
ROLL NUMBER =  1
NAME =  Priya
FEES =  99999.0
GRADE =  A
```

3. **Write a program to calculate the area of a triangle using Heron's formula.**
   (<u>Hint:</u> Heron's formula is given as: area = sqrt(S*(S–a)*(S–b)*(S–c)))

```
a = float(input("Enter the first side of the triangle : "))
b = float(input("Enter the second side of the triangle : "))
c = float(input("Enter the third side of the triangle : "))
print(a,b,c)
S = (a+b+c)/2
area = (S*(S-a)*(S-b)*(S-c))**0.5
print("Area = ",area)
```

OUTPUT

```
Enter the first side of the triangle : 6
Enter the second side of the triangle : 8
Enter the third side of the triangle : 10
6.0 8.0 10.0
Area =  24.0
```

4. **Write a program to calculate the distance between two points.**

```
x1 = (int(input("Enter the x coordinate of the first point : ")))
y1 = (int(input("Enter the y coordinate of the first point : ")))
x2 = (int(input("Enter the x coordinate of the second point : ")))
y2 = (int(input("Enter the y coordinate of the second point : ")))
distance = ((x2-x1)**2+(y2-y1)**2)**0.5
print("Distance = ", distance)
```

OUTPUT

```
Enter the x coordinate of the first point : 1
Enter the y coordinate of the first point : 1
Enter the x coordinate of the second point : 5
Enter the y coordinate of the second point : 5
Distance = 5.656854249492381
```

5. **Write a program to perform addition, subtraction, multiplication, division, integer division, and modulo division on two integer numbers.**

```
num1 = int(input("Enter two numbers : "))
num2 = int(input("Enter two numbers : "))
add_res = num1+num2
sub_res = num1-num2
mul_res = num1*num2
idiv_res = num1//num2
modiv_res = num1%num2
fdiv_res = float(num1)/num2
print(num1, " + ", num2," = ", add_res)
print(num1, " - ", num2, " = ", sub_res)
print(num1, " * ", num2, " = ", mul_res)
print(num1," / ",num2," = ",idiv_res," (Integer Division)")
print(num1," // ",num2," = ",fdiv_res," (Float Division)")
print(num1," % ", num2," = ",modiv_res," (Modulo Division)")
```

OUTPUT

```
Enter two numbers : 25
Enter two numbers : 4
25  +  4  =  29
25  -  4  =  21
25  *  4  =  100
25  /  4  =  6  (Integer Division)
25  //  4  =  6.25  (Float Division)
25  %  4  =  1  (Modulo Division)
```

6. **Write a program that demonstrates the use of relational operators.**

```
x = 30
y = 10
print(x," < ", y, " = ", x<y)
print(x, " == ", y, " = ", x==y)
print(x," != ",y," = ", x!=y)
print(x," > ",y," = ",x>y)
print(x," >= ",y," = ",x>=y)
print(x," <= ",y," = ",x<=y)
```

OUTPUT

```
30 < 10 = False
30 == 10 = False
30 != 10 = True
30 > 10 = True
30 >= 10 = True
30 <= 10 = False
```

7. **Write a program to calculate the volume of a cylinder.**

```
radius = float(input("Enter the radius : "))
height = float(input("Enter the height : "))
volume = 3.14*radius*radius*height
print("VOLUME = %.2f"%volume)
```

OUTPUT

```
Enter the radius : 7
Enter the height : 14
VOLUME = 2154.04
```

8. **Write a program to print the digit at one's place of a number.**

```
num = int(input("Enter any number : "))
digit_at_ones_place = num%10
print("The digit at ones place is : ",digit_at_ones_place)
```

OUTPUT

```
Enter any number : 12345
The digit at ones place of  12345 is 5
```

9. **Write a program to swap two numbers without using a temporary variable.**

```
n1 = int(input("Enter the first number : "))
n2 = int(input("Enter the second number : "))
n1, n2 = n2, n1
print("The first number is = ",n1," and the second number = ",n2)
```

OUTPUT

```
Enter the first number : 6
Enter the second number : 9
The first number is =  9  and the second number =  6
```

10. **Write a program to calculate the average of two numbers. Print their deviation.**

```
n1 = int(input("Enter the two numbers : "))
n2 = int(input("Enter the two numbers : "))
avg = (n1+n2)/2
dev1 = n1-avg
dev2 = n2-avg
print("AVERAGE = ",avg)
print("Deviation of first num =",dev1)
print("Deviation of second num =",dev2)
```

OUTPUT

```
Enter the two numbers : 10
Enter the two numbers : 20
AVERAGE =  15.0
Deviation of first num = -5.0
Deviation of second num = 5.0
```

11. Write a program to convert degrees Fahrenheit into degrees Celsius.

```
Fahrenheit = float(input("Enter the temperature in Fahrenheit : "))
Celsius = (0.56)*(Fahrenheit-32)
print("Temperature in degrees Celsius = %.2f"%Celsius)
```

OUTPUT

```
Enter the temperature in Fahrenheit : 100
Temperature in degrees Celsius = 38.08
```

Key Terms

Variable: Variable means something that may change. In Python programs, any piece of information can be stored in a variable and the information may change.

Identifiers: Names given to identify a variable, function, class, module or any other object.

Lvalue: Expressions that comes on the left side of the assignment operator

Rvalue: Expressions that comes on the right side of the assignment operator.

Keywords: Reserved words in a programming language that have a pre-defined meaning.

Operators: Constructs used to manipulate the value of operands.

Operands: Values on which the operator is applied.

Expression: An expression in a programming language is any valid combination of tokens that represents a value.

Chapter Highlights

- To create a variable in Python, just assign a value to the identifier using the equal to sign.
- When we create a variable, Python creates labels referring to those values.
- Variables can hold values of different types called data types.
- Based on the data type of a variable, the interpreter reserves memory for it and also determines the type of data that can be stored in the reserved memory.
- The five standard data types supported by Python include numbers, string, list, tuple, and dictionary.
- In Python, you can reassign variables as many times as you want to change the value stored in them. You may even store the value of one data type in a statement and then the value of another data in a subsequent statement.
- The `type()` function is used to determine the data type of an object.
- Trying to reference a variable that has not been assigned any value causes an error. This may happen if you have mistakenly used a variable without assigning it a value prior to its use or have deliberately deleted or removed a variable using the `del` statement and then tried to use it later in your code.
- A variable of Boolean type can have one of the two values – True or False.
- Comments are added in a program to describe the statements in the program code. They make the program easily readable and understandable by the programmer as well as other users who are seeing the code.
- To take input from the users, Python makes use of the `input()` function.
- Whitespace at the beginning of the line is called indentation. These whitespaces at the beginning of the logical line determine the indentation level of that logical line.
- Comparison operators, also known as relational operators, are used to compare the values on its either side and determine the relation between them.
- Python supports two types of membership operators – in and not in. These operators test for membership in a sequence such as strings, lists, or tuples.

Review Questions

1. What are identifiers? List some rules that must be kept in mind while naming an identifier.
2. With the help of a diagram, explain what happens when a variable is created in Python.
3. With the help of an example, explain how variables can be re-assigned values in Python.
4. Can we re-assign a value of another data type to a variable? If yes, why?
5. Differentiate between lvalue and rvalue.
6. What do you understand by the term 'multiple assignment'?
7. What are Boolean variables? How are they created?
8. What are comments? How are they written in Python?
9. What is a docstring? How is it defined in a Python program?
10. Why is indentation necessary in Python?
11. Will the statement print "Python # Programming" will be executed? If yes justify its output.

    Hint: The # is inside a string, so it is just considered as a character and not as a comment.
12. Differentiate between = and ==.

    Hint: The = is used to assign value but the == is used to test if two things have the same value.
13. Which data type will you use to represent the following data values?

    a. Number of days in a week. b. The circumference of a circle
    c. Your school fees d. Distance between moon and the earth
    e. Your favorite book f. Whether or not you will take the entrance exam
14. Which type of value will you use for storing the following information?

    a. Employee ID b. Employee Name c. Employee Salary d. Phone Number
15. Which of the following are correct type conversions?

    a. `int (8.2+6.3)` b. `str (5.6 * 6.7)`
    c. `float ("12"+"3.4")` d. `str ( 6/4 )`
16. Express the following floating-point numbers in scientific notation:

    a. `123.456789` b. `0.000123456` c. `1.234567`
17. Evaluate the following arithmetic expressions using the rules of operator precedence in Python.

    a. `4+5*10` b. `6+7*2+5` c. `20//4*2` d. `5*6**3`
    e. `24//6//3` f. `4**2**3` g. `100-(15*3)` h. `50%7`
    i. `-(100/6)+5`
18. Write the following values in the exponential notation.

    a. `1230.4567` b. `0.00000056009`
    c. `7000809.000000000003`
19. Identify the correct arithmetic expression in Python.

    a. `10(13+76)` b. `(15*16)(47+18)`
    c. `14*(33-52)` d. `15***2`
20. Write the data types of the following:

    a. `type(5+4)` b. `(20*345)` c. `type(987/45)` d. `type(2345//12)`
    e. `type(123%34)`

21. Identify the data types of the following literals: 9, 29.4, 5j, 3+7i

22. Evaluate the following expressions:
    a. `True and False`
    b. `(100<10) and (100>50)`
    c. `True or False`
    d. `(100<10) or (100>200)`
    e. `not(True) and False`
    f. `not (100<10) or (100>50)`
    g. `not(True and False)`
    h. `not (100<10 or 100>50)`
    i. `not True and False`
    j. `100<10 and not 100>50`
    k. `not True and False or True`
    l. `not (100<10 or 50<200)`

23. Which of the following results in True?
    a. `>>>90 == 90 and 11==11`
    b. `>>>31==51 and 71==31`
    c. `>>>72!=12 and 25==25`
    d. `>>>54<51 and 61>86`
    e. `15<20 or 20`

24. Write the following expressions in Python:
    a. $\dfrac{-b \pm \sqrt{b^2 - 4ac}}{2a}$
    b. $\sqrt{a^2 + b^2}$
    c. $\dfrac{\pi}{2} rh$
    d. $x^2 yz$
    e. $(a-b)^2 = a^2 - 2ab + b^2$
    f. $d = a^{mn}/a^{-3}$
    g. $(e^m)^n = e^{mn}$

Programming Exercises

1. Write a program to calculate the Body Mass Index (BMI) of a person. (BMI = kg/m^2, where kg is a person's weight and m is his/her height in metres).
2. Write a program to demonstrate printing a string within single quotes, double quotes and triple quote.
3. Write a program to read a character in upper case and then print it in lower case.
4. Write a program to swap two numbers using a temporary variable.
5. Write a program to read the address of a user. Display the result by breaking it in multiple lines.
6. Write a program to calculate simple interest and compound interest.
7. Write a program that prompts users to enter two integers `x` and `y`. The program then calculates and displays x^y
8. Write a program that prompts the user to enter his first name and last name and then displays a message `"Greetings!!! First name Last name"`
9. Energy is calculated as, $e = mc^2$, where m is the mass of the object and c is its velocity. Write a program that accepts an object's mass (in kilograms) and velocity (in metres per second) and displays its energy.
10. Write a program that calculates the number of seconds in a day.
11. Write a program that prompts the user to enter the first name and the last name. Then display the following message.

```
Hello firstnamelastname
Welcome to Python!
```

Fill in the Blanks

1. A line in Python can have maximum ____ characters.
2. ____ are used to store values.
3. Names given to identify a variable, function, class, module or any other object are generally known as ________.

4. A variable in Python is assigned a value by using the ________ operator.
5. When we create a variable, Python creates _____ referring to those values.
6. Variables can hold values of different types called ________.
7. ________ are those objects to which values can be assigned and appear on the left side of an expression.
8. To take input from the users, Python uses the _______ function.
9. The _____ function is used to convert a non-integer value to an integer.
10. In Python, multi-line comments are also known as _______.
11. The level of ______ groups statements to form a block of statements.
12. Values on which the operator is applied are called ________.
13. ________ expressions operate in a shortcut (or lazy) fashion and stop the evaluation when it knows the final outcome for sure.
14. 123.45E-9 is equal to _______.
15. ___________ converts an integer to a floating-point number.
16. The ___ operator returns the quotient after division.
17. To find *xy*, you will use _____ operator.
18. ________ is a group of characters.
19. Variable names can contain only ________, __________ and ___________.
20. >>>90 != 70 gives output _______.
21. 29%0 = ________.
22. int("10"+"20") will give ______.
23. >>> print (format(12356.265901, '.3f')) will result in the value ______.

State True or False

1. In Python, a semi-colon is used to terminate every statement.
2. Python allows writing multiple statements in a single line.
3. The first character of an identifier must be a dollar sign ($).
4. Python is a case-sensitive language.
5. Based on the data type of a variable, the interpreter reserves memory.
6. While re-assigning values to a variable, the data type must not change.
7. Python variables do not have specific data types.
8. Comments are written to make the program easily readable and understandable.
9. Comments are the executable statements in a program.
10. When the program is run, comments are not displayed.
11. All keywords are written in uppercase characters.

12. Statements in a block must have the same indentation level.
13. Arithmetic operators also known as relational operators.
14. Relational operators can be used to compare strings.
15. INT = 2; print(INT) will give an error.

Multiple Choice Questions

1. Which of the following is a valid identifier in Python?
   a. _AaBb b. 1A_Bb
   c. @AaBB d. Aa-Bb
2. Which of the following can be the first character of a valid identifier in Python?
   a. # b. @
   c. _ d. -
3. Which of the following is known as the string concatenation symbol?
   a. + b. *
   c. , d. -
4. Which function is used to is determine data type of object?
   a. `data()` b. `type()`
   c. `val()` d. `str()`
5. A variable can be removed by using the ________ statement.
   a. `remove` b. `erase`
   c. `del` d. `delete`
6. Boolean variables are created using which of the following operator(s)?
   a. Equality b. assignment
   c. Both a and b. d. None of these.
7. The input function takes user's input as a/an _______.
   a. integer b. floating-point
   c. string d. None of these.
8. All characters following the ______ symbol and up to the end of the line are part of the comment.
   a. # b. ____
   c. % d. @
9. Which operator is used for integer division?
   a. / b. %
   c. // d. \
10. If both the inputs are 1 then the result is 1, else 0. Identify the logical operator giving this result.
    a. AND b. NOT
    c. OR d. XOR
11. Which operator returns True if a variable is found in the specified sequence and False otherwise?
    a. is b. not is
    c. in d. not in
12. Identify valid assignment statements.
    a. $x = y + 2$ b. $a = a$++
    c. $x + y$ =10 d. $x + 10 = y$

13. Which line of code produces an error?

a. "one" + "2"
b. 'one' + 2
c. 1 + 2
d. "1" + "two"

14. abc ="AABBCC"; print(abc*3)

a. abcabcabc
b. "abcabcabc"
c. ABCABCABC
d. AABBCCAABBCCAABBCC

15. Identify the correct variable creation statement.

a. my_var =7
b. 123my_var =10
c. my var = 12
d. 10 = myvar

16. Logical operator should not be used on which data type?

a. Integer
b. float
c. string
d. All of these.

17. Which operator is also known as string repetition operator?

a. +
b. *
c. &
d. ^

18. The following statement will produce __ lines of output.
print('Python \n Programming \n is\n ---Fun')

a. 1
b. 2
c. 3
d. 4

19. Identify the expression that may result in arithmetic overflow.

a. a*b
b. a**b
c. a/b
d. a+b

20. Which operations dos not result in 9?

a. 95 // 10
b. 130 % 11
c. 3 **3
d. 81 * * 0.5

21. _________ is not a keyword in Python.

a. `import`
b. `if`
c. `print`
d. `for`

22. Which operator in Python is used to find pow(2,3).

a. **
b. *
c. ^
d. #

23. To print "Good Morning#World", which is not the right way?

a. print("Good " + "Morning" + "#World")
b. print("Good " + "Morning" + "#" + World")
c. print("Good " + "Morning" + "#"*1 + "World")
d. None of these.

Give the Output

1.
```
x,y,z = 10,20,30
y,z,x = x+5, y+7, z-3
print("x = ",x, " y = ",y, "z = ",z)
```

2.
```
x,y = 10,20
y,z = x+5, y-20
print("x = ",x, " y = ",y," z = ",z)
```

3. `>>>350 + 230 - 170`

4. `>>> (51 + 9.7 - 4) * 100`

5. `>>> 110%(95//3)`

6. `>>>'Python Programming is fun... '`

7. `>>>"Python Programming is fun..."`

8.
```
>>>'''Python... \n
   Programming?'''
```

9. `>>> print("Python \n Programmiung")`

10. `>>> print("PYTHON !!!!"*3)`

11. `>>>x = 100 ; x *= 3  ; print(x)`

12. `>>> s1 = "HELLO"     ;      s1 += "WORLD"      ;          print(s1)`

13.
```
days = "Mon Tue Wed Thu Fri Sat Sun"
months = "Jan\nFeb\nMar\nApr\nMay\nJun\nJul\nAug"
print("Days are : "+ days)
print("Months are: "+ months)
print(""" There's a new dream today.
I'll tell you some other day.
Come on, let's enjoy. """)
```

14.
```
# print ABCD
Nothing
```

15.
```
>>>n1 = 20
>>>n2 = 30
>>>del num1
>>>n2 = 40
>>>n1 = 50
>>>print(num1 - num2)
```

16.
```
>>> num1 = "7"
>>> num1 += "10"
>>> num2 = int(num1) + 3
>>> print (float(num2))
```

17.
```
name = input("Enter a word :")
print ('HELLO' + name)
```

18.
```
n1 = 90
n2 = n1 + 50
n2 = int(str(n2) + "40")
print(num2)
```

19. `>>>abs(100-200) * 3`

20. `>>>float("5678" * int(input("Enter a number:")))`

21. `>>> int = 2;  print(int)`

22.
```
a,b = 10,20
b,a = a *5, b /2
print("a = ",a, " and b = ", b)
```

23.
```
a,b = 10,20
a,b,a = a*10, b*5,a*20
print("a = ",a, " and b = ", b)
```

24. `10 ** 3 ** 2`

25. `7 -5 -12 > -5 *3 +8`

26. `bool('0') and (10 < 20)`

27. `23%5 is 23%5`

28. `10 == 10.0`

29. `10 == int(10)`

30. `str(10)==str('10.0')`

31. `'R' == 'R'`

32. `70/(7-(2+4))or 4<5`

33. `len("abcd") == 30/6 or 30/10`

34. `2 * (5 *(len("007")))`

35. `N = 1 + 1 + 1 == 0.3; print(N)`

36.
```
print(bool(int('0')))
print(bool(str(0)))
print(bool(float('0.0')))
print(bool(str(0.0)))
```

37.
```
a,b,c = 12,13,16
d = a + b *c/b
print(d)
```

38. `"abc" or ""`

39. `'' or ''`

40. `'k' or 'r'`

41. `20 or len(20)`

42. `70/(7-(2+4))or 4<5`

43. `5 < 9 or 60/(10-(6+4))`

Find the Error

1. `>>>10+'20'+30+'40'`
2. `>>>'10'*'20'`
3. `>>>'PYTHON'*7.0`
4. ```
   x = 10
   print(x)
   ```
5. ```
   x = 123.456
   print('%'+x)
   ```
6. ```
   x = 1; y = 2;
   print(x+y+z)
   ```
7. `if = 5; print(if)`
8. `a = 10; b = 20; print(a;b)`
9. ```
   x =10
   y = x * 30
   x = "PYTHON"
   z = x/10
   ```
10. ```
    name = int(input("Enter your name : "))
    print("HELLO", name)
    ```
11. `print(len(bool(0)))`
12. `>>> print("HELLO"/2)`
13. `>>> print(type(int("HELLO")))`

AI Lab Session – Interplay Mode

Interplay Mode is a Google experiment that allows users to make videos interactive with AI. With online education, students often learn something new from videos. But videos have a limitation of being a one-way communication mode. Therefore, the Interplay mode is extremely useful as it enables users to write alongside the video and practice what you have just learnt. So, now there is interplay between the user and the video creator, to facilitate communication and feedback. Visit the given link to launch the Interplay Mode application by Google.

https://experiments.withgoogle.com/interplay-mode/view/

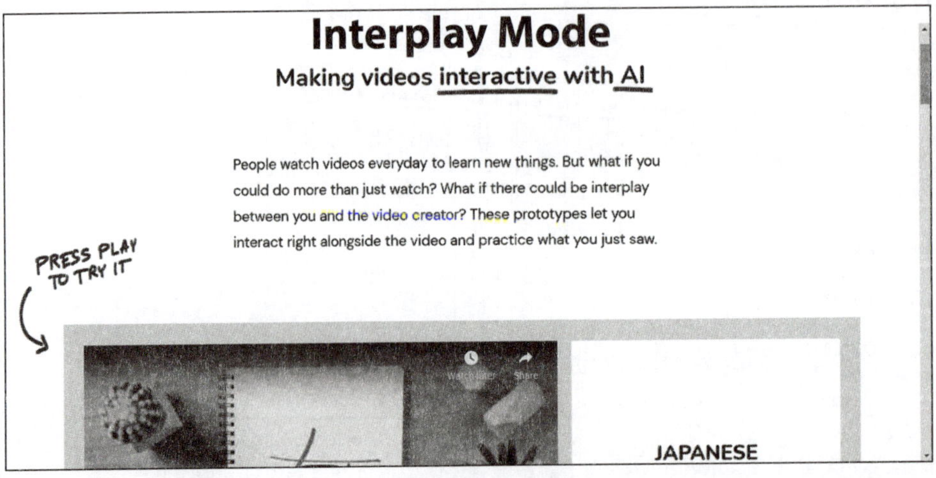
    ```

Answers

Fill in the Blanks

1. 79
2. Variables
3. identifiers
4. assignment
5. labels
6. data types
7. lvalues
8. `input()`
9. `int()`
10. docstring
11. indentation
12. operand
13. Logical
14. 0.00000012345
15. `float()`
16. / or //
17. **
18. String
19. underscore, upper case, lower case character
20. True
21. ZeroDivisionError
22. 1020
23. 12356.266

State True or False

1. False
2. True
3. False
4. True
5. True
6. False
7. True
8. True
9. False
10. True
11. False
12. True
13. False
14. True
15. False

Multiple Choice Questions

1. a
2. c
3. a
4. b
5. c
6. c
7. c
8. a
9. c
10. a
11. c
12. a
13. b
14. d
15. a
16. b
17. b
18. d
19. b
20. c
21. c
22. a
23. d

Give the Output

1. x = 27 y = 15 z = 27
2. x = 10 y = 15 z = 0
3. 410
4. 5670.0
5. 17
6. 'Python Programming is fun… '
7. 'Python Programming is fun…'
8. 'Python… \n Programming?'
9. Python Programming
10. PYTHON !!!!PYTHON !!!!PYTHON !!!!
11. 300
12. HELLOWORLD
13. Days are : Mon Tue Wed Thu Fri Sat Sun
    Months are: Jan
    Feb
    Mar
    Apr
    May
    Jun
    Jul
    Aug
    There's a new dream today.
    I'll tell you some other day.
    Come on, let's enjoy.
14. No output
15. NameError: name 'num1' is not defined
16. 713.0
17. HELLO(input)
18. NameError: name 'num2' is not defined
19. 300
20. inf
21. 2
22. a = 10.0 and b = 50
23. a = 200 and b = 100
24. 1000000000
25. False
26. True
27. True
28. True
29. True
30. False
31. True
32. 70.0
33. 3.0
34. 30
35. False
36. False True False True
37. 28.0

38. 'abc'
39. ''
40. 'k'
41. True
42. 70.0
43. True

Find the Error

1. `TypeError: unsupported operand type(s) for +: 'int' and 'str'`
2. `TypeError:can't multiplay sequence by non-int of type 'str'`
3. `TypeError: can't multiply sequence by non-int of type 'float'`
4. `Error! Tab at the start of the line`
5. `TypeError: cannot concatenate 'str' and 'float' objects`
6. `NameError: name 'z' is not defined`
7. `SyntaxError: invalid syntax`
8. `SyntaxError: invalid syntax`
9. `TypeError: unsupported operand type(s) for /: 'str' and 'int'`
10. `ValueError: invalid literal for int() with base 10: 'ABC'`
11. `TypeError: object of type 'bool' has no len()`
12. `TypeError: unsupported operand type(s) for /: 'str' and 'int'`
13. `ValueError: invalid literal for int() with base 10: 'HELLO'`

Decision Control Statements

7

Chapter Objectives

The chapter discusses a very crucial set of statements that may alter the sequence of program flow. These statements include conditional branching statements such as:

- The `if` statement
- The `if-else` statement
- The nested `if` statement
- The `if-elif-else` statement

Until now, we have executed simple statements in Python. Such statements are executed sequentially from the first line of the program to the last. That is, the second statement is executed after the first, the third statement is executed after the second, and so on. This way of execution is known as **sequential control flow**.

However, in some cases we may want to either execute only a selected set of statements (i.e., selection control) or execute a set of statements repeatedly (i.e., iterative control). In such cases, decision control system comes into picture.

A ***decision control statement*** is a statement that determines the flow of control in a program. Flow of control means deciding on which instruction would be executed next. A decision control statement can either skip one or more instructions. The three fundamental methods of control flow in a programming language are *sequential, selection, and iterative control.*

Selection and iterative control are a part of decision control system. Thus, a decision control statement can alter (change) the flow of a sequence of instructions. And this type of conditional processing helps users to extend the usefulness of programs.

Programmers can make programs that determine which statements of the code should be executed and which should be ignored in certain circumstances. Figure 7.1 shows the categorization of decision control statements.

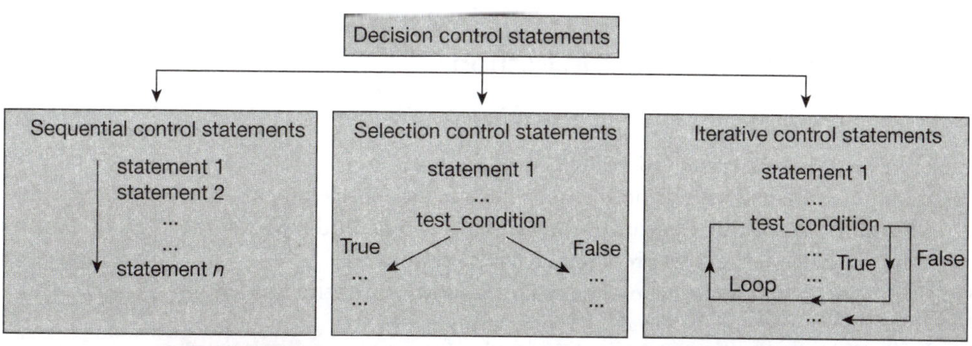

Figure 7.1 Categorization of decision control statements

7.1 SELECTION/CONDITIONAL BRANCHING STATEMENTS

The decision control statements usually jump from one part of the code to another depending on whether a particular condition is satisfied or not. That is, they execute statements selectively based on certain decisions. Such type of decision control statements is known as ***selection control statements*** or *conditional branching statements*. Python language supports different types of conditional branching statements, which are as follows:

- `if` statement
- `if-else` statement
- Nested `if` statement
- `if-elif-else` statement

7.2 `if` STATEMENT

An `if` statement is the simplest form of decision control statement that is frequently used in decision making. An `if` statement is a selection control statement based on the value of a given Boolean expression. The general form of a simple if statement is shown in Fig. 7.2.

SYNTAX OF IF STATEMENT

```
if text_expression:
    statement1

    ........ .

    Statement n
statement x;
```

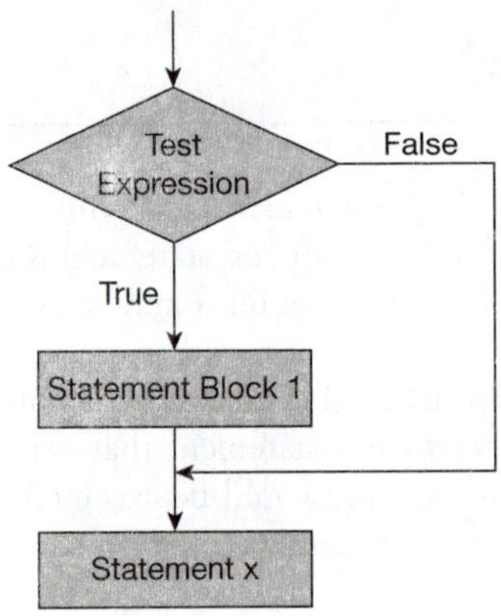

Figure 7.2 `if` statement construct

The `if` block may include 1 or more statements. According to the figure, first the test expression is evaluated. If the test expression is true, the statements of `if` block (statements 1 to *n*) are executed; otherwise, these statements will be skipped and the execution will jump to statement *x*.

> Python is a case-sensitive language. So, `if` is not same as `IF`.

7.2.1 Implementing `if` Statement in Python

Always remember the following points while implementing an `if` construct in Python:

- The statement in an `if` block is any valid statement in Python.
- The test expression is any valid expression that may include logical operators.
- **A header in Python is a specific keyword followed by a colon.** In the figure, the `if` statement has a header, "**if text_expression:**" having keyword `if`.
- The group of statements following a header is called a **suite**. After the header, all instructions that are indented at the same level form a suite.
- While four spaces are commonly used for each level of indentation, any number of spaces may be used.

> Header and its suite are together known as a clause.

Example 7.1 **Program to increment a number if it is positive.**

```
x = 10    #Initialize the value of x
if(x>0): #test the value of x
      x = x+1  #Increment the value of x if it is > 0
print(x)  #Print the value of x
```

> Remember to properly indent the statements that are dependent on the previous statements.

OUTPUT

```
x = 11
```

In the above code, we take a variable *x* and initialize it to 10. In the test expression, we check if the value of *x* is greater than 0 or not. If the test expression evaluates to true, then the value of *x* is incremented and is printed on the screen. Note that the print statement will be executed even if the test expression is false.

Python uses indentation to form a block of code. Other languages such as C and C++, use curly braces to accomplish this.

Example 7.2 **Write a program to determine whether a person is eligible to vote.**

```
age = int(input("Enter the age :"))
if(age>=18):
        print("You are eligible to vote")
```

OUTPUT

Enter the age : 35
You are eligible to vote

Example 7.3 **Write a program to determine the character entered by the user.**

```
char = input("Press any key : ")
if(char.isalpha()):
         print("The user has entered a character")
if( char.isdigit()):
         print("The user has entered a digit")
if(char.isspace()):
         print("The user entered a white space character" )
```

OUTPUT

Press any key : 7
The user has entered a digit

7.3 if-else STATEMENT

Though `if` statement plays a vital role in conditional branching, its usage is very limited. Its simplicity is also its drawback. In the `if` statement, the test expression is evaluated; if the result is true, the statement(s) followed by the expression is/are executed. But if the expression is false, nothing useful happens. So, using an `if-else` statement solves our problem. The general form of a simple `if-else` statement is shown in Fig. 7.3.

SYNTAX OF IF-ELSE STATEMENT

```
if test_expression:
     statement block 1

else:
     statement block 2


statement x;
```

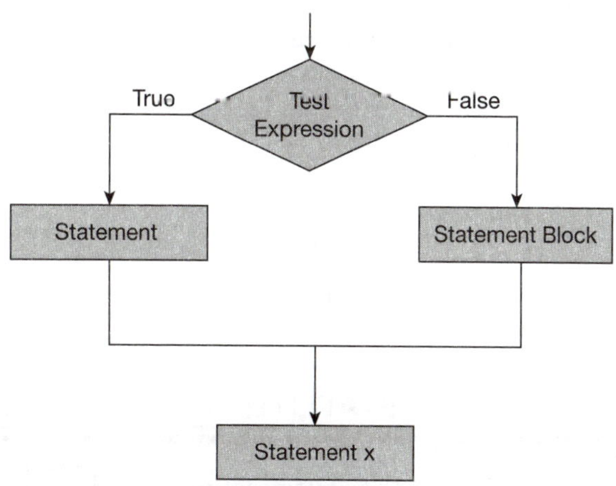

Figure 7.3 `if-else` statement construct

In the above syntax, we have written the statement block. A statement block may include one or more statements. According to the `if-else` construct, first the test expression is evaluated. If the expression is true, statement block 1 is executed and statement block 2 is skipped. Otherwise, if the expression is false, statement block 2 is executed and statement block 1 is ignored. In any case, after the statement block 1 or 2 gets executed the control will pass to statement x. Therefore, statement *x* is executed in every case.

Example 7.4 **Write a program to determine whether a person is eligible to vote or not. If he is not eligible display how many years are left to be eligible.**

```
age = int(input("Enter the age : "))
if(age>=18):
        print("You are eligible to vote")
else:
    yrs = 18 - age
    print("You have to wait for " + str(yrs) + " years")
```

OUTPUT

Enter the age : 10
You have to wait for 8 years

Example 7.5 **Write a program to find larger of two numbers.**

```
a = int(input("Enter the value of a : "))
b = int(input("Enter the value of b : "))
if(a>b):
        large = a
else:
        large = b
print("Large = ",large)
```

OUTPUT

Enter the value of a : 50
Enter the value of b : 30
Large= 50

7.4 NESTED `if` STATEMENTS

A statement that contains other statements is called a ***compound statement***. To perform more complex checks, `if` statements can be nested, that is, they can be placed one inside the other. In such a case, the inner `if` statement is the statement part of the outer one. Nested `if` statements are used to check if more than one condition is satisfied. Consider the code given below to understand this concept.

Example 7.6 **Program that prompts the user to enter a number and then print its interval.**

```
num = int(input("Enter any number from 0-30: "))
if(num>=0 and num<10):
      print(" It is in the range 0-10")
elif(num>=10 and num<20):
      print("lt is in the range 10-20")
elif(num>=20 and num<30):
      print("lt is in the range 20-30")
```

OUTPUT

Enter any number from 0-30: 25
It is in the range 20-30

> `if` statements can be nested resulting in multi-way selection. You can do the same program using `if-else` and `if-elif-else` statements.

7.5 `if-elif-else` STATEMENT

Python supports `if-elif-else` statements to test additional conditions apart from the initial test expression. The `if-elif-else` construct works in the same way as a usual `if-else` statement. It is also known as **nested `if` construct**. The `elif` (short for `else if`) statement is a shortcut to `if` and `else` statements. ***A series of `if` and `elif` statements have a final `else` block, which is executed if none of the `if` or `elif` expressions is True.*** Its syntax is given in Figure 7.4.

> **Comparing Floating-point Numbers**
> Never test floating-point numbers for exact equality. This is because floating-point numbers are just approximations, so it is always better to test floating-point numbers for 'approximately equal' rather than testing for exactly equal. We can test for approximate equality by subtracting the two floating-point numbers (that are to be tested) and comparing their absolute value of the difference against a very small number, epsilon.

SYNTAX OF IF-ELIF-ELSE STATEMENT

```
if (test expression 1)
        statement block 1
elif (test expression 2)
        statement block 2
............................

elif (test expression N)
       statement block N
else
       statement block x
statement y
```

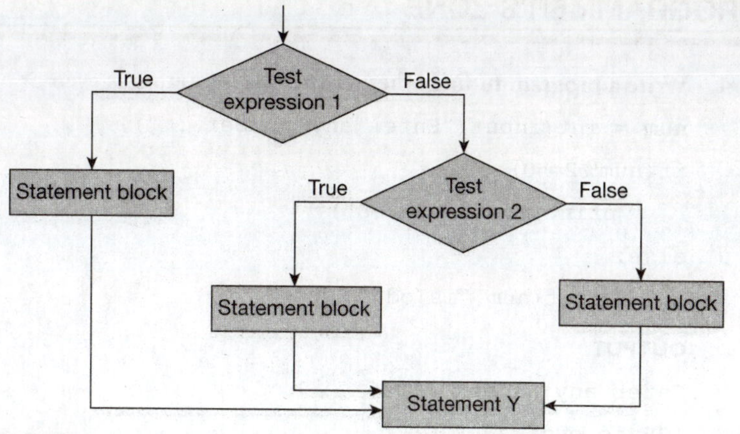

Figure 7.4 `if-elif-else` syntax

Note that it is not necessary that every `if` statement should have an `else` block as Python supports simple `if` statements also. After the first test expression or the first `if` branch, the programmer can have as many `elif` branches as he wants depending on the expressions that have to be tested. The final `else` block is called if none of the `if` or `elif` expressions is True.

> Remember that the `elif` and `else` parts are optional.

Example 7.7 **To test whether a number entered by the user is negative, positive or equal to zero.**

```
num = int(input("Enter any number : "))
if(num==0):
     print("The value is equal to zero")
elif(num>0):
     print("The number is positive")
else:
     print("The number is negative")
```

OUTPUT

Enter any number : -10
The number is negative

Example 7.8 **Write a program to determine whether the character entered is a vowel or not.**

```
ch = input("Enter any character : ")
if(ch=="A" or ch=="E" or ch=="I" or ch=="O" or ch=="U"):
     print ch,"is a vowel")
elif(ch=="a" or ch=="e" or ch=="i" or ch=="o" or ch=="u"):
     print(ch,"is a vowel")
else:
     print(ch, "is not a vowel")
```

OUTPUT

Enter any character: h
h is not a vowel

In the program to test whether a number is positive or negative, note that if the first test expression evaluates a true value, then rest of the statements in the code will be ignored and after executing the print statement that displays "The value is equal to zero", the control will jump to return 0 statement.

Python assumes any non-zero and non-null values as TRUE. Similarly, all values that are either zero or null, are assumed as FALSE value.

> Use the AND/OR operators to form a compound relation expression. In Python, the following expression is invalid.
>
> ```
> if (60 ≤ marks ≤ 75) :
> ```
>
> The correct way to write is,
>
> ```
> if ((marks ≥ 60) and (marks ≤ 75) :
> ```

> Keep the logical expressions simple and short. For this, you may use nested `if` statements.

PROGRAMMER'S ZONE

1. **Write a program to find whether the given number is even or odd.**

```
num = int(input("Enter any number : "))
if(num%2==0):
    print(num,"is even")
else:
    print(num,"is odd")
```

OUTPUT

```
Enter any number : 125
125 is odd
```

2. **Write a program to enter any character. If the entered character is in lower case, then convert it into upper case and if it is a upper case character, then convert it into lower case.**

```
ch = input("Enter any character : ")
if(ch >= 'A' and ch <='Z'):
    ch = ch.lower()
    print("The entered character was in upper case. In lower case it is : " + ch)
else:
    ch = ch.upper()
    print("The entered character was in lower case. In upper case it is : " + ch)
```

OUTPUT

```
Enter any character: c
The entered character was in lower case. In upper case it is: C
```

3. **A company decides to give bonus to all its employees on Diwali. A 5% bonus on salary is given to the male workers and 10% bonus on salary to the female workers. Write a program to enter the salary of the employee and sex of the employee. If the salary of the employee is less than Rs 10,000 then the employee gets an extra 2% bonus on salary. Calculate the bonus that has to be given to the employee and display the salary that the employee will get.**

```
ch = input("Enter the sex of the employee (m or f) : ")
sal = int(input("Enter the salary of the employee : "))
if (ch=='m'):
    bonus = 0.05*sal
else :
    bonus = 0.10*sal
amt_to_be_paid = sal+bonus
print(" Salary = ",sal)
print(" Bonus = ",bonus)
print(" ************************************")
print("Amount to be paid : ",amt_to_be_paid)
```

OUTPUT

```
Enter the sex of the employee (m or f) : f
Enter the salary of the employee : 50000
 Salary =  50000
 Bonus =  5000.0
 ********************************
Amount to be paid :  55000.0
```

4. **Write a program to find whether a given year is a leap year or not.**

```
year = int(input("Enter any year : "))
if((year%4==0 and year %100!=0) or (year%400 == 0)):
    print("Leap Year")
else:
    print("Not a Leap Year")
```

OUTPUT

```
Enter any year : 2000
Leap Year
```

5. **Write a program to find the greater of two numbers.**

```
x = int(input("Enter the first number : "))
y = int(input("Enter the second number : "))
if(x==y):
        print("The two numbers are equal")
elif(x>y):
        print(x,"is greater than",y)
else:
        print(x,"is less than",y)
```

OUTPUT

```
Enter the first number : 6
Enter the second number : 3
6 is greater than 3
```

6. **Write a program to find the greatest number from three numbers.**

```
num1 = int(input("Enter the first number : "))
num2 = int(input("Enter the second number : "))
num3 = int(input("Enter the third number : "))
if(num1>num2):
    if(num1>num3):
        print(num1,"is greater than",num2,"and",num3)
    else:
        print(num3,"is greater than",num1,"and",num2)
```

```
elif(num2>num3):
    print(num2,"is greater than",num1,"and",num3)
else:
    print("The three numbers are equal")
```

OUTPUT

```
Enter the first number : 13
Enter the second number : 43
Enter the third number : 25
43 is greater than 13 and 25
```

7. **Write a program that prompts the user to enter a number between 1–7 and then displays the corresponding day of the week.**

```
num = int(input("Enter any number between 1 to 7 : "))
if(num==1): print("Sunday")
elif(num==2): print("Monday")
elif(num==3): print("Tuesday")
elif(num==4): print("Wednesday")
elif(num==5): print("Thursday")
elif(num==6): print("Friday")
elif(num==7): print("Saturday")
else :
print("Wrong input")
```

OUTPUT

```
Enter any number between 1 to 7 : 5
Thursday
```

8. **Write a program to calculate tax, given the following conditions:**

```
If income is less than 1,50, 000 then no tax
If taxable income is 1,50,001-300,000 then charge 10% tax
If taxable income is 3,00,001-500,000 then charge 20% tax
If taxable income is above 5,00,001 then charge 30% tax
MIN1 = 150001
MAX1 = 300000
RATE1 = 0.10
MIN2 = 300001
MAX2 = 500000
RATE2 = 0.20
MIN3 = 500001
RATE3 = 0.30
income = int(input("Enter the income : "))
taxable_income = income - 150000
if(taxable_income <= 0):
    print("No tax")
```

```
elif(taxable_income>=MIN1 and taxable_income<MAX1):
    tax = (taxable_income - MIN1) * RATE1
elif(taxable_income>=MIN2 and taxable_income<MAX2):
    tax = (taxable_income - MIN2) * RATE2
else:
    tax = (taxable_income-MIN3)*RATE3
print("TAX = ",tax)
```

OUTPUT

```
Enter the income : 2000000
TAX =  404999.7
```

9. Write a program to take input from the user and then check whether it is a number or a character. If it is a character, determine whether it is in upper case or lower case.

```
ch = input("Enter the character : ")
if(ch>="A" and ch<="Z"):
    print("Upper case character was entered")
elif(ch>='a' and ch<='z'):
    print("Lower case character was entered")
elif(ch>='0' and ch<='9'):
    print "A number was entered"
```

OUTPUT

```
Enter any character : C
Upper case character was entered
```

10. Write a program to enter the marks of a student in four subjects. Then calculate the total, aggregate and display the grade obtained by the student. If the student scores an aggregate that is greater than 75%, then the grade is Distinction. If aggregate is 60>= and <75, then the grade is First Division. If aggregate is 50>= and <60, then the grade is Second Division. If aggregate is 40>= and <50, then the grade is Third Division. Else, the grade is Fail.

```
marks1 = int(input("Enter the marks in Mathematics : "))
marks2 = int(input("Enter the marks in Science : "))
marks3 = int(input("Enter the marks in Social Science : "))
marks4 = int(input("Enter the marks in Computers : "))
total = marks1+marks2+marks3+marks4
avg = float(total)/4
print("Total = ",total,"\t Aggregate = ",avg)
if(avg>=75):
        print("Distinction")
elif(avg>=60 and avg<75):
        print("First Division")
elif(avg>=50 and avg<60):
        print("Second Division")
else:
        print("Fail")
```

> While forming the conditional expression, try to use positive statements rather than using compound negative statements.

OUTPUT

```
Enter the marks in Mathematics : 90
Enter the marks in Science : 91
Enter the marks in Social Science : 92
Enter the marks in Computers : 93
Total = 366    Aggregate = 91.5
Distinction
```

11. Write a program that prompts the user to enter three angles. Check whether the angles are that of a triangle or not.

```
ang1= int(input("Enter the first angle : "))
ang2= int(input("Enter the first angle : "))
ang3= int(input("Enter the first angle : "))
if (ang1 + ang2 + ang3) == 180:
    print("The angles are angles of a triangle")
else:
    print("The angles are not the angles of a triangle")
```

OUTPUT

```
Enter the first angle : 120
Enter the first angle : 40
Enter the first angle : 20
The angles are angles of a triangle
```

Key Terms

Sequential control flow: A programming style in which the statements in a program are executed one after the other.

Flow control: Flow control means control on which statement would be executed next.

Decision control flow: A type of flow control in which either a selected set of statements is executed or a particular set of statements is executed repeatedly.

Selection control statements: Decision control statements that allow the flow control to jump from one part of the code to another depending on whether a particular condition is satisfied or not. Since they execute statements selectively based on certain decisions, such type of decision control statements is known as selection control statements or *conditional branching statements*.

Clause: Combination of a header and its suite.

Suite: Group of statements following the header.

Nested (or compound) statement: A statement that contains other statements is called a compound statement.

Chapter Highlights

- A test expression is any valid expression that may include logical operators.
- After the header, all instructions that are indented at the same level form a suite.
- Python uses indentation to form a block of code.
- An `if-else` statement specifies what has to be done if the statement is true as well as when it is false.

- Nested `if` statements are used to check if more than one condition is satisfied.
- A series of `if` and `elif` statements have a final `else` block, which is executed if none of the `if` or `elif` expressions is True.

Review Questions

1. What is flow control?
2. Differentiate between sequential control flow and selection control flow.
3. Why do we need decision control statements?
4. With the help of a flowchart, explain the syntax of the following statements:
   a. `if` b. `if-else` c. `if-el-if` d. nested `if`
5. What are conditional branching statements? How does Python support such statements?
6. How will you identify the suite of an `if` statement?
7. With the help of an example explain why `if-else` statement is better than a simple `if` statement.
8. What do you mean by a nested `if` statement? How is it implemented in Python?
9. Why should we not use floating-point numbers to test for exact equality?
10. Change the indentation to make the code syntactically correct.

```
if condition1:
statement1
elif condition2:
statement2
elif condition3:
statement3
elif condition4:
statement4
```

11. Under what conditions, Programming will be printed?

```
if a < 10:
  print("Python")
elif a < 20:
  print("Programming")
else:
  print("is fun..")
```

Programming Exercises

1. Write a program to check whether a number is divisible by 10 or not. If the number is not divisible, then print how much should be added to it to make it completely divisible by 10.
2. Write a program to verify whether a candidate is eligible to appear for an exam or not. The minimum and maximum age of person appearing for the exam is 21 and 35 respectively.
3. Write a program that prompts the user to enter an angle and then prints its quadrant.
4. Write a program that prompts the user to enter a number between 1–12 and then displays the corresponding month of the year.
5. Write a menu-driven program that prompts the user to enter two sides of a rectangle. The user can then choose from a given set of options, if he/she needs to calculate perimeter, area or diagonal of the rectangle.
6. Write a program that prompts users to enter a character (A, B, C, D, E). Then using `if-elif-else` construct display Outstanding, Very Good, Good, Average and Fail respectively.

7. Write a program that prompts the user to enter two integers. Divide the greater number with the smaller one and print the remainder and quotient thus obtained.
8. Write a program that prompts the user to enter his/her age (15–18 years) and then display the perfect height and weight for that age.

Age	Weight (kg)	Height (cm)
15	56	170
16	60	173
17	64	175
18	66	176

9. Write a program that prompts user to enter his/her body temperature. Check and display whether the user has normal body temperature, high fever or low fever.
10. Write a program that prompts the user to enter a number. Display the square root of the number. Remember that square root of negative numbers is not defined.
11. Write a program that prompts the user to enter the lengths of three sides. Check whether these are the sides of a triangle.
    <u>**Hint**</u>: Sides of a triangle follow the rule, a + b > c. Similarly, b + c > a and a + c > b.
12. Write a program that prompts the user to enter the angles of a triangle. Check whether the triangle is acute-, obtuse- or right-angled.
13. Write a program to check whether a number entered by the user is positive, negative or equal to zero.
14. Write a program that prompts users to enter status code '`S`', '`M`', '`D`', or '`U`' and returns the string '`Separated`', '`Married`', '`Divorced`', or '`Unmarried`', respectively. In case an inappropriate letter is passed, print an appropriate message.
15. An employee's total weekly pay is calculated by multiplying the hourly wage and number of regular hours plus any overtime pay, which, in turn, is calculated as total overtime hours multiplied by 1.5 times the hourly wage. Write a program that takes as inputs the hourly wage, total regular hours, and total overtime hours and prints an employee's total weekly pay.

Fill in the Blanks

1. __________ means control on which statement would be executed next.
2. __________ is the simplest form of decision control statements.
3. Header and its suite together form a __________.
4. Python uses __________ to form a block of code.
5. A __________ statement contains other statements.
6. A series of `if` and `elif` statements have a final ________ block.
7. ______ and ______ operators are used to form a compound relational expression.
8. ________ is a short form of `else if` statement.
9. Python uses __________ to form a block of code.
10. A series of `if elif` statements have a final ______ block, which is executed if none of the `if` or `elif` expressions is True.
11. Python assumes any non-zero and non-null values as ________.
12. ________ begins with a keyword and ends with a colon.

13.
```
x = 10
y = 20
__x>y__
print print("In if")
________
     print ("In else")
```

14. Fill the blanks to print *Python* on the screen.
```
x = 10
y = 50
if x>10 __ y<100:
___("Python")
```

State True or False

1. A sequential control program can skip one or more statements.
2. In selection control statements, all the statements are executed from the first one to the last.
3. A group of statements following the header is known as a clause.
4. After the header, all instructions that are indented at the same level forms a suite.
5. It is mandatory to use four spaces to define each level of indentation.
6. The final `else` block in an `if-elif-else` statement is executed when none of the `if` or `elif` expressions is True.
7. You can use floating-point numbers for checking for equality in the test expression.
8. Indentation identifies a statement block.
9. Statements within a suite can be indented at different levels.
10. `elif` and `else` blocks are optional.

Multiple Choice Questions

1. Which part of if statement should be indented?
   a. The first statement　　b. All the statements
   c. Statements within the `if` block　　d. None of these.
2. A programming style in which the statements in a program are executed one after the other.
   a. Sequential　　b. Decision control
   c. Iterative control　　d. None of these.
3. A test expression must have a/an ________ operator.
   a. arithmetic　　b. logical
   c. unary　　d. assignment
4. In an `if` statement, which of the following headers are optional?
   a. `if`　　b. `elif`
   c. `else`　　d. Both b and c.
5. Logical expression should not be ________.
   a. simple　　b. long
   c. positive　　d. Both b and c.
6. Which of the following is placed after the `if` condition?
   a. ;　　b. .
   c. :　　d. ,

Give the Output

1.
```
if(5.0 < 9.0):
print("DONE")
```

2.
```
years = 99
if(years == 100):
    print("Century")
elif(years == 75):
    print("Platinum Jublee")
elif(years == 50):
    print("Half Century")
elif(years == 25):
    print("Silver Jublee")
elif(years == 10):
    print("Decade")
else:
    print("Long way to go....")
```

3.
```
years = 99
if years > 30:
    print("30")
if years < 50:
    print("50")
if years == 7:
    print("70")
```

4.
```
num = int((10*6 + 10 - 20) > 0)
if num == 50:
else:
    print("Try Again")
```

5.
```
num = 3
if (num ** 3) > (5%2 - 3 * 4 /2):
    if (num // 4) >= 2:
        print("You win")
    else:
        print("Try Again")
```

6.
```
num = 3
if num == 2:
    print("Yes")
elif num == 4:
    print("Yes")
elif num == 8:
    print("Yes")
else:
    print("Number is not an even number")
```

7.
```
if(10 == 100) and (100 + 200 > 300):
    print("Win Win..")
else:
    print("Oh No !!!")
```

8.
```
if not True:
        print("WRONG")
elif not((10+10 - 20 * 3) == 30):
        print("Really !")
else:
        print("May Be")
```

9.
```
if (10 << ((41 - 40 // 2 + 1)%2)) == 60:
        print("WoW")
else:
        print("Gosh")
```

10.
```
a = 5
b = 70
if not 10 + 10 == b or a == 40 and 70== 80:
        print("Yeah")
elif a != b:
        print("Nope")
```

11.
```
num = 10
if num > 30:
        if num > 40:
                print("Python")
        else:
                print("Programming")
elif num < 20:
        if(num!=0):
                print("is fun..")
print("Isnt it !!!")
```

12.
```
weather = 'foggy'
if weather == 'sunny':
        print("Take your shades")
elif weather == 'raining':
        print("Take your umbrella")
else:
        print("Stay at home")
```

AI Lab Session – NeuralCandy

NeuralCandy is an interesting experiment in which a machine dispenses candy when the user displays the requested image in front of the trained image model. The application prompts the user for a random image to be placed in front of the camera module. If the image matches the request, then the motor of the candy dispenser is activated to release the reward.

You can use a smartphone to search on Google for the requested target image and put it in front of the Pi camera. The game can be started by visiting the URL https://experiments.withgoogle.com/neuralcandy

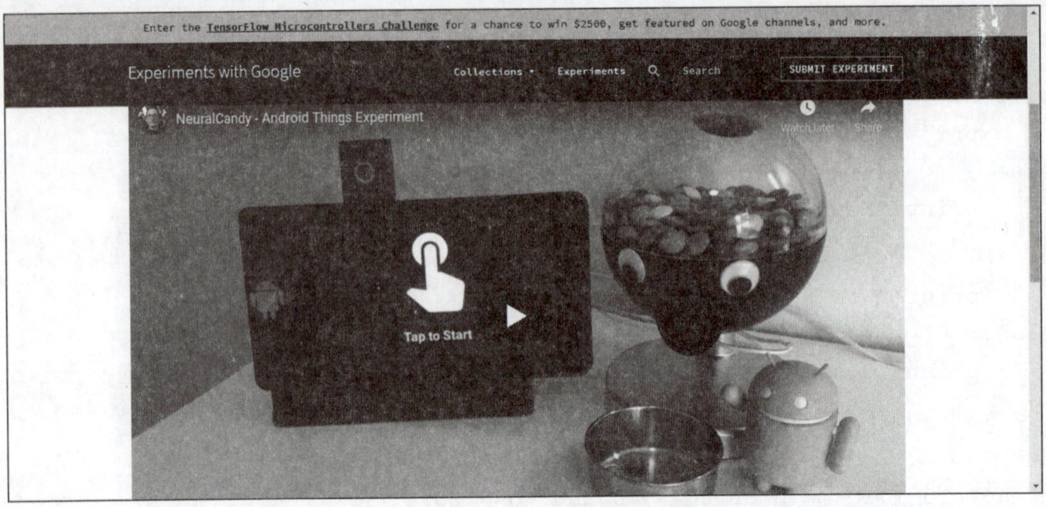

Answers

Fill in the Blanks

1. Flow control
2. `If` statement
3. clause
4. indentation
5. compound/nested
6. `else`
7. `and`, `or`
8. `elif`
9. indentation
10. `else`
11. True
12. Header
13. `if`, `:`, `else:`
14. `or`, `print`

State True or False

1. False
2. False
3. False
4. True
5. False
6. True
7. True
8. True
9. False
10. True

Multiple Choice Questions

1. b
2. a
3. b
4. d
5. b
6. c

Give the Output

1. Done
2. Long way to go....
3. 30
4. Try Again
5. Try Again
6. Number is not an even number
7. Oh No !!!
8. Really !
9. Gosh
10. Yeah
11. is fun..
    Isnt it !!!
12. Stay at home

Basic Loop Structures/Iterative Statements

8

Chapter Objectives

This chapter elucidates the concept of iterative statements in Python. Like decision control statements, the iterative statements may also change the flow of program control. Here, we shall learn about:

- `while` loop
- `for` loop
- The `range()` function
- Nested loops
- The technique to choose an appropriate loop for the given situation
- Path breaking statements like `break`, `continue`, `pass` and `else`

Python supports basic loop structures. Iterative statements are used to repeat the execution of one or more statements. In Python, iterative statements are implemented through `while` loop and `for` loop.

8.1 `while` LOOP

The `while` loop provides a mechanism to repeat one or more statements while a particular condition is true. Figure 8.1 shows the syntax and general form of representation of a `while` loop.

SYNTAX OF `while` LOOP

```
statement x

while (condition):
    statement block

statement y
```

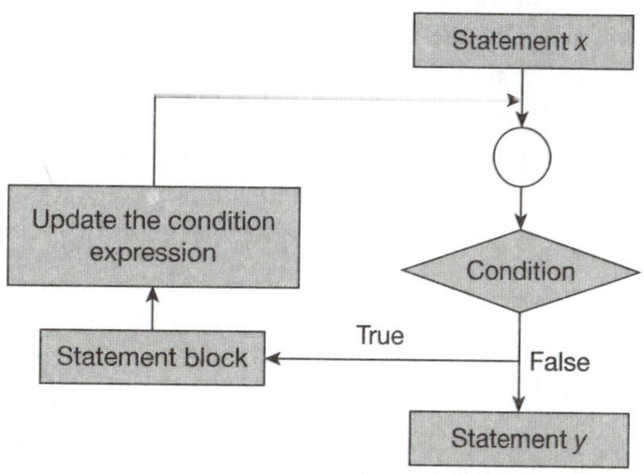

Figure 8.1 The `while` loop construct

> Iterative statements are used to repeat the execution of a list of statements, depending on the value of the integer expression.

Note in the `while` loop, the condition is tested before any of the statements in the statement block is executed. If the condition is true, only then the statements will be executed; otherwise if the condition is false, the control will jump to statement *y*, which is the immediate statement outside the `while` loop block.

We must update the condition with every iteration of the loop. This is necessary because it is this condition which determines when the loop will end. If we do not update the condition, then it will never become false. This will result in an infinite loop, which is never desirable.

A `while` loop is also referred to as a top-checking loop since control condition is placed as the first line of the code. If the control condition evaluates to false, then the statements enclosed in the loop are never executed. Look at the following example code.

Example 8.1 **To print the first 10 numbers using a `while` loop.**

```
i = 0
while(i< =10}:
      print(i,end=' ')
      i = i+1
```

OUTPUT

0 1 2 3 4 5 6 7 8 9 10

Example 8.2 **Write a program to calculate the sum and average of the first 10 numbers.**

```
i = 0
s = 0
while(i<=10):
   s = s+i
   i=i+1
avg = float(s}/10
print("The sum of first 10 numbers is : ",s)
print("The average of first 10 numbers is :",avg)
```

OUTPUT

The sum of the first 10 numbers is : 55

In the program, initially $i = 0$ and is less than 10; that is, the condition is true. So in the `while` loop, the value of *i* is printed and the condition is updated so that with every execution of the loop, the condition becomes more approachable. Always remember that when writing a `while` loop,

First, the loop control variable must be initialized before entering the loop.

Second, the test expression that decides whether the statement(s) in the loop will be executed or not is evaluated.

Third, the statement(s) inside the loop are executed if the test expression is True.

Fourth, the loop control variable is updated.

`while` loop is very useful for designing interactive programs in which the number of times the statements in loop has to be executed may or may not be known in advance. Let us look at a program which results in an infinite loop. Though the program is supposed to calculate the average of the first 10 numbers, the condition never becomes false, and the desired output is *not* generated. If you clearly observe the code, you will see that the statement updating the value of loop control variable (*i*) is missing here. So, every time the loop executes, the value of *i* is zero. In no way, will the value of *i* become equal to or greater than 10. Hence, an infinite loop – a loop that never ends is entered. Once you have entered the infinite loop, either press Ctrl + C keys on the keyboard or press the close button of the Python shell window.

```
i = 0
sum =0
avg = 0.0
while(i<=10):
    sum = sum + i
avg = sum/10
print("\n The sum of first 10 numbers=", sum)
print("\n The average of first 10 numbers = ", avg)
```

> The infinite loop is a loop which never stops running. Its condition always True.

8.2 `for` LOOP

Like the `while` loop, the `for` loop provides a mechanism to repeat a task until a particular condition is true. `for` loop is usually known as a determinate or definite loop because the programmer knows exactly how many times the loop will repeat. The number of times the loop has to be executed can be determined mathematically, by checking the logic of the loop.

The `for..in` statement is a looping statement used in Python to iterate over a sequence of objects, i.e., go through each item in a sequence. Here, by sequence we mean just an ordered collection of items. The flow of statements in a `for` loop can be given as in Fig. 8.2.

FLOW OF STATEMENTS IN FOR LOOP

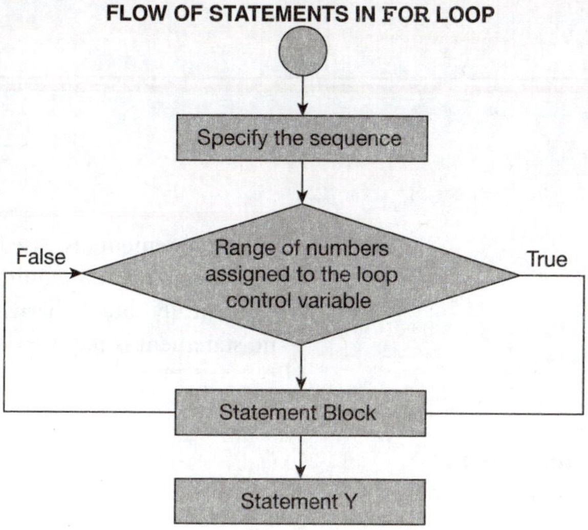

SYNTAX OF FOR LOOP

```
for loop_contol_var in sequence:
    statement block
```

Figure 8.2 for loop construct

When a `for` loop is used, a range of sequence is specified (only once). The items of the sequence are assigned to the loop control variable one after the other. The `for` loop is executed for each item in the sequence. With every iteration of the loop, a check is made to ensure if the loop control variable has been assigned all the values in the sequence. If all the values have not been assigned, the statement block of the loop is executed; else, the statements comprising the statement block of the `for` loop are skipped and the control jumps to the immediate statement following the `for` loop body. Note that every iteration of the loop must make the loop control variable closer to the end of the sequence.

Let us print all the characters in a string using the `for` loop. We know that a string is a sequence of characters. So, the `for` loop statement(s) will be executed for each character in the string.

```
for i in "PYTHON":
    print(i, end = ' ')
Ans. P Y T H O N
```

8.3 THE `range()` FUNCTION

The `range()` is a built-in function in Python that is used to iterate over a sequence of numbers. The syntax of `range()` is **`range(beg, end, [step])`**

> Step can be either positive or negative but cannot be zero.

The **`range()`** generates a sequence of numbers starting with **beg** (inclusive) and ending with one less than the number **end**. The **step** argument is optional (hence, written in brackets). By default, every number in the range is incremented by 1 but we can specify a different increment using `step`. It can be both negative and positive, but not zero.

Programs to print first n numbers using the `range()` in a `for` loop

```
for i in range (1, 5):
    print (i, end = ' ')
```

Print numbers in the same line

OUTPUT

1 2 3 4

beg step

```
for i in range (1, 10, 2):
print (i, end = ' ')
```

end

OUTPUT

1 3 7 9

The `range()` function had produced values 1, 2, 3 and 4. Did you notice that the statement(s) of the `for` loop is executed for each value of the loop control variable (which is *i*, here). Initially, *i* is 1, in the next iteration it is 2, and so on. The loop continues until all the values in the sequence are processed.

PROGRAMMER'S ZONE

1. **Write a program to print 10 horizontal hyphens (-).**

```
i = 1
while(i<=10):
    print("-",end=' ')
    i = i+1
```

> `Pass` statement is used when a statement is required syntactically but otherwise no statement is required.

OUTPUT

```
__________
```

2. **Write a program to calculate the sum of numbers from `m` to `n`.**

```
m = int(input("Enter the value of m : "))
n = int(input("Enter the value of n : "))
s = 0
while(m<=n):
    s = s+m
    m = m+1
print("SUM = ",s)
```

OUTPUT

```
Enter the value of m : 3
Enter the value of n : 9
SUM =  42
```

3. **Write a program to calculate the average of numbers entered by the user.**

```
S = 0
count = 0
print "Enter -1 to stop"…."
num = 0
while(num != -1):
    s = s+num
    num = int(inp"t("Enter the marks": "))
    count  = count+1
avg = float(s)/count
print "TOTAL MARKS": ""s,"\tAVERAGE MARKS": ",avg
```

OUTPUT

```
Enter -1 to stop....
Enter the marks : 90
Enter the marks : 98
Enter the marks : 97
Enter the marks : 89
```

```
Enter the marks : 79
Enter the marks : 96
Enter the marks : -1
TOTAL MARKS :  549   AVERAGE MARKS :  78.4285714286
```

4. Write a program to find whether the given number is an Armstrong number or not.
Hint: An Armstrong number of three digits is an integer such that the sum of the cubes of its digits is equal to the number itself. For example, 371 is an Armstrong number since 33 + 7**3 + 1**3 = 371.**

```
n = int(input("Enter the number : "))
s = 0
num = n
while(n>0):
    r = n%10
    s = s+(r**3)
    n = n/10
if(s==num):
    print("The number is Armstrong")
else:
    print("The number is not Armstrong")
```

OUTPUT

```
Enter the number : 373
432 is not an Armstrong number
```

5. Write a program to enter a number and then calculate the sum of its digits.

```
sumOfDigits = 0
num = int(input("Enter the number : "))
while(num!=0):
    temp=num%10
    sumOfDigits = sumOfDigits+temp
    num=num/10
print("The sum of digits is :",sumOfDigits)
```

OUTPUT

```
Enter the number : 456
The sum of digits = 15
```

6. Write a program to calculate the GCD of two numbers.

```
num1 = int(input("Enter the two numbers : "))
num2 = int(input("Enter the two numbers : "))
if(num1>num2):
    dividend = num1
    divisor = num2
else:
    dividend = num2
    divisor = num1
```

```
while(divisor!=0):
      remainder = dividend%divisor
      dividend = divisor
      divisor = remainder
print("GCD of",num1,"and",num2,"is",dividend)
```

> To stop an infinite loop, press Ctrl + C keys or close the IDLE.

OUTPUT

```
Enter the first number : 40
Enter the second number : 10
GCD of 64 and 14 is = 10
```

7. Write a program to print the reverse of a number.

```
num = int(input("Enter the number : "))
print("The reversed number is :",)
while(num!=0):
      temp = num%10
      print(temp, end=' ')
      num = num/10
```

OUTPUT

```
Enter the number : 678
The reversed number is : 8 7 6
```

8. Write a program using for loop to calculate the average of first n natural numbers.

```
n = int(input("Enter the value of n : "))
avg = 0.0
s = 0
for i in range(1,n+1):
      s = s+i
avg = s/i
print("The sum of first",n,"natural numbers is",s)
print("The average of first",n,"natural numbers is",avg)
```

OUTPUT

```
Enter the value of n : 10
The sum of first n natural numbers = 55
n The average of first n natural numbers = 5.500
```

9. Write a program to print the multiplication table of n, where n is entered by the user.

```
n = int(input("Enter any number : "))
print("Multiplication table of", n)
print("*********************************")
for i in range(1,11):
      print(n,"X",i,"=",n*i)
```

OUTPUT

```
Enter any number : 5
Multiplication table of 5
```

```
***********************
5 X 0 = 0
5 X 1 = 5
...
5 X 20 = 100
```

10. Write a program using for loop to print all the numbers from m - n thereby classifying them as even or odd.

```
m = int(input("Enter the value of m : "))
n = int(input("Enter the value of n : "))
for i in range(m,n+1):
    if(i%2==0):
        print(i,"is even number")
    else:
        print(i,"is odd number")
```

OUTPUT

```
Enter the value of m : 10
Enter the value of n : 15
10 is even number
11 is odd number
12 is even number
13 is odd number
14 is even number
15 is odd number
```

11. Write a program using for loop to calculate the factorial of a number.

```
num = int(input("Enter the number : "))
if(num==0):
    fact = 1
fact = 1
for i in range(1,num+1):
    fact = fact*i
print("Factorial of",num,"is",fact)
```

OUTPUT

```
Enter the number : 6
Factorial of is : 720
```

12. Write a program using while loop to read the numbers until –1 is encountered. Also count the number of prime numbers and composite numbers entered by the user.

```
total_prime = 0
total_composite = 0
while(1):
    num = int(input("Enter no. "))
    if(num == -1):
        break
```

> `break` statement is used to break out of (or discontinue) a loop. It is placed within an `if` statement to jump out of the loop when a particular condition is met.

```
    is_composite = 0
    for i in range(2,(num-1)/2):
        if(num%i == 0):
            is_composite = 1
            break
    if(is_composite):
        total_composite+=1
    else:
        total_prime+=1
print("total composite : ",total_composite)
print("total prime : ",total_prime)
```

OUTPUT

```
Enter no. 12
Enter no. 17
Enter no. 15
Enter no. 27
Enter no. 39
Enter no. 29
Enter no. 37
Enter no. -1
total composite :  4
total prime :  3
```

13. Write a program to calculate `pow(x,n)`.

```
num = int(input("Enter the number : "))
n = int(input("Till which power to calculate?"))
result = 1
for i in range(n):
    result = result*num
print(num,"raised to the power",n,"is",result)
```

OUTPUT

```
Enter the number : 3
Till which power to calculate : 5
3 raised to the power 5 is 243
```

14. Write a program to sum the series: 1+ 1/2 + ... + 1/n.

```
n = int(input("Enter the number : "))
s = 0.0
for i in range(1,n+1):
    a = 1.0/i
    s = s+a
print("The sum of 1,1/2.....1/"+str(n)+" is "+str(s))
```

OUTPUT

```
Enter the number : 7
The sum of 1,1/2......1/5 is  2.5928571428571425
```

15. Write a program to sum the series: $1/1^2 + 1/2^2 + \ldots 1/n^2$.

```
n = int(input("Enter the number : "))
s = 0.0
for i in range(1,n+1):
    a = 1.0/(i**2)
    s = s+a
print("The sum of series is",s)
```

OUTPUT

```
Enter the number : 7
The sum of series is  1.511797052154195
```

16. Write a program to sum the series: 1/2 + 2/3 + ... n/(n+1).

```
n = int(input("Enter the number : "))
s = 0.0
for i in range(1,n+1):
    a = float(i)/(i+1)
    s = s+a
print("The sum of 1/2+2/3......n/(n+1) is",s)
```

OUTPUT

```
Enter the number : 7
The sum of 1/2+2/3......n/(n+1) is  5.2821428571428575
```

17. Write a program to sum the series: $1/1 + 2^2/2 + 3^3/3 + \ldots n^2/n$.

```
n = int(input("Enter the value of n : "))
s = 0.0
for i in range(1,n+1):
    a = float(i**i)/i
    s = s+a
print("The sum of the series is",s)
```

OUTPUT

```
Enter the value of n : 7
The sum of the series is  126126.0
```

18. Write a program to calculate sum of cubes of numbers from 1 – n.

```
n = int(input("Enter the value of n : "))
s = 0
for i in range(1,n+1):
    a = i**3
    s = s+a
print("The sum of cubes is",s)
```

OUTPUT

```
Enter the value of n : 4
The sum of cubes is 100
```

19. Write a program to sum of the squares of odd numbers.

```
n = int(input("Enter the number : "))
s = 0
for i in range(1,n+1):
      if(i%2!=0):
          term = i**2
      else:
          term = 0
      s = s+term
print("The sum of squares of odd number less than",n,"is",s)
```

OUTPUT

```
Enter the number : 10
The sum of squares of even number less than 10 is 165
```

Key Terms

Iterative statement: Statements that repeat the execution of a block of statements depending on the value of an integer expression.

Definite repetition loop: A counter-controlled loop in which the counter is assigned a constant or a value is also known as a definite repetition loop.

Nested loop: A loop that is placed inside another loop.

Chapter Highlights

- In Python, iterative statements are implemented through `while` loop and `for` loop.
- The `while` loop provides a mechanism to repeat one or more statements while a particular condition is true.
- The value of the loop control variable is updated with every iteration of the loop.
- The `for` loop provides a mechanism to repeat a task until a particular condition is true.
- The `for..in` statement is a looping statement used in Python to iterate over a sequence of objects.
- The `range()` is a built-in function in Python that is used to iterate over a sequence of numbers.

Review Questions

1. With the help of a flowchart, explain the construct of a `while` loop.
2. Why is the value of the loop control variable updated with every iteration of the loop?
3. With the help of a flowchart, explain the construct of a `for` loop.
4. With the help of an example, explain the use of `range()` function.

5. Fill in the blanks to complete the code:

   a. create a loop that increments the value of x by 3 and prints the odd values from 0–100.

```
x = 0
____x <= ____
____(x)
x += 2
```

   b. to create a for loop that prints only the even values in the range 0–50:

```
____ i in range(______):
print(____)
```

6. Identify the definite and indefinite loop.

   a.
```
n = input('Enter a number: ')
while n != -1:
        n = input('Enter a number:  ')
```

   b.
```
x = 0
while x<10:
        print 10**num
n = n+1
```

7. Correct the code to produce the desired output.

   a.
```
for i in range(10,0):
    print(i)
```

   b.
```
i=10
while(i>0):
    print(i)
    i-1
```

   c.
```
i=10 ;  result = 1
while(i>0):
result = result + i**2
i = i+1
print(result)
```

8. The following for loops are written to print numbers from 1 to 10. Are these loops correct? Justify your answer.

   a.
```
for i in range(10):
    print(i)
```

   b.
```
for i in range(10):
    num = i+1
    print(num)
```

   c.
```
for i in range(10):
    print(i)
    i = i+1
```

9. Write the following piece of code using for loop.

```
i = 20
while i>0:
    print(i)
    i = i-2
```

Programming Exercises

1. Write a function that accepts two positive numbers n and m where m<=n, and returns numbers between 1 and n that are divisible by m.
2. Write a program to convert time in hours into minutes and vice-versa.
3. Write a program to calculate conveyance charges to be paid by the users. Enter the type of car as a character (like s for sedan, p for prime, m for mini) and distance in kms. Calculate charges as given below:

   sedan – 17 Rs per km, prime – 12 Rs per km, mini – 10 Rs per km.
4. Write a program to sum the series $1^2/1 + 2^2/2 + 3^2/3 + \ldots + n^2/n$.
5. Write a program that prints the cube of numbers in the range (1,n).
6. Write a program that prompts the user to enter the distance between his/her home and school. If the distance is in kilometres, display it in metres and vice-versa.

7. Write a program that displays Python Programming as
   a. `python programming` b. `PYTHON PROGRAMMING`
   c. `pYTHON pROGRAMMING`
8. Write a program that prompts users to enter numbers. Once the user enters `-1`, it displays the count, sum and average of even numbers and that of odd numbers.
9. Write a program to display the `sin(x)` value where `x` ranges from `0` to `360` in steps of 45.
10. Write a program that displays all the numbers from `1-100` that are not divisible 7 as well as by 11.
11. Write a program that accepts any number and prints the number of digits in that number.
12. Write a program that prints numbers from 100 to 1 in steps of 4.
13. Write a program that reads integers until the user wants to stop. When the user stops entering numbers, display the largest of all the numbers entered.
14. Write a program to generate the Fibonacci series.
15. Write a program to print first 20 even numbers in descending order.
16. Write a program to print the sum of the following series: `-x + x2 - x3 + x4 + ....`

Fill in the Blanks

1. __________ statements are used to repeatedly execute one or more statements in a block.
2. In Python, iterative statements are implemented through _______ and _______ loops.
3. An __________ loop will occur if the condition of `while` loop never becomes false.
4. The `for` loop provides a mechanism to repeat a task until a particular condition is _______.
5. The ________function in Python is used to iterate over a sequence of numbers.

State True or False

1. The `while` loop repeats one or more statements while a particular condition is false.
2. An iterative statement repeats the execution of a block of statements depending on the value of an expression that evaluates to an integer value only.
3. In the `while` loop, the condition is tested after the statement block is executed at least once.
4. The value of the loop control variable is updated with every alternate iteration of the loop.
5. An infinite loop will occur if the condition of `while` loop is always false.
6. The `for` loop is executed for each item in the sequence.
7. Every iteration of the loop must make the loop control variable farther from the end of the sequence.
8. The step argument in the `range()` function is optional.
9. The number of times the loop control variable is updated is equal to the number of times the loop iterates.
10. In a `while` loop, the loop control variable is initialized in the body of the loop.

Multiple Choice Questions

1. Which keys are not pressed to exit from the infinite loop?
   a. Alt + C b. Ctrl + C
   c. Alt + F4 d. Ctrl + Q
2. The step argument in the `range()` function cannot be ______.
   a. less than zero b. greater than zero
   c. zero d. None of these.
3. `range(1,5)` will generate numbers ________.
   a. 0, 1, 2, 3, 4, 5 b. 0, 1, 2, 3, 4
   c. 1, 2, 3, 4 d. 1, 2, 3, 4, 5
4. By default, every number in the range is incremented by ____.
   a. 0 b. 1
   c. 2 d. 3
5. In a `while` loop, if the body is executed n times, then the test expression is executed _____ times.
   a. n – 1 b. n
   c. n + 1 d. 2n
6.
```
i = 1
while i > 0:
print("loop")
```
   The above loop is the best example of a __________ loop.
   a. nested b. infinite
   c. counter-controlled d. condition-controlled
7. How many numbers will be printed?
```
i = 5
while i>=0:
print(i)
i=i-1
```
   a. 5 b. 6 c. 4 d. 0
8. How many numbers will be printed?
```
i = 10
while True:
    print(i)
    i = i - 1
    if i<=7:
        break
```
   a. 1 b. 2 c. 3 d. 4
9. How many lines will be printed by this code?
```
while False:
    print("Hello")
```
   a. 1 b. 0 c. 10 d. Countless
10. The output of `for I in range(5,7):` will be _______
    a. 5, 6, 7 b. 5, 6 c. 6, 7 d. 5

Give the Output

1.
```
i=1
while i<=6:
        print(i),
i=i+1
print("Done")
```

2.
```
i=0
while i<10:
  i = i + 1
  if(i == 5):
    print("\n Continue")
    continue
  if(i==7):
    print"\n Breaking"
    break
  print i,
print("\n Done")
```

3.
```
for i in range(5):
        print("hello!", end= " ")
```

4.
```
for i in range(10):
        if not i%2==0:
                print(i+1)
```

5.
```
for i in range(10,0,-1):
    print(i, end = ' ')
```

6.
```
for i in range(5,25,3):
    print(i, end = ' ')
```

7.
```
for i in "PYTHON":
    print(i,'-',end='')
```

8.
```
for i in range(10):
    pass
print(i)
```

9.
```
while True:
    str = input("Enter a string (Bye to exit) : ")
    if str == "bye":
        break
    print(str)
else:
    print("Exiting......")
```

10.
```
while(i<10):
    print(i)
```

11.
```
while(4>5):
    print("DONE")
else:
    print("NOT DONE")
```

12.
```
while(5*2 > 10):
    print("JUST DO IT")
else:
    print("DONE")
```

13.
```
a = 10; b = 0
while(a>b):
    print(a,b)
    a=a-1
    b=b+1
```

14.
```
run = True
a = 100
while run == True:
    print(a)
    a = a - 10
    if a < 40:
        run = False
```

15.
```
for i in range(100,50,-10):
    print(i)
```

16.
```
for i in range(100,50,-10):
    print(i)
```

17.
```
x = 10; y = 5
for i in range(x-y*2):
    print("%")
```

AI Lab Session – Shadow Art

Shadow Art is an application by Google that allows users to use AI to play with the ancient art of shadow puppetry. To play with this game, users have to create shadow puppets with hands in front of a laptop or phone camera. The puppets correspond to one of the lunar cycle's 12 zodiac symbols. The ML model identifies the animal formed by the user's hands. If the user is accurately able to form the first puppet within the specified time, then the next zodiac symbol has to be tried until all 12 puppets are correctly formed by the user. Visit the link to launch the Google experiment: https://experiments.withgoogle.com/shadow-art.

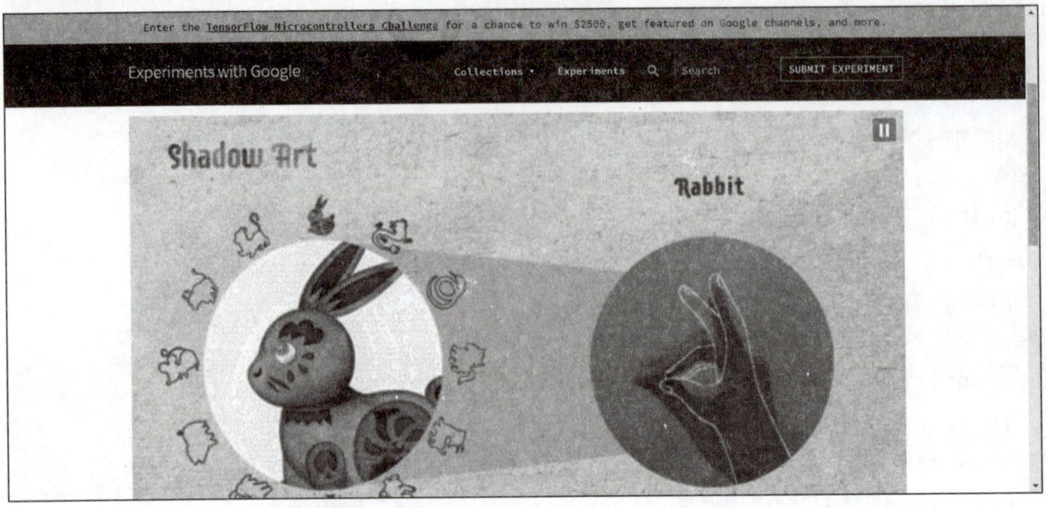

Answers

Fill in the Blanks

1. Flow control
2. `while`, `for`.
3. infinite
4. true
5. `range()`

State True or False

1. False
2. True
3. False
4. False
5. False
6. True
7. False
8. True
9. True
10. False

Multiple Choice Questions

1. a
2. c
3. c
4. b
5. c
6. b
7. b
8. c
9. b
10. b

Give the Output

1. 1 2 3 4 5 6 Done
2. 1 2 3 4
Continue 6 Breaking Done
3. hello! hello! hello! hello! hello!
4. 2 4 6 8 10
5. 10 9 8 7 6 5 4 3 2 1
6. 5 8 11 14 17 20 23
7. P -Y -T -H -O -N -
8. 9
9. No output when bye is entered.
10. NameError: name 'i' is not defined
11. NOT DONE
12. DONE
13. 10 0
14. 100 90 80 70 60 50 40
15. 100 90 80 70 60
16. No output
17. No output

9 Lists

Chapter Objectives

This chapter introduces list as an important and very powerful data structure in Python. The reader will get to learn the following things in this chapter:

- Creating lists
- Accessing and updating its values
- Relational operations
- Nested lists
- The `eval()` function
- Creating deep copies and shallow copies of a given list
- Difference between list cloning and list aliasing
- List operations and methods

List is a versatile data type available in Python, in which elements are written as a list of comma-separated values (items) between square brackets. Lists in Python are mutable as we can change the value of their elements. This is in striking contrast with strings, which are immutable.

The key feature of list is that it can have elements that belong to different data types. The syntax of defining a list can be given as, **List_variable = [val1, val2,.....]**

`list_A = [1,2,3,4,5]`
`print(list_A)`
`[1, 2, 3, 4, 5]`
	`list_B = ['A', 1, 'C', 2, 'E']`
	`print(list_B)`
	`['A', 1, 'C', 2, 'E']`

`list_C = ["HELLO","WORLD")`
`print(list_ C)`
`['HELLO', 'WORLD']`
	`list_D = [1, 'a ', 'HELLO')`
	`print( list_ D)`
	`[1, 'a ', 'HELLO']`

We can even create an empty list by writing **list_variable** = []. An empty list is equivalent to False when used with logical operators.

```
>>> list = []
>>> list == True
False
```

9.1 ACCESSING VALUES IN LISTS

Like strings, lists can also be sliced and concatenated. To access values in a list, square brackets are used to slice along with the index or indices to get the value stored at that index. As discussed earlier, the syntax for the slice operation is, **seq = List[start:stop:step]**

For example, seq = List[::2] *# get every other element, starting with index 0*
seq = List[10::3] *# gets every third element, starting with index 10*
seq = List[-3] *# get third element from the end*
seq = list_A[-3] *# 3rd element from the end*
seq = List[3:] *# get all elements starting from the third index from the beginning*

Example 9.1

```
num_list = [2,4,6,8,10,12,14,16,18,20]
print("num_list is:", num_list)
print("First element in the list is",
num_list[0])
print("num_list[2:5] = ", num_list[4:7])
print("num_list[::2] = ", num_list[::3])
print("num_list[1::3] = ", num_list[1::2])
```

OUTPUT

```
num_list is : [2, 4, 6, 8, 10, 12,
14, 16, 18, 20]
First element in the list is 2
num_list[2:5] = [10, 12, 14]
num_list[::2] = [2, 8, 14, 20]
num_list[1::3] = [4, 8, 12, 16, 20]
```

If the `start` and end values of the slice operation are beyond the size of the list, then all the elements within the specified range are returned. For example, consider the example given below in which the `start` and end values are out of range of the size of the list.

Note that the valid index range of the list is 0–4. Values -9 and 9 are beyond the size of the list, so the entire list is returned as 0 to 4 lies within the range -9 to 9. But in the second case, when start = -3 and end = 9, -3 lies in the valid range which is the third element from the end; hence the result.

```
I = [1,2,3,4,5]
print(l[-9:9])
```

OUTPUT

```
[1, 2, 3, 4, 5]
```

```
I = [1, 2,3,4,5]
print(I[-3:9])
```

OUTPUT

```
[3, 4, 5]
```

9.2 UPDATING VALUES IN LISTS

Once created, one or more elements of a list can be easily updated by giving the slice on the left-hand side of the assignment operator. You can also append new values in the list and remove existing value(s) from the list using the `append()` method and `del` statement respectively.

Example 9.2

```
num_list = [2,4,6,8,10,12,14,16,18,20]
print("List is : ", num_list)
num_list[5] = 100
print("List after udpation is : ", num_list)
num_list.append(200)
print("List after appending a value is ", num_list)
del num_list(3]
print("List after deleting a value is ", num_list)
```

OUTPUT

```
List is : [2, 4, 6, 8, 10, 12, 14, 16, 18, 20]
List after udpation is : [2, 4, 6, 8, 10, 100, 14, 16, 18, 20]
List after appending a value is [2, 4, 6, 8, 10, 100, 14, 16, 18, 20, 200]
List after deleting a value is [2, 4, 6, 10, 100, 14, 16, 18, 20, 200
```

If you know exactly which element(s) to delete, use the `del` statement; otherwise use the `remove()` method to delete the unknown elements.

Example 9.3

```
num_list = [2,4,6,8,10,12,14,16,18,20]
del num_list[3:6] #deletes numbers at index 3,4,5
print(num_list)
del num_list[:] #deletes all the numbers from the list
print(num_list) # an empty list is printed
```

OUTPUT

```
[2, 4, 6, 14, 16, 18, 20]
[]
```

```
del(num_list)
print(num_list)  # the list no longer exists
```

OUTPUT

```
Traceback (most recent call last):
  File "C:\Users\Reema\Python\Python37\try.py", line 5, in <module>
  print(num_list) #the list no loger exists
NameError: name 'num_list' is not defined
```

Note that when we write del num_list, the entire variable is deleted. If you make any attempt to use this variable after the `del` statement, then an error will be generated.

9.3 RELATIONAL OPERATIONS ON LISTS

We can compare two list objects using relational operators like ==, >,<,>=,<=, !=, etc. Python compares elements of a list in lexicographical order. Each element of the list is compared with the corresponding element in the other list. However, to use operators like >=, <=, >, <, the two values must be of compatible type; otherwise an error will be generated.

Example 9.4

```
l1 = [1,2,3]
l2 = [1,2,3]
l3 = [1,[2,3]]
print(l1==l2)
print(l1==l3)
```

OUTPUT

```
True
False
```

```
l1 = [1,2,3]
l2 = [1,3,3]
print(l1>=l2)
print(l1<=l2)
```

OUTPUT

```
False
True
```

```
l1 = [1,2,3,4]
l2 = [1,3,3]
print(l1>=l2)
```

OUTPUT

```
True
```

```
l1 = [1,2,3,4]
l2 = ['a','b','c']
l3 = [1.0,2.0,3.0)
print(l1>=l3)
print(l2>=l3)
```

OUTPUT

```
True
Traceback (most recent call last):
  File "C:\Python37\try.py",line 5,
in <module>
print(l2>=l3) Type Error: '>=' not
supported between instances of 'str'
and 'float'
```

Example 9.5

```
I =[1,2,3,4,5,6,7,8,9,10)
print(I)
#deleting third element
del I[2]
print(I)
#deleting fourth, fifth, sixth and seventh
elements from the list
del1[2:6]
print(I)
#deleting the entire list
print("Deleting List ........ ")
del I
print(I)
```

OUTPUT

```
[1, 2, 3, 4, 5, 6, 7, 8, 9, 10)
[1, 2, 4, 5, 6, 7, 8, 9, 10)
[1, 2, 8, 9, 10)
Deleting List ....... .
Traceback (most recent call last):
File "C:\Python37\try.py", line 12, in
<module> print(I)
NameError: name 'I' is not defined
```

9.4 DELETING ELEMENTS

We can delete one or more elements from the list by using the **`del`** statement. The syntax to remove a single element from the list is **`del list_variable[index]`**. And to remove more than one element from the list, we use the syntax, **`del[start:stop]`**. Finally, to remove the entire list, we need to write **`del list_variable`**.

9.5 BASIC LIST OPERATIONS

Lists behave in the similar way as strings when operators like + (concatenation) and * (repetition) are used. Common operations on lists are discussed in Table 7.1.

Table 9.1 Operations on lists

Operation	Description	Example	Output
len	Returns the length of the list	`len([1,2,3,4,5,6,7,8,9,10])`	`10`
concatenation	Joins two lists	`[1,2,3,4,5] + [6,7,8,9,10]`	`[1, 2, 3, 4, 5, 6, 7, 8, 9, 10]`
repetition	Repeat elements in the list	`"Love", "Python"*2`	`['Love', 'Python', 'Love', 'Python']`
in	Checks if the value is present in the list	`'a' in ['a','e', 'i','o','u']`	`True`
not in	Checks if the value is not present in the list	`9 not in [0,2,4,6,8]`	`True`
max	Returns maximum value in the list	`>>> num_list = [1,0,3,7,4,2,4,9]` `>>> print(max(num_list))`	`9`
min	Returns minimum value in the list	`>>> num_list = [1,0,3,7,4,2,4,9]` `>>> print(min(num_list))`	`0`
sum	Adds the values in the list that has numbers	`num_list = [1,2,3,4,5,6,7,8,9,10]` `print("SUM = ", sum(num_list))`	`SUM = 55`

9.6 LIST METHODS

Python has various methods to help programmers work efficiently with lists. Some of these methods are summarized in Table 9.2.

Table 9.2 List methods

Method	Description	Syntax	Example	Output

append()	Appends an element to the list. In `insert()`, if the index is 0, then element is inserted as the first element and if we write, `list.insert(len(list), obj)`, then it inserts obj as the last element in the list. That is, if `index= len(list)` then `insert()` method behaves exactly the same as `append()` method.	`list.append(obj)`	`num_list = [1,2,3,4]`
			`num_list.append(5)`
			`print(num_list)`
				`[1,2,3,4,5]`

count()	Counts the number of times an element appears in the list	`list.count(obj)`	`num_list = [1,2,3,4,3,2,4,6]` `print( num_list.count(4))`	`1`
index()	Returns the lowest index of obj in the list. Gives a ValueError if obj is not present in the list	`list.index(obj)`	`num_list = [1,2,3,4,3,2,4,6]` `print(num_list.index(3))`	`2`

insert()	Inserts obj at the specified index in the list.	`list.insert(index, obj)`	`num_list = [1,2,3,4,5]`
			`num_list.insert(3, 0)`
			`print(num_list)`
				`[1,2,3,0,4,5]`

remove()	Removes or deletes obj from the list. ValueError is generated if obj is not present in the list. If multiple copies of obj exist in the list then the first value is deleted.	`list.remove(obj)`	`num_list = [0,1,2,3,4,5]`
			`num_list.remove(0)`
			`print(num_list)`
				`[1, 2, 3,4,5]`

reverse()	Reverse the elements in the list.	`list.reverse()`	`num_list = [1,2,3,4]`
			`num_list.reverse()`
			`print num_list`
				`[4,3,2,1]`

sort()	Sorts the elements in the list	`list.sort()`	`num_list = [3,5,0,4,1]`
			`num_list.sort()`
			`print(num_list)`
				`[0,1,3,4,5]`

You must be confused between a method and a function. Observe the above two tables. Clearly, a **function** is a piece of code that is directly called by name. It may or may not accept parameters and may or may not return data. All data that is to be used by a function is explicitly passed (or made global). Example, *len(list1)*.

However, a **method** is a piece of code that is called by name of the object followed by a dot operator and name of the method. Example, *list1.sort()*.

PROGRAMMER'S ZONE

1. **Write a program that creates a list of numbers from 1-20 that are either divisible by 2 or divisible by 4 without using the filter function.**

```
div_2_4 = []
for i in range(2, 22):
    if(i%2 == 0 or i%4 == 0):
        div_2_4.append(i)
print(div_2_4)
```

> The `sort()` method uses ASCII values to sort the values in the list.

OUTPUT

```
[2, 4, 6, 8, 10, 12, 14, 16, 18, 20]
```

2. **Write a program to print the index at which a particular value exists. If the value exists at multiple locations in the list, then print all the indices. Also count the number of times that value is repeated in the list.**

```
num_list = [1,2,3,4,5,6,5,4,3,2,1]
num = int(input("Enter the value to be searched :
   "))
i=0
count = 0
while i<len(num_list):
    if num == num_list[i]:
        print(num, " found at location", i)
        count += 1
    i += 1
print(num, " appears ", count, " times in the list")
```

> An error is generated if you try to delete an element from the list or insert an element that is not present in the list.

> It is safer to avoid aliasing when you are working with mutable objects.

OUTPUT

```
Enter the value to be searched : 4
4  found at location 3
4  found at location 7
4  appears  2  times in the list
list_words = []
```

> When using slice operation, an IndexError is generated if the index is outside the list.

3. **Write a program that forms a list of first character of every word in another list.**

```
list1 = ["Hello", "Welcome", "To", "The", "World", "Of", "Python"]
letters = []
for word in list1:
    letters.append(word[0])
print(letters)
```

> The index must be an integer. If you specify a non-integer number as the index, then TypeError will be generated.

OUTPUT

```
['H', 'W', 'T', 'T', 'W', 'O', 'P']
```

4. **Write a program that counts the number of times each word is repeated in a list.**

```
words
=["abc","def","ghi","lmn","lmn","def","pqr","rst","abc","lmn","def","xyz"]
length = len(words)
```

```
dups = []
uniq = []
i = 0
for word in words:
    count = words.count(word)
    print(word,count, end = ' ')
    words.remove(word)
```

OUTPUT

```
abc 2    ghi 1    lmn 3    pqr 1    abc 1    def 3
```

5. Write a program to create a list of numbers in the specified range in particular steps. Reverse the list and print its values.

```
num_list = []
m = int(input("Enter the starting of the range : "))
n = int(input("Enter the ending of the range : "))
o = int(input("Enter the steps in the range : "))
for i in range(m,n, o):
    num_list.append(i)
print("Original List :", num_list)
num_list.reverse()
print("Reversed List : ", num_list)
```

OUTPUT

```
Enter the starting of the range : 2
Enter the ending of the range : 30
Enter the steps in the range : 3
Original List : [2, 5, 8, 11, 14, 17, 20, 23, 26, 29]
Reversed List :  [29, 26, 23, 20, 17, 14, 11, 8, 5, 2]
```

> `append()` and `insert()` methods are list methods. They cannot be called on other values such as string or integers.

6. Write a program that prints the largest and the second largest value in a list of numbers.

```
list = eval(input("ENter the list elements : "))
length = len(list)
largest = sec_largest = list[0]
for i in range(1,length-1):
    if(list[i]>largest):
        sec_largest = largest
        largest = list[i]
print("LARGEST = ", largest,"SECOND LARGEST = ",sec_largest)
```

OUTPUT

```
ENter the list elements : [9,4,0,2,11,7,6,5]
LARGEST =  11 SECOND LARGEST =  9
```

Key Terms

Immutable data: Data which cannot be modified. Assigning values to elements or slices of immutable data, results in a runtime error.

Mutable data value: Data which can be modified.

List: A mutable data structure that can have elements that belong to different data types.

Chapter Highlights

- List is a versatile data type available in Python, in which elements are written as a list of comma-separated values (items) between square brackets.
- Like strings, lists can also be sliced and concatenated.
- Once created, one or more elements of a list can be easily updated by giving the slice on the left-hand side of the assignment operator.
- We can append new values in the list and remove existing value(s) from the list using the `append()` method and del statement respectively.
- Lists behave in a similar way as strings when operators like + (concatenation) and * (repetition) are used.

Review Questions

1. What is a list?
2. How can we define a list in Python?
3. With the help of an example, demonstrate how a list can be sliced to access its values.
4. Explain the syntax of the slice operation.
5. What is the role of `del` statement with list variables?
6. Differentiate the use of `del` statement and `remove()` function?
7. Explain the purpose of the following functions:
   a. `sorted()` b. `sum()` c. `min()`
8. Name the function or the operator that can be used for the following tasks:
   a. Return length of list
   b. Repeat elements in the list
   c. Join two lists
   d. Check if the value is present in the list
   e. Return maximum value in the list.
9. Name the methods that can be used in the following situations:
   a. Append an element to the list
   b. Count the number of times an element appears in the list
   c. Returns the lowest index of obj in the list.
10. Explain the purpose of the following methods in Python:
    a. `insert()` b. `reverse()` c. `extend()`
11. Given a list, l = [1,2,3,4,5], write instructions for the following tasks:
    a. Set the third element to 100
    b. Insert 200 at the second index
    c. Append 300 to the list
    d. Remove the fourth element from the list
    e. Sort the list
    f. Reverse the list.

Programming Exercises

1. Write a program that creates a list of numbers in the series 2^n-1. Display only the even-indexed values in this list.
2. Write a program that prints the elements along with their indices from the start and end of the list.
3. Write a program that adds the corresponding elements of two lists.

4. Make a list of first ten letters of the alphabet, then using the slice operation do the following operations:
   a. Print the first three letters from the list.
   b. Print any three letters from the middle.
   c. Print the letters from any particular index to the end of the list.
5. Write a program that prints the maximum value of the second half of the list.
6. Write a program that finds the sum of all the numbers using a `while` loop.
7. Write a program that finds the sum of all even numbers in a list.
8. Write a program to find whether a particular element is present in the list using a loop.
9. Write a program that prompts a number from the user and adds it in a list. If the value entered by user is greater than 100, then add "EXCESS" in the list
10. Write a program that counts the number of times a value appears in the list. Use a loop to do the same.
11. Write a program to insert a value in a list at the specified location using `while` loop.
12. Write a program that creates a list of numbers from 1–50 that is either divisible by 3 or divisible by 6.
13. Write a program to create a list of numbers in the range 1 to 20. Then delete all the numbers from the list that are divisible by 3.

Fill in the Blanks

1. ___________ defines a particular way of storing and organizing data in a computer.
2. When using slice operation, __________ is generated if the index is outside the list.
3. [10,20] < [20,10] will return _______.
4. The `sort()` method uses ________ values to sort the values in the list.
5. Fill in the blanks to create a list and print its second element.
```
List = ___10, 20, 30, 40]
print(list[___])
```
6. Fill in the blanks to create a list, reassign its third element and print the list.
```
List = [1,2,3,4,5__
List[__] = 30
print(__)
```
7. Fill in the blanks to print "Hello" if the list contains 'H':
```
Letters = ['W', 'G', 'H']
__ 'H'__ Letters:
   print("_______")
```
8. Fill in the blanks to add 'G' to the end of the list and print the list's length.
```
Letters._____('G')
print(__ ___)
```
9. Fill in the blanks to print the letters in the list.
```
Letters = ['H', 'E', 'L', 'L','O']
___ i __Letters__
print(i)
```
10. Fill in the blanks to print the second element of the list, if it contains odd number of elements.
```
List =[10, 20, 30, 40, 50]
If ___(list)%2__0__
   print(List[__])
```

11. Fill in the banks to print the first two elements of the list:

```
List = [1,2,3,4,5,6]
print(list[0_])
```

12. The range of index values for a list of 10 elements will be ____.
13. `print(len([1,2,3] +[4,5]))` will print ________.

State True or False

1. The index value starts from zero.
2. List is an immutable data structure.
3. Once created, one or more elements of a list can be easily updated
4. It is possible to edit, add and delete elements from a list.
5. Slice operation can be used to insert items from another list or sequence at a particular location.
6. Items in a list can be deleted by assigning an empty list to a slice of elements.
7. If you specify a non-integer number as the index, then IndexError will be generated.
8. Python sorts the original list with the help of `sorted()` function.
9. In Python, the index of the first element in a list is zero.

Multiple Choice Questions

1. If `List = [1,2,3,4,5]` then `List[5]` will result in _____.
   a. 4　b. 3　c. 2　d. `Error`
2. If `List = [1,2,3,4,5]` and we write `List[3] = List[1]`, then what will be `List[3]` ?
   a. 1　b. 3　c. 2　d. 4
3. `type(x)` will print _____.
   a. `<class 'list'>`　b. `<class 'tuple'>`
   c. `<class 'int'>`　d. `Error`
4. If `List = [1,2,3,4,5,6,7,8,9,10]`, then print `List[8:4:-1]` will give _____.
   a. `[2,3,4,5]`　b. `[9,8,7,6]`
   c. `[6,7,8,9]`　d. `[5,4,3,2]`
5. If `List = min([sum([10,20]),max(abs(-30),4)])`, then List = _____.
   a. 10　b. 20　c. 30　d. 4
6. Which slice operation will reverse the list?
   a. `Lists[-1::]`　b. `numbers[::-1]`
   c. `numbers[:-1:]`　d. `List[9:8:1]`
7. If `List = (12,8,7,5)`, then `print(max(min(List[:2]),abs(-6)))` will print _____.
   a. 12　b. 8　c. 7　d. 5
8.
```
l1 = [1,2,3]
print(l1.append([4,5,6]))
print(l1)
```
   a. [1,2,3,4,5,6]　b. [1, 2, 3, [4, 5, 6]]
   c. [[1,2,3,4,5,6]]　d. None of these.

Give the Output

1. ```
   colors = ['red', 'blue', 'green']
   print(colors[2])
   print(len(colors))
   ```
2. ```
   list = ['abc', 'def', 'ghi', 'jkl']
   print(list[1:-1])
   list[0:2] = 'xyz'
   print(list)
   ```
3. ```
   list = ['abc', 'def', 'ghi', 'jkl', [1,2,3,4,5]]
   print(list[4][2])
   ```
4. ```
   list = ['p','r','o','g','r','a','m','m','i','n','g']
   print(list[2:5])
   print(list[:-5])
   print(list[5:])
   print(list[:])
   ```
5. ```
   even = [2,4,6]
   print(even + [10, 12, 14])
   print(even*2)
   even.insert(1,0)
   print(even)
   del even[2]
   print(even)
   ```
6. ```
   list = ['p','r','o','g','r','a','m']
   list.remove('p')
   print(list)
   ```
7. ```
   list = [9,4,3,8,0,2,3,6]
   print(list.index(3))
   print(list.count(8))
   list.sort()
   print(list)
   list.reverse()
   print(list)
   print(0 in list)
   ```
8. ```
   list = [10, 20, 30, 40, 50, 60, 70, 80, 90]
   print(list[-4:-1])
   print(list[-1:-4])
   print(list[-5:])
   print(list[-6:-2:2])
   print(list[::-1])
   ```
9. ```
   list = [[10, 20, [30, 40, [50, 60]]]]
   print(list[0])
   print(list[0][2])
   print(list[0][2][2])
   print(list[0][0])
   print(list[0][2][1])
   print(list[0][2][2][0])
   ```
   ```

10.
```
List = [100, 90, 80, 70, 60, 50]
List[2] = List[1] - 20
if 30 in List:
   print(List[3])
else:
   print(List[4])
```

11.
```
List = list(range(2, 20, 3))
print(List[5])
```

12.
```
str = "abcdefghijklmno"
for i in range(0, len(str), 2):
   print(str[i], end = ' ')
```

13.
```
print([ord(ch) for ch in 'PYTHON'])
```

14.
```
l1 = [1,2,3]
l2 = ['a','b','c']
l3 = [1.2,3.4,5.6]
l4 = l1 + l2 + l3
print(l4)
```

15.
```
print([1,2,8,9] < [1,2,8,9,10])
```

16.
```
l = [1,2,3,4,5,6,7,8,9,10]
print(l[-1])
print(l[l[0]])
print(l[l[-8]])
print(l[l[l[0]+1]]+2)
```

17.
```
msg = ["PYTHON","is","a",["simple","iterpreted","OOP"],"language"]
print(msg[2:4])
print(msg[2:4][1][2])
print(msg[2:4][1][2][1])
print("im" in msg[2:4][1][2][1])
print(msg[2:4][1][1][3:])
print(msg[1]+msg[4])
```

18.
```
>>> [1,2,3] +[1,2,3] == [1,2,3]*2
```

19.
```
l = [1,2,3]
l * 3 == [1,1,1]
```

20.
```
msg = ["PYTHON","is","a",["simple","interpreted","OOP"],"language"]
print(msg[::2])
print('n' in msg[4])
print(msg[2] in msg[4])
```

21.
```
l = [1,2,3]
print((l + [4,5,6])[3])
```

22.
```
[1,2] == [1,2]
```

23.
```
[1,2] is [1,2]
```

24.
```
L = [1,2,3,4,5,6,7,8,9,10,11,12,13,14]
print(L[::-1])
print(L[-1:-2:-3])
```

Find the Error

1. ```
   list = ['abc', 'def', 'ghi', 'jkl']
   print list[2.0]
   ```
2. ```
   even = [2,4,6]
   del even
   print(even)
   ```
3. ```
   list = [(1, 2), [3, 4], '56', 78, 9.0]
   list.remove('abc')
   ```
4. ```
   msg = "Hello"
   msg.append("World")
   print(msg)
   ```
5. ```
   [1,2,3] + 2
   ```
6. ```
   L = [1,2,3,4]
   L.remove(7)
   ```
7. ```
   [1,2,3] * 3.0
   ```

AI Lab Session – Imaginary Soundscape

Imaginary Soundscape is a Web-based sound installation on Google Street view. Created using deep-learning models, the application facilitates users to imagine sounds by taking a glance at a photo. For example, a beach scene is displayed with the sound of crashing waves. Similarly, when viewing a busy road, the sounds of horns and street advertising can be heard. "Imaginary Soundscape" allows users to freely walk around Google Street View and immerse themselves into imaginary soundscapes generated using deep-learning techniques. To use this application, visit the URL: http://www.imaginarysoundscape.net/

   ```

Answers

Fill in the Blanks

1. Data structure
2. `IndexError`
3. True
4. ASCII
5. `[, 1`
6. `], 2, List`
7. `if, in, Hello`
8. `append, len, (, Letters,)`
9. `for, in,:`
10. `len, !=, :, 1`
11. `:2`
12. 0–10
13. 5

State True or False

1. True
2. False
3. True
4. True
5. True
6. True
7. False
8. True
9. True

Multiple Choice Questions

1. b
2. c
3. d
4. b
5. c
6. b
7. b
8. b

Give the Output

1. green, 3
2. ['def', 'ghi']
   ['xyz', 'ghi', 'jkl']
3. 3
4. ['o', 'g', 'r']
   ['p', 'r', 'o', 'g', 'r', 'a']
   ['a', 'm', 'm', 'i', 'n', 'g']
   ['p', 'r', 'o', 'g', 'r', 'a', 'm', 'm', 'i', 'n', 'g']
5. [2, 4, 6, 10, 12, 14]
   [2, 4, 6, 2, 4, 6]
   [2, 0, 4, 6]
   [2, 0, 6]
6. ['r', 'o', 'g', 'r', 'a', 'm']
   o
   ['r', 'g', 'r', 'a', 'm']
   m
   ['r', 'g', 'r', 'a']
7. 2
   1
   [0, 2, 3, 3, 4, 6, 8, 9]
   [9, 8, 6, 4, 3, 3, 2, 0]
   True
8. [60, 70, 80]
   []
   [50, 60, 70, 80, 90]
   [40, 60]
   [90, 80, 70, 60, 50, 40, 30, 20, 10]
9. [10, 20, [30, 40, [50, 60]]]
   [30, 40, [50, 60]]
   [50, 60]
   10
   40
   50
10. 60
11. 17
12. a c e g i k m o
13. [80, 89, 84, 72, 79, 78]
14. [1, 2, 3, 'a', 'b', 'c', 1.2, 3.4, 5.6]
15. True
16. 10 2 4 6
17. ['a', ['simple', 'iterpreted', 'OOP']]
    OOP O False rpreted islanguage
18. True
19. False

20. ['PYTHON', 'a', 'language']

True

True

21. ['PYTHON', 'a', 'language']

True True

22. True

23. False

24. [14, 13, 12, 11, 10, 9, 8, 7, 6, 5, 4, 3, 2, 1]

[14]

Find the Error

1. `TypeError: list indices must be integers, not float`
2. `NameError: name 'even' is not defined`
3. `ValueError: list.remove(x): x not in list`
4. `AttributeError: 'str' object has no attribute 'append'`
5. `TypeError: can only concatenate list (not "int") to list`
6. `ValueError: list.remove(x): x not in list`
7. `TypeError: can't multiply sequence by non-int of type 'float'`

Tuples and Dictionaries

10

Chapter Objectives

In this chapter, we shall discuss three more very important data structures in Python. These are tuples, dictionaries and sets. Each of them supports a different set of functionalities and thus has a unique utility. Here, we will cover the technicalities in:

- Creating a tuple
- Accessing values and performing basic operations on a tuple
- Creating dictionaries and accessing values stored in it
- Adding, deleting and traversing a dictionary
- Working with sets

A tuple is very similar to lists but differs in two things.

- First, a tuple is an immutable object. This means that while you can change the value of one or more elements in a list, you cannot change the values in a tuple.
- Second, tuples use parentheses to define their elements whereas lists use square brackets.

10.1 CREATING TUPLE

Creating a tuple is very simple and almost similar to creating a list. You need to just put the different comma-separated values within a parenthesis.

#Creates an empty tuple **Tup1 = ()** print(Tup1) **OUTPUT** ()	**#Creates tuple with a single element** **Tup1 = (5,)** print(Tup1) **OUTPUT** 5	**#Tuple of integers** **Tup1 = (1,2,3,4,5)** print(Tup1) **OUTPUT** (1, 2, 3, 4, 5)
#Creates a tuple of **#mixed values** Tup5 = (1,"abc" ,2.3,'d') print(Tup5) **OUTPUT** (1, 'abc', 2.3, 'd')	**#A tuple of characters** Tup1 = ('a','b','c','d') print(Tup1) **OUTPUT** ('a', 'b', 'c', 'd')	**# Creates a tuple of strings** Tup1 = ("abc",''def",''ghi") print(Tup1) **OUTPUT** ('abc', 'def', 'ghi')
#Tuple of floating-point **#numbers** Tup1 = (1.2,2.3,3.4,4.5) print(Tup1) **OUTPUT** (1.2, 2.3, 3.4, 4.5)		

Key points to remember

- Any set of comma-separated values written without an identifying symbol like brackets or parentheses, etc., is treated as a tuple by default.
- If you want to create a tuple with a single element, you must add a comma after the element. In the absence of a comma, Python treats the element as an ordinary data type.
- We can use the `eval()` function to input a tuple. But while specifying the input elements, enclose them within parentheses as shown in Example 10.3.

Example 10.1

```
print('A', "bed", 5, 6.7)
```

OUTPUT

```
A bcd 5 6.7
```

```
a,b,c = 10, 20,30
print(a,b,c)
```

OUTPUT

```
10 20 30
```

Example 10.2

```
# comma after first element
Tup = (15,)
print type(Tup)
```

OUTPUT

```
<type 'tuple'>
```

```
#comma missing
Tup = (10)
print type(Tup)
```

OUTPUT

```
<type 'int'>
```

Example 10.3

```
#eval() Function to read Tuple
Tup = eval(input("Enter values of the tuple :"))
print(Tup)
print(type(Tup))
```

OUTPUT

```
Enter values of the tuple: (1,2,'a','bcd',7.8)
(1, 2, 'a', 'bcd', 7.8)
<class 'tuple'>
```

- We can also use the `tuple()` function to create a tuple with the specified sequence.

Example 10.4

```
#Using the tuple() Function
tup = tuple("abc")
print(tup)
tup = tuple ([1, 2,3))
print(tup)
```

OUTPUT

```
('a' , ' b ', 'c ")
(1, 2 , 3)
```

10.2 UTILITY OF TUPLES

In real-world applications, tuples are extremely useful for representing *records* or structures as we call in other programming languages. These structures store related information about a subject together. The information belongs to different data types. For example, a tuple that stores information about a student will have roll_no, name, course, total_marks, avg, etc. If you carefully observe these individual elements, you will see that they belong to different data types. For example, roll_no can be an integer or an alphanumeric value, name and course will be string, total_marks and avg can be floating-point numbers.

Example 10.5

```
Program to illustrates divmod() function
quo, rem = divmod(157,4)
print("Quotient = ",quo)
print("Remainder = ",rem)
```

OUTPUT

```
Quotient= 39
Remainder= 1
```

Some built-in functions return a tuple. For example, the **divmod()** function returns two values – quotient as well as the remainder after performing the divide operation.

Example 10.6

```
Tup1 = (1,20,3,40,5,60,7,80,9,100,11,120)
print("Tup[4:8] = ", Tup1[4:8])
print("Tup[:5] = ", Tup1[:5])
print("Tup[3:] = ", Tup1(3:])
print("Tup[:] = ", Tup1[:])
print("Tup[:-4] =", Tup1[:-4])
print("Tup[-1:5] =", Tup1[-1:5])
print("Tup[::-2] =", Tup1[::-2])
```

OUTPUT

```
Tup[4:8] = (5, 60, 7, 80)
Tup[:5] = (1, 20, 3, 40, 5)
Tup[3:] = (40, 5, 60, 7, 80, 9, 100, 11, 120)
Tup[:] = (1, 20, 3, 40, 5, 60, 7, 80, 9, 100, 11, 120)
Tup[:-4] = (1, 20, 3, 40, 5, 60, 7, 80)
Tup[-1:5] = ()
Tup[::-2] = (120, 100, 80, 60, 40, 20)
```

10.3 ACCESSING VALUES IN A TUPLE

Again, like other sequences (like strings and lists), indices in a tuple start at 0. Slice operation, concatenation and other operations possible with other sequences can also be applied on tuples.

In the slice operation, we can also use negative indices, strides and even expressions.

When accessing a tuple, if the index is out of the range of legal indices of the tuple, then Python raises an IndexError.

The start and stop parameters of the slice operation specify the boundaries of elements to be accessed. All elements falling within the boundary are returned.

Example 10.7

```
#Slice operation on a tuple
tup = (1,'a',2,'bcd',3.4,5,'e',6.7,'efg')
print(tup[3])
print(tup[10 - 4 *2 + 5])
print(tup[-5])
print(tup[3:6])
print(tup[2:7:2])
print(tup[-10:10])
```

OUTPUT

```
bcd
6.7
3.4
('bcd', 3.4, 5)
(2, 3.4, 'e')
(1, 'a', 2, 'bed', 3.4, 5, 'e', 6.7, 'efg')
```

Example 10.8

```
tup = (1,2,3)
print(tup[10])
```

OUTPUT

```
Traceback (most recent call last):
  File "C:\Python37\try.py",line 2, in <module>
print(tup[10])
IndexError: tuple index out of range
```

```
tup = (1,2,3)
print(tup[ -10: 10])
```

OUTPUT

```
(1, 2, 3)
```

10.4 UPDATING TUPLE

We have already said that ***tuple is immutable***. So, you cannot change the value(s) in the tuple. You can only extract values from a tuple to form another tuple.

Example 10.9

```
#Updating tuple
tup = (1,'a ',2,'bcd',3.4,5,'e')
tup[3] = 'Not Possible'
print(tup)
```

OUTPUT

```
Traceback (most recent call last):
  File "C:\Python37\try.py",line 2, in <module>
    tup(3] = 'Not Possible'
TypeError: 'tuple' object does not support item assignment
```

10.5 DELETING ELEMENTS IN TUPLE

Since tuple is an immutable data structure, you cannot delete value(s) from it. Of course, you can create a new tuple that has all elements in your tuple except the ones you don't want (those you wanted to be deleted). However, the entire tuple can be deleted by using the `del` statement.

Example 10.10

```
Tup1 = (1,2,3,4,5)
Tup2 = (6,7,8,9,10)
Tup3 = Tup1 + Tup2
print(Tup3)
```

OUTPUT

```
(1, 2, 3, 4, 5, 6, 7, 8,
9, 10)
```

```
Tup1 = (1,2,3,4,5)
del Tup1[3) #delete an element
print(Tup1)
```

OUTPUT

```
Traceback (most recent call last):
  File "C:\Users\Python37\try.py", line 2, in <module>
    del Tup1[3]
Type Error: 'tuple' object doesn't support item deletion
```

```
Tup1 = (1,2,3,4,5)
#delete tuple
de1Tup1
print(Tupl)
```

OUTPUT

```
Traceback (most recent call last):
  File "C:\Users\Python37\try.py", line 4, in <module>
    print(Tupl)
NameError: name 'Tupl' is not defined
```

10.6 BASIC TUPLE OPERATIONS

Like strings and lists, you can also perform operations such as concatenation, repetition, etc., on tuples. The only difference is that a new tuple should be created when a change is required in an existing tuple. Table 10.1 summarizes some operations on tuples.

Table 10.1 Operations on tuples

Operation	Expression	Output
Length	`len((1,2,3,4,5,6))`	`6`
Concatenation	`(1,2,3) + (4,5,6)`	`(1, 2, 3, 4, 5, 6)`
Repetition	`('Python..')*3`	`Python.. Python.. Python..'`
Membership	`5 in (1,2,3,4,5,6,7,8,9)`	`True`

Iteration	`for i in`
	`(1,2,3,4,5,6,7,8,9,10):`
	`    print(i,end=' ')`
		`1,2,3,4,5,6,7,8,9,10`

Comparison (Use >, <, ==)	`Tup1 = (1,2,3,4,5)`
	`Tup2 = (1,2,3,4,5)`
	`print(Tup1>Tup2)`
		`False`

Maximum	`max(1,9,3,6,4,0)`	`9`
Minimum	`min(1,9,3,6,4,0)`	`0`
Convert to tuple (converts a sequence into a tuple)	`tuple("PYTHON")` `tuple([1,2,3,4,5])`	`('P', 'Y', 'T', 'H', 'O', 'N')` `(1, 2, 3, 4, 5)`

While using the **`max()`** and **`min()`** functions, remember that the values in the tuple must be of the same type. if the values are not of the same type, then **TypeError** will be returned.

Example 10.11

```
# Finding largest and smallest value
tup = (23,75,12,90,82)
print("Largest Value= ",max(tup))
print("Smallest Value = ",min(tup))
```

OUTPUT

```
Largest Value = 90
Smallest Value = 12
```

```
#Finding largest and smallest value in a tuple
tup = (23,'a',12.56,90,'bcd')
print("Largest Value= ",max(tup))
print("Smallest Value = ",min(tup))
```

OUTPUT

```
Traceback (most recent call last):
  File "C:\Python37\try.py", line 3, in <module>
    print("largest Value = ",max(tup))
TypeError: '>'not supported between instances
of 'str' and 'int'
```

10.7 TUPLE ASSIGNMENT

Tuple assignment is a very powerful feature in Python. It allows a tuple of variables on the left side of the assignment operator to be assigned values from a tuple given on the right side of the assignment operator. Each value is assigned to its respective variable.

In case an expression is specified on the right side of the assignment operator, first that expression is evaluated and then assignment is done. This feature makes tuple assignment quite versatile. The codes given below show the different ways of tuple assignment.

Example 10.12

```
#An unnamed tuple of values assigned to values of
#another unnamed tuple
(val1, val2, val3) = (10,20,30)
print(val1, val2, val3)
Tupl = (10, 20, 30)
(val1, val2, val3) = Tupl #tuple assigned to
another tuple
print(val1, val2, val3)
```

OUTPUT

```
10 20 30
10 20 30
```

```
#Expressions are evaluated
before assignment
(val1, val2, val3, val4)= (1+2,
4/3 - 5 , 6%7, 8 ** 2)
print(val1, val2, val3, val4)
```

OUTPUT

```
3 -3.666666666666667 6 64
```

Example 10.13

```
(val1, val2, val3, val4)= (1+2, 6%7, 8 ** 2)
print(val1, val2, val3, val4)
Traceback (most recent call last):
  File "C:\Users\Python37\try.py", line 1, in <module>
    (val1, val2, val3, val4)= (1+2, 6%7, 8 ** 2)
ValueError: not enough values to unpack (expected 4, got 3)
```

Note that ***when assigning values to a tuple, you must make sure that the number of values on both the sides of the assignment operator must be same.*** Otherwise, an error will be generated as shown in Example 10.13.

10.8 DICTIONARIES

Dictionary is a data structure in which we store values as a **pair of key and value.** Each key is separated from its value by a colon (:), and consecutive items are separated by commas. The entire set of items in a dictionary is enclosed in curly braces ({}). The syntax for defining a dictionary is

```
dictionary_name = {key_1: value_1, key_2: value_2, key_3: value_3}
```

If there are many keys and values in dictionaries, then we can also write just one key-value pair on a line to make the code easier to read and understand. This is shown below.

```
dictionary_name = {key_1: value_1,
                   key_2: value_2,
                   key_3: value_3,
                  }
```

> Using a mutable object as a dictionary key causes a TypeError.

While keys in the ***dictionary must be unique and be of any immutable data type (like strings, numbers, or tuples), there is no stringent requirement for uniqueness and type of values.*** That is, value of a key can be of any type. Remember that dictionaries are not sequences, rather they are **mappings**. Mappings are collections of objects that store objects by key instead of by relative position.

Dictionary is like an associative array (also known as hashes) in which any key of the dictionary can be associated or mapped to a value.

10.9 CREATING A DICTIONARY

The syntax to create an empty dictionary can be given as **`dictionary_variable = []`**, and the syntax to create a dictionary with key-value pairs is: `dictionary_variable = {key1 : val1, key2 : val2, ...}`. In this syntax, we can specify key-value pairs separated by a colon in curly brackets as shown in Example 10.14.

Example 10.14

```
#To create an empty dictionary
Dict = {}
print Dict
```

OUTPUT

```
{}
```

```
#Create a dictionary with key-value pairs
Dict = {'EMP NO' : '123', 'Name' : 'Aaditya',
'Department': 'SALES'}
print(Dict)
```

OUTPUT

```
{'EMP NO': '123', 'Name': 'Aaditya',
'Department': 'SALES'}
```

10.9.1 Creating Dictionary Using dict() Method

To create a dictionary with one or more key-value pairs you can also use the `dict()` function. The `dict()` creates a dictionary directly from a sequence of key-value pairs. For example, the line of code given in Example 10.15 creates a dictionary using a list of key-value pairs.

Example 10.15

```
#Creating a dictionary using dict() function
Dict = dict([('EMP _NO', '123'),('Name', Aaditya'),('Department', 'SALES')])
print(Dict)
```

OUTPUT

```
{'EMP NO': '123', 'Name': 'Aaditya', 'Department': 'SALES'}
```

We can enclose the keys and values in a separate tuple and then use them as argument in the `zip()` function. The output of the zip function can then be passed as an argument to the `dict()` function so that the dictionary can be created using the two tuples.

Note that in the program, the `zip()` function clubs the first value from the heads tuple with the first value in the `vals` tuple; then the second value from both the tuples are clubbed; and finally the third value is clubbed.

Example 10.16

```
#Creating dictionary using keys and values that
#are stored as tuples
heads = ('Roll No','Name','Marks')
vals = ('101','Mishti',99)
Student = dict(zip(heads,vals))
print(Student)
```

OUTPUT

```
{'Roll No': '101', 'Name': 'Mishti', 'Marks': 99}
```

10.10 ACCESSING VALUES IN A DICTIONARY

To access values in a dictionary, square brackets are used along with the key to obtain its value. Note that if you try to access an item with a key, which is not specified in the dictionary, a KeyError is generated.

Example 10.17

```
#Accessing dictionary values
Dict= {'EMP NO' : '123', 'Name' : 'Aaditya',
'Department' : 'SALES'}
print("Dict[EMP NO) = ", Dict['EMP_NO'])
print("Dict[Name) = ", Dict['Name'])
print("Dict[Department] =", Dict['Department'])
```

OUTPUT

```
Dict[EMP_NO) = 123
Dict[Name] = Aaditya
Dict[Department] = SALES
```

```
# Accessing key which is not present in dictionary
Dict= {'EMP NO' : '123', 'Name' : 'Aaditya'}
print("Dict[EMP_NO) =", Dict['EMP_NO'])
print("Dict[Name] = ", Dict['Name'])
print("Dict[Department] =", Dict['Department'])
```

OUTPUT

```
Dict[EMP NO)= 123
Dict[ Name]= Aaditya
Traceback (most recent call last):
  File "C:\Users\Python37\try.py", line 4, in <module>
    print("Dict[Department] =",Dict['Department'])
KeyError: 'Department'
```

10.11 ADDING AN ITEM IN A DICTIONARY

To add a new entry or a key-value pair in a dictionary, just specify the key-value pair as you had done for the existing pairs. The syntax to add an item in a dictionary is, **dictionary_variable[key] = val.**

10.12 MODIFYING AN ITEM IN A DICTIONARY

To modify an entry, just overwrite the existing value with the new value.

Example 10.18

```
# adding and modifying values in a dictionary
Dict= {'EMP _NO' : '123', 'Name' : 'Aaditya'}
print("Original dictionary", Dict)
Dict['Department']= 'Sales' #new key-value pair added
Dict['Name']= 'Aadi' #existing value modified
print("Updated Dictionary",Dict)
```

OUTPUT

```
Original dictionary {'EMP_NO': '123', 'Name': 'Aaditya'}
Updated Dictionary {'EMP_NO': '123', 'Name': 'Aadi', 'Department': 'Sales'}
```

10.13 DELETING ITEMS

One or more items in a dictionary can be deleted using the **del** keyword. To delete or remove all the items in just one statement, use the **clear()** function. Note that the clear() method does not delete the dictionary, it just deletes all the elements inside the dictionary. To remove an entire dictionary from the memory, we can again use the del statement as **del Dict_name**. The syntax to use the del statement can be given as, **del dictionary_variable[key]**.

Example 10.19

```
#deleting entries and the entire dictionary
Dict= {'EMP _NO': '123', 'Name': 'Aaditya','Department': 'Sales'}
print("Original Dictionary", Dict)
del Dict['EMP _ NO'] #a particular key-value pair deleted
print("After deleteing EMP _NO", Dict)
```

```
Dict.clear() #all entries deleted
print("After deleteing all entries ", Dict)
del Dict #delete dictionary
print("Printing Dictionary after deleting it", Dict)
```

OUTPUT

```
Original Dictionary {'EMP NO': '123', 'Name': 'Aaditya', 'Department': 'Sales'}
After deleteing EMP _NO {'Name': 'Aaditya', 'Department': 'Sales'}
After deleteing all entries {}
Traceback (most recent call last):
  File "C:\Users\Python37\try.py", line 8, in <module>
    print("Printing Dictionary after deleting it", Dict)
NameError: name 'Dict' is not defined
```

10.14 TRAVERSING A DICTIONARY

Looping over a dictionary can be done to access only values, only keys or both, using the `for` loop. We can use the `items()` method that returns a list of tuples (key-value pair). The `keys()` method returns a list of keys in the dictionary. The `values()` method returns a list of values in the dictionary.

Example 10.20

```
#Program to access items in a dictionary
Dict: = {'EMP _ NO' : '123', 'Name' : ' Aaditya'.'Department' : 'Sales',
'EMP_NO' : '456'}
print:("KEYS : " ,end = ' ')
for key in Dict:
  print:(key, end ='') #accessing only keys
print("\nVALUES : ", end = ' ')
for val in Dict:.values():
  print(val, end = ' ') # accessing only values
print("\nDICTIONARY . ", end = ' ')
for key, val in Dict.items():
  print:(key, val, "\t", end = ' ') # accessing keys and values
```

OUTPUT

```
KEYS : EMP_NO Name Department
VALUES : 456 Aaditya Sales
DICTIONARY : EMP_NO 456    Name Aaditya    Department Sales
```

10.15 SETS

Sets is another data structure supported by Python. Basically, sets are same as lists but with a difference that sets are lists with no duplicate entries. Technically, a set is a mutable and an unordered collection of items. This means that we can easily add or remove items from it.

10.15.1 Creating a Set

A set is created by placing all the elements inside curly brackets `{}`, separated by comma or by using the built-in function `set()`. The syntax of creating a set can be given as,

```
set_variable = {val1, val2, …}
```

For example, to create a set you can write,

```
>>> s = {1,2.0,"abc"}
>>> print( s)
set([1, 2.0,'abc'])
```

A set can have any number of items and they may be of different data types. For example, the code given in Example 10.21 creates a set using the `set()` function. The code converts a list of different types of values into a set.

The program given in Example 10.22 demonstrates different ways of creating sets, that is, sets being created by using a list, tuple or string.

> If we add the same element multiple times in a set, they are removed because a set cannot have duplicate values.

Example 10.21

Program to convert a list of values into a set.

```
s = set([1,2,'a','b',"def",4.56])
print(s)
```

OUTPUT

```
set(['a', 1, 2, 'b', 4.56, 'def'])
```

Example 10.22

```
List1 = [1,2,3,4,5,6,5,4,3,2,1]
print(set(List1))  # list is converted into a set
Tup1 = ('a','b','c','d','b','e','a')
print(set(Tup1))   # tuple is converted into a set
str = "abcdefabcdefg"
print(set(str))              # string is converted into a set
# forms a set of words
print(set("She sells sea shells on the sea shore".split()))
```

OUTPUT

```
set([1, 2, 3, 4, 5, 6])
set(['a', 'c', 'b', 'e', 'd'])
set(['a', 'c', 'b', 'e', 'd', 'g', 'f'])
set(['on', 'shells', 'shore', 'She', 'sea', 'sells', 'the'])
```

As in the case of mathematical sets, Python sets are also powerful tools as they have the ability to calculate differences and intersections between other sets. Figure 10.1(a–d) given below demonstrates various set operations.

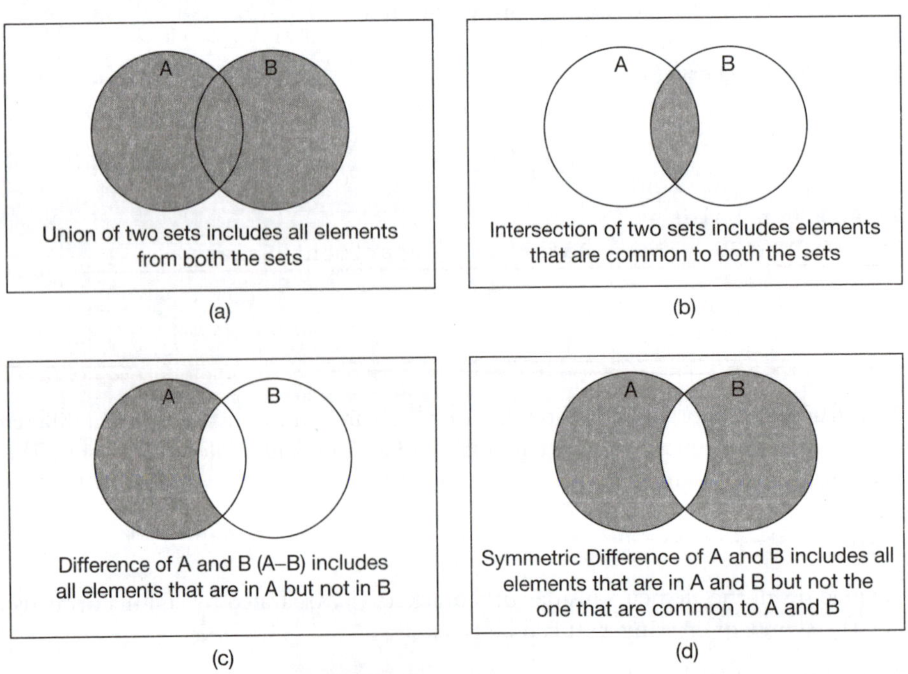

Figure 10.1 Set operations

Example 10.23 Program to find intersection, union, and symmetric difference between two sets.

```
Coders = set(["Arnav","Goransh","Mani","Parul"])
Analysts = set(["Krish","Mehak","Shiv","Goransh","Mani"])
print("Coders : ", Coders)
print("Analysts : ", Analysts)
print("People working as codes as well as analysts : ", Coders.intersection(Analysts))
print("People workinga s Coders or Analysts : ", Coders.union(Analysts))
print("People working as Coders but not Analysts : ", Coders.difference(Analysts))
print("People working as Analysts but not Coders : ", Analysts.difference(Coders))
print("People working in only one of the groups : ", Coders.symmetric_
difference(Analysts))
```

OUTPUT

```
Coders :  set(['Arnav', 'Parul', 'Mani', 'Goransh'])
Analysts :  set(['Shiv', 'Goransh', 'Krish', 'Mani', 'Mehak'])
People working as codes as well as analysts :  set(['Mani', 'Goransh'])
People workinga s Coders or Analysts :  set(['Krish', 'Parul', 'Goransh', 'Arnav',
'Mani', 'Mehak', 'Shiv'])
People working as Coders but not Analysts :  set(['Arnav', 'Parul'])
People working as Analysts but not Coders :  set(['Krish', 'Shiv', 'Mehak'])
People working in only one of the groups :  set(['Krish', 'Parul', 'Mehak',
'Arnav', 'Shiv'])
```

Some other operations that can be performed on sets are discussed in Table 10.2. But before going through this table, it is good to remember the following points.

- Two sets are equal if and only if every element in each set is contained in the other
- A set is less than another set if and only if the first set is a subset of the second set
- A set is greater than another set if and only if the first set is a superset of the second set.

> The `update()` method can take tuples, lists, strings or other sets as its argument.

Table 10.2 Set operations

Operation	Description	Code	Output

`s.update(t)`	Adds elements of set t in the set s provided that all duplicates are avoided	`s = set([1,2,3,4,5])`
		`t = set([6,7,8])`
		`s.update(t)`
		`print(s)`
			`(1, 2, 3, 4, 5, 6, 7, 8)`

`s.add(x)`	Adds element x to the set s provided that all duplicates are avoided	`s = set([1,2,3,4,5])`
		`s.add(6)`
		`print(s)`
			`(1, 2, 3, 4, 5, 6)`

`s.remove(x)`	Removes element x from set s. Returns KeyError if x is not present	`s = set([1,2,3,4,5])`
		`s.remove(3)`
		`print(s)`
			`(1, 2, 4, 5)`

`len(s)`	Returns the length of set	`s = set([1,2,3,4,5])` `print(len(s))`	`5`

(Continued)

<table>
<tr><th>Operation</th><th>Description</th><th>Code</th><th>Output</th></tr>
<tr><td>x in s</td><td>Returns True if x is present in set s and False, otherwise</td><td>s = set([1,2,3,4,5])
print(3 in s)</td><td>True</td></tr>
<tr><td>x not in s</td><td>Returns True if x is not present in set s and False, otherwise</td><td>s = set([1,2,3,4,5])
print(6 not in s)</td><td>True</td></tr>
<tr><td>s.issubset(t) or s<=t</td><td>Returns True if every element in s is present in set t and False, otherwise</td><td>s = set([1,2,3,4,5])
t =
set([1,2,3,4,5,6,7,8,9,10])
print(s<=t)</td><td>True</td></tr>
<tr><td>s.issuperset(t) or s>=t</td><td>Returns True if every element in t is present in set s and False, otherwise</td><td>s = set([1,2,3,4,5])
t =
set([1,2,3,4,5,6,7,8,9,10])
print(s.issuperset(t))</td><td>False</td></tr>
<tr><td>s.union(t) or s|t</td><td>Returns a set s that has elements from both sets s and t</td><td>s = set([1,2,3,4,5])
t =
set([1,2,3,4,5,6,7,8,9,10])
print(s|t)</td><td>(1, 2, 3, 4, 5, 6, 7, 8, 9, 10)</td></tr>
<tr><td>s.intersection(t) or s&t</td><td>Returns a new set that has elements which are common to both the sets s and t</td><td>s = set([1,2,3,4,5])
t =
set([1,2,3,4,5,6,7,8,9,10])
z = s&t
print(z)</td><td>(1,2,3,4,5)</td></tr>
<tr><td>s.intersection_update(t)</td><td>Returns a set that has elements which are common to both the sets s and t</td><td>s = set([1,2,10,12])
t =
set([1,2,3,4,5,6,7,8,9,10])
s.intersection_update(t)
print(s)</td><td>(1, 2, 10)</td></tr>
<tr><td>max(s)</td><td>Returns the maximum value in a set</td><td>s = set([0,1,2,3,4,5])
print(max(s))</td><td>5</td></tr>
<tr><td>min(s)</td><td>Returns the minimum value in a set</td><td>s = set([0,1,2,3,4,5])
print(min(s))</td><td>0</td></tr>
<tr><td>sum(s)</td><td>Returns the sum of elements in the set</td><td>s = set([0,1,2,3,4,5])
print(sum(s))</td><td>15</td></tr>
<tr><td>sorted(s)</td><td>Returns a new sorted list from the elements in the set. It does not sort the set as sets are immutable.</td><td>s = set([5,4,3,2,1,0])
print(sorted(s))</td><td>[0, 1, 2, 3, 4, 5]</td></tr>
</table>

PROGRAMER'S ZONE

1. **Write a program that has a dictionary of metropolitan cities and their codes. Add another city in the pre-defined dictionary; print all the items in the dictionary and try to print the code for a city that does not exist. Set a default value prior to printing.**

```
Codes = {'Delhi' : '011', 'Mumbai' : '022', 'Chennai' : '044'}
Codes['Kolkatta'] = '033'       # add another state
Codes.setdefault('','Sorry, no idea')
print("Code for Kolkatta is : ", Codes['Kolkatta'])
print("-" * 5, "CODES", "-" * 5)
for i in Codes.items():
    print(i)
print("Code for Mumbai : ", Codes.get('Mumbai'))
```

OUTPUT

```
(Code for Kolkatta is :  033
----- CODES -----
('Delhi', '011')
('Mumbai', '022')
('Chennai', '044')
('Kolkatta', '033')
('', 'Sorry, no idea')
Code for Mumbai :  022
```

> Dictionary keys are case-sensitive. Two keys with same name but in different case are not the same in Python.

2. **Write a program that creates a dictionary of squares and cubes of numbers entered by the user .**

```
print("Enter -1 to exit....")
Squares = {}
while True:
    r = int(input("Enter number : "))
    if r == -1:
        break
    else:
        Dict = {r:[r*r , r*r*r]}
        Squares.update(Dict)
print(Squares)
```

> In Python, "None" is a special value like null or nil, which means no value.

OUTPUT

```
Enter -1 to exit....
Enter number : 3
Enter number : 5
Enter number : 2
Enter number : 7
Enter number : -1
{3: [9, 27], 5: [25, 125], 2: [4, 8], 7: [49, 343]}
```

3. **Write a program that has a set of words in English language and their corresponding words in Hindi. Define another dictionary that has a list of words in Hindi and their corresponding words in Urdu. Take all words from the English language and display their meanings in both the languages.**

```
E_H = {'Friend' : 'Mitr', 'Teacher' : 'Shikshak', 'Book' : 'Pustak', 'Queen' : 'Rani'}
H_U = {'Mitr' : 'Dost', 'Shikshak' : 'Adhyapak', 'Pustak' : 'Kitab', 'Rani' : 'Begum'}
for i in E_H:
    print(i, "in Hindi means", E_H[i], "and in Urdu means", H_U[E_H[i]])
```

OUTPUT

```
Book in Hindi means Pustak and in Urdu means Kitab
Teacher in Hindi means Shikshak and in Urdu means Adhyapak
Friend in Hindi means Mitr and in Urdu means Dost
Queen in Hindi means Rani and in Urdu means Begum
```

4. **Write a program to count the number of characters in the string and store them in a dictionary data structure.**

```
str = "Python is a wonderful programming language"
len = len(str)
Dict = {str:len}
print(Dict)
```

Trying to index a key that isn't part of the dictionary returns a KeyError.

A KeyError occurs on an invalid access of a key, like when a key that is used is not present in dictionary.

OUTPUT

```
{'Python is a wonderful programming language': 42}
```

5. **Write a program that finds whether or not a particular value is present in the dictionary or not. Do not use the `values()` method.**

```
Dict = {"Amna":4,"Brij":2,"Chaitanya":5,"Divyanka":3}
v = int(input("Enter the value to be searched : "))
flag = 0
for i in Dict:
    if(Dict[i] == v):
        print(i)
        flag = 1
if(flag == 0):
    print("Value not present")
```

`sorted ()` takes any sequence as a parameter and returns a new list with the same elements but in a different order.

OUTPUT

```
Enter the value to be searched : 5
Chaitanya
```

6. **Write a program that has a dictionary of states and their codes. Add another state in the pre-defined dictionary; print all the items in the dictionary and try to print the code for a state that does not exist. Set a default value prior to printing.**

```
states = {'Delhi' : 'DL', 'Maharashtra' : 'MH', 'Tamil Nadu' : 'TN', 'Rajasthan'
    : 'RJ'}
states['Tamil Nadu'] = 'TN'      # add another state
states.setdefault('Karnataka','Sorry, no idea')
print("Code for Rajasthan is : ", states['Rajasthan'])
print("-" * 5, "CODES", "-" * 5)
```

```
for i in states.items():
    print(i)
print("Code for Karnataka : ", states.get('Karnataka'))
```

7. **Write a program that has a list of countries. Create a set of the countries and print the names of the countries in sorted order.**

```
countries = ['India', 'Russia', 'China', 'Brazil', 'England']
C_set = sorted(set(countries))
Print(C_set)
```

OUTPUT

```
['Brazil', 'China', 'England', 'India', 'Russia']
```

Key Terms

Tuple: An immutable data structure that stores related items together.

Dictionary: A collection of key-value pairs that maps the keys to values. While a key can be of any immutable type, there is no such restriction on its associated value, which can be of any type.

Key: Data that is *mapped to* a value in a dictionary. Keys are unique data items that are used to look-up values in a dictionary.

Key-value pair: A pair of items in a dictionary. Key is used to look-up for a value stored in the dictionary.

Chapter Highlights

- A tuple is an immutable object. This means that while you can change the value of one or more elements in a list, you cannot change the values in a tuple.
- Tuples use parentheses to define their elements, whereas lists use square brackets.
- Any set of comma-separated values written without an identifying symbol like brackets or parentheses, etc., is treated as a tuple, by default.
- The `tuple()` function is used to create a tuple with the specified sequence.
- When accessing a tuple, if the index is out of the range of legal indices of the tuple, then Python raises an IndexError.
- Since tuple is an immutable data structure, you cannot delete value(s) from it.
- Python has a built-in function `sorted()` which takes any sequence as a parameter and returns a new list with the same elements but in a different order.
- Keys must have unique values. Keys should not be duplicated in a dictionary.
- While keys in the dictionary must be unique and be of any immutable data type (like strings, numbers, or tuples), there is no stringent requirement for uniqueness and type of values.
- Dictionaries are not sequences; rather, they are mappings.
- To create a dictionary with one or more key-value pairs, the `dict()` function is used.
- To access a value in a dictionary, square brackets are used along with the key to obtain its value.
- If an item with a key, which is not specified in the dictionary, is accessed, a KeyError is generated.
- One or more items in a dictionary can be deleted using the `del` keyword.

Review Questions

1. With the help of an example, explain the significance of + and * operators, when used with tuples.
2. Can we change the value of one or more elements in a tuple? Justify your answer.
3. How is a tuple different from a list?
4. Can we add or delete values from a tuple?
5. What are nested tuples?
6. Explain the different ways of defining a tuple?
7. How will you join two tuples?
8. With the help of an example, differentiate between packing and unpacking a tuple.
9. Why do we use the `index()` function?
10. Demonstrate the use of membership operators on a tuple.
11. Explain the use of `zip()` function.
12. List some advantages of using tuple over lists.
13. List some restrictions which you will keep in mind when creating a dictionary.
14. Draw a comparison between a list and a dictionary.
15. What is a dictionary?

Programming Exercises

1. Write a program that has a predefined list. Create a copy of this list in such a way that only those values that are in valid_tuple are added in the new list.
2. Create a nested tuple that has marks of at least 5 students obtained in three subjects. Now, perform the following operations on it:
   a. Display the marks of the fourth student.
   b. Display the marks obtained by the second student in the first subject.
   c. Display the total marks obtained by each student.
   d. Display the average (or mean) marks obtained by each student.
   e. Using the average marks obtained by each student, calculate the average marks obtained by all the students (finding the mean of means).
   f. For each student, display the maximum and minimum marks obtained.
3. Write a program that concatenates the first tuple at the end of the second tuple.
4. Write a program that creates the following tuples.
   a. Squares of first 10 natural numbers
   b. Cube of first 10 odd numbers
   c. First 10 multiples of 7
   d. –5, –3, –1, 1, 3
5. Write a program that has two tuples. Check if the first tuple is a super-set of the second tuple.
6. Create a dictionary of products purchased and their MRPs. Calculate the bill and display it to the customer.
7. Write a program that has a dictionary of your friends' name (as keys) and their birthdays. Print the items in the dictionary in a sorted order. Prompt the user to enter a name and check if it is present in the dictionary. If the name does not exist, then ask the user to enter DOB. Add the details in the dictionary.

8. Write a program to check whether a dictionary has some key-value pairs stored in it or not.
9. Write a program that prints keys with different values in the dictionary.
10. Create a dictionary which has name of the student as key and his total marks as value. Now, perform the following operations on this dictionary:
    a. Display the marks obtained by a particular student.
    b. Display the names of all the students who scored 90 and above.
    c. Display all key-value pairs sorted by keys.
    d. Display all key-value pairs sorted by marks.
11. Create a dictionary storing names of months as keys and the number of days as values.
12. Make two sets of random integers and apply all set operations on them.

Fill in the Blanks

1. _______ use parentheses to define its elements.
2. To add a single element in the set, use the _____ method and to add multiple elements in the set, use the ________ method.
3. The _______ function creates a tuple with the specified sequence.
4. The entire tuple can be deleted by using the ________ statement.
5. If `tup = ("abc", "def", "ghi", "jkl")`, `tup[-1]` will print _______.
6. We can access an individual element of a tuple by using its _______.
7. _______ are used to return more than one value from a function.
8. The ______ method returns the number of elements with a specific value in a tuple.

State True or False

1. You cannot perform operations like concatenation, repetition, etc., on tuples.
2. It is possible to specify a list within a tuple.
3. If a sequence is specified without parenthesis, it is treated to be a list, by default.
4. Lists are faster than tuples.
5. A tuple can be sliced.
6. Once created, one or more elements of a tuple can be easily updated.
7. It is possible to edit, add and delete elements from a tuple.
8. Tuples can store information that belongs to different data types.
9. Numbers or any other type values cannot be added to a tuple.
10. `max()` and `min()` functions can be used on a tuple if the values in it are of different data types.
11. Tuples cannot be divided or subtracted.
12. Keys of a dictionary can be sorted using the `sorted()`.
13. The key-value pairs can be specified as a list or as a tuple.
14. Keys in the dictionary must be of any mutable data type.

15. Tuples can be used as keys for a dictionary but lists cannot be used as keys.
16. Values in a dictionary must be unique.
17. Slicing and concatenation operations are not possible on dictionaries.
18. Dictionary keys are case insensitive.

Multiple Choice Questions

1. If `tup = ("abc", "def", "ghi", "jkl")`, then `tup("def")` will return ____.
   a. 1 b. 2
   c. 0 d. Error
2. `print((0, 10, 20) < (0, 30, 40))` will print ____.
   a. True b. False
   c. Equal d. Error
3. Which data structure allows you to return multiple values from a function?
   a. List b. Tuple
   c. Dictionary d. Set
4. Which of the following functions can be used to input a tuple?
   a. `input()` b. `eval()`
   c. `tuple()` d. `raw_input()`
5. Indices in a tuple start at _____.
   a. -1 b. 0
   c. 1 d. 10
6. Which error is returned when index is out of the range of legal indices of the tuple?
   a. ValueError b. TypeError
   c. IndexError d. SliceError
7. Which error is returned when we try to modify the value of an element in a tuple?
   a. ValueError b. TypeError
   c. IndexError d. NameError
8. Which error is returned if we divide two tuples?
   a. ValueError b. TypeError
   c. IndexError d. NameError
9. Identify the function or method which is not supported on tuples.
   a. `sorted()` b. `reverse()`
   c. `count()` d. `index()`
10. A _______ cannot be used as a key in the dictionary.
    a. string b. number
    c. tuple d. list
11. Which error will be generated if the key of the dictionary is a list?
    a. TypeError b. KeyError
    c. NameError d. IndexError
12. Which data structure does not allow duplicate values?
    a. List b. Tuple
    c. Dictionary d. Set
13. Which data structure does not support indexing?
    a. List b. Tuple
    c. Dictionary d. Set

14. Using a mutable object as dictionary will result in which error?
   a. TypeError b. KeyError
   c. NameError d. IndexError

15. Which error is returned if an item with a key, which is not specified in the dictionary, is accessed?
   a. TypeError b. KeyError
   c. NameError d. IndexError

Give the Output

1.
```
tup1 = (1,2,3)
tup2 = (1.0,2.0,3.0)
print(tup1 == tup2)
```

2.
```
Tup = ("abc", "def")
(key, value) = Tup
print(key, value)
```

3.
```
Tup = (1,2,3)
Add_Tup = Tup + Tup
print(Add_Tup)
Mul_Tup = Tup * 3
print(Mul_Tup)
```

4.
```
Tup  = (1, 'abc')
List = [1, 'abc']
print(Tup == List)
print(Tup == tuple(List))
print(list(Tup) == List)
print((1, 2) + (3, 4))
```

5.
```
Tup = ('Good',)
for i in range(4):
    Tup = (Tup,)
    print(Tup)
```

6.
```
Tup1='a','bcd',12.34
Tup2=Tup1,(5,6,7,8)
print(Tup2)
```

7.
```
t = (1,2,3,'a')
l = list(t)
l
```

8.
```
tup = (1,2,3,4,5,6,7,8,9)
print(tup[3:5]*3)
```

9.
```
tup = (10,7,8,9,6,3,4,5,0,1,2)
print(tup[0])
print(tup[tup[3]])
print(tup[-4])
print(tup[tup[-2]])
print(tup[tup[tup[7]]-4])
print(tup[10*2-15+3])
```

10.
```
t = (1,2,3)
a,b,c = (x,y,z) = t
print(a,b,c)
print(x,y,z)
```

11.
```
t=('a')
print(type(t))
t=('a',)
print(type(t))
```

12.
```
t = (1,2,3)
tup = ('GO',) + t
print(tup)
```

13.
```
t1 = (1,2,3)
t2 = (4,5)
print(t1 + t2)
```

14.
```
t1 = (1,2,3)
t2 = t1 * (3)
print(t2)
```

15.
```
t1 = (1,2,3)
t2 = ('1','2')
print(t1 + t2)
```

16.
```
t = (78,98,80,76,53,54,78,98,87,74)
print(t[3:])
print(t[:6])
print(t[-4:])
print(t[-4:4])
print(t[:])
```

17.
```
t1 = 'a','b'
t2 = ("a","b")
print(t1==t2)
```

18.
```
t = ('a',('b',('c',('d',))))
print(len(t))
print(t[1][0])
print('c' in t)
```

19.
```
t = ((1,2),)*7
print(t)
print(len(t[3:8]))
```

20.
```
tup = ("abc","def")
x,y = tup
print(x, y)
```

21.
```
List = [10,10,10,20,30,30,20,40,40,40]
counts= {}
L= []
for i in List:
    if i not in L:
        L.append(i)
        counts[i] = 1
    else:
        counts[i] += counts[i]
print(counts)
```

22.
```
List = [10,10,10,20,30,30,20,40,40,40]
counts = {}
for i in List:
    if i in counts:
        counts[i] += 1
    else:
        counts[i] = 1
print(counts)
```

23.
```
Dict = {"Amna":4,"Brij":2,"Chaitanya":5,"Divyanka":3}
n = ''
for i in Dict:
    if n < i:
       n = i
print(n)
```

24.
```
Dict = {"Amna":4,"Brij":2,"Chaitanya":5,"Divyanka":3}
n = 'Chaitanya'
v = 10
if n in Dict:
    Dict[n] = v
print(Dict)
```

25.
```
Dict = {'a':1, 'b':2, ('c','d'):3}
print(Dict)
```

26.
```
Dict = {'a':1, 'b':2, 'c':3,'d':4}
v = Dict['c']
if v in Dict:
    print("FOUND")
else:
    print("NOT FOUND")
```

27.
```
Toppers = {}
Toppers['Mitanshi'] = 97
Toppers['Harshita'] = 92
Toppers['Pritika'] = 89
print('Harshita got ' + str(Toppers.get('Harshita')) + ' marks.')
```

28.
```
Dict = {"India":"New Delhi", "Nepal":"Kathmandu", "USA":"Washington DC"}
print(Dict.get("Russia"))
print(Dict.get("Pakistan", "No Idea"))
```

29.
```
IT_studs = set(['Dev', 'Era', 'Francis', 'Geet'])
Elec_studs = set(['Geet', 'Harman', 'Susan', 'Janak'])
CS_studs = set(['Era', 'Francis', 'Susan', 'Krishnav'])
students = IT_studs | Elec_studs | CS_studs
print("Students : ", students)
It_Elec_studs = IT_studs & Elec_studs
CS_studs.add('Loveya')
print("Is Students Superset of IT : ", students.issuperset(IT_studs))
CS_studs.update(Elec_studs)
print("CS Students : ", CS_studs)
```

30.
```
x = set()
x.add("abc")
x.add("def")
x.update(["ghi","jkl"])
print(x)
```

Find the Error

1.
```
tup = ("abc", "def", "ghi", "jkl")
tup.append("mno")
```

2.
```
Tup1 = (9,8,7,6,5)
Tup2 = (1,2,3,4,5)
print(Tup1 - Tup2)
```

3.
```
tup.remove("abc")
```

4.
```
Tup = ('abc', 'def', 'ghi','jkl')
Tup[2] = 'xyz'
```

5.
```
x, y = 10, 20, 30
```

6.
```
x = {1, 2, 3, 4, 5}
x.add([6,7,8])
print(x)
```

7.
```
tup1 = (1,2,3)
tup2 = tup1 + (2)
print(tup2)
```

8.
```
(a,b,c,d) = (10,20,30)
```

9.
```
t = (1,2,3,4,5)
print(t[10])
```

10.
```
t1 = (1,2,3)
t2 = (1,2)
print(t2-t1)
```

11.
```
t1 = (1,2,3)
t2 =  t1 *(4,)
print(t2)
```

12.
```
t = (1,)*3
t[0] = 2
print(t)
```

13.
```
Tup = (1,2,3,4.0,"abc")
print(min(Tup))
```

14.
```
Dict = {"India":"New Delhi",
"Nepal":"Kathmandu"}
print(Dict["USA"])
```

15.
```
Dict = {}
print(Dict[0])
```

16.
```
Dict={'a':1, 'b':2, ['c','d']:[3,4]}
print(Dict)
```

17.
```
msg = "How are you doing?"
counts = {}
for c in msg:
    counts[c] = counts[c] + 1
print(counts)
```

18.
```
Dict = {}
Dict[(1,2,3)] = 10
Dict[[3,2,1]] = 20
print(DIct)
```

19.
```
Dict = {'a':1,'b':2,'c':3,'d':4}
print(Dict['a','b'])
```

AI Lab Session – Talk to Books

Talk to Books is an AI-powered application that allows users to browse passages from books, thereby providing an absolutely new way to interact with books. Users can speak directly with all 100,000 books, ask questions or make statements. Users can even filter their search results depending on category of books. Visit the link to use this application: https://experiments.withgoogle.com/talk-to-books

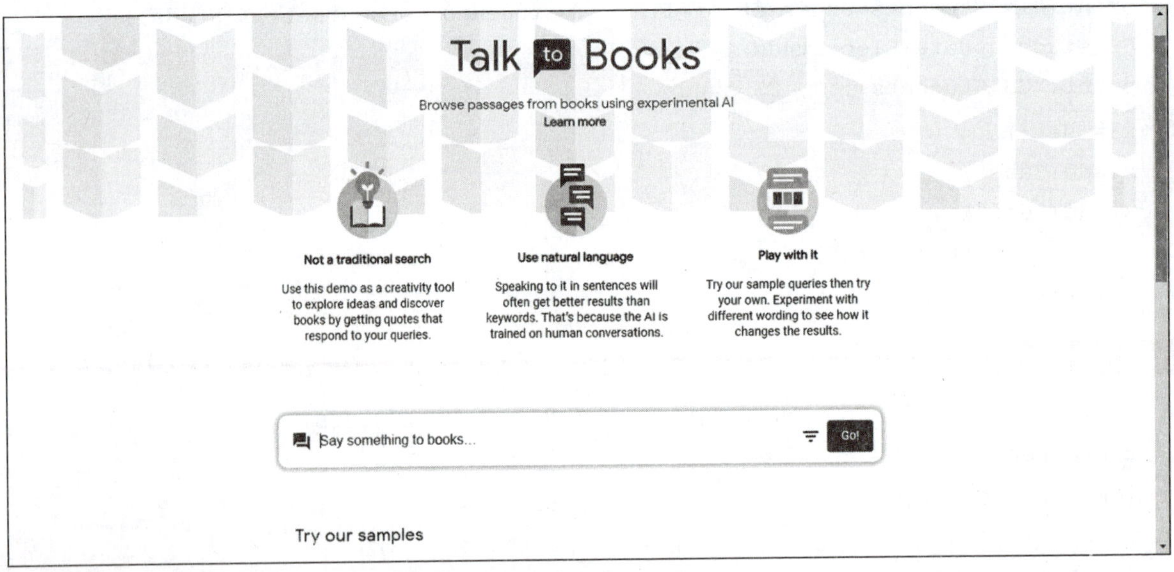

Answers

Fill in the Blanks

1. Tuples
2. `add()`, `update()`
3. `tuple()`
4. `del`
5. `jkl`
6. index
7. Tuples
8. `count()`

State True or False

1. False
2. True
3. False
4. False
5. True
6. False
7. False
8. True
9. True
10. False
11. True
12. True
13. True
14. False
15. True
16. False
17. True
18. False

Multiple Choice Questions

1. d
2. a
3. b
4. b
5. b
6. c
7. b
8. b
9. b
10. d
11. a
12. d
13. d
14. a
15. b

Give the Output

1. True

2. abc def

3. (1, 2, 3, 1, 2, 3)
(1, 2, 3, 1, 2, 3, 1, 2, 3)

4. False
True
True
(1, 2, 3, 4)

5. ((‘Good’,),)
(((‘Good’,),),)
((((‘Good’,),),),)
(((((‘Good’,),),),),)

6. ((‘a’, ‘bcd’, 12.34), (5, 6, 7, 8))

7. [1, 2, 3, ‘a’]

8. (4, 5, 4, 5, 4, 5)

9. 10 1 5 7 2 0

10. 1 2 3
1 2 3

11. <class ‘str’> <class ‘tuple’>

12. (‘GO’, 1, 2, 3)

13. (1, 2, 3, 4, 5

14. (1, 2, 3, 1, 2, 3, 1, 2, 3)

15. (1, 2, 3, ‘1’, ‘2’)

16. (76, 53, 54, 78, 98, 87, 74)
(78, 98, 80, 76, 53, 54)
(78, 98, 87, 74)
()
(78, 98, 80, 76, 53, 54, 78, 98, 87, 74)
[‘programming’, ‘is’]
False
(‘but’, ‘fun’)
False

17. True

18. 2 b False

19. ((1, 2), (1, 2), (1, 2), (1, 2), (1, 2), (1, 2), (1, 2)) 4

20. abc def

21. {10: 4, 20: 2, 30: 2, 40: 4}

22. {10: 3, 20: 2, 30: 2, 40: 3}

23. Divyanka

24. {‘Amna’: 4, ‘Brij’: 2, ‘Chaitanya’: 10, ‘Divyanka’: 3}

25. `{‘a’: 1, ‘b’: 2, (‘c’, ‘d’): 3}`

26. NOT FOUND

27. Harshita got 92 marks.

28. None
No Idea

29. Students : {‘Francis’, ‘Geet’, ‘Harman’, ‘Dev’, ‘Janak’, ‘Susan’, ‘Krishnav’, ‘Era’}
Is Students Superset of IT : True
CS Students : {‘Francis’, ‘Geet’, ‘Loveya’, ‘Janak’, ‘Harman’, ‘Susan’, ‘Krishnav’, ‘Era’}

30. {‘def’, ‘ghi’, ‘jkl’, ‘abc’}

Find the Error

1. `AttributeError: 'tuple' object has no attribute 'append'`

2. `TypeError: unsupported operand type(s) for -: 'tuple' and 'tuple'`

3. `NameError: name 'tup' is not defined`

4. `TypeError: 'tuple' object does not support item assignment`

5. `ValueError: too many values to unpack (expected 2)`

6. `TypeError: unhashable type: 'list'`

7. `TypeError: can only concatenate tuple (not "int") to tuple`

8. `ValueError: not enough values to unpack (expected 4, got 3)`

9. `IndexError: tuple index out of range`

10. `TypeError: unsupported operand type(s) for -: 'tuple' and 'tuple'`

11. `TypeError: can't multiply sequence by non-int of type 'tuple'`

12. `TypeError: 'tuple' object does not support item assignment`

13. `TypeError`

14. `KeyError: 'USA'`

15. `KeyError`

16. `TypeError: unhashable type: 'list'`

17. `KeyError: 'H'`

18. `TypeError: unhashable type: 'list'`

19. `KeyError: ('a', 'b')`

Data Science

11

Chapter Objectives

Data science is all about analyzing data systematically in a variety of ways. In this chapter, we will look into:

- Applications of data science
- Life cycle
- Data science components
- Descriptive statistics
- Visualization using charts
- *K*-nearest neighbor algorithm

Data is a collection of facts that is processed to obtain information. This data can be anything including numbers, words, measurements, observations, etc. In this chapter, our focus will therefore be to understand the importance of data and learn how this data can be structured and analyzed to derive useful information.

11.1 DATA AND ITS PURPOSE

Data can exist in different forms – numbers or text on paper or on a computer. Irrespective of the industry, collection and analysis of data has changed the way we do things today. For example, data is analyzed to study symptoms and arrive at appropriate treatment for a disease, increase the revenue of a company, generate targeted ads, etc.

Data helps companies to make better decisions. These days, all businesses generate a lot of data. Any business with a website, presence on social media, or involvement in any kind of electronic payment is collecting data about customers, user demographics, and more. Businesses can harness this data to make decisions about:

- Finding new customers
- Increasing customer retention
- Improving customer service
- Managing marketing efforts
- Tracking social media interaction
- Predicting sales trends.

Thus, data helps business leaders make smart decisions about where to take their companies.

Figure 11.1 Data for analyzing market trends and making stragetic decisions

11.2 IMPORTANCE OF DATA

- Data helps companies to solve problems. For example, companies can analyze their data to find out if there is a drop in sales, and observe the effectiveness of their marketing campaign. Such sales-related problem(s) can be easily tracked and reviewed by analyzing data from business processes. Data helps business managers to know which of their products are performing well and what steps are to be taken to increase the profits of those items that are lagging behind.

- Data helps companies to monitor business performance and improve business processes. This will help companies to efficiently utilize time and money.
- Data helps companies understand their consumers and strategically develop their theories. It also facilitates business groups to get better **return on investments**
- All in all, data improves quality of life of not only business employees but also of customers and all those who support business.
- Companies also use data to know how they should design their next product. For this, they collect and extract keywords to learn exactly what features or solutions, the customers are looking for.
- Business organizations get information about current trends in the industry by monitoring the relative change in keyword frequencies. This can then be used to predict trends in customer behaviour.

Figure 11.2 Data for preparing budgets, setting goals and monitoring performance

11.3 DATA SCIENCE

Data Science is a science that includes a detailed study of the flow of information from massive amounts of data present in an organization's repository. It tends to obtain useful insights from raw and unstructured data by processing it using analytical, programming, and business skills.

Today, the entire world is moving towards a digital space in which organizations are working with zettabytes and yottabytes of structured and unstructured data every day. With newer and still evolving technologies, critical data can be stored at relatively low costs. Therefore, there is a huge need for skilled and certified Data Scientists. In fact, data scientists are among the highest-paid professionals in the IT industry these days. Looking at the increasing demand of data scientists, McKinsey has predicted that there will be a 50 percent gap in the demand and supply of Data Scientists in the next few years.

In addition to organizations' ever-growing data, recent years have also witnessed a massive growth in the field of Internet of Things (IoT) which is alone producing 90 percent of the data that has been generated. Approximately 2.5 quintillion bytes of data are being generated each day. This data is coming from sources such as:

- Sensors used in shopping malls to collect shoppers' information
- Posts, pictures, videos shared on social media platforms
- Text, pictures and videos in our smart phones and tablets
- Purchase transactions completed through e-commerce websites
- Data collected by IoT devices
- Our location data when we use Google Maps and other such apps.
- Every time we login to a website, data is generated.

This data is known as big data. Every company that has huge amounts of data looks out for ways in which it can analyze and utilize this data in the best possible way.

Problem	Solution
Companies have huge amounts of data.	The data scientist identifies opportunities in the data to make better decisions that meet the customer needs.
It is very challenging to extract valuable information from the voluminous data.	Data can be visualized for better understanding.

It is here that the concept of Data Science comes into picture. *Data Science encompasses skills from multiple disciplines like statistics, mathematics, business domain knowledge and machine learning, to name a few.* The overlap of various domains in Data Science is illustrated in Fig. 11.3 Data Science enables organizations to:

- Reduce costs
- Enter new markets
- Tap on different demographics
- Take informed and data-driven decisions
- Estimate and analyze the effectiveness of a marketing campaign
- Launch a new product or service
- Optimally utilize resources.

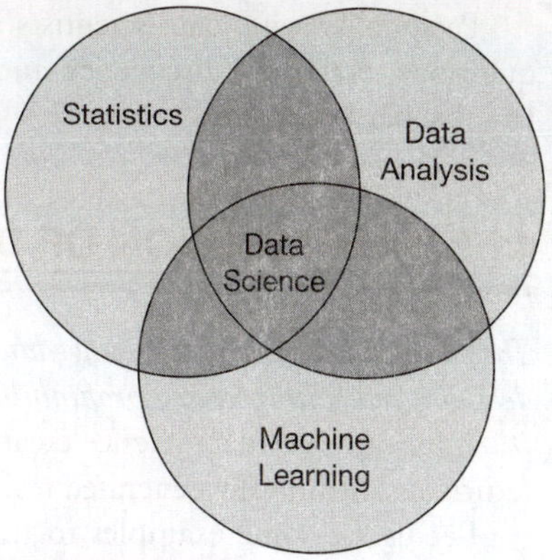

Figure 11.3 Data Science is an overlap of multiple disciplines

Irrespective of the industry vertical, Data Science plays a crucial role in any organization's success. Table 11.1 lists some more applications of data science.

Table 11.1

Areas	Purpose
Sales	Dynamic pricing, discount offers, demand forecasting
Travel	Predicting flight/train/bus delays
Social media	Digital marketing, sentiment analysis
Automation	Self-driving cars, pilotless aircrafts and drones
Marketing	Cross-selling and up-selling, predicting loyalty of customers
Healthcare	Analyzing effectiveness of medication, disease prediction
Credit Card Industry	Fraud and risk detection

11.4 DEFINING A DATA SCIENTIST

Data is everywhere and ever expanding. Special technical skills are required for mining, cleaning, analyzing and interpreting this data. In this scenario, a data scientist comes into the picture.

The term "data scientist" was first coined in the year 2008 when companies realized the need for data professionals who are skilled in organizing and analyzing massive amounts of data. A data scientist must be capable of collecting relevant data, understand the data, process it to extract value from it, visualize it and communicate it through business reports or other visualization tools.

To identify relevant data from a multitude of different data sources, organize it, translate the results into solutions, and communicate the findings in a way that positively affects business decisions is not at all an easy task. Special training is required to perform these tasks. A data scientist with this skill set is in great demand in almost all industries.

Data scientists must possess a combination of analytical, machine learning, data mining, coding and statistical skills. They must be able to draw digital information from a growing list of channels and sources, including smartphones, Internet of Things (IoT) devices, social media surveys, purchases, and Internet searches, to name a few.

> Do you know that LinkedIn listed data scientist as one of the most promising jobs in 2017 and 2018? Moreover, in 2020 the demand of data scientists increased by 28%.

When given an organization problem, a data scientist acts like a detective investigating data to understand the pattern or characteristics that lie within it. This task demands analytical creativity and business acumen.

Personality wise, data scientists are deep thinkers with intense intellectual curiosity. They continuously ask new questions, make new discoveries, and learn new things. They are passionate about using their capabilities and creativity to solve hard problems.

11.5 APPLICATION OF DATA SCIENCE BY TOP INDUSTRY PLAYERS

The main advantage of applying data science in an organization is that it facilitates data-driven decision-making. Such decisions result in increased profitability, improved operational efficiency and better business performance.

Application of data science creates a "data product". Such a product takes data as input, and processes the data to return algorithmically generated results. This data product is developed, tested, refined and deployed by data scientists.

Let us see some examples to understand how and where data science (or data product) is applied in different organizations.

- The sales and marketing team of any organization uses data science to identify and refine target audiences.
- The HR team of organizations use data science techniques to assist them in recruitment process. For example, data science can be used to process applications, conduct and evaluate data-driven aptitude tests and games to make quicker and more accurate selections during the hiring process.
- Streaming services like Netflix and Amazon Prime use data science to determine what its users are interested in so that they can determine what TV shows or films to produce. Data science is also used to create personalized recommendations based on a user's viewing history.
- Shipment companies like DHL, FedEx and UPS use data science to find the best delivery routes, times and mode of transport for shipment.
- Google hires data scientists on a large scale as all its applications are mostly driven by Data Science, Artificial Intelligence, and Machine Learning techniques.
- Amazon extensively uses data science to find out customer mindset and increase the reach of its e-commerce and cloud computing applications.
- Spotify uses data science to recommend music to its users.
- Gmail's spam filter uses data science to processes incoming mail and determine if a message is junk or not.
- Computer vision used for self-driving cars is also a data product – machine learning algorithms are able to recognize traffic lights, other cars on the road, pedestrians, etc.
- Visa, an online financial gateway for most companies, uses data science to generate more revenue, check fraudulent transactions, and customize products and services as per customer requirements.
- Proctor & Gamble utilizes time series models to predict future demand so that it can plan for production levels more optimally.

Thus, we see that data science does much more than merely providing data insights to take better decisions.

11.6 DATA SCIENCE LIFE CYCLE

To better understand Data Science Life Cycle, assume that you are the owner of a retail store and currently your focus is on increasing the sales. For this, you are trying to find out answers to the following questions.

- Which are the most profitable products in the store?
- How are the in-store promotions working?
- Are the product placements effectively deployed?

Of course, the answer to these questions can be obtained by analyzing the sales of products over the last several years. So, you appoint a Data Scientist who will use the data science life cycle to discover answers to these questions.

Data Discovery The first phase in any data science project life cycle is data discovery. It includes ways to discover data from various structured or unstructured sources. While structured sources include text files or database files, unstructured sources may include emails, PDF files, videos or images. Organizations are also using social networking sites to better understand the user's requirements.

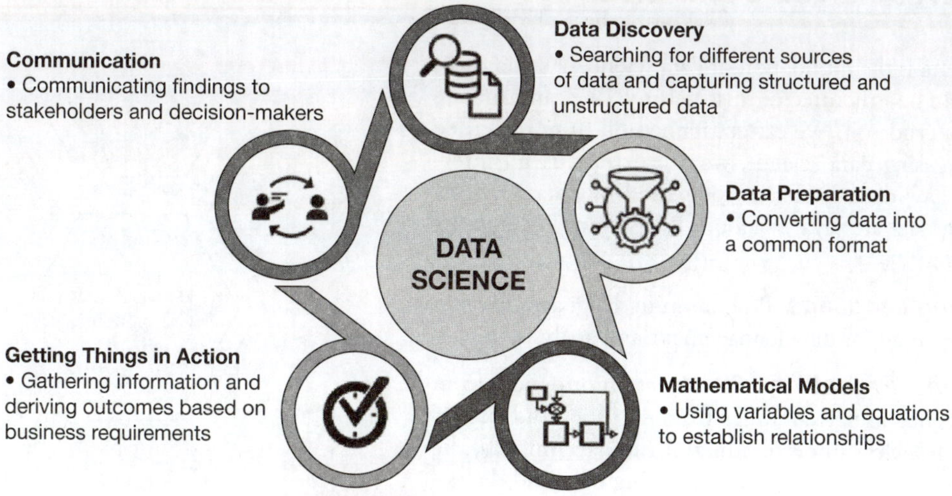

Figure 11.4 Data science life cycle

Coming to our case study, to boost the sales of your business, you should first identify the factors affecting sales. These factors may include:

- store location
- staff satisfaction, working hours
- product placement, pricing, promotions
- the competitors' location and promotions, etc.

After identifying these factors, you know exactly what data you want for analysis.

Data Preparation The next phase in a data science project is data preparation. It includes converting disparate data (data in different formats as they may have been taken from different sources) into a common format. This process involves cleaning data, filling any missing value(s), merging two or more tables that may store different information about the same object, summarizing fields in a table using aggregation, etc.

Mathematical Models Data processing means the process of converting raw data to meaningful information. This information may help to resolve a problem or improve an existing scenario. At the heart of mining a data science project lies the ability to view the data through a quantitative lens. For this, several dimensions and correlations in data are expressed mathematically.

Every data science project is driven by a certain mathematical model. Data scientists develop the most appropriate model that best suits the specific need of the business organization. Therefore, a data science project applies various mathematical domains including statistics, logistic regression, linear regression, differential and integral calculus, etc. Various tools like R programming language, Python programming language, SAS advanced analytical tools, SQL and various data visualization tools like Tableau and QlikView can be used.

For many projects, one model may not be sufficient. We may need to use two or more models. Even after developing one or more models, the data scientist may have to revise the parameters and fine-tune them. This process of revision and creating models continues until the Data Scientist finds the best model. The output of a mathematical model is usually expressed in appropriate forms like diagrams, reports, graphics, text or a combination of all this.

Getting Things in Action Once the data is cleaned and prepared and the models have been developed, the model is practically brought into use to obtain the desired results. Even at this time, there may be several discrepancies for which troubleshooting may be required. So, in this phase, the model must be evaluated to determine its performance.

Communication In the final stage of the life cycle, the results of the findings are communicated to key stakeholders and decision-makers in the organization so that actions can be taken based on the recommendations of the Data Scientist.

11.7 DATA SCIENCE COMPONENTS

Data Raw data is the foundation of data science. As said earlier, this data can be structured or unstructured. We can compare raw data with crude oil. We extract refined oil from the crude oil. Similarly, using data science, we can extract useful information from raw data. Different tools used by data scientists to process big data are Java, Hadoop, R, Python, Pig, Apache Spark, etc.

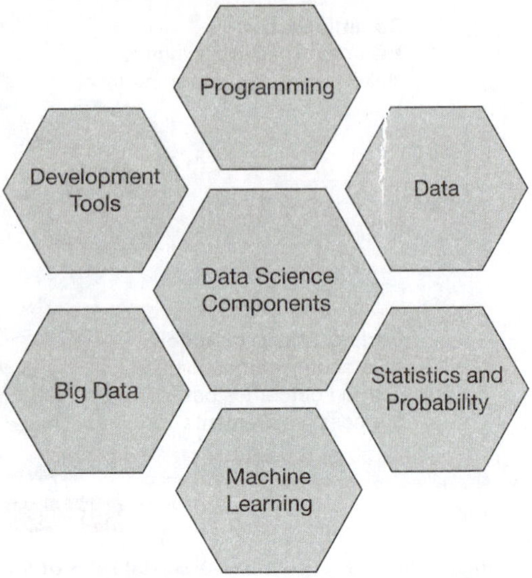

Figure 11.5 Data science components

Programming Language Programming languages like Python and R are used for data management and analysis.

Statistics and Probability To extract information from data, data science uses techniques from statistics and probability. Without a clear understanding of these techniques, the data scientist may end up in misinterpreting data and deducing incorrect conclusions.

Machine Learning A data scientist applies machine learning algorithms such as regression and classification. So, a data scientist must have a good knowledge of machine learning algorithms to gain valuable insights from available data.

11.7.1 Structured, Semi-structured and Unstructured Data

Massive amount of data available today can be categorized into three groups – structured data, semi-structured data, and unstructured data.

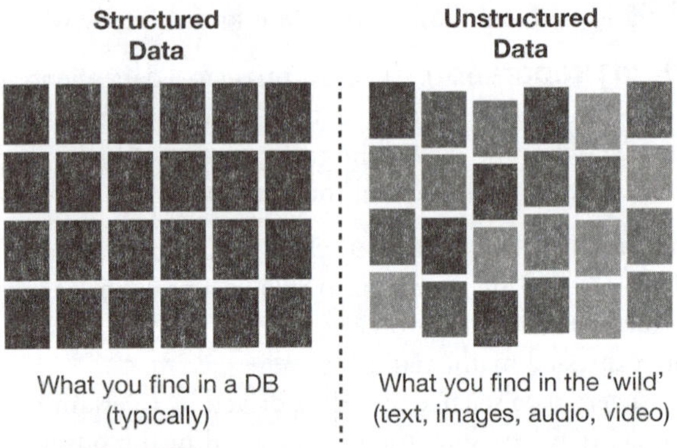

Figure 11.6 Structured vs. unstructured data

Structured data Structured data, also referred to as quantitative data, is that data which can be used for effective analysis. It is stored in a database and has a well-defined structure and format. However, the downside of structured data is that it lacks flexibility in data storage and analysis techniques. There is a fixed format and storage and retrieval is limited to a pre-defined format. *Example*: SQL tables.

Semi-structured data Semi-structured data is not stored in a database. So, analysing such data is not that easy. However, after processing this data, it can be stored in a database to make it convenient for further usage. *Example*: XML data.

Unstructured data: Unstructured data, also referred to as qualitative data, is not available in a pre-defined format. This data cannot be stored in a database. For example, data stored in Word Processing applications (like MS Word), PDF files, social media posts, presentations, chats, IoT sensor data, satellite imagery, audio and video files, text messages, locations are all important sources of unstructured data. Though this type of data has the freedom to be stored in different formats, it is however difficult to analyze. Special expertise and tools are required for data storage and retrieval for analysis.

The graph shown in Fig. 11.7 illustrates that applications these days generate more of unstructured data rather than structured data and this trend is going to be seen in the years to come. Table 11.2 summarizes the difference between structured and unstructured data.

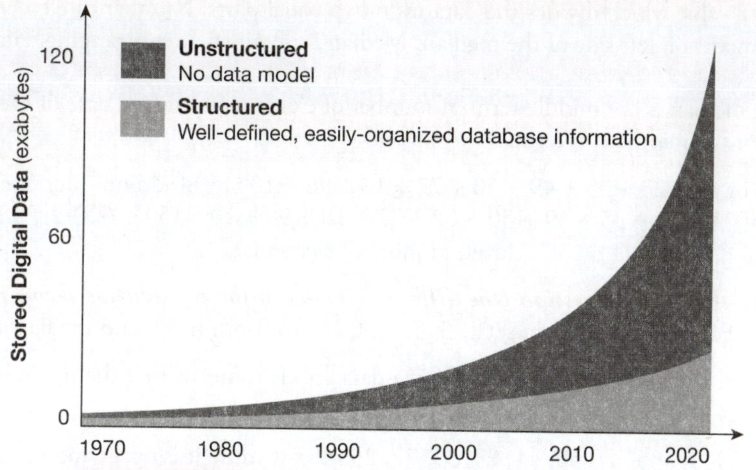

Figure 11.7 Constant increase in unstructured data

Source: https://www.researchgate.net/

Table 11.2 Comparison between structured and unstructured data

Properties	Structured Data	Unstructured Data
Characteristics	Predefined format	Raw/native format
Ease of searching	Easy and straight-forward	Difficult
Data types	Defined data types	Many varied data types
Storage	Relational databases	Cannot be stored in relational databases
Flexibility	Not flexible; schema-dependent	Flexible; not schema-dependent
Availability	Approx. 20% of data	Approx. 80% of data
Examples	Excel, Google Sheets, SQL, customer data, phone records, transaction history	Text data, social media comments, phone calls transcriptions, various logs files, images, audio, video

11.8 DESCRIPTIVE STATISTICS

Descriptive statistics are evaluated to summarize and organize data for better understandability. As the name suggests, descriptive statistics describes data, but they do not make inferences from the sample to the whole population. There are two types of descriptive statistics – measures of central tendency and measures of variability (spread).

11.8.1 Measure of Central Tendency

Central tendency indicates that there is one number that best summarizes the entire set of measurements. This number is "central" to the set.

Mean/Average Mean or Average is a central tendency of the data. In other words, it is a number around which a whole data is spread out. It is that single number which can estimate the value of the whole data set. Mean is calculated by dividing the sum of all elements by the number of elements.

$$\overline{X} = \frac{1+2+3+4+5+6+7+8+9+10}{10} = 5.5$$

Median Median is the value which divides the data in to two equal parts. Number of elements on right side of it is same as number of elements on left side of the median. Median is obtained after arranging data either in ascending or descending order.

To make it simple, median is the middle term, if number of elements is odd. In case of even number of elements, median is the average of the middle two terms.

Median of 11 + 23 + 35 + 49 + 50 + 77 + 18 + 96 + 10 = 50 (odd number of elements)
Median of 11 + 23 + 35 + 49 + 50 + 62 + 77 + 18 + 96 + 10 = (50 + 62)/2 = 112/ 2 = 56
(even number of elements)

When values are in arithmetic progression (the difference between the consecutive terms is constant), median is always equal to mean. For example, in data set 1, 3, 5, 7, 9, 11, 13. Both mean and median are same.

Mode Mode is the term appearing most frequently in a data set. This means that the mode has highest frequency of occurrence in the data set.

Mode of 11, 23, 39, 35, 41, 50, 41, 23, 39, 77, 23 = 23 because it is occurring thrice in the data.

Key points to remember

- In some data sets, there can be no mode at all as all values appear same number of times.
- If two values appear for the same maximum number of times then the data set is said to be **bimodal**.
- If three values appear for the same maximum number of times then the data set is said to be **trimodal**. Similarly, for *n* values appearing most frequently, the data set is said to be **multimodal**.

11.8.2 Measure of Spread/Dispersion

Measure of Spread refers to the idea of variability within your data.

Standard deviation Standard deviation measures the average distance between each value and the mean. This gives a clarity about how data is spread out from mean. A low standard deviation indicates that values are closer to the mean of the data set, while a high standard deviation means that the data values are spread out over a wider range of values.

Standard deviation is calculated as,

$$\text{S.D.} = \sqrt{\frac{1}{n}\sum_{i=0}^{n}(x-\mu)^2}$$

where μ is mean of a population.

Example 11.1 **Consider the data set given below.**

12, 7, 8, 11, 5, 4, 10, 9, 6, 9, 4, 9, 2, 5, 4, 9, 3, 7, 4, 12

$$\text{Mean of the values} = \frac{\text{Sum of all values}}{\text{Number of values}} = 7$$

For each number, subtract the Mean and square the result
This is the part of the formula that says: $(x_i - \mu)^2$

$$x_1 = 12, x_2 = 7, x_3 = 8, \text{ etc.}$$

For each value, subtract the mean and square the result, as shown below.

$$(12 - 7)^2 = (5)^2 = 25$$
$$(7 - 7)^2 = (0)^2 = 0$$
$$(8 - 7)^2 = (1)^2 = 1$$
$$(11 - 7)^2 = (4)^2 = 16$$
$$(5 - 7)^2 = (-2)^2 = 4$$
$$(4 - 7)^2 = (-3)^2 = 9$$

$$(10-7)^2 = (3)^2 = 9 \; (9-7)^2 = (2)^2 = 4$$
$$(6-7)^2 = (-1)^2 = 1$$
$$(9-7)^2 = (2)^2 = 4$$
... etc ...

Now, find the mean of these squared differences. For this, add up all the values, then divide by number of values. In our data set, the mean of squared differences = 178

Finally, divide this mean by number of values and find its squared root. So,

Mean of squared differences = (1/20) × 178 = 8.9

Standard Deviation, $\sigma = \sqrt{(8.9)} = 2.983$

Variance Variance is calculated as the square of average distance between each quantity and mean. This means that variance is the square of standard deviation.

$$\text{Variance} = (\text{S.D.})^2$$

Range Range is calculated as the difference between lowest and highest value.

Range of 11, 23, 39, 35, 41, 50, 41, 23, 39, 77, 23 = 77 – 11 = 60

Example 11.2 **Let us write a Python program to compute the descriptive statistics. For this, we will use the statistics module.**

Remember that to access a function in a module we use the dot operator. This means that to use the `mean ()` function of the statistics module, we will write `statistics.mean()`.

```
import statistics
L = [80,97,83,92,95,90,89]
print("Length of the list = ", len(L))
print("Sum of List Elements = ", sum(L))
print("Minimum Value in List = ", min(L))
print("Maximum Value in List = ", max(L))
print("Range of Values= ", max(L) - min(L))
print("Mean of Values= ", statistics.mean(L))
print("Median of Values= ", statistics.median(L))
print("Mean of Values= ", statistics.mode{L))
print("Variance of Values= ", statistics.variance(L))
print("Standard deviation of Values= ", statistics.stdev(L))
```

OUTPUT

```
Length of the list = 7
Sum of List Elements = 626
Minimum Value in List = 80
Maximum Value in List = 97
Range of Values = 17
Mean of Values = 89.42857142857143
Median of Values = 90
Mean of Values = 80
Variance of Values = 37.61904761904762
Standard deviation of Values = 6.133436852128472
```

11.9 VISUALIZING DATA THROUGH PLOTS

We study statistics to collect and organize data. This data must be properly organized and presented in such a way that it is easily and clearly interpreted. For this reason, we can either organize data in the form of tables or present it pictorially using bar charts, histograms, frequency plots, scatter plots, box plots, etc. Visualizing data through charts helps users to easily understand and interpret even complex and/or large amount of data in one glance.

In this chapter, we will be using pyplot module which is, in turn, a sub-module of the matplotlib module. So before drawing charts, make sure you have installed the matplotlib module in your computer. Matplotlib is the most widely used scientific plotting library in Python. To install matplotlib, use the `pip` command by writing, **pip install matplotlib.**

The pyplot module provides an interface for graphing data. It contains over 100 functions and, to use them, you must import this module by writing, import matplotlib.pyplot as plt where, plt is the standard variable name used. This module allows users to,

- Create a plot
- Visualize data effectively
- Customize the plot with focus on plot legends and text, titles, axes labels and plot layout.
- Save the plot for future use
- Show the plot
- Clear the plot area
- Close the plot.

11.10 BAR CHART

A bar chart or bar graph is a chart or graph that presents categorical data with rectangular bars. These bars can be drawn either vertically or horizontally. The height or length of the bars is proportional to the values they represent.

In a bar graph, while one axis of the chart shows the specific categories being compared, the other axis, on the other hand, represents a measured value. The main advantage of plotting a bar graph is that it depicts comparisons among discrete categories.

11.10.1 Drawing a Bar Graph in Python

The pyplot module in the Matplotlib provides the **`bar()`** function that can be used to plot a bar graph. The syntax of this function can be given as,

```
bar(x, height)
```

where,
x is a sequence of values representing the x-coordinates of the bars.
`height` represents the sequence of values representing the height(s) of the bars.

The code given below plots a bar graph.

```
import numpy as np
import pandas as pd
from pandas import Series, DataFrame
import matplotlib.pyplot as plt
data = [27,45,36,18,72,81,108,19,9]
x = range(1,10)
plt.bar(x, data)
plt.show()
```

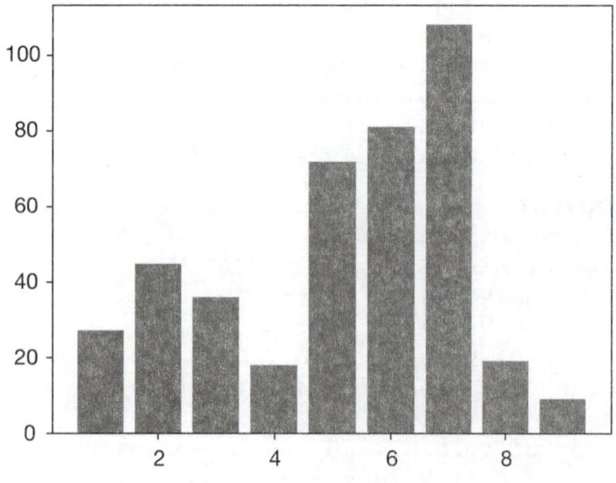

11.11 PLOTTING HISTOGRAMS

Histogram is a graphical representation which is quite similar to a bar graphs. It is a great tool for assessing a probability distribution of a continuous variable that can be easily understood.

Histogram plots the frequency distribution of a numeric array by splitting it to small equal-sized bins. It is an excellent tool for visualizing and understanding the probabilistic distribution of not only numerical data bust also image data.

To construct a histogram, we need to keep in mind three basic steps.

Step 1: Bin the range of values.
Step 2: Divide the entire range of values into a series of intervals.
Step 3: Count how many values fall into each interval.

Remember that the bins are usually specified as consecutive, non-overlapping intervals of a variable.

To plot a histogram, the `hist()` function of matplotlib and pyplot module is used. The syntax of this function is,

```
plt.hist(data, bins = number of bins)
```

The function accepts the data and number of bins as arguments. Setting bins = "auto" gives the "ideal" number of bins.

Example 11.3 **The code given below draws a simple histogram of 100 random integer data values. A histogram uses its bin edges on the x-axis and the corresponding frequencies on the y-axis.**

```
import matplotlib.pyplot as plt
from random import seed
from random import randint
# seed random number generator
seed(1)
data = []
# generate some integers
for i in range(100):
        value = randint(0, 100)
        data.append(value)
print(data)
plt.hist(data, bins=25)
plt.show()
```

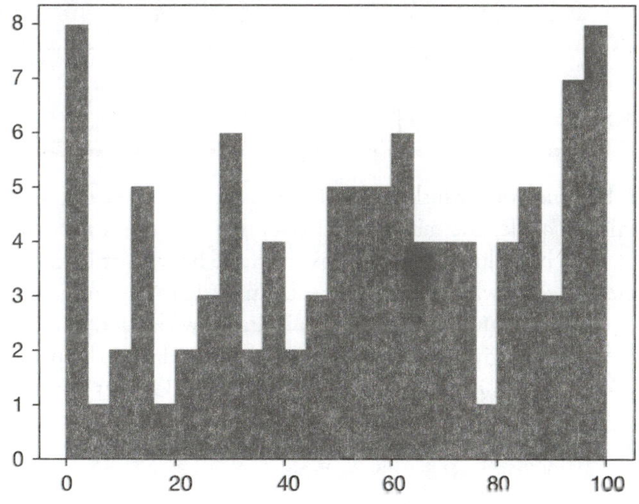

11.12 FREQUENCY POLYGON

A frequency polygon is a graphical form of representation of data. It gives an idea about the shape of the data and the trends that a particular data set follows. It can be used to compare two sets of data and are best for comparing two data sets that have the same sample size.

We usually draw a frequency polygon with a histogram but it can be drawn even without a histogram. The basic steps to draw a Frequency Polygon include:

Step 1: On the horizontal axis (x-axis), mark the class intervals. Frequency will be plotted on the vertical axis (y-axis).
Step 2: Calculate the class_mark for each class interval by using the formula.

```
class_mark = (Upper limit + Lower limit) / 2
```

Step 3: Mark all the class marks on the horizontal axis.
Step 4: Corresponding to each class mark, plot the frequency. The height always depicts the frequency. Note that the frequency is plotted against the class mark and not the upper or lower limit of any class.
Step 5: Join all the plotted points using a line segment. The curve obtained will be kinked. This resulting curve is called the frequency polygon.

The above steps are used to draw a frequency polygon without drawing a histogram. To draw a frequency polygon with a histogram, first draw rectangular bars against the given class intervals. Then, join the midpoints of the bars to obtain the frequency polygon.

Example 11.4 **Consider the data set and the corresponding frequency plot given below.**

Test scores	Frequency	Cumulative frequency
49.5–59.5	5	5
59.5–69.5	10	15
69.5–79.5	30	45
79.5–89.5	40	85
89.5–99.5	15	100

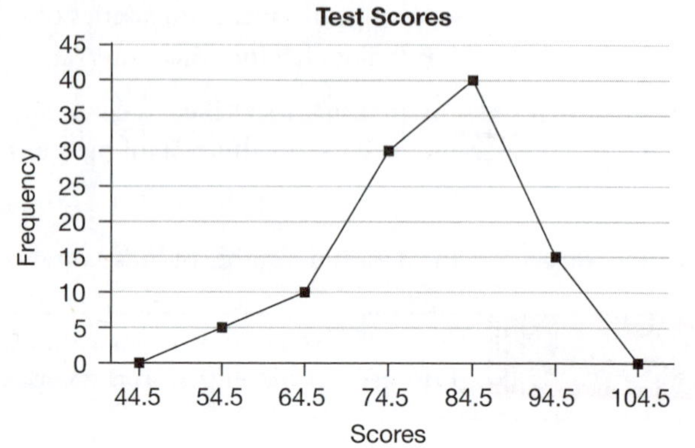

11.13 BOX PLOT

A box plot or a whisker plot displays the summary of a set of data containing the minimum, first quartile, median, third quartile, and maximum. Recall that quartile is a measure of central tendency that divides a data set in to 4 parts.

In a box plot, we draw a box from the first quartile to the third quartile. A vertical line goes through the box at the median. The whiskers go from each quartile to the minimum or maximum.

The median (percentile 50%) is drawn with a red line. The box represents Q1 and Q3 (percentiles 25 and 75), and the whiskers give an idea of the range of the data. The position of the whiskers is set by default to 1.5 * IQR (where, IQR = Q3 - Q1) from the edges of the box. Outlier points are those past the end of the whiskers.

In a boxplot, the x-axis has the data for which the box plot has to be drawn and the y-axis denotes the frequency distribution.

11.13.1 Understanding a Boxplot

A boxplot can be very useful when comparing the distribution of data across data sets. In such a case, different boxplots can be drawn for each data in the data set.

Example 11.5 **Let us draw a boxplot of the following data which represent the ages of people working on a crucial project.**

24, 27, 28, 28, 29, 33, 34, 34, 36, 37

Step 1: Sort the data. Our sample data is already sorted.

Step 2: Find the median. So, here median is (29 + 33) / 2 = 64 / 2 = 32.

Step 3: Find the quartiles.

The first quartile would be the median of the data points to the *left* of the median.

In our data, the first quartile is the median of 24, 27, 28, 28, 29. Therefore, the first quartile, $Q_1 = 28$.

The third quartile would be the median of the data points to the *right* of the median.

In our data, the third quartile is the median of 33, 34, 34, 36, 37. Therefore, the third quartile, $Q_3 = 34$.

Step 4: Find the min and max values. In our data set, min = 24 and max = 37.

Step 5: Label the axis and mark the scales with a five-number summary.

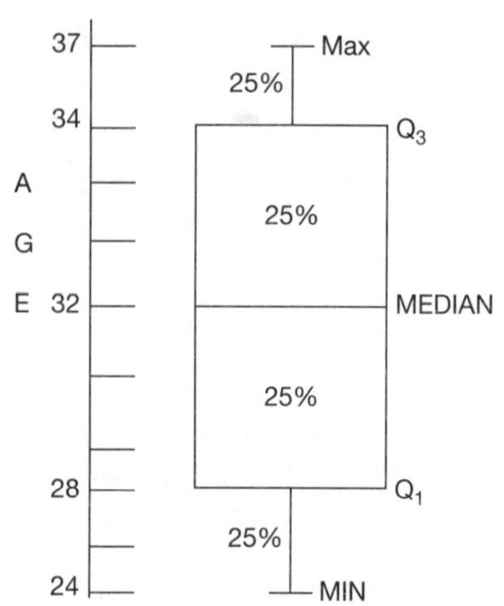

Step 6: Draw a box from Q_1 to Q_3 with a line passing through the median.
Step 7: Draw a whisker from Q_1 to min and another whisker from Q_3 to the max. Now, once our boxplot graph is ready, let us interpret the information presented by it. The boxplot says that 25% of the people working on the project are below the age of 25 and 75% are above the age of 28.

> The span from first quartile to the third is called IQR (Inter Quartile Range).

Correspondingly, 25% of the people are above the age of 34. Moreover, half of the people are below the age of 32.

11.13.2 Use of Box Plot Graph

Box plots are very useful to identify the outliers. John Tukey has provided a precise definition for two types of outliers:

Outliers are either 3 × *IQR* or more above the third quartile, or 3 × *IQR* or more below the first quartile.

Suspected outliers are slightly more central versions of outliers. They are either 1.5 × *IQR* or more above the third quartile or 1.5 × *IQR* or more below the first quartile.

If any outlier is present then the inner fence on that side of the whisker is taken as 1.5 × *IQR* from the quartile. All suspected outliers are displayed as unfilled circles and outliers are filled circles. From the figure, it is clear that the outer fence is 3 × *IQR* from the quartile.

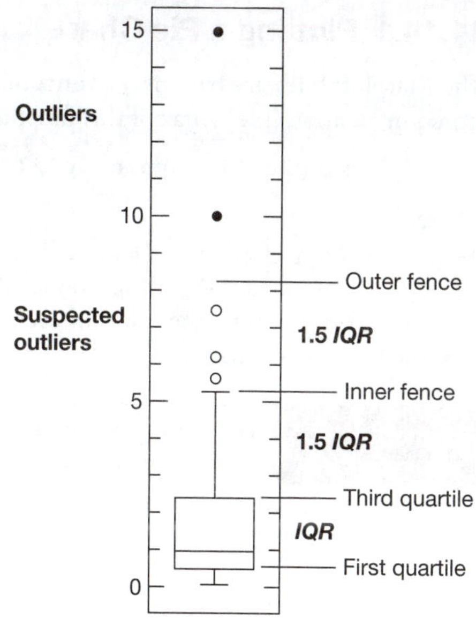

Usually, suspected outliers are not uncommon in large normally distributed data sets (for example, those having more than 100 data-points). Outliers are expected in normally distributed data sets with more than about 10,000 data-points.

We should never treat the outliers as bad data points as many a time, most useful information in the data set is depicted by them. They should never be discarded or removed from the data set. Rather, they may deserve special consideration as they may be the key to the phenomenon under study or the result of human errors.

Thus, a box plot can be used to make the following observations:

- Key values like the mean, median, minimum, maximum, 25th percentile etc.
- Outliers and suspected outliers, if any.
- How tightly the data is grouped

11.13.3 Creating a Boxplot

The `boxplot()` function of the pyplot module is used to draw a boxplot. The syntax of this function can be given as, `boxplot(x)`

Example 11.6 **Let us create a data set with some random integer values and then plot a box plot using this data.**

```
import matplotlib.pyplot as plt
from random import randint
data = []
# generate some integers
for i in range(1000):
        value = randint(0, 1000)
        data.append(value)
plt.boxplot(data)
plt.show()
```

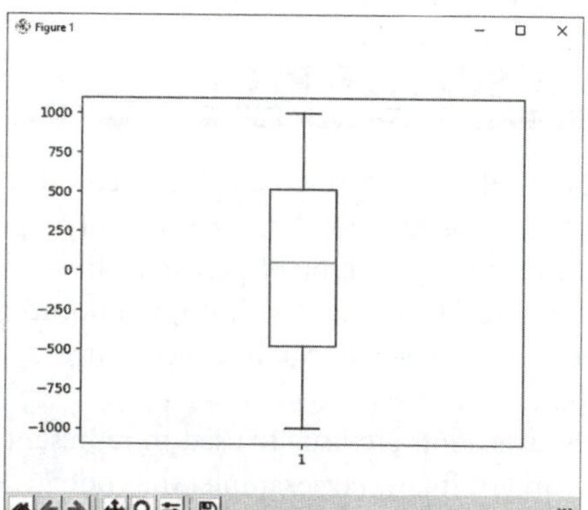

11.14 PIE CHART

We have been drawing and interpreting pie charts in Mathematics. Did you ever notice that a pie chart displays one series of data? It shows the size of items in one data series, proportional to the sum of the items. The area of the whole chart represents 100% or the whole of the data. This means that data points in a pie chart are shown as a percentage of the whole pie. The slices of the pie are called **wedges**.

The `pie()` function in the Matplotlib library is used to create a pie chart in which the fractional area of each wedge is calculated using the formula, **x/sum(x)**. Since pie charts provide a quick summary, they are commonly used in business presentations like sales, operations, survey results, news articles, and resource usage diagrams like disk and memory.

11.14.1 Plotting a Pie Chart

The Matplotlib library has `pie()` function in the pyplot module that is used to create a pie chart representing data stored in an array. The syntax of this function is,

```
matplotlib.pyplot.pie(data, labels=None, colors=None, autopct=None)
```

where,

`data` is the array of values to be plotted. The fractional area of each slice is calculated as, **data/sum(data)**.
`labels` is a list containing strings to the labels of each wedge.
`color` is used to specify the color for each wedge.
`autopct` is a string that labels wedges with their numerical value.

Example 11.7 **The code given below plots a pie chart to show the contribution of each subject's marks in the total marks obtained by a student.**

```
import matplotlib.pyplot as plt
Marks = [80,90,60,85,100]
my_labels =
'Math','Science','English','Social
Science','Painting'
plt.pie(Marks,labels=my_
labels,autopct='%1.1f%%')
plt.title('Marks Obtained')
plt.axis('equal')
plt.show()
```

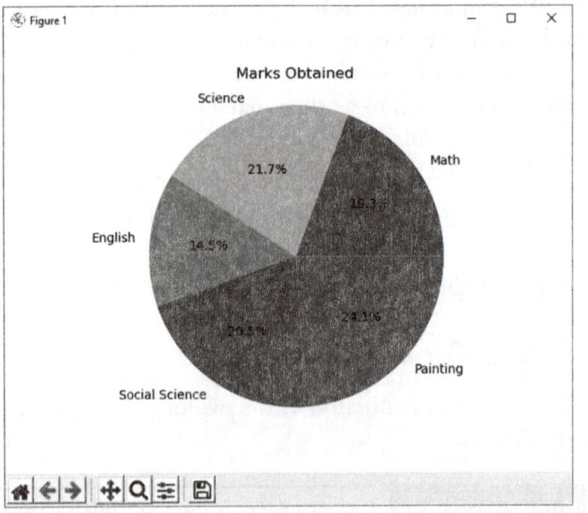

11.15 SCATTER PLOT

A scatter plot is a chart which plots each value in the data set using a dot. A scatter plot is drawn using the `scatter()` function. This function has the capability to render a different size and/or colour for each point.

Scatter plot is a type of plot that shows data as a collection of points. To draw a scatter plot, we need two arrays of the same length. The position of a point depends on its two-dimensional value, where each value is a position on either the x- or y-axis. So, one of the arrays species denotes the values of the x-axis, and the other denotes the values of the y-axis.

Scatter Plots are usually used to represent the correlation between two or more variables. It also helps us to identify outliers, if any. For example, the code given below draws a scatter plot to depict marks obtained by 15 students in a test.

```
import numpy as np
import matplotlib.pyplot as plt
from random import seed
from random import randint
x = []
y = []
# generate some integers
for i in range(20):
        value = randint(0, 100)
        x.append(value)
        value = randint(0, 100)
        y.append(value)
plt.scatter(x, y)
plt.show()
```

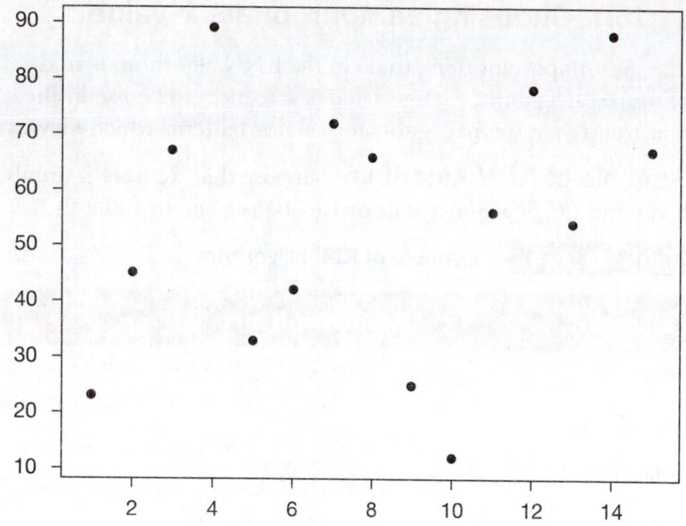

Scatter plots are used to plot data points on horizontal and vertical axis in an attempt to show how much one variable is affected by another.

11.16 K-NEAREST NEIGHBOR ALGORITHM

The *k*-nearest neighbor algorithm (KNN) is a supervised learning algorithm in which the output value of data is known but how the way of getting the output is not known. For example, if we have several groups of labelled samples and all items available are homogeneous, then to find which group an item with unknown label belongs, we will find similarities between the item (at hand) and with items in each group. Finally, we will conclude that the item belongs to the group to which it is most similar. The KNN algorithm works in exactly the same way.

The *k*-nearest neighbor algorithm stores all available cases and classifies new cases by a majority vote of its *k* neighbors. The algorithm segregates unlabelled data values into well-defined groups. The value for a new instance (*x*) is predicted by searching the training set for the *k* most similar cases (neighbors) and summarizing the output values for those *k* cases. In other words, this is the mode (or most common) value.

Example 11.8 **To better understand the concept, look at Fig. 11.8. There are two groups of data and a new data point whose label is unknown. We will calculate the number of nearest neighbors of the new point from Group A and its nearest neighbors from Group B. The group having a greater number of neighbors is the group to which the new point belongs.**

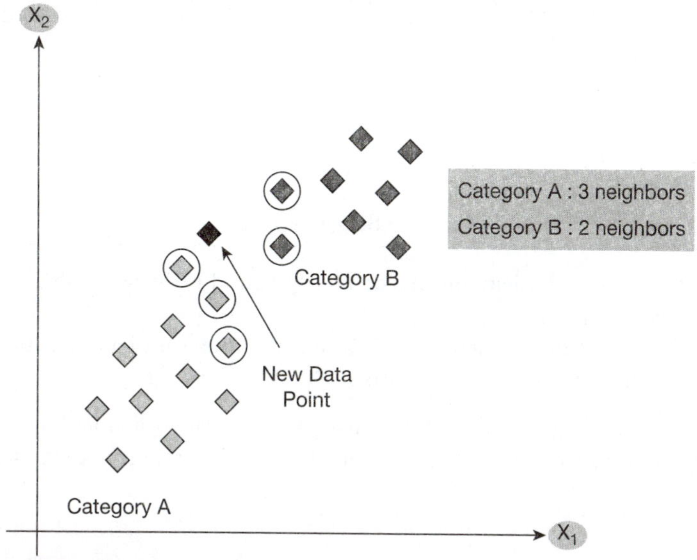

Figure 11.8 Data segregation using k-nearest neighbor algorithm

11.16.1 Choosing an Appropriate *k*-value

The most important thing to do in the KNN algorithm is to determine an appropriate value of k, that is, the number of nearest neighbors. A large value of k reduces the noise in the data. But, if we have more number of data points in one group then we may ignore the smaller patterns which may have useful insights.

Example of KNN Algorithm Suppose that we have n number of students rated on two parameters – Academic Score and EC Score on a scale of 1 to 10 as given in Table 11.3.

Table 11.3 (a) Example of KNN algorithm

Name	Academic Score	EC Score	Grade
Ria	8	8	Outstanding
Khushank	9	1	Academically Sound
Mehar	4	8	Sporty
Nagma	2	1	Below Average

Then, Academic Score is an indication of how well the student performs academically and EC Score is the score obtained by the student in extra-curricular activities.

Now, if we have a new student to categorize, then we will calculate the distance between 'New Student' and its nearest neighbors ('Outstanding', 'Sporty', 'Academically Sound' and 'Below Average') using the Euclidean distance formula.

Assuming that co-ordinates of the New Student are (8,2), we calculate the distance between Below Average (2,1) and New Student as:

```
dist(Below Average, New Student) = 6.08
```

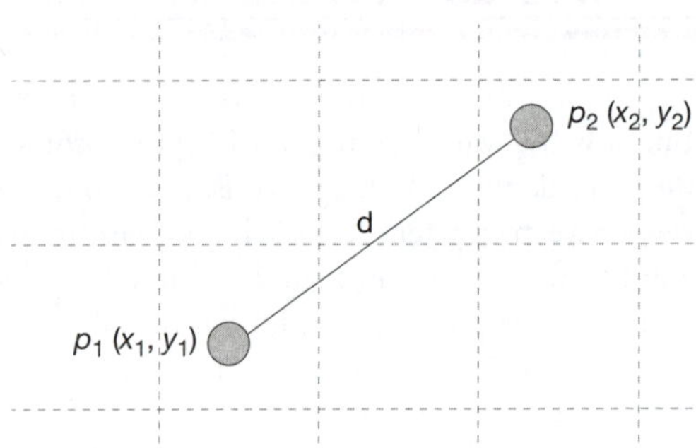

Euclidean distance (d) = $\sqrt{(x_2 - x_1)^2 + (y_2 - y_1)^2}$

Similarly, calculate the distance of New Student from each of its nearest neighbors as shown in Table 11.3 (b).

Table 11.3 (b) Example of KNN algorithm

Name	Academic Score	EC Score	Grade	Distance to New Student
Ria	8	8	Outstanding	6.08
Khushank	9	1	Academically Sound	1.41
Mehar	4	8	Sporty	7.21
Nagma	2	1	Below Average	6.08

We see that distance between New Student and Academically Sound is the least. So the New Student belongs to the group of academically sound students.

KNN algorithm can also be used for prediction. It is extensively used in pharmaceutical industry to detect the growth of oncogenic (cancer) cells or presence of a disease.

Choosing the *k* value Consider Fig. 11.9. If we have two classes – class A denoted by stars and class B indicated by triangles, then to classify a new square object, the value of k plays an important role. If $k = 3$, then according to the figure, the 3 nearest neighbors belong to class B. So, the new object is placed in class B. However, if we take $k = 7$, then the new object will be a member of class A. If we take $k = 1$, then the new object will belong to class B. Hence, the value of k greatly influences the classification.

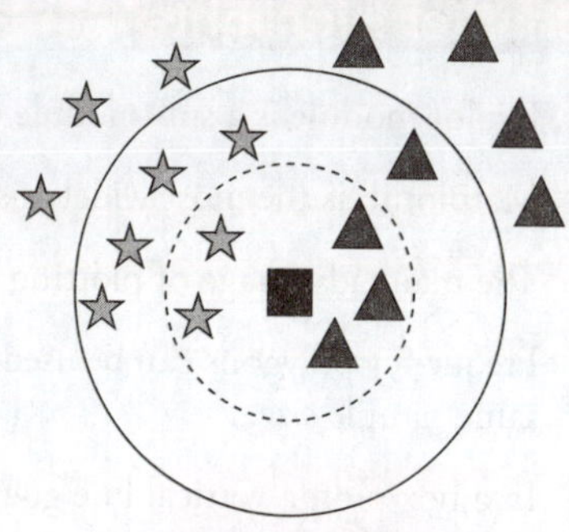

Figure 11.9

Pros and Cons of KNN Algorithm

Pros

- The KNN algorithm is a very simple and effective algorithm.
- Users can easily implement the algorithm; this has made the algorithm quite popular with data professionals.
- The algorithm is highly unbiased in nature and does not make any prior assumption of the underlying data.
- The KNN algorithm works well with multi-class algorithms
- The algorithm can be applied to both classification and regression.

The k-nearest neighbor can be used for regressionwhen the dependent variable is continuous. In this case, the predicted value is the average of the values of its k nearest neighbors.

Cons

- Simple things are usually not very powerful. Same is the case with KNN algorithm.
- Although the algorithm trains the model really fast, the prediction time is high.
- Many a time, useful insights may get ignored.
- The algorithm is sensitive to the scale of data; so data must first be standardized
- The performance of the algorithm deteriorates when there are multiple independent variables
- The algorithm requires more memory and is computationally expensive
- It does not work well if the target variable is skewed
- The accuracy of the algorithm depends on k value. For any given problem, a small value of k will lead to a large variance in predictions. And setting k to a large value may lead to a large model bias.

Key Terms

Bar chart: A bar graph is a chart or graph that presents categorical data with rectangular bars.

Histogram: A graphical representation which is quite similar to a bar graph. It is a great tool for assessing the probability distribution of a continuous variable that can be easily understood by the people looking at it.

Frequency polygon: A graphical form of data representation that gives an idea about the shape of the data and the trends that a particular data set follows.

Box plot: Also known as a whisker plot, it displays a summary of a set of data containing the minimum, first quartile, median, third quartile, and maximum.

Scatter plot: A chart which plots each value in the data set by a dot.

Data: Raw facts or figures which are processed to give useful information.

Data science: Science that includes a detailed study of the flow of information from massive amounts of data present in an organization's repository.

Data scientist: Professionals who are skilled in organizing and analyzing massive amounts of data.

Data processing: The process of converting raw data to meaningful information.

Multimodal data set: Data set in which n values appear most frequently.

K-nearest neighbor algorithm: A supervised learning algorithm in which the output value of data is known but the way of getting the output is not known.

Chapter Highlights

- Pyplot module is a sub-module of the matplotlib module.
- Matplotlib is the most widely used scientific plotting library in Python.
- The main advantage of plotting a bar graph is that it depicts comparisons among discrete categories.
- Frequency polygons can be used to compare two sets of data and are best for comparing two data sets that have the same sample size.
- In a box plot, a vertical line goes through the box at the median. The whiskers go from each quartile to the minimum or maximum.
- The main advantage of applying data science in an organization is that it facilitates data-driven decision-making. Such decisions result in increased profitability, improved operational efficiency and better business performance.
- The first phase in any data science project life cycle is data discovery.
- Descriptive statistics are evaluated to summarize and organize data for better understandability.
- Central tendency indicates that there is one number that best summarizes the entire set of measurements. This number is "central" to the set.
- Measure of Spread refers to the idea of variability within a given set of data.
- Visualizing data through charts helps users to easily understand and interpret even complex and/or large amount of data in one glance.
- A box plot or a whisker plot displays a summary of a set of data containing the minimum, first quartile, median, third quartile, and maximum.
- We should never treat the outliers as bad data points as many a time, most useful information in the data set is depicted by them. They should never be discarded or removed from the data set.

Review Questions

1. How is plotting graphs helpful in statistics?
2. What is data? Give any three uses of analyzing data.
3. Define the term data science and discuss its relevance in the current scenario.
4. Mention any five sources of data.
5. Name any five organizations that extensively use Data Science. Also elaborate in what ways they apply data science.
6. Explain the Data Science Life Cycle.
7. Differentiate between structured and unstructured data.
8. Why should we visualize data using different types of charts?
9. How does KNN algorithm classify a new data point?
10. Why is the value of *k* so important for the accuracy of the KNN model?

Fill in the Blanks

1. Pyplot module is a sub-module of the ________ module.
2. In a box plot, we draw a box from the first quartile to the ______ quartile.
3. ________ are usually used to represent the correlation between two or more variables.
4. ___________ studies the flow of information throughout the organization.
5. The job of a _________ is to collect relevant data, understand the data, process it to extract value from it, visualize it and communicate it through business reports or other visualization tools.
6. ______ and ______ are two popularly used programming languages for data science applications.
7. _________ data is not available in a pre-defined format.
8. In a _________ data set, *n* values appear most frequently.
9. _________ is calculated as the square of average distance between each quantity and mean.
10. The height or length of the bars is proportional to the ______ they represent.
11. Histogram plots data by dividing it into equal-sized _____.
12. Values above or below 3 × IQR are known as ________.
13. The slices of the pie are called ________.

State True or False

1. A bar graph presents categorical data with rectangular bars.
2. In a bar graph, bars can be drawn only vertically.
3. Histograms assess probability distribution of a non-continuous variable.
4. Histogram plots the frequency distribution of a numeric array by splitting it to small equal-sized bins.
5. Frequency polygon is always drawn along with a histogram.
6. When drawing a frequency plot, frequency is plotted on x-axis.
7. Data product is developed, tested, refined and deployed by data scientists.
8. Emails, PDF files, videos or images are examples of structured data.
9. Median is obtained after arranging data either in ascending or descending order.
10. In some data sets, there can be no mode at all.
11. A high standard deviation indicates that values are closer to the mean of the data set.
12. Variance is the square root of standard deviation.
13. Bar charts can be drawn vertically or horizontally.
14. Histogram bins are specified as consecutive, non-overlapping intervals of a variable.
15. In a box plot, we draw a box from the first quartile to the third quartile.
16. Outliers are bad data and must be discarded or removed from the data set.
17. The *k*-nearest neighbor algorithm is a supervised learning algorithm.

Multiple Choice Questions

1. Which of the following plot displays the summary of a set of data containing the minimum, first quartile, median, third quartile, and maximum?
   a. Bar chart b. Histogram
   c. Box plot d. Scatter plot

2. In a box plot, a vertical line goes through the box at the ________.
   a. median b. first quartile
   c. third quartile d. fourth quartile

3. Which of the following plot is used to identify the outliers?
   a. Bar chart b. Histogram
   c. Box plot d. Scatter plot

4. Which plot shows data as a collection of points?
   a. Bar chart b. Histogram
   c. Box plot d. Scatter plot

5. IQR is calculated as _______.
   a. Q1 + Q3 b. Q3 – Q1
   c. (Q1 – Q3)/2 d. (Q1 + Q3)/2

6. A data scientist must possess __________ skills.
   a. Analytical b. Machine Learning
   c. Statistical d. All of these.

7. Cleaning data, filling any missing value(s), merging two or more tables, summarizing fields in a table using aggregation, etc., are all done in the ________ phase.
   a. Data Discovery b. Data Preparation
   c. Mathematical Models d. Communication

8. Data _________ means the process of converting raw data to meaningful information.
   a. Discovery b. Preparation
   c. Processing d. Visualization

9. ________ is a single number which can estimate the value of the whole data set.
   a. Mean b. Median
   c. Mode d. Variance

10. _______ is the value which divides the data into two equal parts.
    a. Mean b. Median
    c. Mode d. Variance

11. _________ is calculated as the difference between lowest and highest value.
    a. Mean b. Median
    c. Range d. Variance

12. A box plot does not display ________.
    a. First quartile b. Median
    c. Third quartile d. None of these.

13. Which chart shows the size of items in one data series, proportional to the sum of the items?
    a. Bar b. Box plot
    c. Pie d. Scatter plot

Group Decision

Discuss how data science can be used by companies for sales and marketing.

Role Play Activity

Imagine that you are Vice President of a very big Fashion Brand. Discuss how you will use the power of data to take your business to new heights.

Project Work

Collect information about any five companies that use data science to promote and enhance their business.

Data Analytics Activity

1. Collect data about your class's performance in the last examination.
   a. Compute descriptive statistics (calculate mean, median, mode, standard deviation and variance)
   b. Create different charts to interpret information from this data
2. Look at the following graphs that are used to monitor business performance and write down the indications they give.

a.

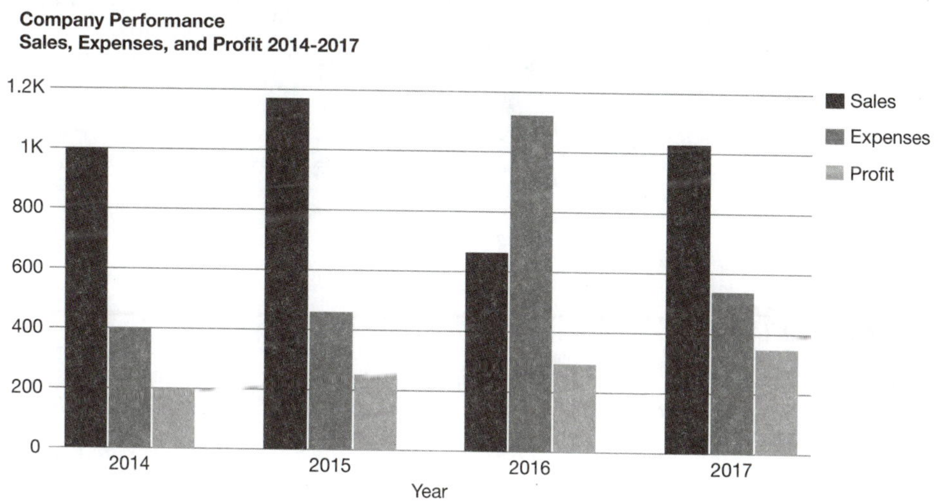

b.

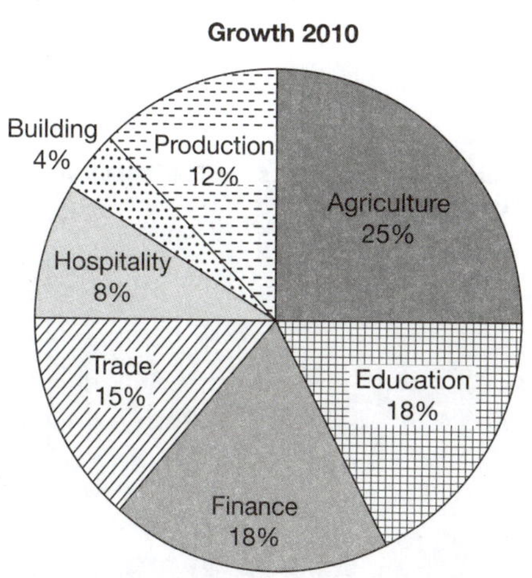

c.

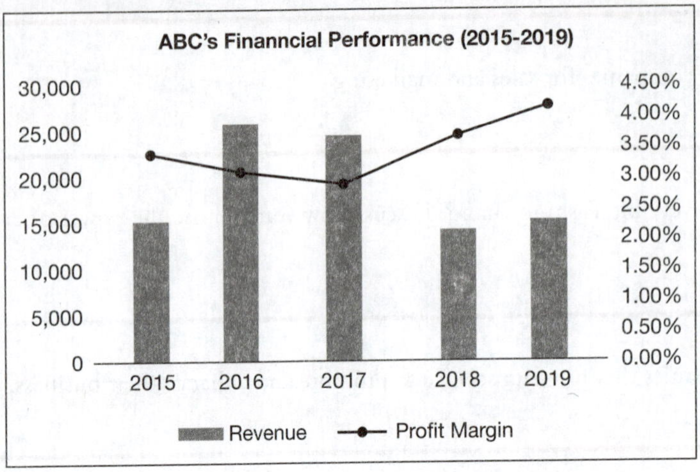

3. Consider the figure given below and write down to which class the new object belongs if the value of $k = 3$ and if $k = 6$ in the KNN model. According to you, which should be the correct classification?

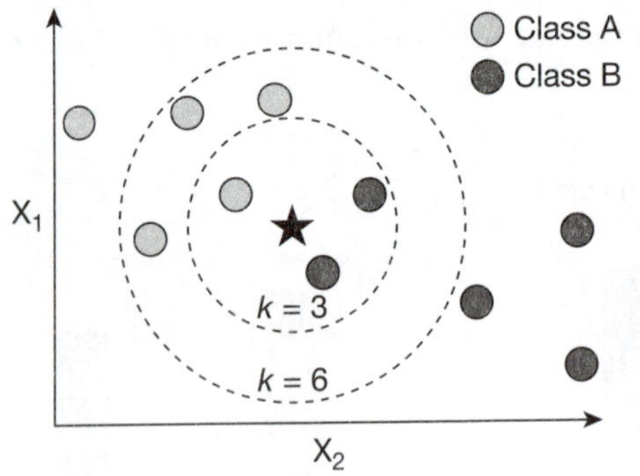

AI Lab Session – Cartoonify

Cartoonify is an experiment by Google that uses Artificial Intelligence to turn a photo into a cartoon using neural networks. For best results, upload images with clear objects on a solid background. Visit the link https://www.kapwing.com/cartoonify to cartoonify yourself!

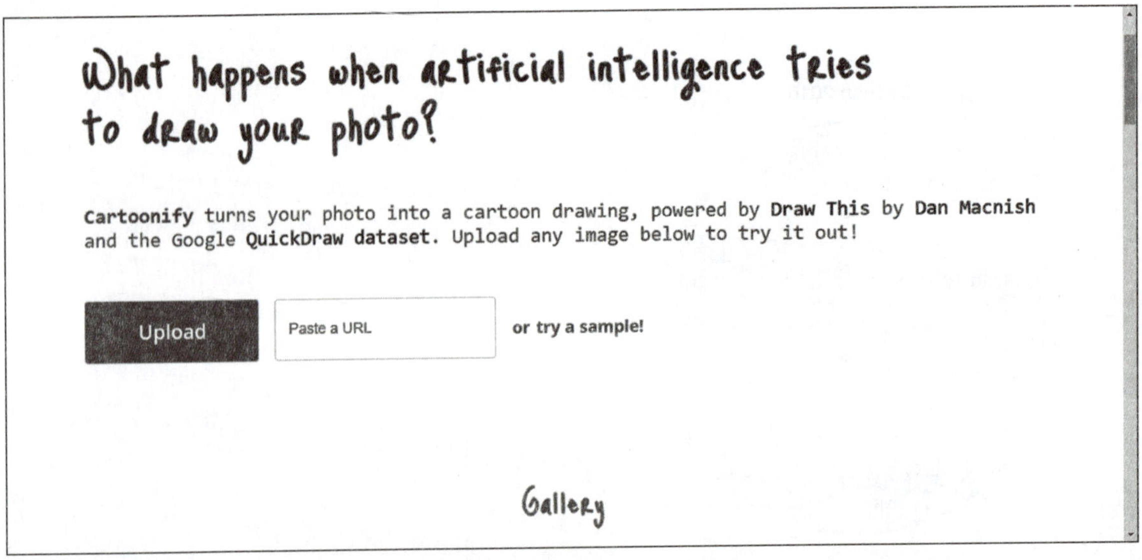

Personality Prediction Activity

Step 1: Create a graph with two axes X and Y as shown below. Honestly write down your name and your classmates names in the quadrant that matches their personality. For example, if a person is a very good passive listener but is otherwise less focused, then his name will come in the second quadrant.

Step 2: Visit the link https://tinyurl.com/discanimal and do a 15-question personality prediction quiz about yourself. Answer all the questions honestly without discussing them with others. After the quiz is completed, the system will predict an animal for you. Just note it down and do not show it to anyone.

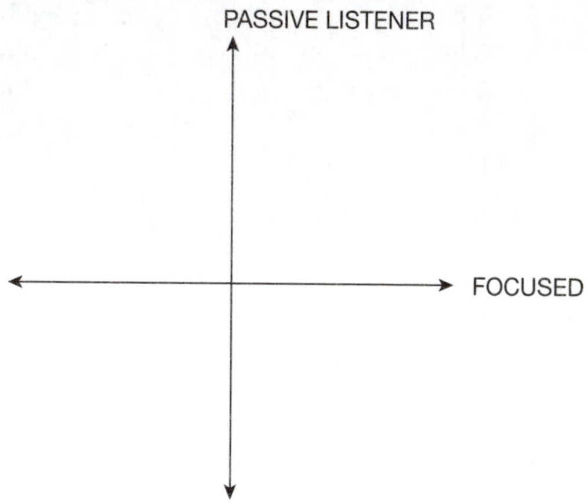

Note that a passive listener listens to people and understands everything that they say, without interruption. Focused people try to deliver the best experience to other people.

Now use the same graph of Step 1 and draw the symbol which corresponds to the animal predicted for you.

Lion	Otter	Golden Retriever	Beaver
♥	●	☺	★

Now use the same graph of Step 1. Every student except 4 students should draw the symbol which corresponds to the animal predicted for them. The 4 students who are not drawing the symbols, must keep the animals predicted for them, secret. On the graph, just write names of these students.

Our task is to use the nearest neighbor algorithm and predict what can be the possible animal(s) for these 4 unknowns. For this, find out which animal is occurring the most in their vicinity. For example, if the lion symbol is occurring the most near their names, then there is a good probability that their animal would also be a lion. Likewise, guess the animals and then ask these 4 students if the guess is right or not.

Answers

Fill in the Blanks

1. matplotlib
2. Third
3. Scatter plots
4. Data Science
5. data scientist
6. R, Python
7. Unstructured
8. multimodal
9. Variance
10. values
11. bins
12. outliers
13. wedges

State True or False

1. True
2. False
3. False
4. True
5. False
6. False
7. True
8. False
9. True
10. True
11. False
12. False
13. False
14. True
15. True
16. False
17. True

Multiple Choice Questions

1. c
2. a
3. c
4. d
5. b
6. d
7. b
8. c
9. a
10. b
11. c
12. d
13. c

Computer Vision

12

Chapter Objectives

The chapter covers one of the most interesting topics of Artificial Intelligence. Interpreting and playing with images excite us all. Therefore, in this chapter, we will understand topics such as:

- Computer vision – evolution, working, tasks, applications, challenges
- Human vision vs computer vision
- Understanding pixels and resolution
- Convolutional neural network
- Working with opencv

Computer Vision (CV) is a field of Artificial Intelligence that helps computers gain a high level of understanding from digital images or videos. It is done by acquiring images, processing them, analyzing them and finally understanding the information they are conveying. If AI allows computers to think, computer vision helps them to see, observe and understand.

12.1 HUMAN VISION VS. COMPUTER VISION

Computer vision works like the human vision. The main advantage of human vision is that we have a brain that automatically learns to tell how far away two objects are, whether they are moving or not, whether there is something wrong in an image and many more questions like that.

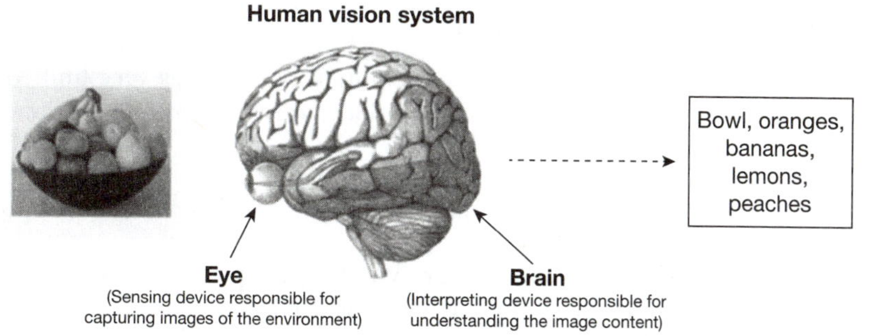

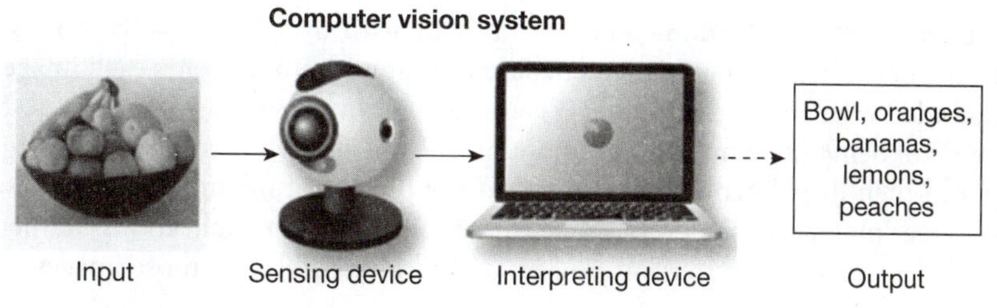

Computer vision techniques, on the other hand, train machines to perform these functions. The main challenge here is that machines have to analyze images coming from cameras using data and algorithms in a very limited time. Once a system is trained to process thousands of images in a minute, it can quickly surpass human capabilities.

12.1.1 How Computer Vision Works

Computer vision algorithms need a large volume of data for analyzing and recognizing images. For this, computer vision makes extensive use of deep learning (next level of machine learning) and Convolutional Neural Network (CNN).

Machine learning or deep-learning algorithms help machines to learn about the context of visual data and learn, by itself, how to identify and differentiate images. CNN complements the machine learning or deep learning model by breaking images down into pixels that are given tags or labels. It uses these labels to perform convolutions (a mathematical operation on two functions to produce a third function) to make predictions about what it is "seeing." Multiple iterations of the neural network are run and the accuracy of their predictions is evaluated. The process is repeated until the computer identifies the image with an acceptable accuracy. At this time, we say that the machine is recognizing or seeing images in a way similar to humans.

Example: We can build a machine learning model to differentiate between two varieties of dogs – Greyhound and Labrador. For this, we need to extract their inherent features like height of the dog, the color of its eyes, hair length, etc.

Greyhound Labrador

As you can see from the figure, Greyhounds are taller than Labradors. However, this is not always true because there are many variations in the world. Therefore, in machine learning projects, we cannot perform classification based on just one feature. We need multiple features to capture different types of information. If only one feature analysis was sufficient, we could have easily done it using a basic `if-else` statement. There would have been no need to build a classifier.

12.1.2 The Evolution of Computer Vision

Prior to deep learning/machine learning, performance of computer vision was very limited as a lot of manual coding and the developer's efforts were required. For example, facial recognition could be done using the following steps.

Create a Database of individual images of all the subjects to be tracked. Store them in a specific format.

Annotate Images by entering key points/features of every individual image. For example, distance between the eyes, the width of nose bridge, distance between upper lip and nose, etc.).

Capture New Images and repeat the measurement process to mark the key points on the image.

All this work was done manually. Automation comes into picture with the application comparing the measurements in the new image with the ones already stored in its database. The application matches each image to the database and tells whether it corresponded with any of the profiles it was tracking. In this scenario, there was very little automation as most of the work was still being done manually. No doubt, the possibility of error was also large in this context.

Machine learning and then deep learning revolutionized the process of solving computer vision problems. Now, developers have to no longer manually code every single rule into their vision applications. Rather, programs are written to extract features to detect specific patterns in images and ultimately classify those images in different categories (Fig. 12.1).

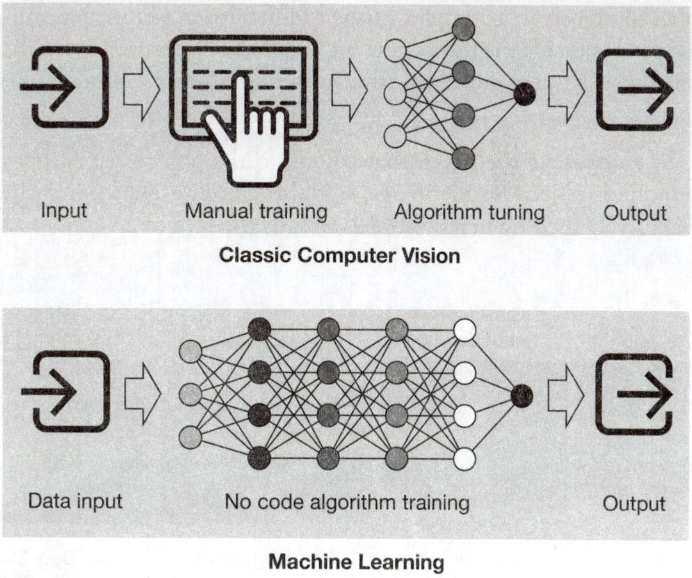

Figure 12.1 Computer vision through classical and machine learning process

12.2 TASKS IN COMPUTER VISION

Computer vision applications recognize things in photographs by using the following techniques.

Object Classification to identify the broad category of object in the photograph.

Object Identification to classify the type of a given object in the photograph

Object Verification to confirm the presence of object in the photograph.

Object Localization to locate the objects in the photograph. The goal of **localization** is to find the location of a single object in an image. Usually, the located object is enclosed within a rectangular box. For example, in the figure, the cat is first classified and then localized. The standard way to perform localization is to define a bounding box enclosing the object in the image.

Object Landmark Detection to understand the key points for the object in the photograph.

Object Detection or Object Identification task involves repeatedly locating and classifying all objects of interest in the image. The main aim here is to find and classify a ***variable number of objects*** in the given image (Fig. 12.2).

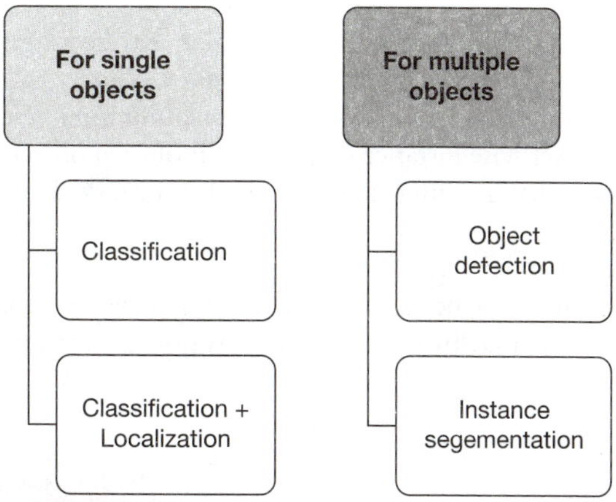

Figure 12.2 Object detection for multiple objects

Identifying unknown number of objects in a complex image is difficult for a human as some objects may be partially visible. These objects may be partly outside the frame, present in different sizes or may overlap each other. For example, object identification is extensively used to monitor real-time images from security cameras to identify a specific person's face.

Object Segmentation to ***enumerate the pixels*** that belong to the object in the image (Fig. 12.3). Instance or object segmentation not only finds objects in the image, but also creates a mask for each detected object that is as accurate as possible. It is extensively used by news channels to blur the face of a victim or any person whose identity is not to be revealed.

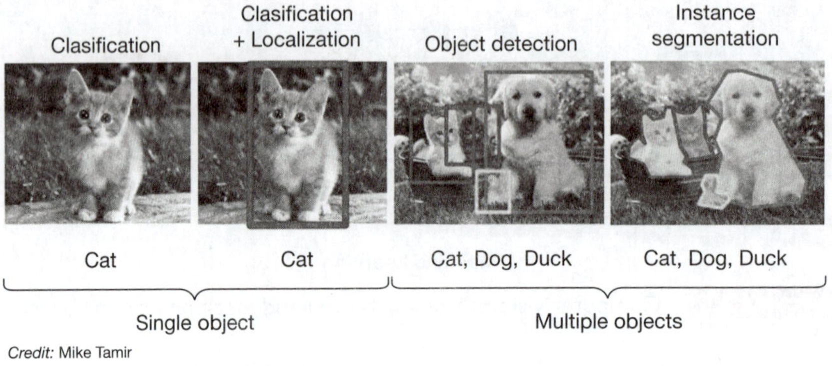

Figure 12.3 Computer vision tasks

Object tracking inputs a video to track an object that is in motion over time. This is essentially useful in robotics (for example, to stop a ball when the robot is used as a goalkeeper), in autonomous vehicles for spatial reasoning and path planning, and in human tracking systems.

Object Tracking applies object detection to capture the object being tracked and then discern the movements of that object.

In addition to the this, computer vision also includes methods for:

Video Motion Analysis to estimate the velocity of objects in a video, or the camera itself.

Scene Reconstruction to create a 3D model of a scene inputted through images or video.

Image Restoration uses filters based on machine learning to remove noise (to remove parts of the image that are blurred).

To better realize the application of computer vision, play the game **Emoji Scavenger Hunt.**

12.3 HOW COMPUTER VISION WORKS WITH DEEP LEARNING

With deep learning and CNN, the entire process of computer vision has been transformed. The steps given below outline a general approach to building a computer vision model using CNNs.

Create a dataset of annotated images or use an existing one. Annotations include image classification, object detection (using bounding boxes), a pixel-wise instance segmentation of each object of interest present in the image.

From each image, **extract features** that are important for the current task. For example, extract facial features to recognize faces.

Train a deep learning model based on extracted features.

Evaluate the model using images that were not used in the training phase and compute the accuracy of the model.

This strategy comes under **supervised machine learning technique** as it requires a dataset from which the model can learn.

12.4 APPLICATIONS OF COMPUTER VISION

Once the images are understood, computer vision is then used in the following areas.

Facial recognition systems to recognize faces in images and videos (Fig. 12.4). Applications like google photos, spam chat, Facebook, Instagram, etc., use facial recognition system to identify people.

Almost every smartphone these days uses facial-recognition algorithms to unlock phones. Facebook uses facial recognition to identify users in the posted pictures. In China, this technology is integrated with **payment technology** to allow users do cashless payment.

Some government agencies in different countries are also using facial-recognition technology for **surveillance**. Though use of this has raised concerns among rights and privacy advocates, the applications of facial recognition techniques are on a constant rise.

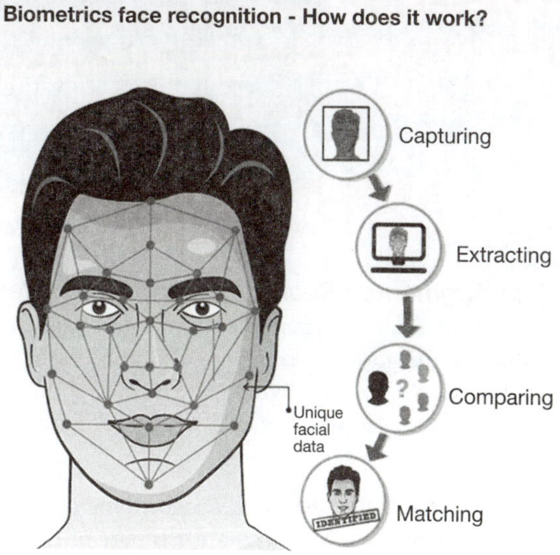

Figure 12.4 Facial recognition sequence

Content-based Image Retrieval Systems identify images by identifying image properties like composition, color, texture etc. Search engines like Google and Bing and software analyzing CT scans and MRIs in hospitals, etc. used CBIR systems.

Computer vision is extensively used in smart interactions to give input to computers. This is especially helpful in **gaming software** and in systems designed for differently abled individuals.

Software used in **home security systems**, office security systems, drone-based surveillance systems etc. also use computer vision techniques.

Computer vision is the heart of **augmented reality apps** that detect physical objects in real-time to place virtual objects within the physical environment.

Many agricultural organizations use computer vision techniques to monitor the harvest and solve common agricultural problems including weeds emergence or nutrient deficiency (Fig. 12.5). Images collected from satellites, drones, or planes are processed by computer vision algorithms to **detect potential problems** in the early phase, thereby avoiding unnecessary loss at later stages.

Figure 12.5 Use of computer vision in agriculture

Self-driving cars (like Tesla) use computer vision to learn from their surroundings. Every smart vehicle has cameras to capture videos from different angles. These videos act as an input to the computer vision software that processes them to detect objects like road marking, pedestrians or other cars, traffic lights, etc.

Websites like Facebook perform **content moderation** using computer vision techniques. Billions of posts uploaded by users every day are reviewed and any images/videos that contain violence, extremism or pornography are immediately removed.

Ninety percent of medical data is present in the form of images. So, most of the diseases can be easily diagnosed by processing images available in the form of **X-rays, MRI, mammography**, etc. For example, computer vision algorithms can detect diabetic retinopathy, which is the most prevalent cause of blindness. Going further, these algorithms can also process pictures of the back of the eye (Fig. 12.6) and rate their severity (in case the disease is detected). Computer vision algorithms can even detect cancer with much higher precision than human doctors.

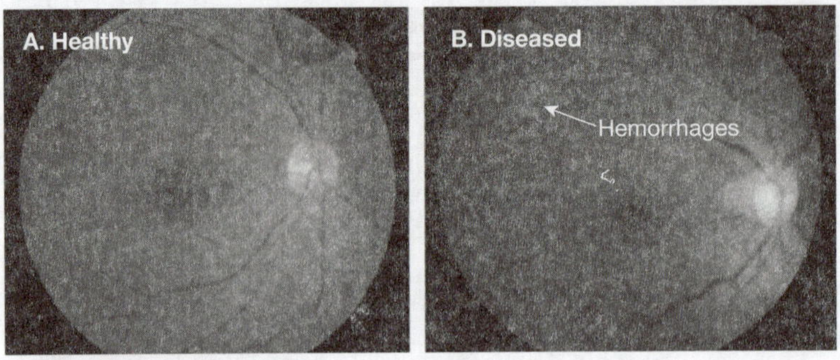

Figure 12.6 Digital retinal imaging for detecting eye diseases

CV in Augmented Reality (AR) and Mixed Reality (MR): In AR and MR, computer vision enables computing devices (like smartphones, tablets and smart glasses) to overlay and embed virtual objects on real-world imagery. For example, CV algorithms can help AR applications detect planes such as tabletops, walls and floors. Moreover, Snapchat Filters that overlay digital images onto your face is an application of AR. Another example of AR is Pokemon Go where users can walk around with their mobile phones and find Pokemon that are overlaid in the environment around the user.

Inventory management: CV algorithms can analyze images from security camera to generate a very accurate estimate of the items available in the store. Results obtained through this analysis can then be used by store managers to check if there is an unusual increase in demand for certain products and react early and efficiently.

> Retailers use Computer Vision techniques to track customers' movements through stores, analyze navigational routes and detect walking patterns.

Manufacturing: In this sector, most losses occur due to problems in machines or because of production of defective components. Computer vision algorithms can be used for **predictive maintenance**. Images obtained through cameras (probably fitted in the eyes of robots) can be analyzed to detect potential problems that may occur. CV can even be helpful to reduce defects. The system can identify defects in components throughout the entire production line and notify the manufacturers to take action in real time.

The system is trained to classify a defect as a serious defect or a mild defect. In case of a serious defect, further production is completely halted until the issue is resolved.

Insurance: CV is used in insurance sector for processing claims. The clients can be asked to share images while documenting and claiming money. The CV system can analyze those images to estimate and adjust repair costs, determine if the insurance covers them and even check for possible fraud. In this way, clients get a better experience as the length of claim-cycle gets shortened due to automation.

A CV system can also be used to **avoid accidents** by preventing collisions, when integrated into industrial machinery, cars, and drones. This provision will have a huge impact on the insurance industry.

Defense and Security: CV systems are used in homes and companies with high security requirements (like banks) to **identify customers** based on analysis of images from security cameras.

Such systems can also be used to improve cargo inspection at ports or for surveillance of sensitive places such as embassies, power plants, hospitals, railroads, and stadiums. In these places, computer vision algorithm analyzes and classifies images, creates a detailed description of a scene in real time to help decision-makers take the right action at the right time. In defense, CV systems can also be used to identify enemy terrain or enemies in images.

> Amazon Go Store uses Computer Vision technique to allow customers who have installed the Amazon Go application on their mobile devices to avoid long queues in the super market. They just go to the store, pick up their items and come back without paying at the kiosks.

Visual Search Engines: A visual search engine retrieves images that meet the specified criteria. For example, Google search engine allow users to present a source image so that it can find all images similar to it. Applications like **Google Lens** can be used to obtain detailed information from images. For example, you can show an image of a dog to get information about its breed, or any other details.

Google's Search by Image feature (Fig. 12.7) gets search results through an image. The underlying Computer Vision algorithm compares different features of the input image to the database of images and gives us the search result after analyzing the various features of the image.

Figure 12.7 Google image search

In the e-commerce market, **Pinterest Lens** can be used to find new ways to wear clothing outfits. For example, when you present a photo of an item, then Pinterest Lens will return outfit ideas that include compatible clothing items that you would like to buy.

Moreover, the **Google Translate App** help users to read signs in a foreign language. Users just have to point their phone's camera at the words and let the Google Translate app tell what it means in their preferred language almost instantly.

Sports Industry: Computer vision algorithms are gradually replacing human eyes to better analyze crucial sports event moments for giving precise scores and accurate judgements. These algorithms are also used in the following areas:

- **Training process** by doing an in-depth analysis of captured actions in swimming, gymnastics, athletics, skiing, and other sports where the technique of performing movements matters the most;
- 3D simulations and for inspecting videos of the off-sides, outs, goals, and photo-finish in mass races, for referring events.
- **Analyzing the performance of a player** during events. For example, the dynamics of players based on their movements and slight gestures can be captured and analyzed. Now, the person recruiting players need not attend competitions or travel to assess their abilities. They just have to watch a video with all the necessary analytics in the office or at home.
- In tennis, cricket and other sports, ball trajectories can be analyzed as well as predicted for further in-depth analytics. The referee can see whether the ball landed in or out of bounds during the game. Predicting ball trajectories supports **100% fair refereeing and reputable sport performance analytics.**
- Cameras are stabilized and smart focus is applied for real-time smoothing-out of action frames (Fig. 12.8 a, b and c).

Figure 12.8 (a) Use of cameras to detect the player's position

Computer Vision algorithms take a piece of motion video content and convert it into a series of images so that players' positions can be closely analyzed. Multiple camera angles and flexible motion capture the essential details to know whether the **ball landed in or out of bounds during the game.**

- Algorithms help sports coaches to build the **best team, develop effective tactics and game strategies** by assessing the actions of each player and their interaction with each other.
- Computer vision in sports analytics goes far beyond just recording a video of a game field. It facilitates mathematical processing of the video stream for analyzing the **position of each player of the opponents' teams at each moment.**
- In sports such as formula-one racing, computer vision algorithms are used for timely detection and prevention of **vehicle malfunctions,** thereby avoiding situations that can be potential life-endangering for the players.
- Another popular use of CV algorithms is that it allows analysts to **analyze the mood of the fans** and their engagement in the game.
- Journalists covering sports events use CV to generate impressive media content and report on the game highlights more precisely.

In addition, CV integrated with NLP can be used to automatically **commentate on events** without the help of live speakers.

Figure 12.8 (b) Use of cameras to detect the player's position

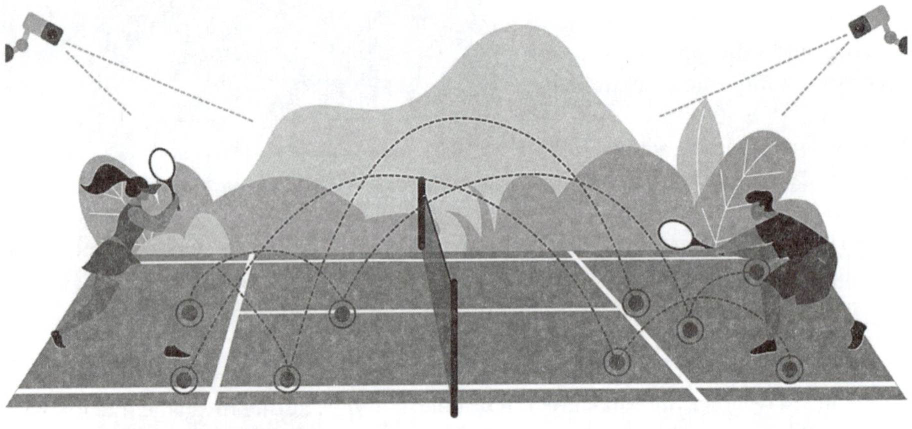

Figure 12.8 (c) Use of cameras to detect the player's position

CV Software Solutions for Sports Analysis: Applications such as Sentio's smart tracking and analytics systems, Stats Perform's SportVU 2.0 with in-depth computer vision-based algorithms, and GAMEFACE.AI with its in-depth analysis of strategic insights and other footage points, are available these days and can be used by simply integrating them with the system's hardware as well as software. Users just have to control the resolution and speed of the cameras. The software does its best to focus on minimizing the volume of video recordings and enhancing the ease of working with them.

12.5 WHICH VISION SUCCEDED?

It is interesting to note that certain experiments were carried out tin Germany to address the void between computer and human vision.

Experiment 1 was conducted to understand how neural networks perceive contours (or boundary). For this, both the human and the AI participant were shown an image and asked whether it has a closed contour or not. The experiment was specifically done to check if deep-learning algorithm can identify closed and open shapes or not.

Results showed that a well-trained neural network could identify a closed contour even when the contour was not made of straight lines.

Experiment 2 was performed to understand whether the deep-learning algorithm could identify the relation between different shapes in the picture or not. While human vision could easily understand this, it was found that deep-learning algorithms that were trained with less data found it difficult to draw a conclusion.

Experiment 3 was specifically carried out to identify the recognition gap that strains computer vision technology to detect an object or a thing from closer proximity when it is zoomed. When we zoom in an image beyond a certain range, we are less likely to understand what it is. But, *deep-learning performed better than humans and could identify minuscule features that are imperceptible to the human eye and detectable only when the image is zoomed in very closely.*

12.6 CHALLENGES IN COMPUTER VISION

Though computer vision has emerged as one of the top fields of machine learning, there are several obstacles that make it difficult to become a leading technology. Human vision is a complicated and highly effective system, which is difficult to replicate through technology.

Given below are certain issues and challenges faced by computer vision algorithms. These are related to the nature of the data or the application to be created and its context. In this section, we will discuss these challenges to make the CV algorithms more robust and efficient.

Real-time processing: Many applications demand computer systems to analyze images and quickly take action without any time delay. Such systems need to be very accurate. Achieving this level of accuracy with specified time constraints is not easy to achieve.

Limited resources: To successfully implement a computer vision algorithm, the computer system needs ample amount of memory, CPU and other computing resources.

Different lighting: Computer vision algorithms collect knowledge about the real-world objects in different kinds of lighting. For example, a white object in red light may look red in the image. Correspondingly, a red object under a red lamp becomes almost invisible.

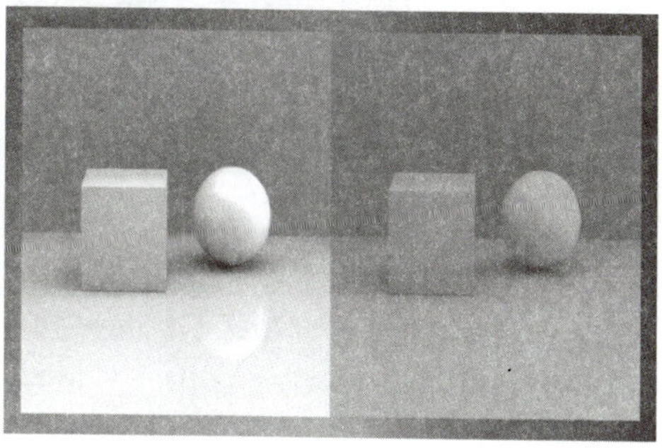

Noise: A noisy image or an image with incomplete/incorrect data makes it hard for computer vision to recognize objects. For example, when an image appears brighter or darker than they should be. Another example of noisy data could be images obtained from videocams on the road, which are much less effective when it is raining or snowing outside.

Unfamiliar angles: An image must be fed in the system from several angles. Otherwise, a computer won't be able to recognize it if the angle changes.

Unfamiliar angles

Overlapping: When there are multiple objects on the image, they may overlap with each other and remain hidden, thereby making it difficult for a machine to recognize them.

Different types of objects: Objects belonging to the same category may look totally different. This makes it very difficult for a machine to successfully recognize them.

Fake similarity: Objects looking same may actually belong to different categories. For example, Samoyed puppies look similar to little polar bears in some pictures.

Adversarial attacks: An attacker can attack a machine learning model to make the machine fail intentionally. These flawed models are difficult to identify and may affect the system adversely.

12.7 UNDERSTANDING IMAGE PIXELS

Pictures displayed on a digital screen like a monitor or are simply in digital form are made up of thousands of tiny dots, also known as pixels.

> Computer vision applications are growing at a very fast pace. Corporate giants like Google, Facebook, Apple and Microsoft are investing huge amounts in computer vision.

A monitor represents each pixel as three strips and varies the intensity of each strip to render what looks like a particular color.

The word 'pixel' means 'picture element' indicating one single dot. In colored images, pixels of different colors are arranged alongside each other to represent different shades of colors. This means that every digitized image is broken up into tiny blocks with a description of a color value at each point. Figure 12.9 shows a pixelated black-and-white image of an army officer.

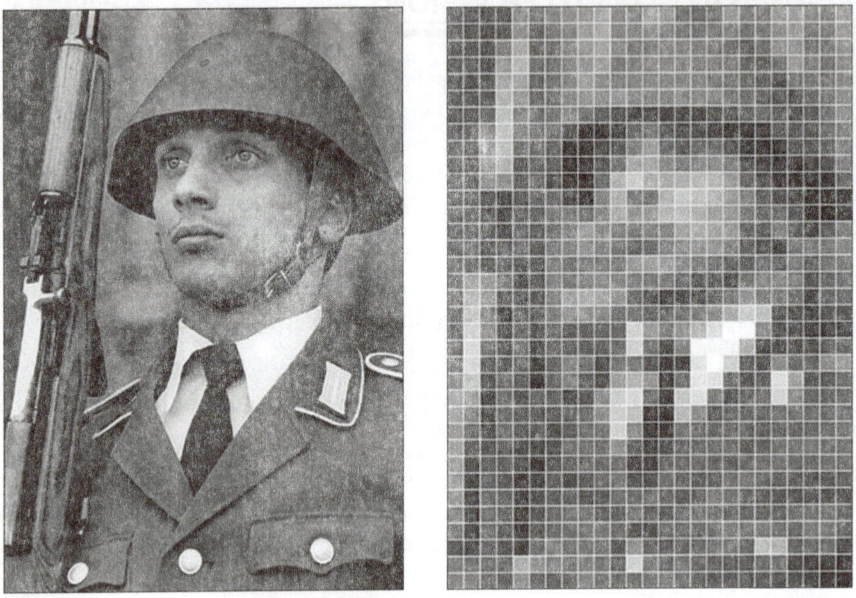

Figure 12.9 Image pixelation

In a colored image, each square or pixel stores the value of just one of the three prime colors of Red, Green and Blue (RGB).

As seen in Fig. 12.10, an image viewed on a screen is made up of pixels. Each pixel comprises of three strips of Red, Green and Blue. The intensity of these strips is changed to represent a color. To be more specific, each pixel contains a series of numbers or digits, hence the term 'digital'. These numbers dictate the color values seen. However, when we see an image, we do not see these digits, we just see the color that they represent.

Figure 12.10 Each pixel is made up of red, green and blue strips

Figure 12.11 shows the digits stored in each pixel in a black-and-white image as well as in a colored image. The black-and-white image stores a '0' for a black pixel and a '1' for white pixel. This is known as a 'bitmap' image as it only requires one bit of information, 0 or 1, to describe the color. But such a representation can be used with only two tones: black and white. Not even shades of gray can be represented using a bitmap. To represent more colors (gray shades), we usually use grayscale images that use a number from 0–255 to indicate the specific color. A grayscale image can represent a total of 256 different colors.

> Like RGB, CMYK is an image format that stores four values for each pixel. The pixel stores values of Cyan, Magenta, Yellow, Black.

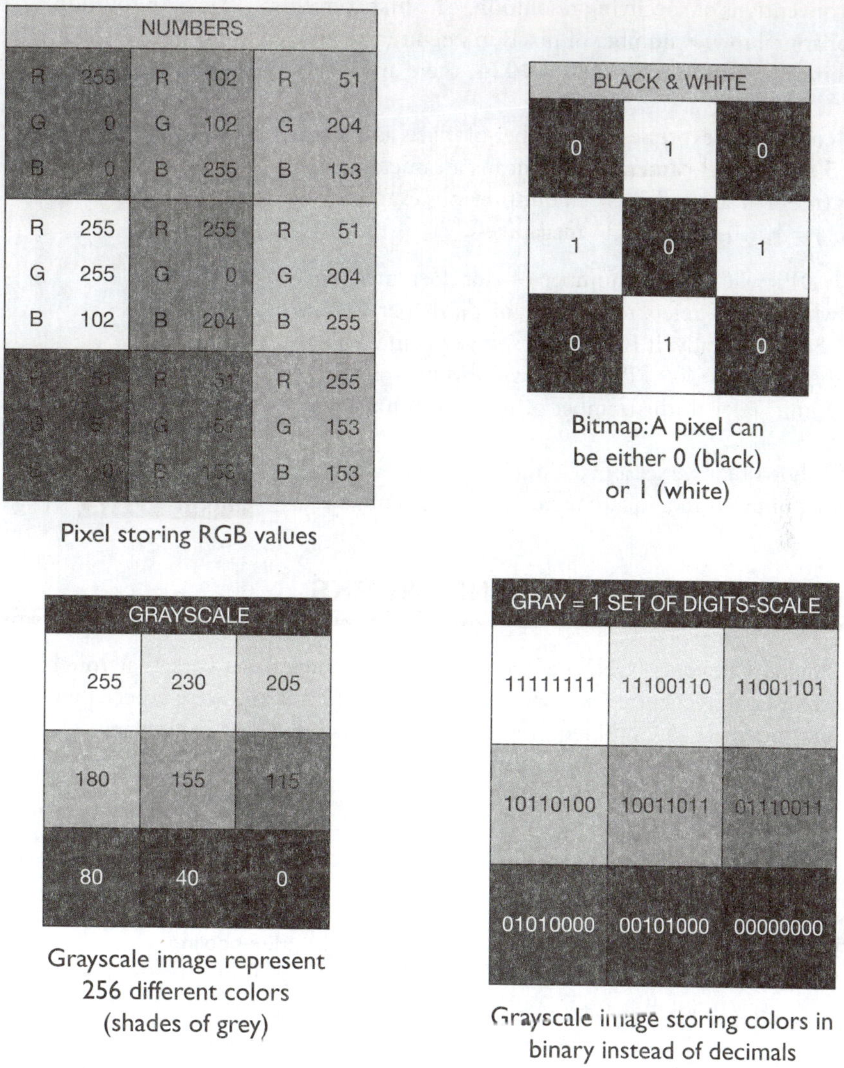

Figure 12.11 The color of an image is dictated by the RGB and bitmap values

12.7.1 What Is Resolution?

Resolution refers to the detail that an image holds. Higher the resolution, the more details the image stores and vice-versa. More details mean better picture clarity. Correspondingly, less details mean less clarity. Image resolution is often measured in Dots Per Inch (DPI) and Pixels Per Inch (PPI).

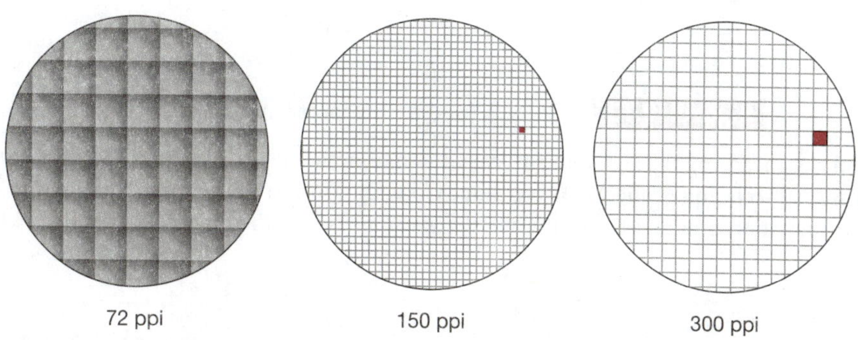

There are two conventions of specifying resolution. The first convention express resolution as the number of pixels in the width (a horizontal row) × number of pixels in height (a vertical column) of the screen. That is, if we say the resolution of the **computer monitor is 1280 × 1024**, there are 1280 pixels in a row from left-to-right and 1024 pixels from top to bottom.

The second convention expresses the number of pixels as a single number, like a **5 mega pixel camera** which means a camera having 5 million pixels (mega means millions). In our previous example, we had 1280 × 1024 = 1,310,720, or 1.31 megapixels.

DPI and PPI DPI refers to the number of dots per inch on a printed image whereas PPI refers to number of pixels per inch in a digital image. So, technically, it is PPI in a soft copy and DPI in a hardcopy of the image. A 300 PPI image will also be a 300 DPI image. Both the units refer to the number of units within a square inch of an image.

Figure 12.12 shows that we see a pixel in greater detail when we have more number of pixels in a square inch.

Figure 12.12 High- and low-res images

12.8 CONVOLUTIONAL NEURAL NETWORKS

Convolutional Neural Networks (CNN) are a special type of neural network that roughly imitates human vision. Initially, they were used to recognize hand-written digits (Fig. 12.13) and were especially used in the postal sectors to read zip codes, pin codes, etc. A CNN requires a large amount of data and computing resources to train.

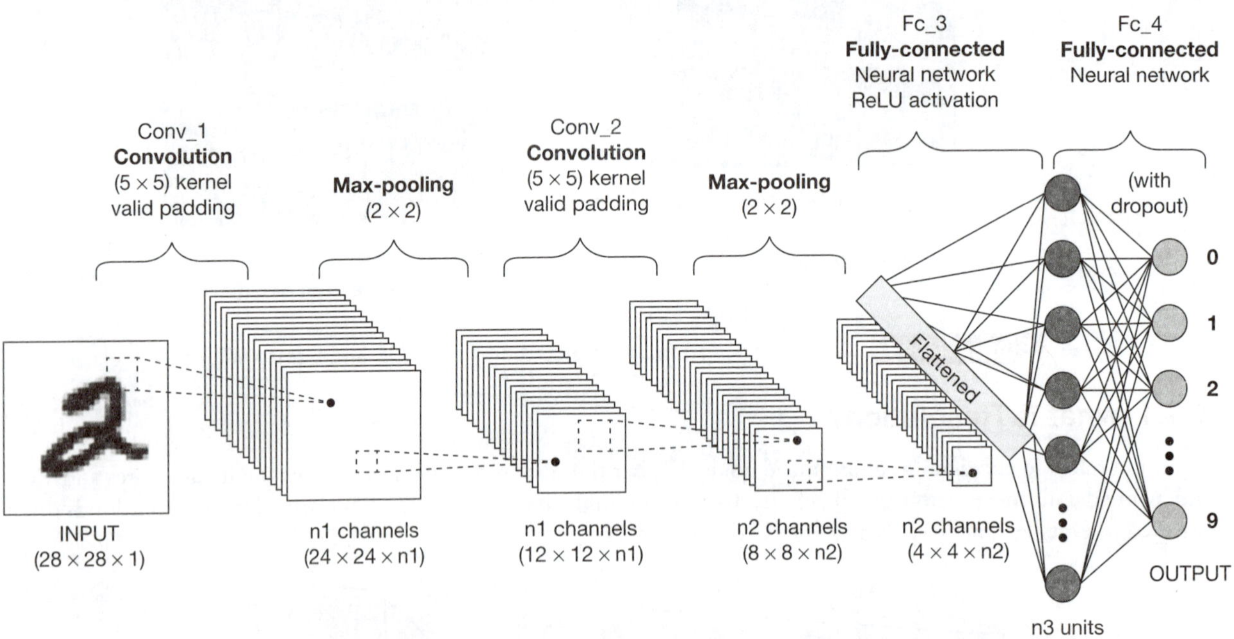

Figure 12.13 CNN is used to interpret hand-written digits

CNN is a branch of deep learning that uses multi-layered neural networks to analyze visual imagery (Fig. 12.14). For this, CNN uses a special technique called Convolution. Convolution is a mathematical operation on two functions that produces a third function that expresses how the shape of one is modified by the other.

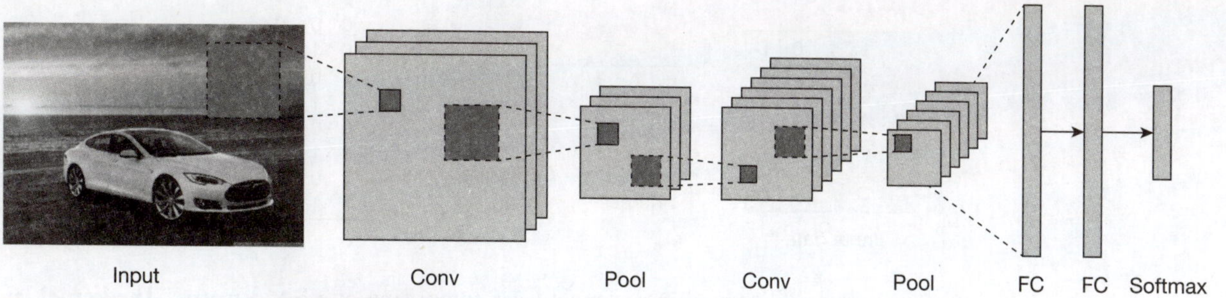

Figure 12.14 CNN processes visual imagery in three layers

We will not discuss the mathematics part required to understand how a CNN works. Just understand that a CNN is a composition of three main types of layers:

- **Convolution layer**, which is the primary building block and performs computational tasks based on convolution function.
- **Pooling layer**, which is arranged next to convolution layer and is used to reduce the size of inputs by removing unnecessary information to speedup computations without losing features that are critical for getting a good prediction.
- **Fully connected layer**, arranged next to the series of convolution and pooling layer to classify input into various categories.

As shown in Fig. 12.15, there are two series of convolution and pooling layer. The convolution layer receives and processes the input to produce the output.

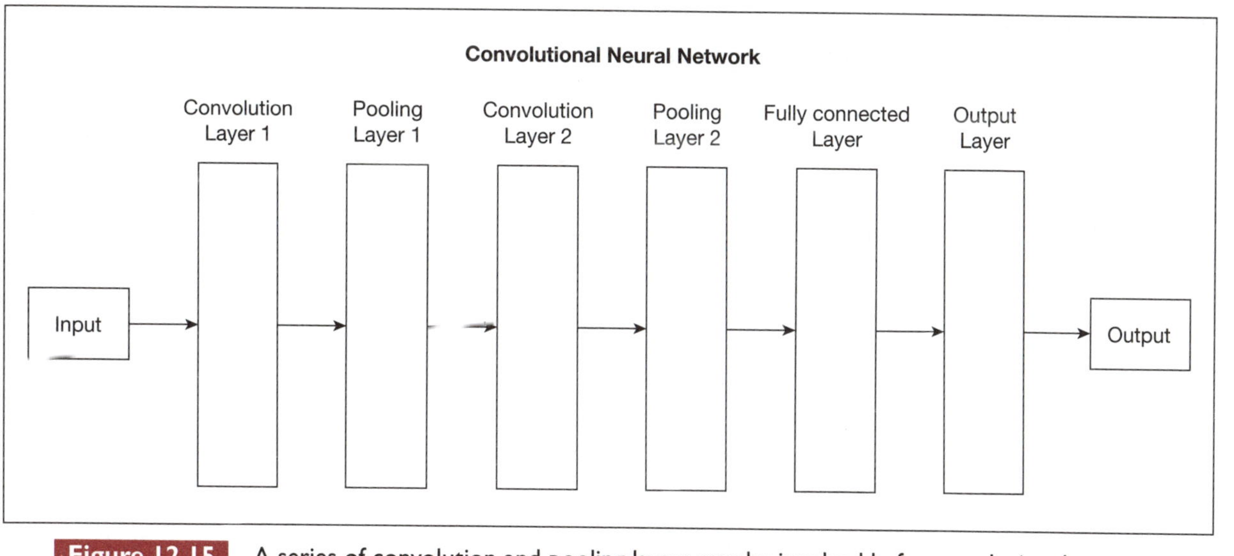

Figure 12.15 A series of convolution and pooling layers may be involved before producing the output

12.8.1 Understanding the Working of a Simple CNN

The Convolution Layer Convolution is a simple mathematical operation that can be applied on image processing operators. Convolution can be done by multiplying two arrays (or lists) of numbers, to produce a third array (or list) of numbers of the same dimension.

An image **convolution is an element-wise multiplication of image arrays and another array called the kernel followed by the sum.**

For simplicity, let us consider a grayscale image that is represented as a pixel of values.

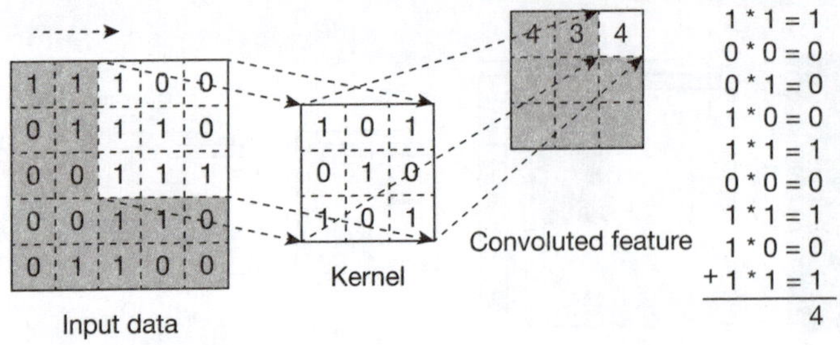

In the above image, we have applied a filter by using a kernel layer comprising of a 3 × 3 matrix. **The kernel layer is applied to the input image to get the convoluted feature.** This convoluted feature is passed on to the next layer.

Thus, we see that a CNN consists of multiple layers of artificial neurons that calculate the weighted sum of multiple inputs in order to output an activation value. When an image is inputted in a CNN, each layer generates several activation functions that are then passed on to the next layer. For example, the first layer extracts basic features such as horizontal or diagonal edges. This output is passed on to the next layer which detects more complex features such as corners or combinational edges. More layers in the network can be used to identify even more complex features such as objects, faces, etc.

Activation map (also known as feature map) generated by the final convolution layer guides the classification layer to produce a set of confidence scores (values between 0 and 1) indicating how likely the image is to belong to a particular class.

Therefore, a **CNN need not be limited to only one convolutional layer**. The first Convolution Layer captures low-level features such as edges, color, gradient orientation, etc. Subsequent layers can extract other high-level features that give a wholesome understanding of images in the dataset. In the convolution layer, **several kernels are used to produce several features.**

The activation or the feature map can then be used to

- reduce the image size so that it can be processed more efficiently.
- focus on certain features of the image that can help in processing the image further. For example, we may need to focus on a person's eyes, nose and mouth to recognize the person rather than focusing on the entire face.

12.8.2 The Pooling Layer

The convolution layer is followed by a pooling layer that can be of two types – max pooling and average pooling.

Max Pooling finds the maximum value of a pixel from a part of the image covered by the kernel. It discards the noisy activations, thereby performing de-noising along with dimensionality reduction.

Average Pooling returns the average of all the values from the part of the image covered by the Kernel. ***Max Pooling performs better than Average Pooling.***

The two techniques of pooling can be better understood from the image shown in Fig. 12.16.

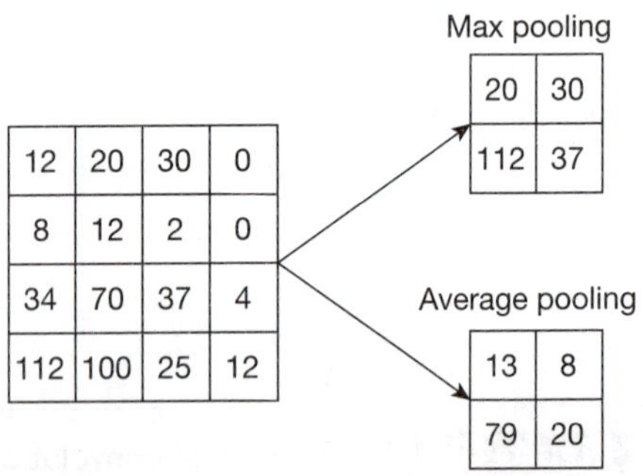

Figure 12.16 Max pooling and average pooling

Limitations The advent of CNN has revolutionized the field of AI in a big way. CNN gives in-depth results and recognizes even minute patterns and details that otherwise go unnoticed by the human eye. However, even after using great amount of computing power while being trained with massive amount of data, CNN is not able to completely identify, block and remove inappropriate content from social media.

CNN also fails to detect objects when they are seen under different lighting conditions and presented from new angles. Table 12.1 highlights the differences between a CNN and a Neural Network, often referred to as ANN or Artificial Neural Network.

Table 12.1 Difference between convolutional and artificial neural network

CNN	ANN
Partially connected layers	Fully connected layers
Can be used for image of any size	Can be used for small images
Considers only a part of the entire image for learning patterns (depending on filters)	Considers the entire image for learning patterns
Comparatively smaller number of parameters used for learning	Large number of parameters used for learning
More efficient technique	Less efficient technique
More computational cost	Less computational cost
Once a CNN has learnt to detect a pattern in one position, it can detect the same pattern even in different locations	Once an ANN has learnt to detect a pattern in one position, it cannot detect the same pattern even in different locations (say, if the image is rotated or shifted)
More number of records/data for training is required	Number of records/ data for training depends on complexity of the task
Success rate is high	Success rate is comparatively low.

Application of Image Features: In computer vision and image processing, a **feature** is a piece of information that is required to solve a computational task in context to a given application. These features may be points, edges or objects. For example, if given six small patches of images, we can make our algorithm identify the location of those image patches in the image. Once developed, we can use this algorithm to find similar images in a huge dataset of images.

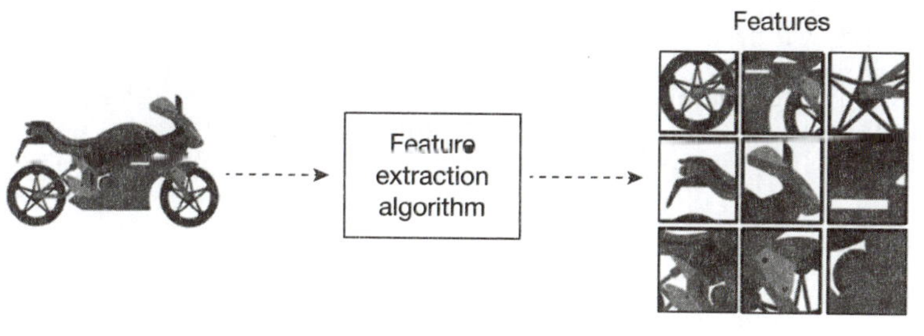

12.9 OPENCV

OpenCV is one of the most popular libraries providing functions for computer vision. The library has functions for the following tasks.

- Reading an image
- Extracting the RGB values of a pixel
- Extracting the Region of Interest (ROI)
- Resizing the image
- Rotating the image
- Drawing a rectangle
- Displaying text

With OpenCV, users can easily do complex tasks such as identifying and recognizing faces and objects, tracking moving objects, stitching images together to generate an entire scene with a high-resolution image, etc.

To install OpenCV on windows using pip command, just write the following command in Window's Command Prompt.

```
pip install opencv-python
```

> The file should be in the working directory or we must give the full path to the image.

Before using the OpenCV package, let us first discuss some important functions that we will be using in this section.

1. The **imread()** function accepts the name of the image to open and a value 1 if the image has to be read as a colored image. Syntax of this function can be given as,

   ```
   cv2.imread(path, flag)
   ```

   Here, path is a string representing the path of the image to be read and flag specifies how the image should be read – 0 for grayscale image and 1 for a colored image.

   The imread() either returns the image loaded from the specified path file (if the image is found), or it returns a matrix.

   Now, type the following program in Python IDLE to read and process images using OpenCV.

Example 12.1 Reading and processing an image

```
import cv2
import numpy as np
#importing the opencv module
img = cv2.imread('Doraemon.png',1)
print(img.shape)
# Resize image
img_resized=cv2.resize(img, (780, 540))
cv2.imshow("Resized",img_resized)
# Rotate image
image = cv2.rotate(img, cv2.ROTATE_90_COUNTERCLOCKWISE)
# Draw a circle on the image
cv2.imshow("Rotated",image)
cv2.circle(img,(80,80), 55, (255,0,0), -1)
cv2.imshow('image',img)
# Draw a rectangle on the image
cv2.rectangle(img,(15,25),(200,150),(0,255,255),15)
cv2.imshow('image',img)
cv2.waitKey(0)
cv2.destroyAllWindows()
```

OUTPUT

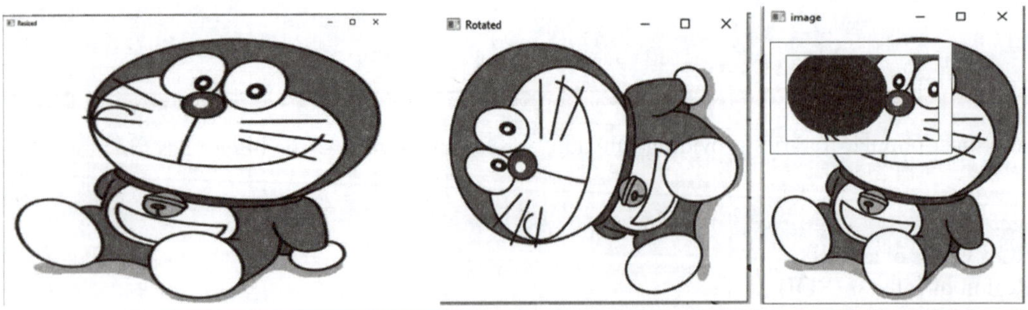

2. The **resize()** is used to change the size of the image. In ML algorithms, increase in number of pixels in an image increases the number of input nodes and thus the complexity of the model. The syntax of resize() is,

   ```
   cv2.resize(s, size)
   ```

   where,

   s is the input image (required).

   size is the desired size for the output image after resizing (required)

3. The **`cv2.rotate()`** method is used to rotate a 2D array in multiples of 90 degrees. The syntax of this method is,

```
cv2.rotate( src, rotateCode[, dst] )
```

where,
src is the image to be rotated.

4. **rotateCode** specifies how to rotate the array. Its values can be cv2.ROTATE_90_CLOCKWISE, cv2.ROTATE_180, cv2.ROTATE_90_COUNTERCLOCKWISE.

5. The **`imwrite ()`** function having syntax,

```
cv2.imwrite(filename, image)
```

is used to save an image on a storage device in the specified location. The function returns a value (or status) indicating success or failure in saving the image. The code given below reads the image in file Doraemon.png and saves it in C:\ → Users → Chikki Folder

```
img = cv2.imread('Doraemon.png',1)
status = cv2.imwrite(r'C:\Users\Chikki\cat.png',img)
print("Image written success? : ", status)
```

If the file is successfully written then this function returns True; otherwise it returns False.

12.10 BASIC OPERATION ON IMAGES

In this section, we will discuss some basic operations that can be performed on the images. These are,

Access Pixel Values and modify them. This can be done by writing

```
img = cv2.imread('Doraemon.png',1)
px = img[50,60]     # accessing a pixel
print( px )
OUTPUT
 [157 166 200]
```

This prints a list containing 3 values, which in turn, specify the color of the pixel – Blue component, Green component and Red component. To modify the values, we can access the pixel and then overwrite it with a new value as shown below:

```
img[50,60] = [250,125,55]
print( img[50,60] )
Output:
 [250 125 55]
```

Access Image Properties like the size (total number of pixels in the image), number of rows, columns, and channels. While `shape()` is used to print the number of rows, columns and colors, `size()` prints the size of the image.

```
print( img.shape )
>>(350, 348, 3)
print( img.size )
>> 4248148
```

Image ROI (Region of interest) to select only a specific region of the image. For example, to detect eyes in an image, we need not search the entire image, we must concentrate only on the face. Thus, here the face is our ROI.

Splitting and Merging Image Channels to split the channels from an image and then work on each channel separately or to merge the channels together.

12.10.1 OpenCV Drawing Functions

OpenCV has functions to allow users to draw certain shapes on an image such as circle, rectangle, ellipse, polylines, convex lines, etc. This is often used to highlight any object in the input image. For example, Facebook identifies a face by drawing a rectangle around it.

Drawing a Circle

`circle()` is used to draw a circle in an image. The syntax of `circle()` is:

```
cv2.circle(image, center_coordinates, radius, color, thickness)
```

where,
image is the input image on which a circle is to be drawn.
center_coordinates specify the x- and y-coordinate values representing the center of the circle.
radius is the radius of the circle.
color specifies the color of the border line of the circle.
thickness indicates the width of the circle border line in px.

Drawing a Rectangle

We use the `rectangle()` to draw a rectangle on the image. The syntax of `rectangle()` is,

```
cv2.rectangle(image, start_point, end_point, color, thickness)
```

where,
image is the input image on which the rectangle is to be drawn.
start_point specifies the top left vertex of x- and y-coordinates of the rectangle.
end_point indicates the bottom right vertex of x- and y-coordinates of the rectangle.
color specifies the color of the border line of the rectangle to be drawn (in the form of BGR).
thickness gives the width of the rectangle border line in px.

Drawing Lines

The `line()` is used to draw lines on an image. Its syntax can be given as,

```
cv2.line(image, start_point, end_point, color, thickness)
```

where,
image is the input image on which the line is to be drawn.
start_point specifies the starting coordinates (x and y values) of the line.
end_point gives the ending coordinates (x and y values) of the line.
Color indicates the color of the line to be drawn in the form of BGR)
thickness is the width of the line in px.

Write Text on an Image

Text can be written on an image by using the `putText()`. The syntax of this function can be given as,

```
cv2.putText(img, text, org, font,fontScale color)
```

where,
img represents the input image on which we want to write text
text is what is to be written on the image.
org denotes the bottom-left corner of the text string on the image. Thus, org is used to set the location of the text on the image
font specifies the font of the text.
fontScale denotes the scale by which the size of the font can be increased or decreased.
color represents the color of the text in BGR form.

Example 12.2 **Code given below places text on an image.**

```
import cv2
import numpy as np
 #importing the opencv module
font = cv2.FONT_HERSHEY_SIMPLEX
img = cv2.imread('Doraemon.png',1)
cv2.putText(img,'DORAEMON',(10,200), font, 1,(200,125,235),2)
#Display the image
cv2.imshow("image",img)
cv2.waitKey(0)
```

Canny Edge Detection

Edge detection is an image processing technique used to identify an object's boundaries within an image. In the code given below, we have used the Canny Edge Detection algorithm. The syntax of `Canny()` can be given as,

`edges = cv2.Canny(img, minVal, maxVal, apertureSize, L2gradient)`

where,
img is the input image whose edges are to be detected.
minVal is the minimum intensity gradient
maxVal is the maximum intensity gradient

As per the syntax, edges with intensity gradient more than maxVal are definitely edges and those with intensity gradient less than minVal are sure to be non-edges and therefore discarded. Edges with values between maxVal and minVal are classified as edges or non-edges based on their connectivity with the 'sure edges'. If the edges are connected to "sure-edges" then they are taken to be a part of the edges. Otherwise, they are treated as non-edges and discarded.

Example 12.3 **Detecting the edges of an image.**

```
#importing the opencv module
import cv2
# using imread('path') and 1 denotes read
as color image
img = cv2.imread('Doraemon.png',1)
edges = cv2.Canny(img,200,300,True)
cv2.imshow("Edge Detected Image", edges)
cv2.imshow("Original Image", img)
cv2.waitKey(0)  # waits until a key is
pressed
cv2.destroyAllWindows() # destroys the
window showing image.
```

OUTPUT

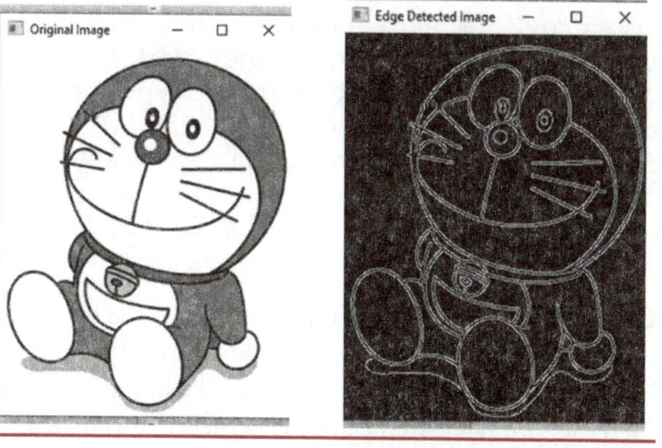

Image Smoothing

Image smoothing is an image processing technique that removes noise from an image. For example, when blurring an image, low-intensity edges are removed. Blurring is often used to hide the details or any confidential information in an image. The different types of blurring techniques supported by OpenCV include: Averaging, median Blur, Gaussian Blur and Bilateral Filter.

In the **averaging technique**, the image is normalized with a box filter. The average of all the pixels in the box area is calculated. The average value then replaces the value of the pixel at the center of the box filter. The `cv2.bur()` in OpenCV is used to perform this operation. Its syntax can be given as,

`cv2.blur(src, ksize)`

where,
src specifies the image to be blurred.
Ksize represents the blurring box area.

```
 #importing the opencv module
import cv2
# using imread('path') and 1 denotes read as
color image
img = cv2.imread('Doraemon.png',1)
cv2.imshow("Original Image", img)
cv2.imshow('cv2.blur output', cv2.blur(img,
(3,3)))
#cv2.imshow('cv2.GaussianBlur output',
cv2.GaussianBlur(img, (5, 5), cv2.BORDER_
DEFAULT))
cv2.waitKey(0)  # waits until a key is
pressed
cv2.destroyAllWindows()  # destroys the window showing image
```

The **median Blur** technique calculates the median of all the pixels under the box area and replaces the value of the central pixel with this median value. `medianBlur()` provided in the OpenCV pakage is used to easily implement this kind of smoothing. The syntax of this function can be given as,

```
cv2.medianBlur(src, dst, ksize)
```

where,
src represents the input image.
dst represents the output image.
ksize represents the size of the kernel (box).

```
import cv2
# using imread('path') and 1 denotes
read as  color image
img = cv2.imread('Doraemon.png',1)
cv2.imshow("Original Image", img)
cv2.imshow('cv2.medianBlur output', cv2.
medianBlur(img,5))
cv2.waitKey(0)  # waits until a key is
pressed
cv2.destroyAllWindows()  # destroys the
window showing image
```

Gaussian Blur technique: Here, instead of the box filter, a Gaussian function is used to blur the image. The width and height of the kernel window should be specified and these values should be positive and odd. The standard deviation in x- and y-coordinates is also specified using the sigmaX and sigmaY parameters respectively. If sigmaX = sigmaY = 0, then they are calculated from the kernel size. The `GaussianBlur()` is used to implement this technique. Its syntax is,

```
GaussianBlur(src, dst, ksize, sigmaX,sigmaY)
```

where,
src is the image to be blurred
dst is the output image of the same size and type as src.
ksize specifies the size of the kernel.
sigmaX and **sigmaY** are double values that represent standard deviation in the x-direction and y-direction respectively.

```
import cv2
# using imread('path') and 1 denotes read as  color image
img = cv2.imread('Doraemon.png',1)
cv2.imshow("Original Image", img)
cv2.imshow('cv2.GaussianBlur output', cv2.GaussianBlur(img, (5, 5), cv2.BORDER_
DEFAULT))
```

```
cv2.waitKey(0)  # waits until a key is pressed
cv2.destroyAllWindows()  # destroys the window showing image
```

Bilateral Filter is a highly effective technique to remove noise but it is slower compared to other filters. The problem with Gaussian filter is that it blurs the edges also, which is not at all desirable. Bilateral filter blurs only the pixels with similar intensities to the central pixel thereby preserving the edges (pixels on edges have large intensity variation). It is implemented using the `cv.bilateralFilter()`.

Key Terms

Computer vision: A field of Artificial Intelligence that helps computers gain a high level of understanding from digital images or videos

Object classification: The process of classifying the broad category of the object in the photograph.

Object identification: The process of identifying the type of a given object in the photograph

Object verification: The process of confirming the presence of an object in the photograph.

Object localization: The process of locating objects in the photograph. The goal of **localization** is to find the location of a single object in an image.

Object detection: The process of repeatedly locating and classifying all objects of interest in the image.

Object segmentation: The process of enumerating the pixels that belong to an object in the image.

Object tracking: The process of detecting an object and then discerning its movements.

Video motion analysis: The process of estimating the velocity of objects in a video, or the camera itself.

Scene reconstruction: The process of creating a 3D model of a scene inputted through images or video.

Image restoration: The process of using filters based on machine learning to remove noise (to remove parts of image that are blurred).

Visual search engines: A search engine that retrieves images meeting the specified criteria.

Noisy image: An image with incomplete/incorrect data, which makes it hard for computer vision to recognize objects.

Adversarial attacks: Attacks in which an attacker intentionally attacks a machine learning model to make the machine fail. These flawed models are difficult to identify and may affect the system adversely.

Convolutional neural networks: A branch of deep learning that uses multi-layered neural networks to analyze visual imagery.

Convolution: A mathematical operation on two functions that produces a third function that expresses how the shape of one is modified by the other.

Chapter Highlights

- A CNN complements the machine learning or deep learning model by breaking images down into pixels that are given tags or labels.
- Computer vision algorithms can be used for **predictive maintenance**. Images obtained through cameras (probably fitted in the eyes of robots) can be analyzed to detect potential problems that may occur. CV can even be helpful to reduce defects.
- Convolutional Neural Networks are a special type of neural network that roughly imitates human vision.
- Edge detection is an image processing technique used to identify an object's boundaries within an image.

Review Questions

1. What do you understand by the term "computer vision"?
2. Explain the tasks involved in computer vision.
3. Computers can detect objects better than humans. Justify this statement.
4. How does computer vision work with deep learning?
5. How can we use computer vision in manufacturing units?
6. Give any four areas where CV is extensively used.
7. List any three challenges faced by computer vision systems.
8. What do you understand by CNN? Explain the different layers that makes up a CNN model.
9. Differentiate between CNN and ANN.
10. Differentiate between a bitmap and a grayscale image.
11. What is image resolution? Discuss two ways in which resolution can be specified.
12. Give any two benefits of using an activation map in a CNN.
13. Why do we need multiple convolution layers?

Fill in the Blanks

1. A ________ neural network is used in computer vision algorithms.
2. __________ is the process of classifying the type of a given object is in the photograph.
3. Object ________ is performed to detect an object and then discern its movements.
4. _________ systems are used to recognize faces in images and videos.
5. Pokemon Go and Snapchat use ________ Reality applications.
6. A _______ search engine retrieves images that meet the specified criteria.
7. ________ Attacks are intentionally done on a machine learning model to make the machine fail.
8. __________ Neural Networks are a special type of neural network that roughly imitates human vision.
9. _________ is one of the most popular libraries providing functions for computer vision.
10. Tiny dots on a monitor are known as ________.
11. _________ refers to the detail that an image holds.

State True or False

1. Computer vision makes extensive use of deep learning techniques.
2. To remove noise from an image, we will use scene reconstruction technique.
3. Computer vision algorithms can detect diseases by analyzing X-rays, MRI, and mammography.
4. Google Lens is used to obtain detailed information from images.
5. The fully connected layer is arranged next to the series of convolution and pooling layer.
6. The pooling layer is followed by a convolution layer.
7. Average Pooling performs better than Max Pooling.
8. An image is rotated in multiples of 90 degrees.
9. Fully connected layers are present in a CNN.
10. Pooling layer is present in a CNN but not in ANN.
11. Pixel means picture element.
12. In a bitmap, every pixel stores the value of RGB components.
13. A bitmap cannot represent shades of gray.
14. Higher the resolution of an image, lesser is its clarity.
15. A 1280 × 1024 pixels camera has a higher resolution than a 3 mega pixel camera.

Multiple Choice Questions

1. Object __________ technique is used by news channels to blur the face of a victim or any person whose identity is not to be revealed.
   a. Identification b. Segmentation
   c. Verification d. Localization
2. The process of repeatedly locating and classifying all objects of interest in the image is known as Object ________.
   a. Verification b. Detection
   c. Localization d. Segmentation
3. The process of creating a 3D model of a scene inputted through images or video is known as ________.
   a. Scene Reconstruction b. Object Tracking
   c. Video Motion Analysis d. Image Restoration
4. _______ is used to estimate the velocity of objects in a video, or the camera itself.
   a. Scene Reconstruction b. Object Tracking
   c. Video Motion Analysis d. Image Restoration
5. Computer Vision cannot be used for _________ systems.
   a. Home Security b. Augmented Reality
   c. Speech Recognition d. Gaming
6. Video cameras placed in/on ________ produces a noisy image.
   a. a dark room b. a road when there is heavy rain
   c. bright sun d. All of these.
7. Overlapping of image occurs when an image has _________.
   a. missing data b. different lighting
   c. one object hidden below another d. been taken from different angles

8. CNN is a branch of ________ learning.
   a. deep
   b. supervised
   c. unsupervised
   d. reinforcement

9. ________ layer reduces the size of inputs by removing unnecessary information to speedup computations.
   a. Convolution
   b. Polling
   c. Fully Connected
   d. All of these.

10. ________ layer performs computational tasks.
    a. Convolution
    b. Polling
    c. Fully Connected
    d. All of these.

11. Which function is sued to change the size of an image?
    a. `imread()`
    b. `resize()`
    c. `rotate()`
    d. `size()`

12. Which function is used to print the size of an image?
    a. `shape()`
    b. `resize()`
    c. `rotate()`
    d. `size()`

13. Which function is used to print the number of rows, columns and colors?
    a. `shape()`
    b. `resize()`
    c. `rotate()`
    d. `size()`

14. Which technique removes noise from an image?
    a. Blurring
    b. Smoothing
    c. Detecting edges
    d. Resizing

15. Which technique used to hide the details or any confidential information in an image?
    a. Blurring
    b. Smoothing
    c. Detecting edges
    d. Resizing

16. An ANN does not have ________ layer.
    a. Input
    b. Output
    c. Convolution
    d. Hidden

17. Which of the following statements is incorrect about a CNN?
    a. CNN is more efficient than ANN and has a higher success rate.
    b. CNN requires more data for training than ANN.
    c. CNN uses a greater number of parameters for learning than ANN.
    d. Computational cost of CNN is more than that of ANN.

18. A grayscale image can store how many different colors?
    a. 2
    b. 256
    c. 20
    d. 16,535

19. A ________ image stores either of two values in a pixel.
    a. Bitmap
    b. Grayscale
    c. Colored
    d. All of these.

20. Image ________ is often measured in Dots Per Inch (DPI) and Pixels Per Inch (PPI).
    a. Width
    b. Height
    c. Resolution
    d. Brightness

21. An image with resolution 2048 × 1536 has ________ number of pixels in a row and ______ pixels in a column.
    a. 2048, 1536
    b. 1536, 2048
    c. 3 mega pixels
    d. All of these.

Identify the Process

Group Discussion

Discuss how you will use computer vision technology to learn techniques by a famous sportsperson playing your favorite sport.

Brain Storming Activity

Ask students to discuss how Computer Vision can be used to detect cheating in assignments, classwork and exam answer sheets submitted by students.

Hint: Compare handwriting.

AI Lab Session – Fontjoy

Fontjoy is an AI-powered Google experiment that allows users to generate font combinations using deep learning techniques. Visit the link https://fontjoy.com/ and click on Generate button to create a new font pairing. Click on the Lock icon to lock fonts that you want to keep, and click on Edit to choose a font manually. The text is editable, so users can replace the default text with their own piece of text, any time.

The application is mainly used to select fonts that share an overarching theme and yet have a pleasing contrast. With this application, we are using neural networks to visualize the fonts that work together.

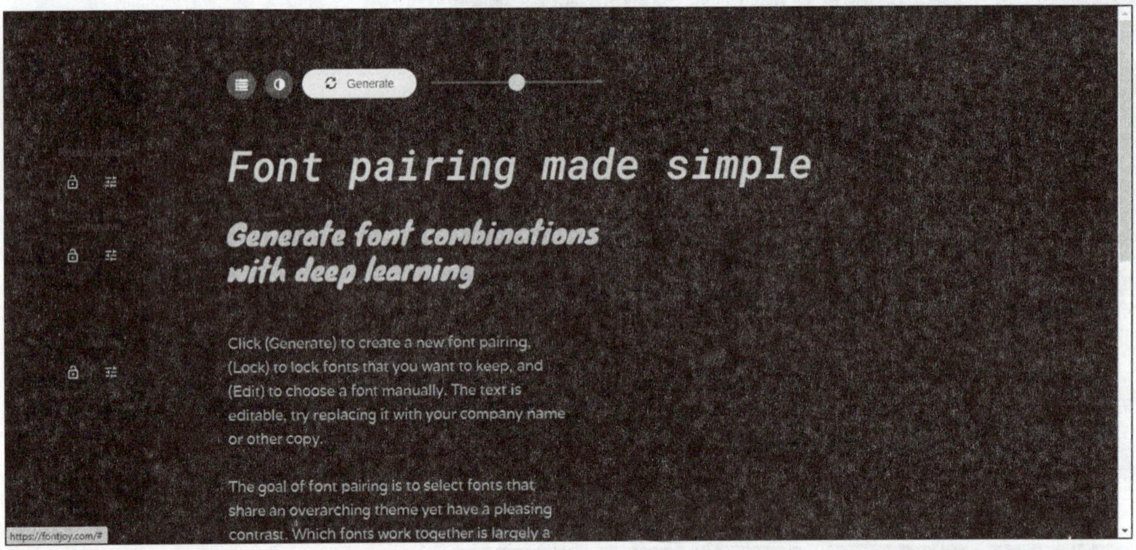

Exploring RGB Colors Activity

RGB color values are supported in all browsers. RGB means Red, Green and Blue. Different values of the three basic colors define the intensity of the color. The value of each color can vary from 0 to 255. For example, RGB (0, 0, 255) is rendered as blue, because the blue parameter is set to its highest value (255) and the others are set to 0.

Visit the link https://www.w3schools.com/colors/colors_rgb.asp and explore the different shades of colors along with their RGB values. Also, can you answer the following questions now:

1. What color is rendered if R = G = B = 255?
2. What color is rendered if R = G = B = 0?
3. What color is rendered if R = 0, G = 255, B = 255?
4. What color is rendered if R = 255, G = 0, B = 255?

5. What color is rendered if R = 255, G = 255, B = 0?
6. What color is rendered if R = 150, G = 150, B = 150?
7. What is the RGB value of your favorite color from the color palette?

Fill in the Missing Value

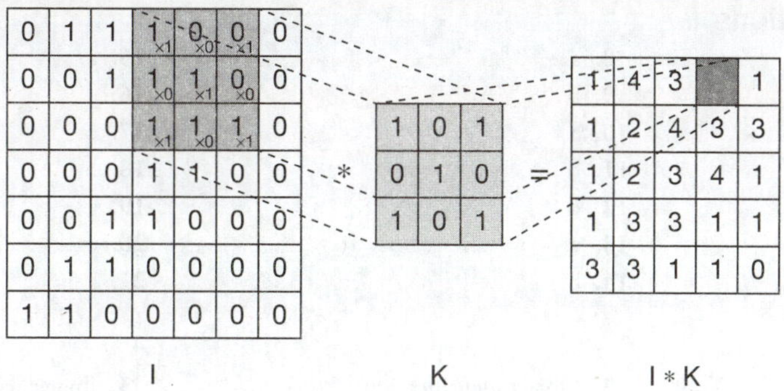

Classifying Images Activity

Visit the link https://www.cs.ryerson.ca/~aharley/vis/conv/flat.html to explore an online application of classifying different numbers. You can visualize how analysis is done using multiple convolution layers to finally classify the input digit.

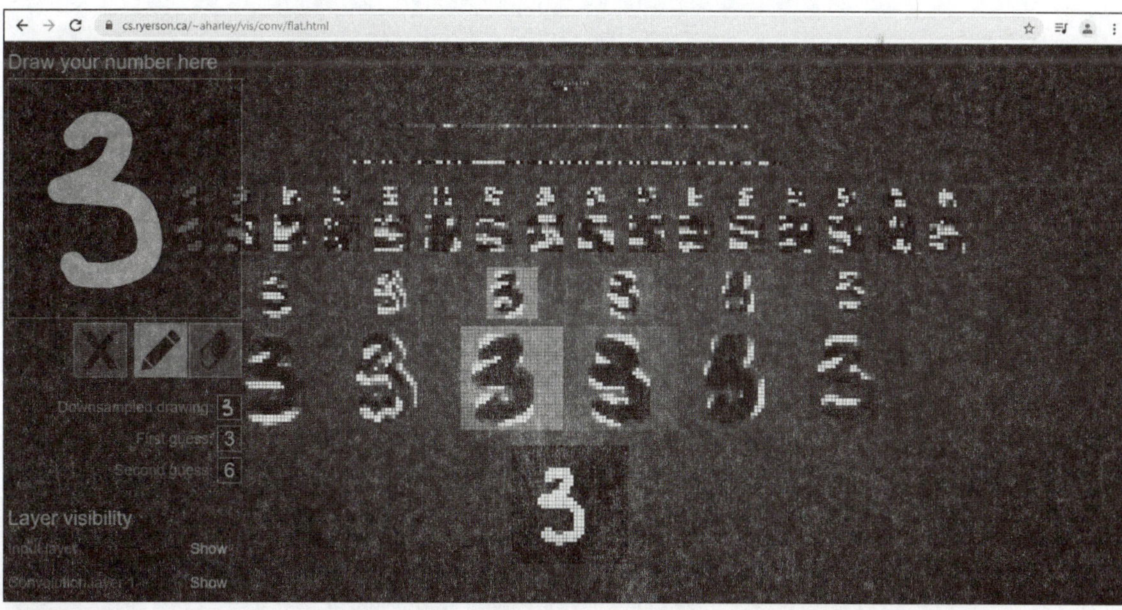

Answers

Fill in the Blanks

1. convolutional
2. Object Identification
3. tracking
4. Facial recognition
5. Augmented
6. visual
7. Adversarial
8. Convolutional
9. OpenCV
10. pixels
11. Resolution

State True or False

1. True
2. False
3. True
4. True
5. True
6. False
7. False
8. True
9. False
10. True
11. True
12. False
13. True
14. False
15. False

Multiple Choice Questions

1. b
2. c
3. a
4. c
5. c
6. d
7. c
8. a
9. b
10. a
11. b
12. d
13. a
14. b
15. a
16. c
17. c
18. b
19. a
20. c
21. a

Identify the Proces

1. Localization
2. Object identification
3. Image Segmentation

Fill in the Missing Value

1. 4

Natural Language Processing

13

Chapter Objectives

This chapter talks about Natural Language Processing – an AI technique that reads, interprets, manipulates to respond in human language. Here, we will read about:

- Examples, applications, components and challenges of NLP systems
- Steps involved in NLP
- The NLTK library

13.1 WHAT IS NATURAL LANGUAGE PROCESSING?

Natural Language Processing (NLP) is the manipulation or understanding of text or speech by a computer software. As humans interact, they understand each other's views and respond with an appropriate answer. Similarly, NLP systems also interact, understand and respond to queries.

Natural Language Processing, a field of artificial intelligence, studies interactions between computers and human (natural) languages. It applies machine learning algorithms to text and speech. For example, NLP can be used to create intelligent systems for speech recognition, machine translation, answering questions, spam detection, document summarization, predictive typing, named entity recognition and autocomplete, to name a few.

These days, smartphones and computers support so many applications that all modern operating systems have a built-in speech recognition module. For example,

Cortana, which is the **virtual assistant** of Microsoft Windows, recognizes **human voice** to set up reminders, open apps, send emails, search information, play games, get latest updates on weather, etc.

Siri, the virtual assistant of the Apple Inc.'s iOS, watchOS, macOS, HomePod, and tvOS help users to perform their tasks with voice commands like starting a call, texting someone, sending an email, clicking a picture, setting up a timer, opening an app, setting up an alarm, using navigation and so on.

Gmail, the most popular email service developed by Google, uses NLP to detect and filter spam emails.

13.2 WHY NLP IS IMPORTANT

Large Volumes of Textual Data: Natural language processing helps computers communicate with humans in their own language. NLP empowers computers to read text, hear speech, interpret it, measure sentiment and determine the parts that are important.

Today's machines are supposed to interact with humans in a consistent, unbiased way without getting tired or fatigued. With increasing use of machines in our day-to-day lives (from medical records to social media), enormous amount of unstructured data is being generated.

Structuring the Unstructured Data: Human language is complex and diverse, as humans express the same thing in infinite ways, both in written and spoken form.

You will be surprised to know that there are 6500 human languages out of which 121 are widely spoken. Every language has its unique set of grammar and syntax rules, terms and slang. Moreover, while writing, we often misspell or abbreviate words, or omit punctuation. Similarly, while speaking, we pronounce different words differently (in regional accents). Some people mumble, stutter and borrow terms from other languages which further increases the complexity of processing natural languages.

Techniques like deep, supervised and unsupervised learning are widely used for modeling human language to resolve ambiguity in language. Table 13.1 lists the difference between natural and computer language.

Table 13.1 Difference between natural language and computer language

Natural Language	Computer Language
Natural language has a very large vocabulary.	Computer language has a very limited vocabulary.
Natural language is easily understood by humans.	Computer language is easily understood by the machines.
Natural language is ambiguous in nature.	Computer language is unambiguous.

13.3 HOW NLP SYSTEMS ARE USEFUL

NLP systems break down text/speech in human language into shorter, elemental pieces, to understand relationships that exist between the pieces for interpreting their meaning. Such systems are then used for the following tasks:

- Generate the summary of a document, generate keywords for efficient searching and indexing
- Accurately capture the meaning and themes in text and use it for optimization and forecasting
- Automatically extract structured information from textual sources
- Perform sentiment analysis to identify the user's opinion within large amounts of text
- Speech-to-text and text-to-speech conversion to transform voice commands into written text, and vice-versa
- Automatic translation of text or speech from one language to another.

> Spam emails are those emails that are sent in bulk to recipients without their permission. They are often sent for commercial purposes.

13.4 EVERYDAY NLP EXAMPLES

Let us look at some of the widely used NLP applications in our everyday lives.

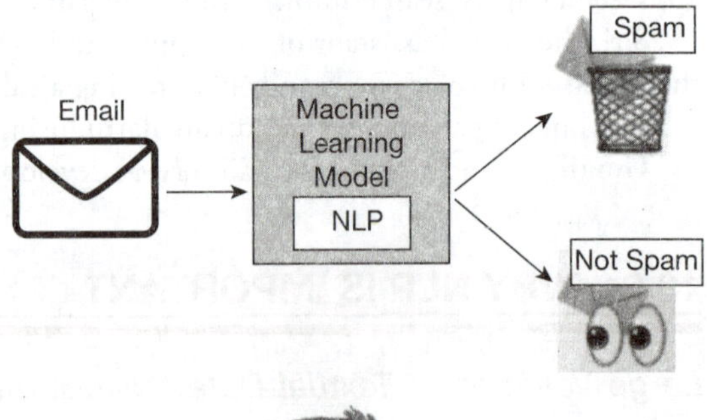

1. Just check the spam folder in your email, it has already separated some emails with common words as spam. Spam filtering uses NLP to compare words in spam email to those present in valid emails to identify junk mail.
2. Whenever you miss a phone call, you get an automatic transcript of the voicemail in your email inbox or smartphone app. This is possible due to NLP's capability to perform speech-to-text conversion.
3. NLP is also the underlying technology when we do a voice search.
4. **Speech Recognition** is used for converting spoken words into text. It is used in applications where the user gives voice commands to smartphones, voice biometrics device, home automation systems, or dictates in software like Microsoft Word, etc. In these systems, NLP is used to give voice commands to devices to perform a particular task (such as to play a song or search information about a topic on a search engine).

5. NLP systems are being used by companies to understand what their customers think and say about them on social media, emails, feedbacks and reviews.
6. Companies perform Sentiment Analysis (also known as opinion mining) to assess the attitude, behavior, and emotional state of the customers. For this, NLP assigns values to the text (positive, negative, or neutral) and also identifies the mood of the context (happy, sad, angry, etc.) in which the customer has written that feedback/review.
7. **Chatbots** are NLP, AI-based systems that are specifically designed to interact with humans through text or speech. They are extensively used these days to offer 24 × 7 assistance to customers by handling their queries. Chatbots actively learn from each interaction to gain a better understanding of the user's intent. This information is used by companies to automate repetitive and time-consuming tasks and allows employees to focus on more fulfilling tasks.
8. **Spelling correction** is a very important tool provided by Microsoft Corporation in its application software like MS-word and PowerPoint. The NLP program embedded in this software automatically checks the spelling in the text. If the spelling is incorrect, it notifies the user and also gives suggestion on what could be the correct spelling.
9. **Topic Classification** uses NLP to organize unstructured text into categories. For example, companies use NLP to analyze hundreds of open-ended responses to surveys to gain insights from customer feedback. Topic classifier will tag all key words in seconds and then automatically route them to the right person for speedy response.
10. NLP is used to translate text/speech written in one language to another. **Example:** Google Translator

13.5 COMPONENTS OF NLP

NLP is a combination of NLU and NLG techniques.

Natural Language Understanding (NLU) deals with mapping the given input in natural language into useful representations.

Natural Language Generation (NLG), on the other hand, uses content in internal representation to produce meaningful sentences in a natural language. NLG is performed using:

Text planning that retrieves relevant content from knowledge base.

Sentence planning that selects required words to form meaningful sentences in the right tone in current context.

Text realization that finally converts a sentence plan into sentence structure.

NLU is harder than NLG. The differences between the two techniques are given in Table 13.2.

Table 13.2 Difference between NLU and NLG

NLU	NLG
Reads and interprets language.	Writes or generates language.
Generates non-linguistic outputs from natural language inputs.	Generates natural language outputs from non-linguistic inputs.

13.6 CHALLENGES IN NLP

Human languages are often ambiguous for machines as one sentence can have different meanings and several sentences may mean the same thing. Hence, we can say that this difficulty mainly persists due to different levels of ambiguity:

Lexical ambiguity that exists due to confusion in different words. For example, whether the word "board" should be treated as a noun or as a verb.

Syntax Level ambiguity that occurs because a sentence can be parsed in different ways. For example, the sentence, "He lifted the beetle with a red cap.", can be interpreted in two ways. First, did he use a cap to lift the beetle? Second, did he lift a beetle that had a red cap?

Referential ambiguity is common when using pronouns. For example, consider the sentences:

Ria met Gauri. She said, "I am going to the school."

Now exactly who is going to the school?

13.7 STEPS IN NLP

There are five general steps in the NLP system.

1. **Lexical Analysis:** Lexicon of a language refers to the collection of words in a language. Lexical analysis therefore identifies and analyzes structure of words by breaking down a big chunk of text into elementary words.
2. **Syntactic Analysis:** Also known as parsing, this type of analysis is done to analyze the words in a sentence to interpret its meaning as per the grammatical rules of the language. For example, the sentence, "I did not do nothing" is rejected by the English syntactic analyzer.

   Syntactic analysis studies how words in a sentence are organized, and how they relate to each other. This is done using ***tokenization*** (breaking a text into elementary words), ***part-of-speech tagging*** (labeling tokens as *verb, adverb, adjective, noun,* etc.), ***lemmatization and stemming*** (reducing words to their base form) and ***Stop word removal*** (removes frequently occurring words that don't add any semantic value, such as *I, they, have, like, yours,* etc.).

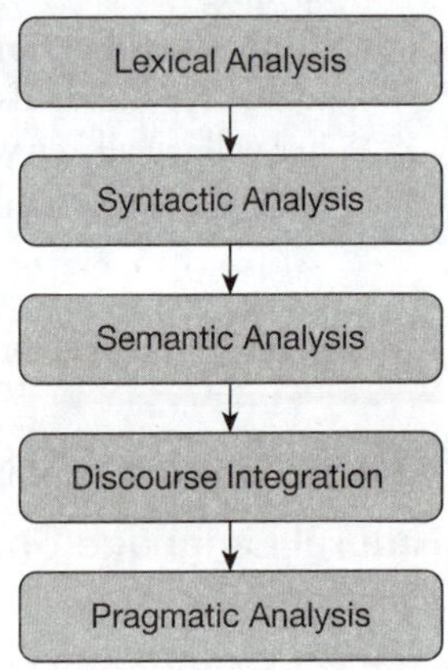

3. **Semantic Analysis:** While syntactic analysis checks whether the sentence is correct as per the grammar of the language, semantic analysis checks to see if the sentence is meaningful or not. Semantic analysis draws the exact meaning from the text. For example, the phrase "hot ice-cream" or "The rat rushed to the school" are syntactically correct but semantically incorrect.
4. **Discourse Integration:** The meaning of any sentence depends upon the meaning of the sentence just preceding it. It also influences the meaning of the sentence immediately succeeding it.
5. **Pragmatic Analysis:** In this step, text is re-interpreted based on what it actually meant. For this, aspects of language requiring real-world knowledge are analyzed. For example, "If you eat all of that food, it will make you **bigger**!" Here, "bigger" can have different meanings (like obese, tall, grown-up as young, etc.) in different contexts.

13.8 NLP, AI, MACHINE LEARNING: THE DIFFERENCE

Artificial Intelligence (AI), Natural Language Processing (NLP), and Machine Learning (ML) are important terms that are often used interchangeably. But you must know that,

NLP and machine learning are both subsets of Artificial Intelligence.

With NLP, machines can understand what the user wrote or spoke and then respond accordingly. NLP uses ML (Machine Learning) algorithms to automate the process of delivering accurate responses.

For example, AI-powered chatbots use NLP to interpret what users say and what they intend to do, and machine learning to automatically deliver more accurate responses by learning from past interactions.

> People's thoughts, research, opinions, facts and feedback transfer into the digital world through social media feeds, legal case files, electronic health records, contact center logs, warranty claims and more. Natural language processing uncovers the insights hidden in the word streams.

13.9 THE NLTK LIBRARY FOR PYTHON

NLTK or the **Natural Language Toolkit** is a free, open-source, community-driven project that is widely used for building Python programs that can process human language data. For this purpose, NLTK has easy-to-use interfaces to use several resources and contains a suite of text-processing libraries that has built-in functions for classification, tokenization, stemming, tagging, parsing, and semantic reasoning.

13.9.1 Processing Natural Language

The basic steps in NLP include:

1. Sentence tokenization
2. Word tokenization
3. Text lemmatization and stemming
4. Stop words
5. Regex
6. Bag-of-words
7. TF–IDF

Step 1: Sentence Tokenization, also known as Sentence Segmentation, divides a string written in a language into its basic components. For example, in languages like English, a sentence can be split at the position of a punctuation mark. The NLTK library has the nltk.sent_tokenize function to perform sentence tokenization.

Example 13.1 **The code given below performs sentence tokenization on a review written for the Jruma app.**

```
import nltk
text = "A very great App for students! I wish to solve more and more quizzes
every day and increase my knowledge! Thank you so much for this App! This App
should be appreciated more and more! Congratulations!!:))"
sentences = nltk.sent_tokenize(text)
for sentence in sentences:
    print(sentence)
```

You can think of stemming and lemmatization as a special case of normalization.

OUTPUT

```
A very great App for students!
I wish to solve more and more quizzes every day and increase my knowledge!
Thank you so much for this App! This App should be appreciated more and more!
Congratulations!!:))
```

Step 2: Word Tokenization or Word Segmentation divides a string of written language into its constituent words. For example, in English, two consecutive words are separated using a space. The `nltk.word_tokenize()` function is used to apply word tokenization on the given string.

```
from nltk import word_tokenize, sent_tokenize
import nltk
text = "A very great App for students! I wish to solve more and more quizzes every
day and increase my knowledge! Thank you so much for this App! This App should be
appreciated more and more! Congratulations!!:))"
words = nltk.word_tokenize(text)
for word in words:
    print(word, end = '###')
```

OUTPUT

```
A###very###great###App###for###students###!###I###wish###to###solve###more###and###
more###quizzes###every###day###and###increase###my###knowledge###!###Thank###you###
so###much###for###this###App###!###This###App###should###be###appreciated###more###
and###more###!###Congratulations###!###!###:###)###)###
```

Step 3: Text Lemmatization and Stemming is used for grammatical reasons to support documents that contain different forms of a word. For example, words like run, runs, running are related words having a similar meaning. In this case, **stemming** *and* **lemmatization** *can be used to* reduce all these related words to a common base.

Thus, 'am', 'are', and 'is' have a common base, 'be'. Similarly, 'run', 'runs', 'running' can be reduced to base form 'run'.

Stemming and lemmatization are special cases of **normalization**. However, they are different from each other.

Lemmatization performs its task with the help of a vocabulary and morphological analysis of the words to return the base or dictionary form of any given word, which is often known as the **lemma**.

Stemmer, on the other hand, operates without knowledge of the context. It cannot understand the difference between words having different meanings in different contexts. However, stemmers are easier to implement and usually run faster. Figure 13.1 clarifies the difference between stemming and lemmatization.

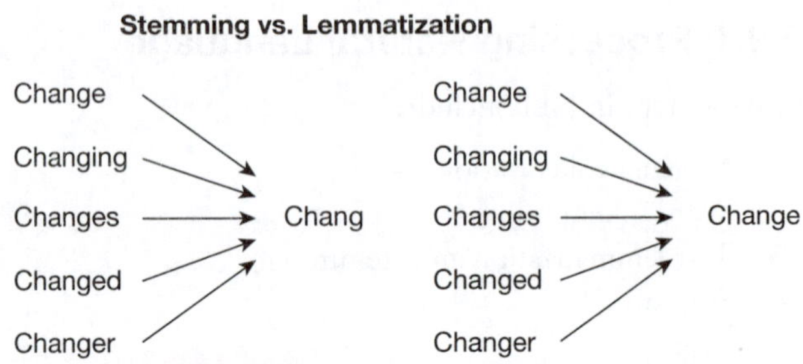

Figure 13.1 Stemming vs. lemmatization

Example 13.2 **Program to demonstrate stemming text.**

```
from nltk.stem import PorterStemmer
stemmer = PorterStemmer()
words = ['run', 'running', 'runs', 'runner']
stemmed = [stemmer.stem(word) for word in words]
print(stemmed)
```

OUTPUT

```
['run', 'run', 'run', 'runner']
```

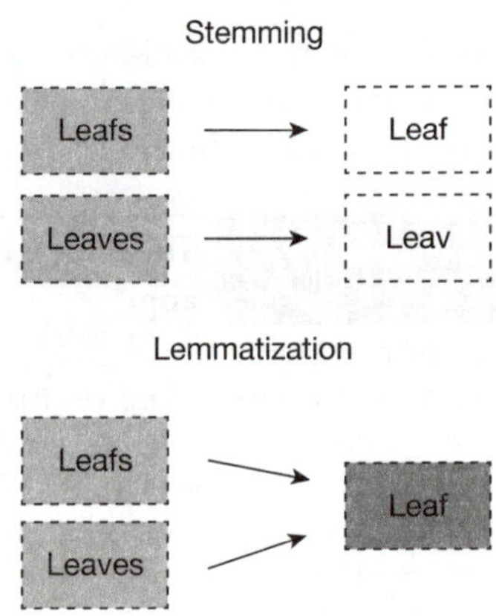

Step 4: Eliminate stop words. These words are usually filtered out before or after processing text. Since these words add a lot of noise, they are treated as irrelevant and must therefore be discarded. Some common stop words in English language are "**and**", "**the**" and "**a**".

The NLTK library has a predefined list of common stop words. However, when using the NLTK library for the first time, you must download the stop words by writing, nltk.download("stop words"). After downloading, the stop words can be loaded from the nltk.corpus package.

While removing stop words, we convert the list into a set because search operation is performed faster on a set than on a list.

Example 13.3 **Let us remove stop words from our text.**

Note that you must first download stop words of English language by writing nltk.download('stop words').

```
from nltk import word_tokenize, sent_tokenize
from nltk.corpus import stop words
import nltk
nltk.download('stop words')
text = "A very great App for students! I wish to solve more and more quizzes
every day and increase my knowledge! Thank you so much for this App! This App
should be appreciated more and more! Congratulations!!:))"
stop_words = stop words.words('english')
words = nltk.word_tokenize(text)
cleaned_text = []
for word in words:
    if word not in stop_words:
        cleaned_text.append(word)
```

```
print("Uncleaned Text : ", text)
print("Cleaned Text : ", cleaned_text)
```

OUTPUT

```
Uncleaned Text :  A very great App for students! I wish to solve more and more
quizzes every day and increase my knowledge! Thank you so much for this App! This
App should be appreciated more and more! Congratulations!!:))

Cleaned Text :  ['A', 'great', 'App', 'students', '!', 'I', 'wish', 'solve',
'quizzes', 'every', 'day', 'increase', 'knowledge', '!', 'Thank', 'much', 'App',
'!', 'This', 'App', 'appreciated', '!', 'Congratulations', '!', '!', ':', ')',
')']
```

POS Tagging or Parts of Speech Tagging, also known as grammatical tagging, is a process that marks words in text format for a particular part of a speech depending on its definition and context. It reads text in a language and assigns some specific token (Parts of Speech) to each word. The steps involved in POS tagging include:

Step 1: Tokenize text
Step 2: Apply pos_tag using nltk.pos_tag(tokenize_text)

Example 13.4 **To tag text using the `pos_tag()` method of NLTK library.**

Note that you need to first download the averaged_perceptron_tagger' before using the po_tag() method.

```
from nltk import word_tokenize, sent_tokenize
from nltk.corpus import stop words
import nltk
nltk.download('averaged_perceptron_tagger')
text = "A very great App for students! I wish to solve more and more quizzes
every day and increase my knowledge! Thank you so much for this App! This App
should be appreciated more and more! Congratulations!!:))"
stop_words = stop words.words('english')
words = nltk.word_tokenize(text)
cleaned_text = []
for word in words:
    if word not in stop_words:
        cleaned_text.append(word)
tagged = nltk.pos_tag(cleaned_text)
print("Tagged Text is : ", tagged)
```

OUTPUT

```
Tagged Text is :  [('A', 'DT'), ('great', 'JJ'), ('App', 'JJ'), ('students',
'NNS'), ('!', '.'), ('I', 'PRP'), ('wish', 'VBP'), ('solve', 'RB'), ('quizzes',
'JJ'), ('every', 'DT'), ('day', 'NN'), ('increase', 'VB'), ('knowledge',
'NN'), ('!', '.'), ('Thank', 'NNP'), ('much', 'JJ'), ('App', 'NNP'), ('!',
'.'), ('This', 'DT'), ('App', 'NNP'), ('appreciated', 'VBD'), ('!', '.'),
('Congratulations', 'NNPS'), ('!', '.'), ('!', '.'), (':', ':'), (')', ')'),
(')', ')')]
```

In the output, VB refers to 'verb', NNS refers to 'plural nouns', DT refers to a 'determiner'.

Steps Involved in the POS tagging example

- Tokenize text (word_tokenize)
- apply pos_tag to the above step, that is, nltk.pos_tag(tokenize_text)

Refer to any website for a list of tags. These tags are almost always accurate but we should be aware that they *can* be inaccurate at times. However, pre-trained models usually assume the English being used is written properly, following the grammatical rules.

Reducing customer complaints with NLP
Royal Bank of Scotland uses text analytics, an NLP technique, to extract important trends from customer feedback in many forms. The company analyzes data from emails, surveys and call center conversations to identify the root cause of customer dissatisfaction and implement improvements.

13.10 WHAT IS A CHATBOT?

Chatbot is an artificial intelligence (AI) program that simulates conversation (or a chat) with a user in natural language through messaging applications, websites, mobile applications or by phone (Fig. 13.2). You must have seen that many websites offer a real-time chat service that helps you to find relevant information on their portals. Such an application provides a pleasant user experience and faster and simpler customer service interaction. At the same time, it also allows companies to improve their operational efficiency by reducing the typical cost of customer service. Employees who were dedicatedly providing customer support can now be utilized to do more fruitful jobs. Companies are now able to save thousands of rupees per month by deploying a chatbot instead of a human employee exclusively for providing customer support. Figure 13.3 shows some of the benefits of chatbot.

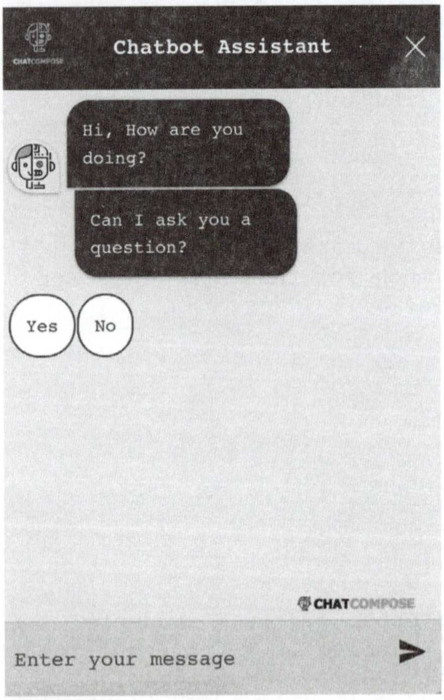

Figure 13.2 A typical chatbot conversation

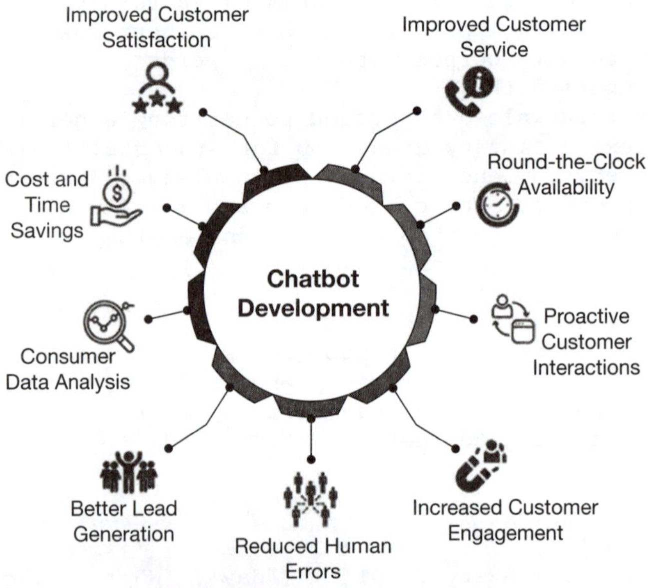

Figure 13.3 Benefits of chatbot

The best part of a chatbot is that it allows users to pick up a conversation from the point where they last left. This has been possible because chatbots have a memory that implicitly learns about the users and stores key information about them for future use.

Users can query about multiple things one after the other without annoying the information provider.

13.10.1 Open and Closed Chatbots

A chatbot can be categorized as open or closed depending on its usage. While open chatbots use ML techniques to learn from their interactions with users, closed chatbots, on the other hand, execute a specific conversation flow.

Thus, open chatbots support a more natural way of conversing with humans. But their success depends on how well they have been trained. Closed chatbots comparatively have a lower risk of providing poor user experience.

13.10.2 Uses of Chatbots

Customer Service: Chatbots can be programmed to collect registration data, provide information, answer frequently asked questions, etc. This gives a pleasant experience to customers. Users can now interact in a simpler and faster way.

Online purchases: Chatbots assist users while shopping online to select a product of their utility and then make the payment easily. They provide information, solve problems faced by users during shopping and perform searches to identify similar products.

They are also useful in **sending information and news about latest updates in products or about discount offers** automatically to customers and potential buyers of the product.

Collect information: Chatbots can be designed to collect some useful information about users, such as email, phone number, etc. This information can be filtered (to select the most appropriate ones in the current context) and then be forwarded to sales representatives for a follow-up conversation.

Make appointments: Chatbots can automatically make appointments by displaying availability on a calendar and allowing the user to select a suitable date.

Healthcare websites deploy chatbots in their websites to provide patient information. A patient can enter his symptoms. The NLP-based chatbot will compare those symptoms with known ailments. After analyzing the basic issues, the chatbot can then *assist patients in booking an appointment, finding a doctor, and more.*

Chatbots also help users to *find an appropriate insurance policy.* For this, the chatbot collects relevant information from the users and then tailors products according to each consumer's needs. These chatbots not only help users to find a suitable policy but also help in follow-up services such as complete the payment for the policy, file for a claim, renew policies, check their coverage and track the status of a policy/claim, to name a few.

Personal counseling: Children of this era, known as Gen Z, are dealing with more mental health, body image, and loneliness issues than all the other people. These *children can use chatbots that can gauge their emotional state based on conversational context and respond with compassion* (Fig. 13.4).

Build trust and improve customer engagement: Chatbots help companies to keep their customers satisfied and well-informed as customers are assisted in everything they do. A chatbot instantly responds 24 × 7 and provides immediate answers to simultaneous users at once.

Figure 13.4 Chatbot helper for counseling

13.11 HOW A CHATBOT WORKS

A chatbot works on request–response model. When a user requests information, the chatbot analyzes the request to identify what information the user exactly wants.

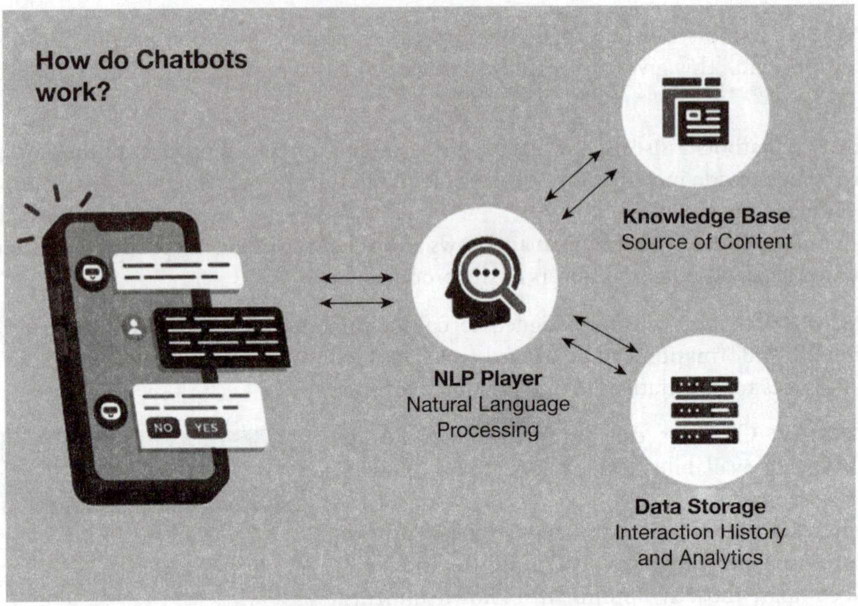

Figure 13.5 Working of a chatbot

Once the intent of user's request is correctly known, the chatbot searches its knowledge base to give the most appropriate response. Many-a-time, the user asks for some information or data. In such cases, the chatbot interacts with the back-end system to retrieve the data required to satisfy the user's request.

If there is no information available in the current context or if the chatbot fails to interpret the user's request, then the chatbot may reply with a generic and predefined text.

13.11.1 Types of Chatbots

Chatbots apply a combination of different AI techniques including natural language processing, machine learning and semantic understanding. There are different types of chatbots, each one serving a different purpose and solving a different issue (Fig. 13.6). Depending on the use-case you want to address, some chatbot technologies are more appropriate than others.

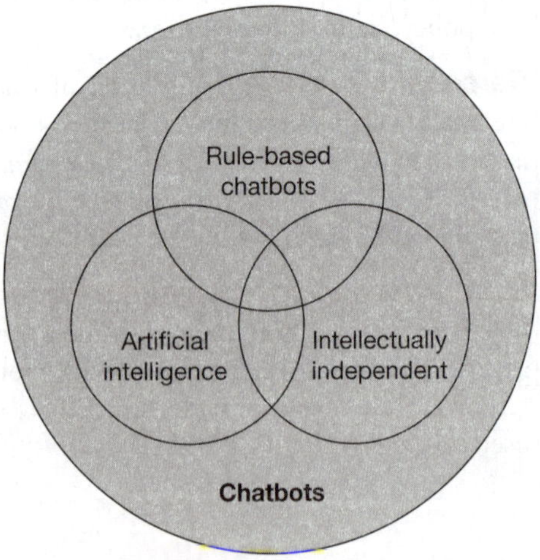

Figure 13.6 Types of chatbots

Rule-based Chatbots As the name suggests, these chatbots follow predefined paths while conversing with the user. As the conversation progresses, the user is offered several options that correspond to their inquiry. Based on the option selected by the user, the chatbot decides the next step in the conversation.

Though these chatbots make the interaction simple for both the user as well as the chatbot program, they can be used only to answer basic customer inquiries (like the status of one's delivery, get some information, etc.).

> AI-powered chatbots get smarter over time.

Menu-based Chatbots These chatbots are a variant of rule-based chatbots and present a menu or buttons showing different options available to the user. Instead of typing text, the user has to click on these buttons or options to interact with the system. Such chatbots lack critical understanding and flexibility. These bots can only automate situations that they have learned and are likely to arise.

Intellectually independent chatbots These chatbots use Machine Learning (ML) algorithms to learn from the user's requests and the bot's reply. During every conversation, the bots use keywords to recognize recurring patterns and common user behaviors to decide what to do when little or no human assistance is available. For example, if the user types "Facing problems in account login", then the bot breaks the sentence into keywords like "problem," "login," and "account," and then provides a predefined answer based on these keywords.

AI-powered chatbots These are hybrid bots that combine the attributes of both rule-based and intellectually independent chatbots. These chatbots extensively use artificial intelligence (AI) techniques to simulate human intelligence, thereby making machines work and think like people.

AI-powered chatbots use a predefined flow to ensure accurate responses to a user's inquiry. If no such path is available, they are also equipped to understand free language.

We can also classify chatbots based on where they are deployed (Fig. 13.7). For example, chatbots can be implemented into messengers, stand-alone applications or on a website.

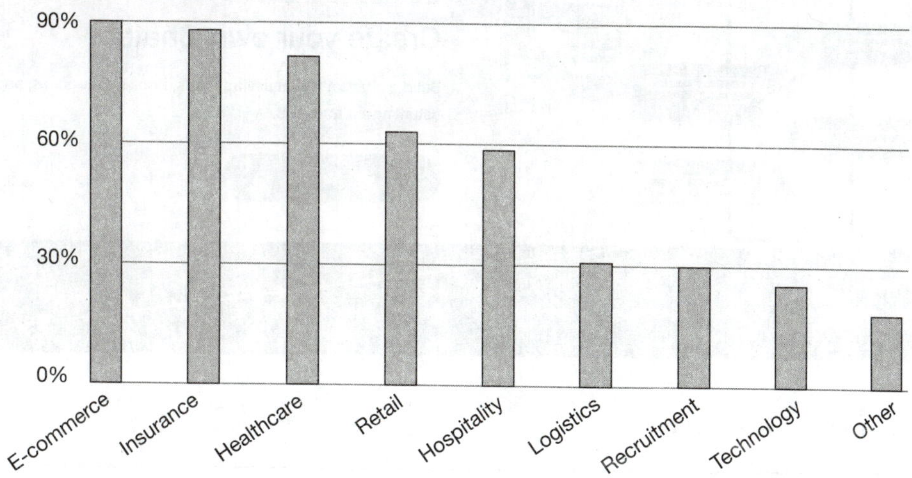

Figure 13.7 Industries that are benefitted most from chatbots

13.12 CREATING A CHATBOT

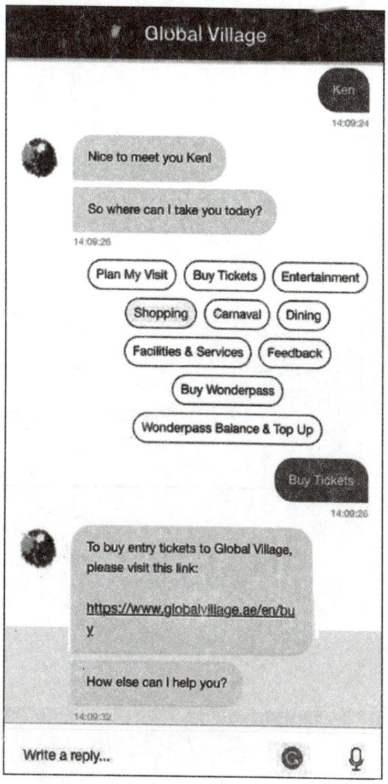

Before creating a chatbot, you must first do a preliminary research to understand the following issues.

Understand your target market. For this, you must know who would use the chatbot, what questions they frequently ask and what tasks they want to accomplish through the chatbot.

Define your goals to have a clarity on what would be the purpose of the chatbot. To get this information, you should know why you are creating the chatbot – to assist in online shopping, just to greet the website visitor, schedule a meeting, check the shipping status, fitness tracking, etc. Based on the goals, we will actually know the time and effort involved in developing the chatbot.

> Chatbots make the user interaction quick and professional, yet casual.

Design your chatbot's personality. For this, use the information collected in Step 1. For example, if it is just a greeting chatbot, then you must think how your audience would like to be treated. Write a script to give your user a pleasant experience. You may even record your voice for the same. The chatbot responses should be simple, polite and yet powerful.

Create diagrams or flowcharts depicting requests and replies. The replies must be short. You may include visual elements like GIFs, emojis, pictures, or videos.

Example 13.5 **Let us create a chatbot using appypie.**

Step 1: Type https://www.appypie.com/chatbot/builder in the address bar of the browser window.

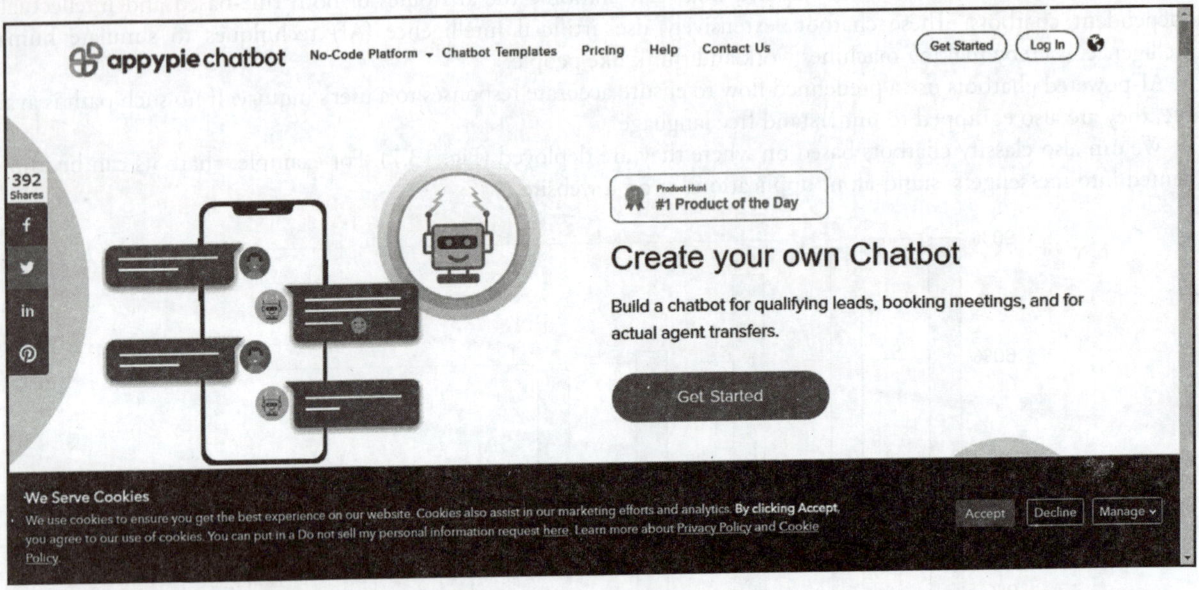

Step 2: Enter the name of your chatbot.

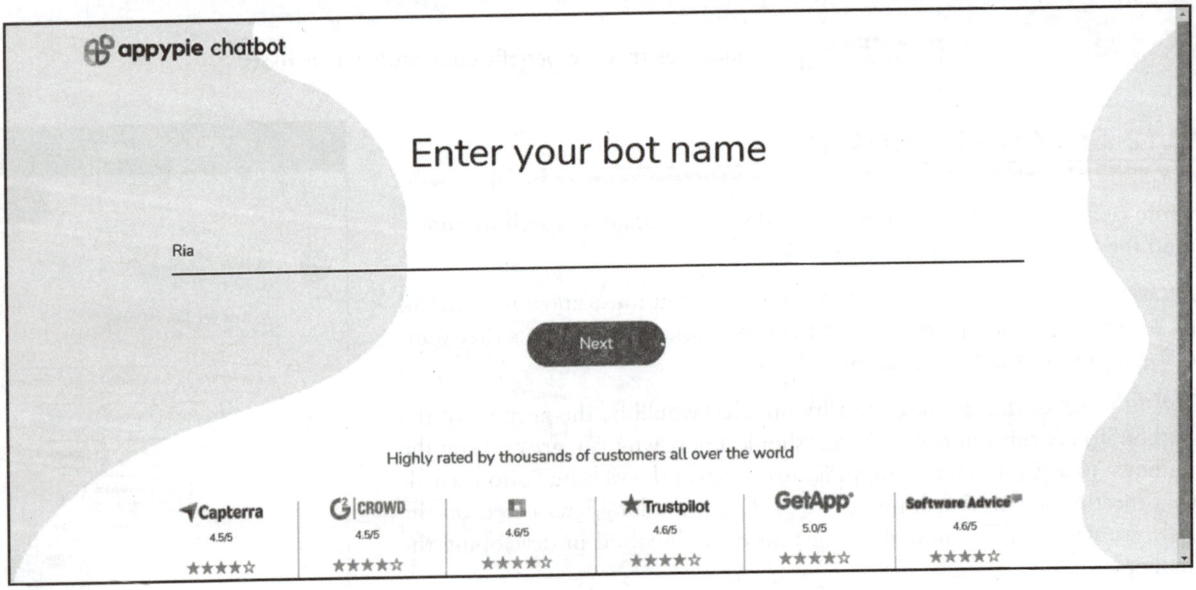

Step 3: Select the type of bot to be created.

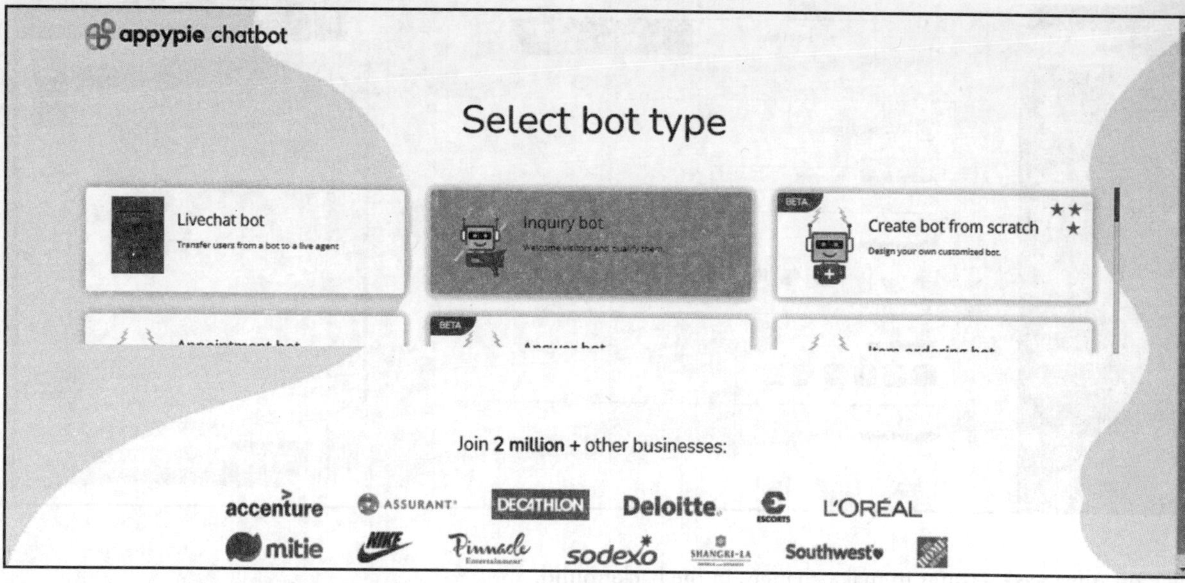

Step 4: Create an account on appypie to register yourself. You can even login through your Google or Facebook account. When you click on Sign Up, a verification code will be sent on your registered email address. Enter the verification code to continue.

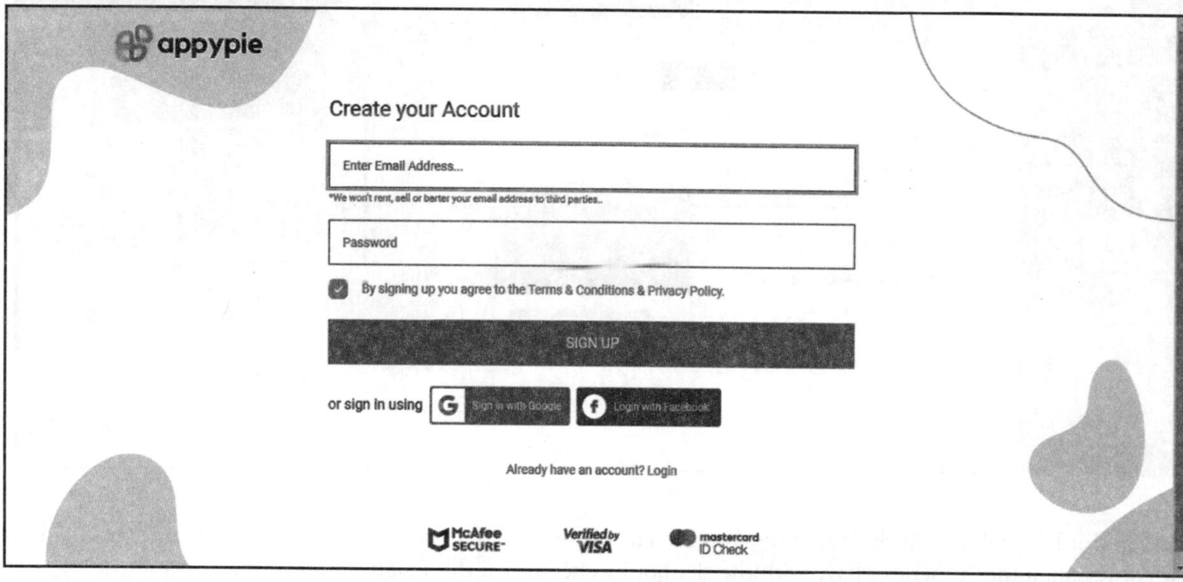

Step 5: When the account is created, you can preview the bot and make design or flow changes in it.

Click on Design Customization tab to change badge style, avtar, theme color and header name. Click on "Save and Next" to save the changes.

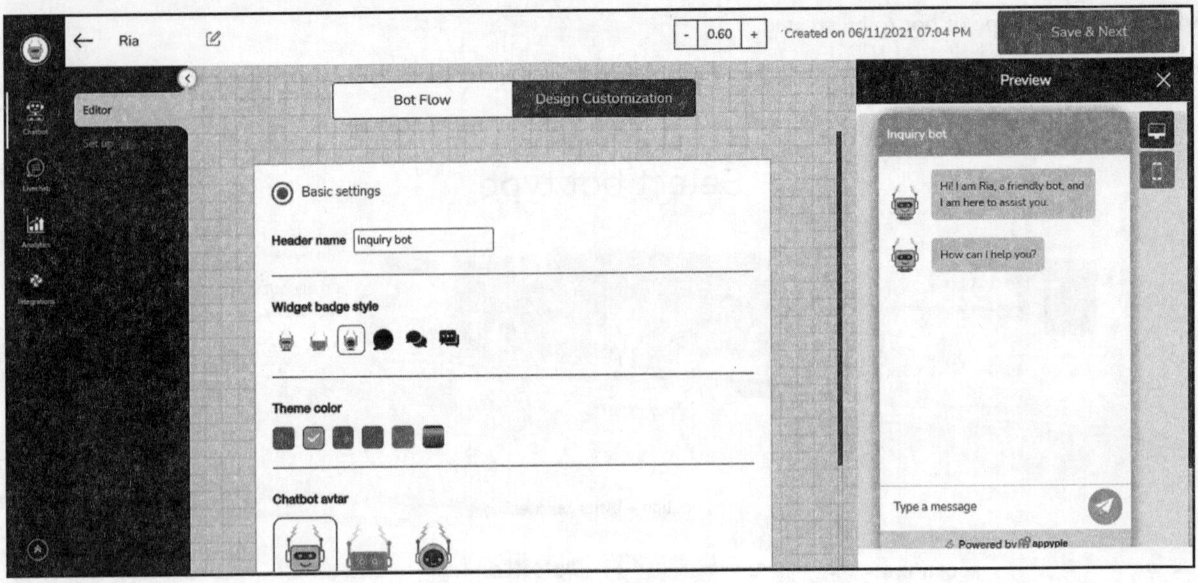

Click on Advanced Settings to make changes in the background.

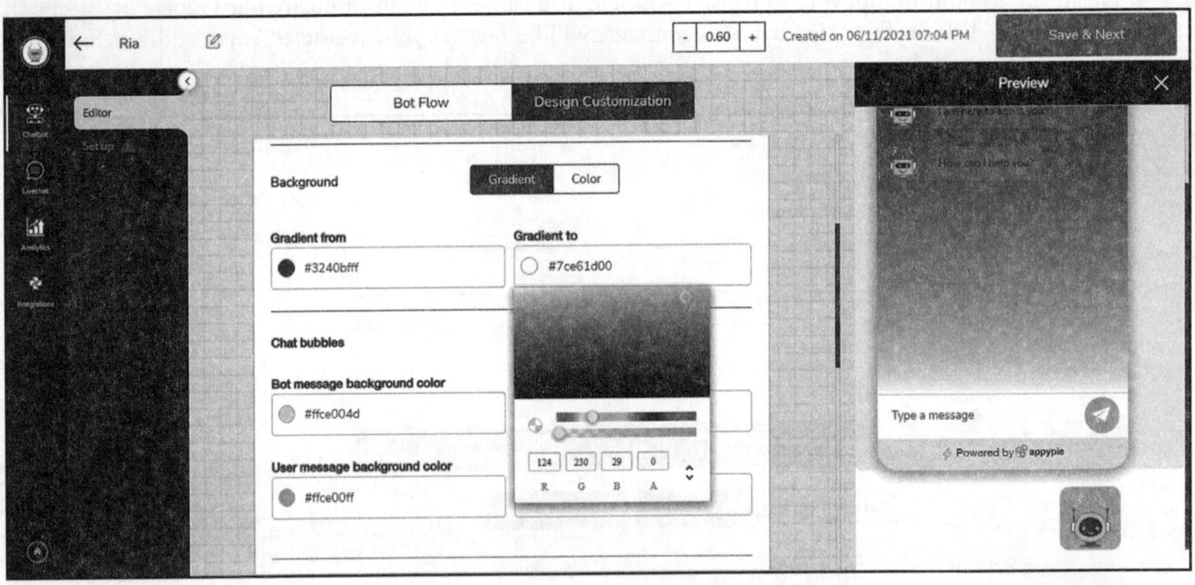

Click on Bot Flow tab to edit the bot's flow. You can edit the pre-written content as per your requirements or add a new conversation that a user can have with the chatbot by clicking on the + sign.

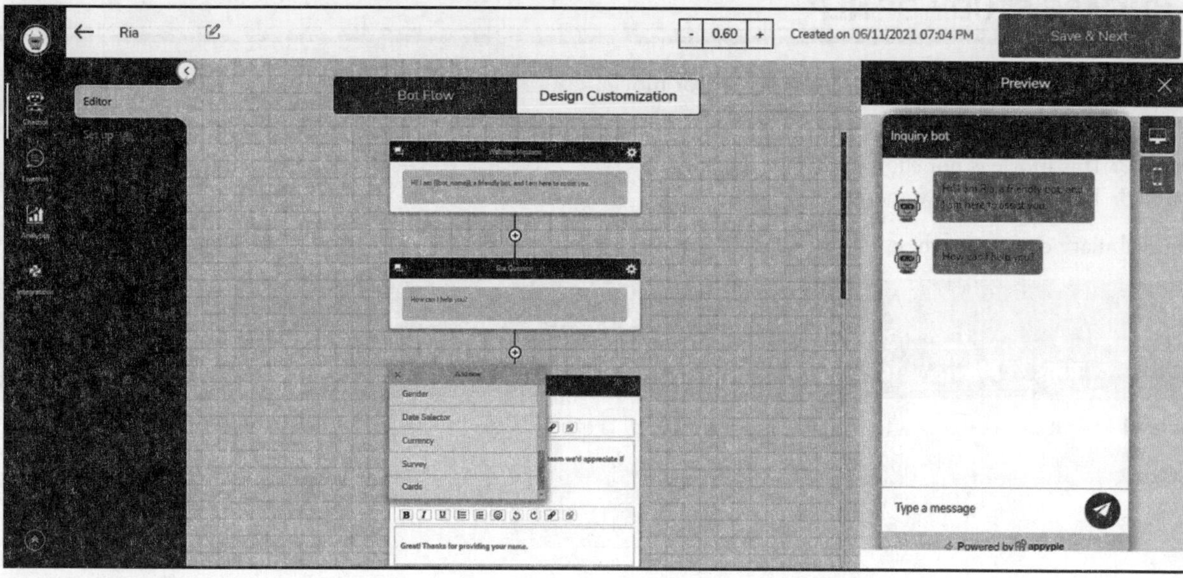

Chatbots thus created can then be deployed on various platforms including Facebook, WhatsApp, Telegram, WeChat, website, native mobile applications, etc.

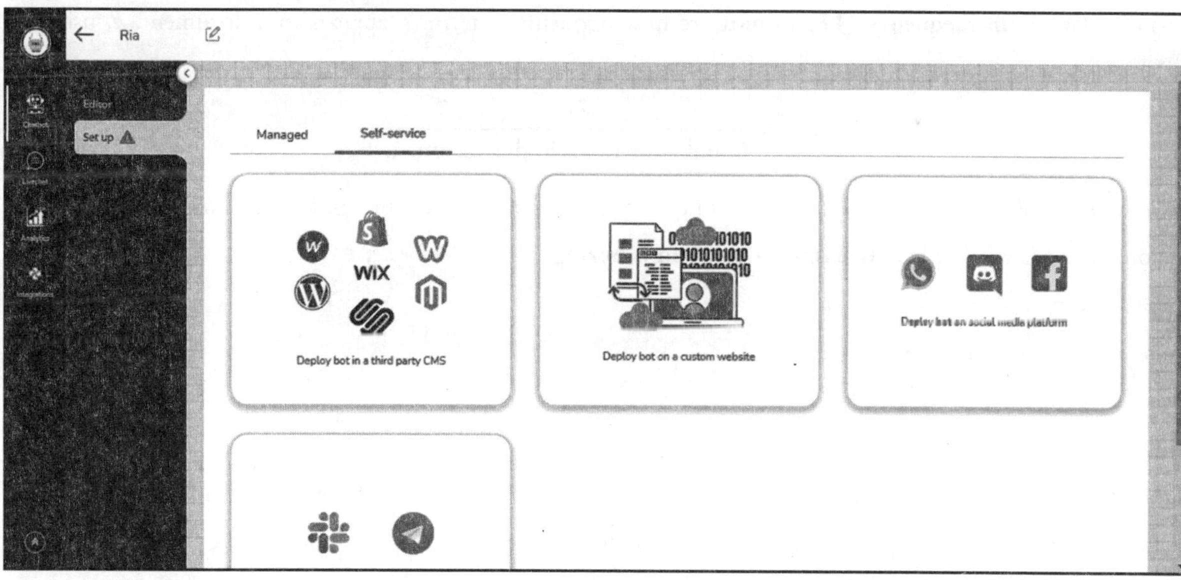

Appypie will give you the code of the chatbot, which you can easily add in your application. For example, I can copy the chatbot code in the Body section of my HTML website.

```
<!-- Appy Chatbot widget, Paste the code in the <body> section -->
<script id="appyWidgetInit" src="https://chatbot.appypie.com/widget/loadbuild.
js?cid=kps7q47r-AGENT1623408869081-BOTID1623418487049&name=mixBuild"></script>
<!-- /. End Appy chatbot widget code -->
```

13.13 CASE STUDY OF NLP

Here is a sample of reviews about a particular horror movie:

Review 1: This movie is very short and good.
Review 2: This movie is not short and is boring.
Review 3: This movie is slow and good.

The vocabulary consists of these 11 words: 'This', 'movie', 'is', 'very', 'short, 'and', 'good', 'not', 'boring', 'slow'

	1 This	2 Movie	3 Is	4 Very	5 Short	6 And	7 Good	8 Not	9 Boring	10 Slow	Length of Review in Words
Review1	1	1	1	1	1	1	1	0	0	0	7
Review2	1	1	2	0	1	1	0	1	1	0	8
Review3	1	1	1	0	0	1	1	0	0	1	6

Vector of Review 1: [1 1 1 1 1 1 1 0 0 0]
Vector of Review 2: [1 1 2 0 1 1 0 1 1 0]
Vector of Review 3: [1 1 1 0 0 1 1 0 0 1]

Let us calculate **Term Frequency (TF)** to measure how frequently a term, *t*, appears in a document, *d*, using the formula,

$$TF_{t,d} = \frac{n_{t,d}}{\text{Number of terms in the document}}$$

Here, *n* is the number of times the term *t* appears in the document *d*. Every document and term has its own TF value.

Therefore, in Review 2, **"This movie is not short and is boring"**

Number of terms = 8

Number of times 'this' appears in review 2 = 1

Hence, TF of 'this' = 1/8 = 1/8

Similarly,

TF('movie') = 1/8 TF('is') = 2/8 = ¼ TF('very') = 0/8 = 0 TF('short') = 1/8

TF('and') = 1/8 TF('good') = 0/8 = 0 TF('not') = 1/8 TF('boring') = 1/8

TF('slow') = 0/8 = 0

We can calculate the term frequencies for all the terms and all the reviews as shown in the table given below.

Term	Review 1	Review 2	Review 3	TF Review 1	TF Review 2	TF Review 3
This	1	1	1	1/7	1/8	1/6
Movie	1	1	1	1/7	1/8	1/6
Is	1	2	1	1/7	1/4	1/6
Very	1	0	0	1/7	0	0
Short	1	1	0	1/7	1/8	0

(*Continued*)

Term	Review 1	Review 2	Review 3	TF Review 1	TF Review 2	TF Review 3
And	1	1	1	1/7	1/8	1/6
Good	1	0	1	1/7	0	1/6
Not	0	1	0	0	1/8	0
Boring	0	1	0	0	1/8	0
Slow	0	0	1	0	0	1/6

Calculate **Inverse Document Frequency (IDF)** to measure how important a term is. It is calculated as,

$$\mathrm{IDF}_t = \log \frac{\text{Number of documents}}{\text{Number of documents with term } t}$$

We can calculate the IDF values for all the words in Review 2, "This movie is not short and is boring."

IDF('this') = log(number of documents/number of documents containing the word 'this') = log(3/3) = log(1) = 0

Similarly,

IDF('movie',) = log(3/3) = 0

IDF('is') = log(3/2) = 0.18

IDF('not') = log(3/1) = log(3) = 0.48

IDF('short') = log(3/1) = 0.48

IDF('and') = log(3/3) = 0

IDF('boring') = log(3/1) = 0.48

We can calculate the IDF values for each word like this. Thus, the IDF values for the entire vocabulary would be:

Term	Review 1	Review 2	Review 3	IDF
This	1	1	1	0.00
Movie	1	1	1	0.00
Is	1	2	1	0.00
Very	1	0	0	0.48
Short	1	1	0	0.18
And	1	1	1	0.00
Good	1	0	1	0.18
Not	0	1	0	0.48
Boring	0	1	0	0.48
Slow	0	0	1	0.48

Hence, we see that words like 'is', 'this', 'and', etc., are reduced to 0 and have little importance; while words like 'good', 'boring', 'short' have more importance and thus have a higher value.

Calculate the TF–IDF score for each word. Words with a higher score are more important than those having a lower score.

$$(\mathrm{TF\text{–}IDF})_{t,d} = \mathrm{TF}_{t,d} * \mathrm{IDF}_t$$

Let us calculate the TF–IDF score for every word in Review 2: "This movie is not short and is boring"

TF–IDF('this', Review 2) = TF('this', Review 2) * IDF('this') = 1/8 * 0 = 0

Similarly,

TF–IDF('movie', Review 2) = 1/8 * 0 = 0

TF–IDF('very', Review 2) = 0 * 0.48 = 0

TF–IDF('and', Review 2) = 1/8 * 0 = 0

TF–IDF('not', Review 2) = 1/8 * 0.48 = 0.06

TF–IDF('boring', Review 2) = 1/8 * 0.48 = 0.06

TF–IDF('is', Review 2) = 1/4 * 0 = 0

TF–IDF('short', Review 2) = 1/8 * 0.18 = 0.023

TF–IDF('good', Review 2) = 0/8 * 0.18 = 0.0

TF–IDF('slow', Review 2) = 0/8 * 0.48 = 0.0

Similarly, we can calculate the TF–IDF scores for all the words with respect to all the reviews:

Term	TF Review 1	TF Review 2	TF Review 3	IDF	TF–IDF Review 1	TF–IDF Review 2	TF–IDF Review 3
This	1/7	1/8	1/6	0.00	0	0	0
Movie	1/7	1/8	1/6	0.00	0	0	0
Is	1/7	1/4	1/6	0.00	0	0	0
Very	1/7	0	0	0.48	0.068	0	0
Short	1/7	1/8	0	0.18	0.025	0.023	0
And	1/7	1/8	1/6	0.00	0	0	0
Good	1/7	0	1/6	0.18	0.025	0	0.03
Not	0	1/8	0	0.48	0	0.06	0
Boring	0	1/8	0	0.48	0	0.06	0
Slow	0	0	1/6	0.48	0	0	0.08

TF–IDF has larger values for less frequent words and is high when both IDF and TF values are high, i.e., the word is rare in all the documents combined but frequent in a single document.

Key Terms

Natural Language Processing: Manipulation or understanding of text or speech by a computer software.

Chatbots: NLP- and AI-based systems that are specifically designed to interact with humans through text or speech.

Lexical analysis: The process of identifying and analyzing the structure of words by breaking down a big chunk of text into elementary words.

Syntactic analysis: The process of parsing a sentence to analyze the words in the sentence to interpret its meaning as per the grammatical rules of the language.

Chapter Highlights

- NLP can be used to create intelligent systems for speech recognition, machine translation, answering questions, spam detection, document summarization, predictive typing, named entity recognition and autocomplete, to name a few.
- While writing using human language, we often misspell or abbreviate words, or omit punctuation. Similarly, while speaking, we pronounce different words differently (in regional accents). Some people mumble, stutter and borrow terms from other languages, which increases the complexity of processing natural languages.

- Techniques like deep, supervised and unsupervised learning are widely used for modeling human language to resolve ambiguity in language.
- NLP systems break down text/speech in human language into shorter, elemental pieces, to understand relationships that exist between the pieces for interpreting its meaning.
- Speech recognition is used for converting spoken words into text.
- Topic classification uses NLP to organize unstructured text into categories.
- Natural Language Understanding (NLU) deals with mapping the given input in natural language into useful representations.
- Natural Language Generation (NLG) uses content in internal representation to produce meaningful sentences in a natural language.
- A chatbot works on request–response model.

Review Questions

1. What do you understand by the term Natural Language Processing?
2. Give the applications of NLP.
3. Discuss some issues faced while dealing with human language.
4. Differentiate between the following:
   a. Natural Language and Computer Language.
   b. NLU and NLG
   c. Open and Closed Chatbot
5. How are NLP systems useful?
6. Give any three real-world applications of NLP.
7. Discuss three ambiguities faced by NLP systems.
8. Discuss the steps involved to perform NLP.
9. What is a chatbot? Give any three uses of a chatbot.
10. How does a chatbot work?
11. Enumerate the different types of chatbots.
12. What steps will you follow to create a chatbot?
13. Identify stemming and lemmatization in the words shown below.

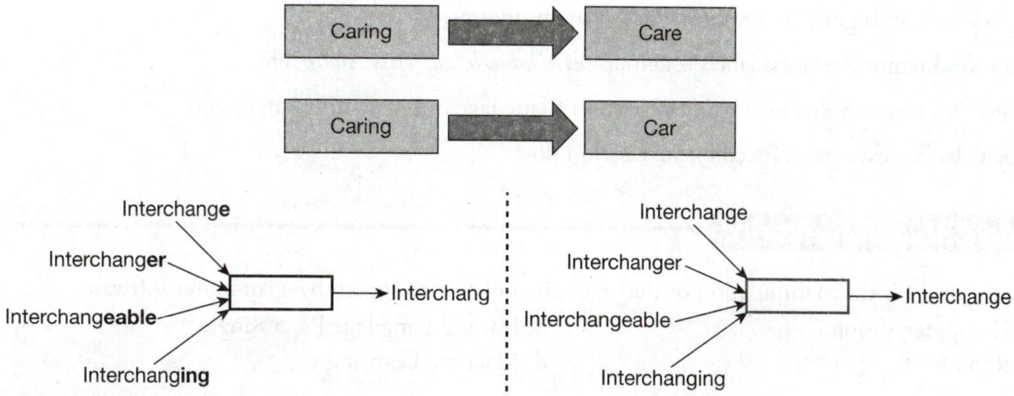

Fill in the Blanks

1. NLP applies machine learning algorithms to ________ and __________.
2. ______ uses NLP to detect and filter spam emails.
3. _________ language is ambiguous in nature.
4. __________ analysis is used to identify the user's opinion within large amounts of text.
5. Speech __________ is used for converting spoken words into text.
6. __________ are NLP-based systems that are specifically designed to interact with humans through text or speech.
7. __________ of a language refers to the collection of words in a language.
8. _________ analysis is done to analyze the words in a sentence to interpret their meaning as per the grammatical rules of the language.
9. _____________ reduce words to their base form.
10. Words like *I, they, have, like* and *yours* are known as ________ words.
11. ____________ refers to having any sentence depend upon the meaning of the sentence just preceding it.
12. NLP and machine learning are both subsets of _________.
13. A chatbot works on __________ model.

State True or False

1. NLP applies machine learning algorithms to process text and speech.
2. Predictive typing uses Computer Vision algorithms to recommend what users should type next.
3. Siri is the virtual assistant of Google.
4. Every language has its unique set of grammar and syntax rules, terms and slang.
5. Computer language has a very large vocabulary.
6. Computer language is easily understood by humans.
7. Chatbots are used to offer 24 × 7 assistance to customers by handling their queries.
8. Chatbots are used to automate repetitive and time-consuming tasks.
9. Natural Language Understanding generates non-linguistic outputs from natural language inputs.
10. NLU is harder than NLG.
11. Syntax-level ambiguity is common when using pronouns.
12. Stop word removal process labels tokens as *verb, adverb, adjective, noun,* etc.
13. Word Tokenization divides a string written in a language into its basic components.
14. Open chatbot executes a specific conversation flow.

Multiple Choice Questions

1. ___________ is the manipulation or understanding of text or speech by a computer software.

   a. Computer Vision b. Natural Language Processing
   c. Robotics d. Machine Learning

2. NLP systems ________ user queries.
   a. Interact to
   b. understand
   c. respond to
   d. All of these.
3. ________ is the virtual assistant of Microsoft.
   a. Alexa
   b. Siri
   c. Cortana
   d. Ymo
4. Sentiment Analysis is used to assess the ___________ of the customers.
   a. attitude
   b. behavior
   c. emotional state
   d. All of these.
5. NLP systems cannot be used for _________.
   a. predictive typing
   b. spelling correction
   c. speech translation
   d. None of these.
6. ________ uses NLP to organize unstructured text into categories.
   a. Document Summarization
   b. Topic Classification
   c. Predictive Typing
   d. Speech Translation
7. _________ uses NLP to analyze hundreds of open-ended responses to surveys to gain insights from customer feedback.
   a. Document Summarization
   b. Topic Classification
   c. Predictive Typing
   d. Speech Translation
8. __________ ambiguity exists due to confusion in using different words.
   a. Lexical
   b. Syntax-level
   c. Referential
   d. Grammatical
9. __________ ambiguity is common when using pronouns.
   a. Lexical
   b. Syntax-level
   c. Referential
   d. Grammatical
10. _________ analysis is the process of identifying and analyzing the structure of words by breaking down a big chunk of text into elementary words.
    a. Lexical
    b. Syntactic
    c. Semantic
    d. Pragmatic
11. _______ means breaking a text into elementary words.
    a. Part of speech tagging
    b. Tokenization
    c. Lemmatization and stemming
    d. Stop word removal
12. __________ analysis draws the exact meaning from the text.
    a. Lexical
    b. Syntactic
    c. Semantic
    d. Pragmatic
13. In _________ step, text is re-interpreted based on what it actually means in the current context.
    a. Lexical
    b. Syntactic
    c. Semantic
    d. Pragmatic
14. __________ chatbots follow predefined paths while conversing with the user.
    a. Rule-based
    b. Menu-based
    c. Intellectually independent
    d. AI-powered

Identify the Ambiguity in the Following Sentences

1. I saw the girl with the binocular.
2. Manya is looking for a match.

Give an Example of Each

1. Different syntax but same semantics.
2. Different semantics but same syntax.
3. Words having multiple meaning.
4. Sentences having correct syntax and incorrect semantics.

Brainstorn Activity

Ask students to generate ideas on how NLP can be used to make lengthy chapters interesting to read, especially a day before the examination.

Hint: Generate a summary of the chapters, extract important keywords for quick revision

Project Work

1. Create a chatbot for a university website to give detailed information about courses offered in a department, their fee and eligibility.
2. Create a chatbot that asks students to answer MCQs. If the answer is correct, the student is asked the next question. For every incorrect answer, the correct answer is displayed.

AI Lab Session – Semnatris

Semantris is a word association game powered by semantic search. The application uses machine learning and more specifically, NLP techniques. Each time the user enters a clue, the AI looks at all the words in the play and chooses the ones it thinks are most related. To develop this game, the AI system was trained on billions of examples of conversational text that span a large variety of topics. So, the application can make many types of accurate associations. Visit the link https://research.google.com/semantris/ to launch this experiment.

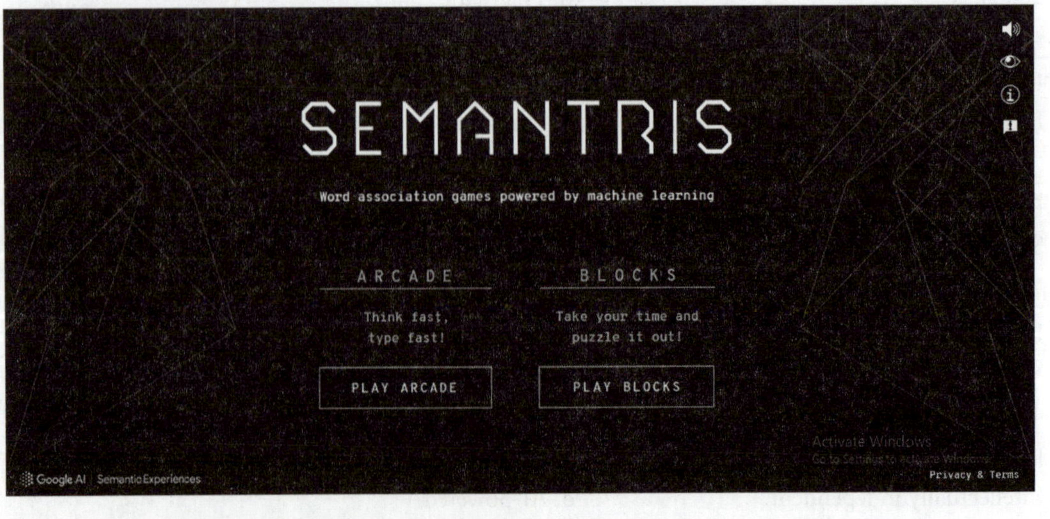

Analyzing the Engligh Language

1. The English language has words that may have multiple meanings. So, knowledge of the context in which those words are being used is very important to understand the correct meaning of a particular piece of text.
   A fly is buzzing around the room.
   She wants to become a pilot to fly high.
   Give two more examples of such sentences.
2. In human language, a perfect balance of syntax and semantics of a sentence is important for a better understanding of the context in which it is said. But when analyzing text written in the English language, the machine may encounter a piece of text that is syntactically correct but conveys no meaning. Such sentences complicate the NLP task. For example, **Ducks are riding the bicycle**, is syntactically correct but adds no additional information. Can you think of any other such sentence?

Answers

Fill in the Blanks

1. text, speech
2. Gmail
3. Natural
4. Sentiment
5. Translation
6. Chatbots
7. Lexicon
8. Syntactic
9. Lemmatization and stemming
10. stop
11. Discourse Integration
12. Artificial Intelligence
13. request–response

State True or False

1. True
2. False
3. False
4. True
5. False
6. False
7. True
8. True
9. False
10. True
11. False
12. False
13. False
14. False

Multiple Choice Questions

1. b
2. d
3. c
4. d
5. d
6. b
7. b
8. a
9. c
10. a
11. b
12. c
13. d
14. a
15. a
16. c
17. c
18. b
19. a
20. c
21. a

Identify the Ambiguity in the Following Sentences

1. Syntactic Ambiguity, because it is not clear: did I have the binoculars? Or did the girl have the binoculars?
2. Lexical Ambiguity, because it is not clear whether Manya is looking for a partner or Manya is looking for a match. (Cricket or any other match)

Evaluation of Models

14

Chapter Objectives

This chapter discusses evaluation models that are used to analyze the accuracy of AI model. Topics discussed in the chapter include:

- Confusion matrix
- ROC curve
- Over-fitting and under-fitting issues
- Bias vs. variance
- *K*-cross validation
- Evaluation metrics like *p*-value, MSE, residuals: F-statistic, RSE, R2, adjusted R2.

Machine learning is increasingly becoming an integral part of computer systems designed to solve real-world problems. However, true benefits from such systems can be obtained only if they give accurate predictions. To calculate the accuracy of a model we must use different ways to evaluate the machine learning model.

Once a model is trained, we need to check how the model performs on new/unseen data. The results from this step will help us to know whether we can trust the predictions made by the machine learning model or not.

Model evaluation techniques use a training data set to train the machine learning model (i.e., make the model learn) and a training data set to evaluate the performance of the model. The test data validates the accuracy of the model.

As a thumb rule, we must not use the same training data to also test the model. In your Mathematics exam, do you get the same questions as given in your text book? No. Because you know all the answers. So, a slight variation in values is necessary to check how accurately you can get the result. Similarly, while evaluating the machine learning model, we take a different data set for testing the model. Like us, the model remembers the whole training set, and will therefore always predict the correct value for any data in the training set. This is known as **over-fitting**.

In this section, we will discuss some popularly used techniques to evaluate an ML model.

14.1 CONFUSION MATRIX

It is a table with four cells that represent Actual vs. Predicted values. Looking at this table, we can easily calculate the accuracy of the model.

	1 (Predicted)	0 (Predicted)
1 (Actual)	True Positive	False Negative
0 (Actual)	False Positive	True Negative

True positives (TP): TP indicates cases in which the classifier predicted 1 when it was actually 1.

True negatives (TN): TN indicates cases when the classifier predicted 0 when it was actually 0.

False positives (FP): FP indicates cases where the classifier predicted 1 when it was actually 0. False positive is also known as "Type I error".

False negatives (FN): FN indicates cases where the classifier predicted 0 but in reality, it was 1. FN is also known as "Type II error."

Accuracy: **Accuracy** is defined as the percentage of correct predictions for the test data. It is calculated by dividing the number of correct predictions by the number of total predictions. Therefore, accuracy of the model can be given as,

$$\frac{\text{True Positive} + \text{True Negatives}}{\text{True Positive} + \text{True Negatives} + \text{False Positives} + \text{False Negatives}}$$

> Higher the diagonal values of the confusion matrix, the better it is.

True Positive Rate (TPR): TPR, also known as **sensitivity or recall,** indicates the number of positive values out of all the positive values that have been **correctly predicted**. That is, TPR is calculated as

$$\frac{TP}{TP + FN}$$

Also,

$$\frac{TPR}{1 - \text{False Negative Rate}}$$

This means that recall value specified the fraction of data that is predicted to belong to a class with respect to all data that truly belong in the class. In simple words, recall value says ***how many extra right ones, the model missed when it showed the right ones.***

False Positive Rate (FPR): FPR indicates the number of negative values out of all the negative values that have been **incorrectly predicted.** FPR is calculated as

$$\frac{FP}{FP + TN}$$

Also,

$$\frac{FPR}{1 - \text{True Negative Rate}}$$

True Negative Rate (TNR): TNR, also known as ***specificity***, indicates the number of negative values out of all the negative values that have been **correctly predicted**. TNR is calculated as

$$\frac{TN}{TN + FP}$$

False Negative Rate (FNR): FNR indicates the number of positive values, out of all the positive values that have been **incorrectly predicted**. FPR is calculated as

$$\frac{FN}{FN + TP}$$

Precision: Precision specifies the number of all the predicted positive values that are actually positive. It is calculated as,

$$\frac{TP}{TP + FP}$$

That is, precision is the percentage of positive values out of the ***total predicted positive*** values. Precision shows ***how much the model is right when it says it is right.***

A good machine learning model must have a high value for True Positives and True Negatives. Correspondingly, a good model must also have False Positives and False Negatives as low as possible. When talking about ratios, TPR and TNR should be very high while FPR and FNR should be very low,

F Score: F score is the harmonic mean of precision and recall. It lies between 0 and 1. Higher the value, better the model. We can calculate the F score as

$$F = 2\frac{\text{Precision} \times \text{Recall}}{\text{Precision} + \text{Recall}}$$

Example 14.1 **Consider the confusion matrix given below. It states that out of 165 employees studied, the classifier predicted that 110 employees will leave the company and 55 will not. But in reality, 105 left the company and 60 did not.**

Using the confusion matrix, we can calculate the metrics as given below.

n = 165	Predicted: NO	Predicted: YES
Actual: NO	50	10
Actual: YES	5	100

Sensitivity or Recall = TP/(TP + FN) = 100/(100 + 5)

Specificity = TN/(TN + FP) = 50/(50 + 10)

Precision = TP/predicted yes = 100/(10 + 100)

Accuracy = (TP + TN)/Total = 100 + 50/165

Note that both precision and recall are useful metrics for evaluating models that work with data in which classes or categories are not evenly distributed.

Example 14.2 **When we type a keyword in Google, we may get 40 pages, out of which only 30 may be relevant.**

So, we can calculate precision as 30/40 = 75%. But do you know that Google actually returned 40 pages out of 100 relevant pages it had for that query. Therefore, **recall is 30/100 = 30%.**

This example clearly shows that precision is "***how useful the search results are***," and recall is "***how complete the results are.***"

Example 14.3 **An ML model that predicts whether the patient has cancer or not works with data that is unevenly distributed.**

Suppose we build a model for a city in which 1% of the population has cancer. Then the model may incorrectly predict that a new patient does not have this disease (assuming even distribution, so it would classify 99% times No Cancer and Cancer in only 1% cases).

But when we calculate both Recall as well as Precision, only then it would be clear how accurate the model is. While Recall ensures that we are not overlooking the patients having cancer, Precision, on the other hand, ensures that the model is not misclassifying too many people as having the disease when they don't.

> Never use accuracy as a measure when dealing with an imbalanced test set. An imbalanced data set has high bias.

Thus, it is important to evaluate both Precision and Recall of a model.

14.1.1 ROC Curve

Receiver Operating Characteristic (ROC) can be used to visualize the performance of an ML model. It evaluates the trade-off between true positive rate and false positive rate. The area under the ROC curve is referred to as **index of accuracy (A)** or the **concordance index**. ***Higher the area under curve, better the predictive power of the model.*** For a perfect predictive model, the ROC has TP equal to 1 and FP equal 0 and will thus touches the top left corner of the graph.

14.2 OVER-FITTING AND UNDER-FITTING PROBLEM IN MACHINE LEARNING ALGORITHMS

In machine learning algorithms, we test the model to ensure that they do not suffer from over-fitting or under-fitting issues.

14.2.1 Over-fitting

Over-fitting means that a model fits the training data too well. It occurs when a model learns the details and noise in the training data to the extent that it negatively impacts the performance of the model on new data. In such a situation, outliers in the training data are picked up and learned as concepts by the model. Thus, an over-fitted model is trained with a lot of data.

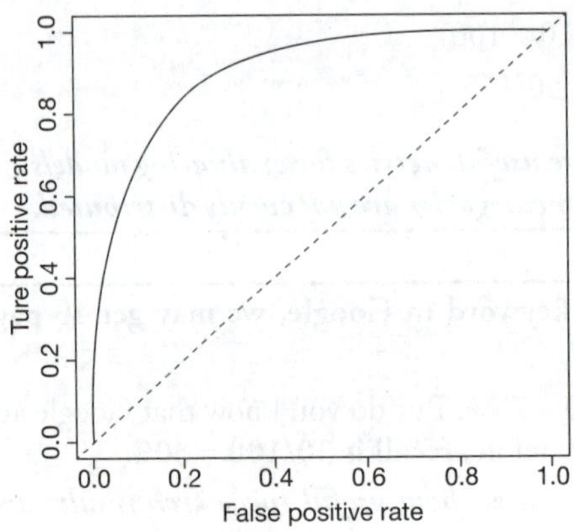

Figure 14.1 ROC curve

Over-fitting is more likely with nonparametric and nonlinear models (like decision trees) that have more flexibility when learning a target function. To rectify this problem, the decision tree must be pruned (that means, some nodes must be removed) after it has learned, so that some of the unnecessary details are removed.

14.2.2 Under-fitting

Under-fitting refers to a model that can neither model the training data nor generalize to new data. An under-fit machine learning model also gives poor performance on the training data.

A machine learning model is said to be under-fitted when it cannot capture the underlying trend of the data. Such a model does not fit the data well enough. It usually happens when we have less data to build an accurate model and also when we try to build a linear model with a non-linear data. An under-fitted model can be avoided by using more data and performing dimensionality reduction.

14.2.3 Good-fit Model

A machine learning model is said to be good if it generalizes any new input data from the problem domain in a proper way. This helps us to make predictions in future data that the data model has never seen. Ideally, the model should be neither under-fitted nor over-fitted. Such a model is at the sweet spot between under-fitting and over-fitting. If we measure the performance of a model over time, the number of errors decreases as the training model learns. However, if we train a model for too long, the performance of the model on the training dataset may continue to decrease due to the problem of over-fitting and learning the irrelevant detail and outliers in the training dataset. Simultaneously, errors in the test data start to rise as the model's ability to generalize decreases.

A good-fit model makes predictions with 0 errors. In order to get a good fit, we will stop at a point just before where the error starts increasing. At this point, the model has good skills on the training dataset as well on the testing dataset.

14.2.4 Limiting Over-fitting Issues

Both over-fitting and under-fitting can result in poor performance. However, the most common problem in applied machine learning is over-fitting. Over-fitting can be limited by using resampling techniques like the *k*-fold cross-validation to estimate model accuracy. The *k*-fold cross-validation allows you to train and test your model *k* times on different subsets of training data and build up an estimate of the performance of a machine learning model on unseen data.

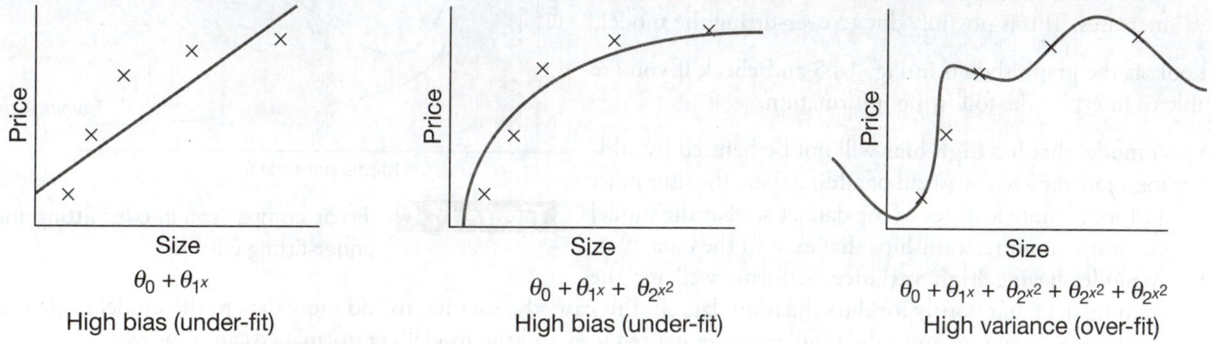

Figure 14.2 Bias and variance of over-fitted and under-fitted curves

Figure 14.2 illustrates that **an over-fitted model *shows* low bias *but* high variance**. An **under-fitted model, on the other hand, *shows* low variance *but* high bias**. While over-fitting results due to a complex model, under-fitting is a result of a very simple model. Both over-fitting and under-fitting lead to **poor predictions** on new data sets.

14.3 BIAS VS. VARIANCE

Some machine learning models have a pre-built rigid structure that limit the model's ability to learn from the examples. For instance, this may be the case when we train a linear model on an exponential dataset.

Models with high bias give less attention to the data thereby resulting in under-fitting. In the previous section, we studied that ***under-fitting also occurs when a model is not fed with enough data to learn from.***

On the other extreme, our machine learning models suffer from over-fitting problems in which the model learns *too much* from the training data. In addition to useful information, the model also learns about noise (or outliers or irrelevant data) that must be discarded otherwise. Such a model is said to have a high **variance**.

Thus, we have seen that ***a model with high bias is limited from learning the true trend and under-fits the data. Correspondingly, a model with high variance learns too much from the training data and over-fits the data.*** The best model lies between the two extremes (Fig. 14.3).

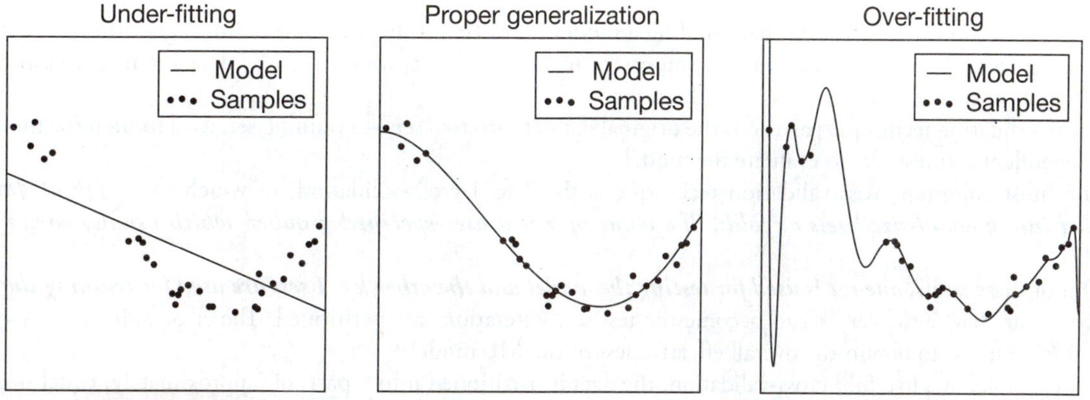

Figure 14.3 Data distribution in under-fit and over-fit models and generalized curve

Look at the graph shown in Fig. 14.4 and observe the following points:

- The model suffers from high bias in the region (under-fitting) where both the training error and validation error are high.
- When the training error decreases, validation error increases. This is possibly due tc over-fitting the model.

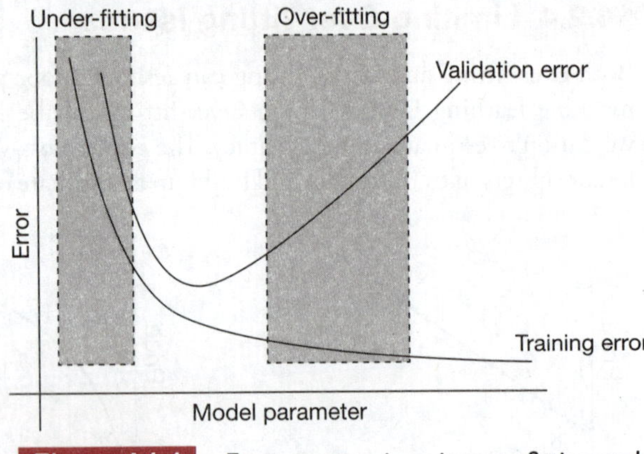

Figure 14.4 Error comparison in over-fitting and under-fitting curves

Look at the graph shown in Fig. 14.5 and check if you are able to interpret the following information.

- A model that has **high bias** will not be befitted by adding more data sets. Instead of adding data, the user must add some more features to the dataset so that the model can learn about relationships that exist in the data.
- A model having **high variance** performs well for the training data, but poorly for the validation data. In this case, the user has to add more data to the model so that the gap between training and validation error can get reduced and the model's performance can improve.

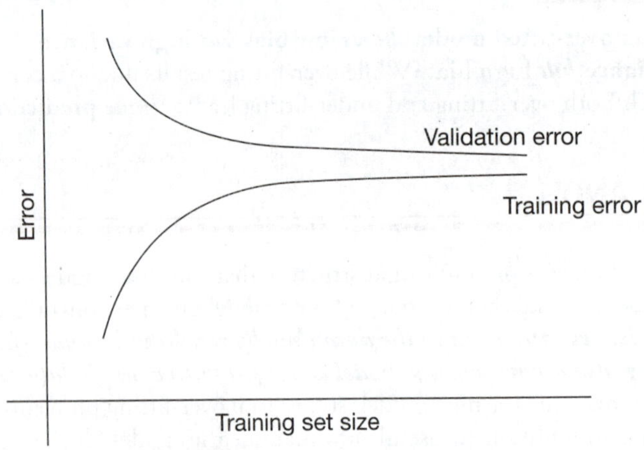

Figure 14.5 Training and validation errors

14.4 *K*-FOLD CROSS-VALIDATION

In the above section, we have seen that building a model is not that difficult. But building a good-fit model can be a challenging task. Cross-validation is a very important technique that is widely used by data scientists to estimate the performance of their model.

Cross-validation technique partitions the original dataset into two sets – a training set, used to train the model, and an independent set (test set) to evaluate the model.

The most common cross-validation technique is the *k*-fold cross-validation, in which the ***original dataset is divided into k equal-sized sets or folds. The value of k is a user-specified number, which usually varies from 5 to 10.***

Out of these *k* sets, ***one set is used for testing the model and the other k – 1 sets are used for training the model.*** To give a fair chance to every set to become the test set, *k* iterations are performed. The error estimation is averaged over all *k* iterations to obtain the overall effectiveness of the ML model.

For example, in a five-fold cross-validation, the data is partitioned into 5 parts of (approximately) equal size. Then, there will be 5 iterations. In the first iteration, the first data set is used as the test set and rest of the four sets are used as training sets. In the second iteration, the second data set is taken as the test set and other four set s are training sets, and so on.

The k-fold cross-validation technique significantly reduces the bias and variance of the model. Thus, the steps in *k*-fold cross-validation are:

Step 1: Split the original training data set into *k* equal subsets. Each subset is called a **fold**. Name these individual folds as $f_1, f_2, \ldots, f_k$.

Step 2: Set $I = 1$

Step 3: Repeat Steps 4–6 while $I <= k$.

Step 4: Use the fold f_i as validation set and all other remaining $k-1$ folds as training set.

Step 5: Train the model using the training set.

Step 6: Calculate the accuracy of the model by validating the predicted results against the validation set.

Step 7: Estimate the accuracy of the model by averaging the accuracies derived in all the *k* cases of cross-validation.

14.5 MODEL EVALUATION METRICS

In this section, we will read about different model evaluation metrics that are used to quantify the performance of the machine learning model. The choice of which evaluation metric to use in the current context will depend on the machine learning task (such as classification, regression, ranking, clustering and topic modeling, among others).

p-Value: *p*-value of individual predictor variables are very useful in machine learning models. These *p*-values should be less than the pre-determined statistical significance level of 0.05. If a variable has *p*-value higher than 0.05, then it means that variable (or feature) has no significance in predicting the output and hence, it should be discarded.

Example 14.4 **Assume that we are creating a machine learning model that predicts the marks obtained by a student in Class X. For this, we have two variables. First, marks obtained in pre-board exam having a *p*-value 0.003 and another variable for the date of exam, having *p*-value 0.09.**

In this scenario, we will use only the first value for predicting the output and discard (or remove) the second variable.

14.5.1 Null and Alternate Hypothesis

Whenever we consider *p*-value, there is always a Null and Alternate Hypothesis associated. The Null Hypothesis (H0) is that the coefficients used in a ML model are equal to zero. The alternate hypothesis (H1) is that the coefficients are not equal to zero.

When the coefficients are not equal to zero then there exists a relationship between the independent variable and the dependent variable. Correspondingly, when the coefficients are equal to zero then there is no relationship between the variables.

14.5.2 Mean Squared Error (MSE)

MSE or Mean Squared Error is calculated as,

$$\text{MSE} = \frac{1}{n}\sum_{i=1}^{n}(\hat{y}_i - y_i)^2$$

where

n is the number of observations (data) in the dataset.

y_i is the actual (or true) value of the ith target value (y^i). This means that y is the value of data i in the data set.

$\hat{y}_i$ is the model's predicted value for y_i.

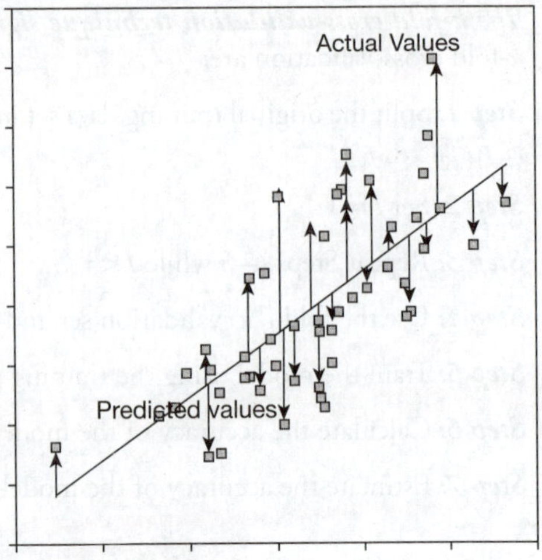

Figure 14.6 Mean squared error

MSE finds the squared sum of all the distances between predicted and true values. Higher MSE indicates a greater sum of squared error; hence, poor quality of model predictions. The key benefits of squaring the error margins are:

- All error values are restricted to be positive.
- The model will penalize a few large error values more than it will penalize many small error values.

14.5.3 Residuals

Another way to test the quality of a model is to look at the residuals or the differences between the real values and the predicted values. For example, a straight line in Fig. 14.6 represents the predicted values and the vertical line from the straight line to the observed data value is the residual. ***The sum of the residuals should be approximately zero or as low as possible.***

The Residual Standard Error (RSE) is an estimate of the standard deviation of $\in$. In other words, it is the average of the extent to which the response will deviate from the true regression line. It is computed by:

$$\text{RSE} = \sqrt{\frac{1}{n-2}\sum_{i=1}^{n}(y_i - \hat{y}_i)^2}$$

where,

$\hat{y}_i$ is the fitted value for observation i.

R^2: Another measure to test the quality of the model is the coefficient of determination or R^2, which is defined by the proportion of the total variability explained by the model. R^2 assumes that every independent variable in the model helps to explain variation in the dependent variable. However, practically, not every variable affects the dependent variable. So, they do not contribute in building a good model. R^2 can be calculated as,

R^2 = Explained variation of the model / Total variation of the model or

R^2 = 1 - (SSE / SST), where

$$\text{SSE} = \sum_{i}^{n}(y_i - \hat{y}_i)^2 \text{ and SST} = \sum_{i}^{n}(y_i - \overline{y}_i)^2$$

$\hat{y}_i$ is the fitted value for observation i and

$\overline{y}_i$ is the mean of Y.

For models that fit the data well, R^2 is near 1.

Models that poorly fit the data have R^2 near 0.

Example 14.5 **If a model has an R^2 of 0.02, then this means that it explains only 2% of the data variability. A model with R^2 of 0.99 is far better than the first one as it explains 99% of the total variability.**

Adjusted R^2: ***At times, a high R^2 may not be as good as a low R^2.*** This is especially important when in some circumstances data points don't fit in a perfectly straight line (for example, you may have two children of the same age with a lot of variation in their heights). In such cases, an R^2 of 0.5 is considered good.

Another problem with multiple R^2 is that it always increases as we add more independent variables to our model. So even if the newly added variable does not add to the predictions, R^2 will increase. For this reason, the adjusted R^2 is used when we add more than one variable to the model. The value of adjusted R^2 increases only if it reduces the overall error of the predictions.

Technically, ***adjusted R^2 measures the proportion of variation explained by only those independent variables that really affect the dependent variable.*** Unlike R^2, adjusted R^2 penalizes for adding independent variable(s) that do not affect the dependent variable.

$$R^2_{adj} = 1 - \left(\frac{(1 - R^2)(n-1)}{n-q} \right)$$

where,
n is the number of observations or the sample size
q is the number of predictors.

Statistic	Criterion
R squared	Higher the better
Adjusted R squared	Higher the better
F-statistic	Higher the better
Standard error	Closer to zero the better

F-statistic: The *F-statistic* test is done to see if at least one predictor variable has a non-zero coefficient. This is especially important when dealing with multiple predictors (variables that affect the prediction) as in multiple linear regression. A larger F-statistic value will produce a statistically significant p-value ($p < 0.05$).

R^2 measures the proportion of variation in dependent variable explained by all the independent variables.

Key Terms

Confusion matrix: A table with four cells that represents actual vs. predicted values

True positives (TP): TP indicates cases in which the classifier predicted 1 when it was actually 1.

True negatives (TN): TN indicates cases when the classifier predicted 0 when it was actually 0.

False positives (FP): FP indicates cases where the classifier predicted 1 when it was actually 0. False positive is also known as "Type I error".

False negatives (FN): FN indicates cases where the classifier predicted 0 but in reality, it was 1.

Over-fitting: Over-fitting means that a model fits the training data too well.

Under-fittng: Under-fitting refers to a model that can neither model the training data nor generalize to new data.

Accuracy: Accuracy is defined as the percentage of correct predictions for the test data. It is calculated by dividing the number of correct predictions by the number of total predictions.

Bias: A systematic error that occurs in the AI model itself due to incorrect assumptions.

Variance: Changes in the model when using different portions of the training data set.

Chapter Highlights

- To calculate the accuracy of a machine learning model, we must use different ways to evaluate it.
- Once a model is trained, we need to check how the model performs on new/unseen data.
- We can trust the predictions made by an evaluated machine learning model.
- Model evaluation techniques use a training data set to train the machine learning model (i.e, make the model learn) and a training data set to evaluate the performance of the model.
- Sensitivity or recall indicates the number of positive values, out of all the positive values, that have been correctly predicted
- A good machine learning model must have a high value for True Positives and True Negatives.
- Higher the area under the ROC curve, better the prediction power of the model.
- An over-fitted model shows low bias but high variance. An under-fitted model, on the other hand, shows low variance but high bias.
- A model with high bias is limited from learning the true trend and under-fits the data. Correspondingly, a model with high variance learns too much from the training data and over-fits the data.

- While over-fitting results due to a complex model, under-fitting is a result of a very simple model. Both over-fitting and under-fitting lead to poor predictions on new data sets.
- The most common cross-validation technique is *k*-fold cross-validation, in which the original dataset is divided into *k* equal-sized sets or folds.

Review Questions

1. Why should we evaluate a machine learning model?
2. Differentiate between training and testing data sets.
3. Why should we have a separate data set for testing the machine learning model?
4. Differentiate between over-fitting and under-fitting issues.
5. Explain the *k*-fold cross-validation technique.
6. Write short notes on the following:
   a. Confusion matrix b. ROC curve
7. Identify the scenario: Under-/Good-/Over-fit model

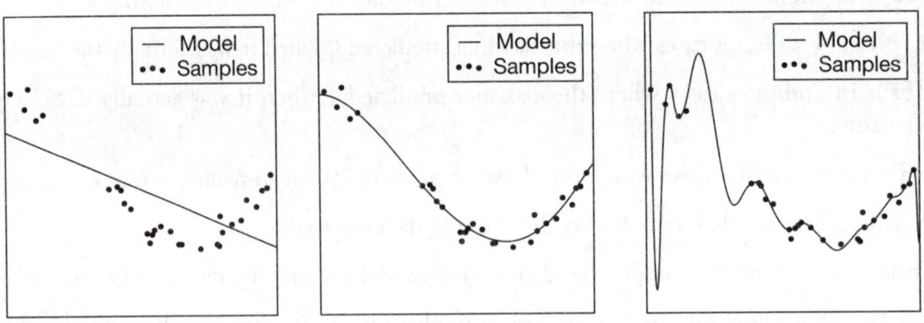

Fill in the Blanks

1. The test data validates the ________ of the model.
2. __________ is a table with four cells that represents actual vs. predicted values.
3. __________ is defined as the percentage of correct predictions for the test data.
4. __________ indicate cases in which the classifier predicted 1 when it was actually 1.
5. __________ indicates number of positive values, out of all the positive values, that have been correctly predicted.
6. A good model must have ______ false positives and false negatives.
7. ________ is the harmonic mean of precision and recall.
8. An imbalanced data set has ________ bias.
9. __________ evaluates the trade-off between true positive rate and false positive rate.
10. To rectify over-fitting issues, the decision tree must be __________.
11. A machine learning model is said to be _______ when it cannot capture the underlying trend of the data.
12. Over-fitting results due to a _________ model.
13. Models with high bias result in an _________ model.
14. In *k*-fold cross-validation, the value of *k* varies from _________.

15. If a variable has p-value higher than ______, then it means that the variable has no significance in predicting the output and hence, it should be discarded.

16. The ________ test is done to see if at least one predictor variable has a non-zero coefficient.

State True or False

1. The training data set validates the accuracy of the model.
2. We must use the training data to also test the model.
3. True negatives indicate cases where the classifier predicted 0 when it was actually 0.
4. Accuracy is calculated by adding the number of correct predictions and the number of total predictions.
5. Higher the diagonal values of the confusion matrix, the better it is.
6. Sensitivity indicates the number of negative values, out of all the negative values, that have been correctly predicted.
7. Higher the area under the ROC curve, better the prediction power of the model.
8. An over-fitted model makes predictions with 0 errors.
9. Under-fitting occurs when a model learns the details and noise in the training data to the extent that it negatively impacts the performance of the model on new data.
10. Under-fitting is a result of a very simple model.
11. When the coefficients are equal to zero, then there exists a relationship between the independent variable and the dependent variable.
12. Higher MSE indicates poor quality of model predictions.
13. Models that poorly fit the data have R^2 near 0.

Multiple Choice Questions

1. Once a model is trained, we need to check how the model performs on _______ data.
   a. new b. unseen
   c. Both of these. d. None of these.
2. _________ indicates cases where the classifier predicted 1 when it was actually 0.
   a. True Positive b. True Negative
   c. False Positive d. False Negative
3. ________ indicates cases where the classifier predicted 0 but in reality, it was 1.
   a. True Positive b. True Negative
   c. False Positive d. False Negative
4. A good machine learning model must have _______ value for True Positives and True Negatives.
   a. High b. low
   c. equal d. Any of these.
5. _________ specifies the number of all the predicted positive values that are actually positive.
   a. Specificity b. Sensitivity
   c. Precision d. Accuracy
6. _______ can be limited by using resampling techniques like the k-fold cross-validation.
   a. Under-fitting b. Over-fitting
   c. Good-fitting d. All of these.

7. Both over-fitting and under-fitting lead to ________ predictions on new data sets.
   a. better b. poor
   c. no change in d. Any of these.
8. A model with high variance results in ________ the data.
   a. under-fitting b. over-fitting
   c. good-fitting d. All of these.
9. ____________ is calculated as the difference between the real values and the predicted values.
   a. Accuracy b. ROC
   c. Residual d. Precision
10. For models that fit the data well, R^2 is near ______.
   a. 0 b. 1
   c. –1 d. infinity

Interpret the Graphs and Fill in the Blanks

1. 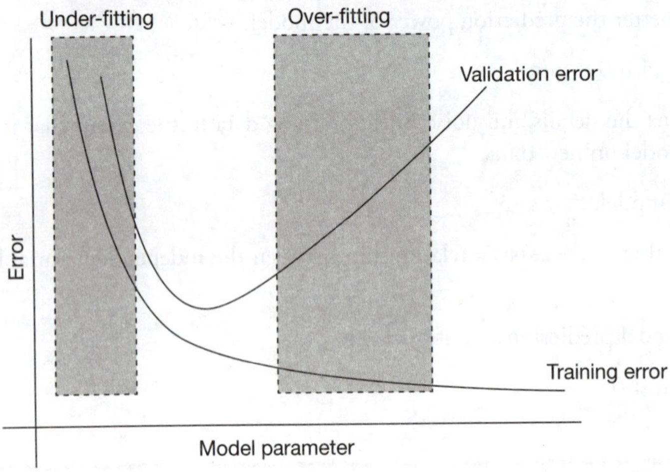

   a. The model suffers from high bias in the region (under-fitting) where both the training error and validation error are _______.
   b. When the training error decreases, validation error _______. This is possibly due to ___________ the model.

2. 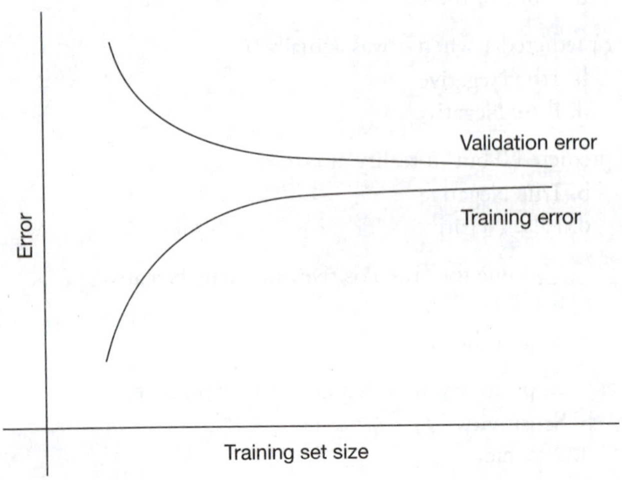

   Adding more data to the model _________ the gap between training and validation error.

Test Your Analytical Skills

1. **Identify whether the statement given below is True Positive, True Negative, False Positive or False Negative.**

   a. You predicted that it would rain today and it did.

   b. You predicted that it would not rain today and it didn't.

   c. You predicted that it would rain today but it didn't.

   d. You predicted that it would not rain today but it did.

   e. A diseased person is diagnosed to be healthy.

   f. A healthy person has been diagnosed as sick.

2. **Fill in the Blanks**

   a.

		Actual	
		Positive	*Positive*
Predicted	*Positive*	**True Positive** *Predicted has cancer* *Has Cancer*	**False Positive** ________
	Positive	**False Negative** ________	**True Negative** *Predicted not cancer* *Does not have cancer*

   b.

Predicted as a hotdog.
This is a case of ________

Predicted not being a hotdog
This is ________

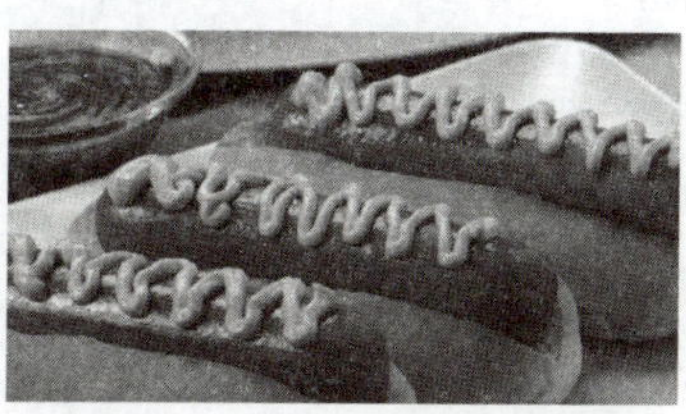

Predicted not being a hotdog
This indicates ________

Predicted Hotdog
This means ________

c.

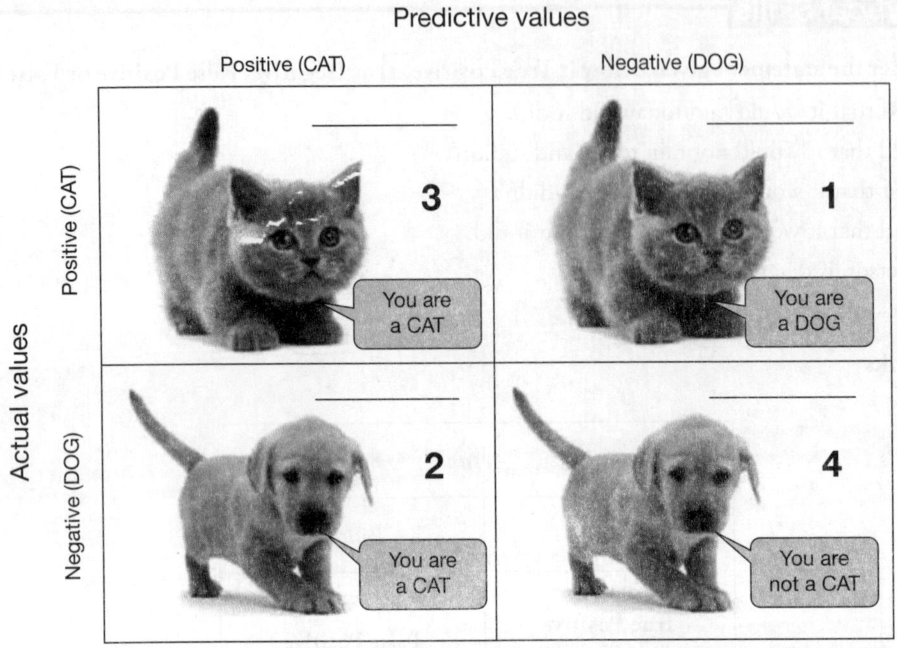

3. Calculate the Accuracy, Recall and Precision from the Confusion Matrix given below.

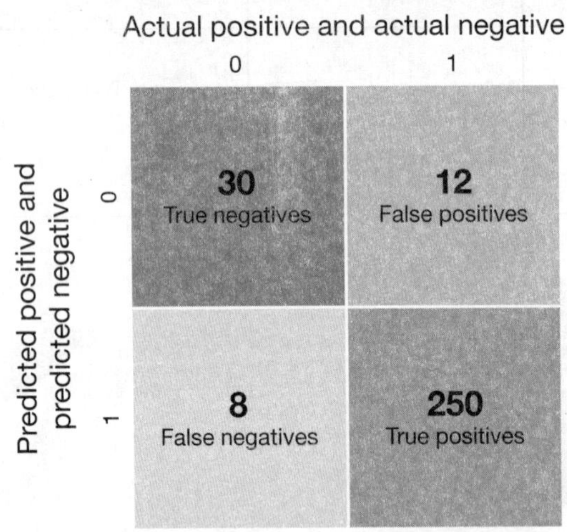

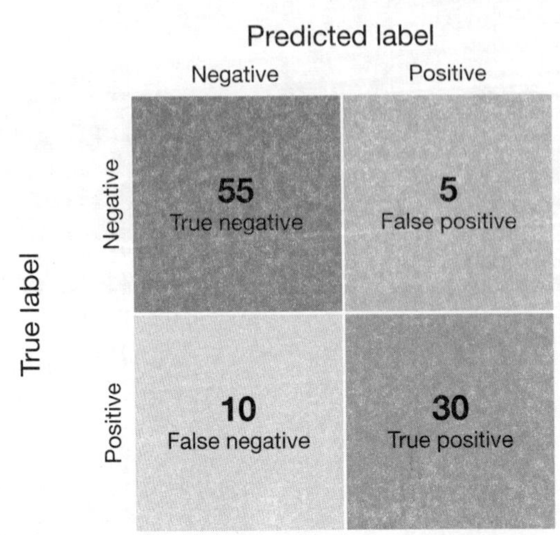

AI Lab Session – Emoji Scavenger Hunt

Emoji Scavenger Hunt is an AI-powered Google experiment that identifies emojis in the real world with the user's device camera. The application uses neural networks to identify the real-world versions of the emojis we use every day. To launch this application, visit the link https://emojiscavengerhunt.withgoogle.com/

Project Work

In Class IX, you have discussed ideas for the projects given below. Now after gaining a good understanding about AI, refine your report to include more details for any one project listed below:

- Detect unacceptable posts on social media
- Detect drowsiness of a person driving a vehicle
- Detect jaundice and recommend precautions to be taken
- Detect depression symptoms. If the user is depressed, recommend some measures to overcome it.
- Predict a user's interest from reading history in library and predict similar types of books which the user may like to read.
- Predict quantity of food and type of food that must be prepared for a wedding function.
  Hint: Prediction depends on factors like guest's preference, count of guests, season, etc.
- Detect rash driving by school bus/cab drivers
  Hint: It depends on the driver's speed, time taken to reach school, congestion, season, etc.

Answers

Fill in the Blanks

1. accuracy
2. Confusion matrix
3. Accuracy
4. True positives
5. Sensitivity or recall
6. low
7. *F*-score
8. high
9. ROC curve
10. pruned
11. under-fitted
12. complex
13. under-fitted
14. 5 to 10
15. 0.05
16. *F*-statistic

State True or False

1. False
2. False
3. True
4. False
5. True
6. False
7. True
8. False
9. False
10. True
11. False
12. True
13. True

Multiple Choice Questions

1. c
2. c
3. d
4. a
5. c
6. b
7. c
8. c
9. c
10. b

Interpret the Graphs and Fill in the Blanks

1. a. high b. increases, over-fitting
2. reduces

Test Your Analytical Skills

1. a. TP
   b. TN
   c. FP
   d. FN
   e. FN
   f. FP
2. TPR = 91.4%
   TNR = 90%
   FPR = 10%
   FNR = 8.6%